PENGUI

HELL

D0358113

Terry Brighton read Politics and Philosophy at Lancaster University and Theology at Birmingham University before serving as an Anglican priest in Herefordshire and Lincolnshire. He has done postgraduate work in Collections Management and Interpretation and is an Associate of the Museums Association and a member of the Crimean War Research Society.

He has worked on the curatorial staff of the Queen's Royal Lancers Regimental Museum, Belvoir Castle, for over twenty years. The Queen's Royal Lancers is the descendant regiment of the 17th Lancers, which rode in the front line of the Charge of the Light Brigade.

Hell Riders

The Truth about the Charge of the Light Brigade

TERRY BRIGHTON

PENGUIN BOOKS

PENGUIN BOOKS

Published by the Penguin Group
Penguin Books Ltd, 80 Strand, London WC2R 0RL, England
Penguin Group (USA) Inc., 375 Hudson Street, New York, New York 10014, USA
Penguin Group (Canada), 10 Alcorn Avenue, Toronto, Ontario, Canada M4V 3B2
(a division of Pearson Penguin Canada Inc.)
Penguin Ireland, 25 St Stephen's Green, Dublin 2, Ireland
(a division of Penguin Books Ltd)
Penguin Group (Australia), 250 Camberwell Road, Camberwell, Victoria 3124, Australia
(a division of Pearson Australia Group Pty Ltd)
Penguin Books India Pvt Ltd, 11 Community Centre, Panchsheel Park, New Delhi – 110 017, India
Penguin Group (NZ), cnr Airborne and Rosedale Roads, Albany, Auckland 1310, New Zealand
(a division of Pearson New Zealand Ltd)
Penguin Books (South Africa) (Pty) Ltd, 24 Sturdee Avenue, Rosebank 2196, South Africa

Penguin Books Ltd, Registered Offices: 80 Strand, London WC2R 0RL, England

www.penguin.com

First published by Viking 2004
Published in Penguin Books 2005
1

Copyright © Terry Brighton, 2004
All rights reserved

The moral right of the author has been asserted

Typeset by Rowland Phototypesetting Ltd, Bury St Edmunds, Suffolk
Printed in England by Clays Ltd, St Ives plc

To R.E. and E.L.

In a moment they were gone:
Like a sudden spark
Struck vainly in the night,
Then returns the dark
With no more hope of light.

Alfred, Lord Tennyson, *Maud*

Contents

List of Illustrations   xi

List of Maps   xv

Acknowledgements   xvii

Introduction   xix

ONE – The Invasion of the Crimea

1. The Bear Hunt *The Light Brigade prepares for war*   3

2. The Ruling Asses *Their lordships Lucan and*   18
   Cardigan take command

3. Journey into Hell *Three trials en route to the Crimea*   31

4. The Invasion of the Crimea *From Kalamita Bay to*   46
   Balaklava

5. Reconnaissance and the Cossacks *The secret*   63
   intelligence that could have saved the Light Brigade

TWO – The Charge of the Light Brigade

6. Towards the Valley of Death *The Russian attack,*   81
   the thin red line and the Heavy Brigade

7. The Charge *Seven minutes into hell with the Light*   105
   Brigade

8. Behind the Guns *The Light Brigade pursues the*   142
   Russian cavalry

9. The Return *The survivors fight their way back*   170

10. Experience and Observation *Death in the valley and*   189
    glory on the heights

THREE – The Last of the Light Brigade

11. The Miserable Remains *The Light Brigade in winter*   205
12. After the Crimea 1. *From the battlefield to the*   223
    workhouse
13. After the Crimea 2. *From the facts to the legend*   229

FOUR – Investigating the Charge

14. Finding Fault *Did Captain Nolan – or one of their*   239
    lordships Raglan, Lucan and Cardigan – lose the Light
    Brigade?
15. The Balaklava Bugle Controversy *Did Henry Joy or*   262
    Billy Brittain – or no one at all – sound the charge of the
    Light Brigade?
16. Lord Cardigan's Retreat *Did Cardigan desert the*   278
    Light Brigade at the Russian guns?
17. Not the Six Hundred *Counting them out and*   290
    counting them in
18. Death or Glory? *Did the charge succeed or fail?*   295
19. The Truth about Scutari *Was Florence Nightingale –*   303
    or Mary Seacole – the true nursing heroine of the Light
    Brigade?
20. Light Brigade Scandals *Murder, suicide and the*   316
    Victoria Cross

CONCLUSION 325

Appendix 1. Researching the Light Brigade *Did* 331
            your ancestor ride in the charge?

Appendix 2. Roll of the Light Brigade *An* 336
            alphabetical list of officers and men

Bibliography 361
Index 365

List of Illustrations

First Section

1. Assistant Surgeon Henry Wilkin, 11th Hussars. Photograph by Roger Fenton, 1855
2. Balaklava harbour. Photograph by James Robertson, 1855
3. Balaklava harbour seen from the end of the wharf. Photograph by Roger Fenton, 1855
4. Balaklava seen from the cavalry camp at Kadikoi. Photograph by Roger Fenton, 1855
5. Looking out across the Balaklava plain from the cavalry camp at Kadikoi. Photograph by Roger Fenton, 1855
6. Field kitchen of the 8th Hussars. Photograph by Roger Fenton, 1855
7. Camp of the 4th Dragoon Guards. Photograph by Roger Fenton, 1855
8. Captain Henry Duberly (8th Hussars) and his wife, Fanny. Photograph by Roger Fenton, 1855
9. Officers and men of the 8th Hussars. Photograph by Roger Fenton, 1855
10. General Lord Raglan, commander-in-chief of the British Army in the Crimea. Photograph by Roger Fenton, 1855
11. Lieutenant General Lord Lucan, commanding the Cavalry Division
12. Major General Lord Cardigan, commanding the Light Brigade
13. Captain Louis Nolan, 15th Hussars, who carried the order from Lord Raglan to Lord Lucan. Drawing by an unknown artist
14. His Highness Prince Menshikov, commander-in-chief of the Russian Army in the Crimea

15. Lieutenant General Liprandi, in command of the Russian attack on Balaklava on 25 October 1854

16. Colonel Prince Obolensky, commanding the Don Cossack battery charged by the Light Brigade

17. *The Thin Red Line*. Photogravure after Richard Gibb published by Archibald Ramsden, London, 1883

18. *The Charge of the Heavy Brigade*. Oil painting by Godfrey Douglas Giles, 1897

Second Section

19. Lord Cardigan leads the charge of the Light Brigade on his charger, Ronald. Oil painting by Alfred de Prades, 1855

20. Sir Briggs, the horse used in the charge by Captain Godfrey Morgan (later Lord Tredegar) of the 17th Lancers. Oil painting by Alfred de Prades, 1856

21. *The Midnight Alarm*. Lithograph by an unknown artist published by Read and Co., London, 1854

22. *The Charge of the Light Brigade*. Lithograph by E. Walker published in *The Seat of War in the East*, Colnaghi, London, 1855

23. *The Charge of the Light Brigade*. Oil painting by Richard Caton Woodville, 1886

24. *The 17th Lancers at Balaklava*. Oil painting by Richard Simkin reproduced by Eyre and Spottiswoode

25. *The Relief of the Light Brigade*. Oil painting by Richard Caton Woodville, 1897

26. *The Rescue of Captain Augustus Webb, 17th Lancers*. Chromolithograph after Harry Payne published by Raphael Tuck and Sons, 1891

27. *Balaklava: The Return*: the survivors make their way back. Oil painting by Lady Butler

28. *Florence Nightingale in the Military Hospital at Scutari*. Lithograph by Joseph Benwell published by the Caxton Press, London, 1856

29. *Our Cavalry, December 1854*. Watercoloured sketch by Lieutenant Henry Wilkinson, 9th Foot, 1854

Third Section

30. Lord Raglan's order to the cavalry
31. The bugle blown by Trumpeter Billy Brittain to sound the charge of the Light Brigade, and the bugle blown by Trumpet Major Henry Joy to sound the advance of the Heavy Brigade
32. *The Death of Captain Nolan*. Oil painting by Thomas Barker, 1855
33. *The Charge*. Oil painting by C. E. Stewart
34. & 35. The mêlée behind the guns. *Illustrated London News*, 18 November 1854
36. *The Roll Call*. Lithograph after Richard Caton Woodville, 1890
37. 'The Charge of the Light Brigade'. Tennyson's first draft of his poem
38. Alfred, Lord Tennyson
39. William Russell, war correspondent of *The Times*. Photograph by Roger Fenton, 1855
40. The Valley of Death. Photograph by Roger Fenton, 1855
41. Four survivors of the charge photographed in August 1855 after their return to the cavalry depot at Brighton
42. Private Benjamin Soley, who rode in the charge with the 17th Lancers
43. & 44. Letter describing the charge written by Private Soley
45. Survivors of the charge with Butcher, one of the few horses to live through both the charge and the winter that followed and to return home
46. Survivors of the charge photographed with Buffalo Bill (Colonel William Cody) at Earls Court, London, in 1903

Illustration Acknowledgements

The author and publishers are grateful to the following for permission to reproduce illustrations: 1, 3–10, 39–40, Fenton Collection, Library of Congress, Washington, DC; 2, 11–13, 17, 22–4, 26, 28, 31, 34–6, 41–4, 46, The Queen's Royal Lancers Museum, Belvoir Castle; 14–16, Sevastopol'tsy, St Petersburg; 18, 20, 21, 25, 29, 30, National Army Museum, London; 19, The Hon. Mrs Brudenell; 27, Manchester Art Gallery; 32, National Gallery of Ireland, Dublin; 33, Cavalry and Guards Club, London; 37–8, Tennyson Research Centre, Lincoln; 45, Wrexham County Archives.

List of Maps

1. The Russian and Turkish empires, 1854   xxiii

2. The Invasion of the Crimea, September 1854   xxiv

3. Sevastopol and Balaklava: cavalry patrols clash by the Chernaya, October 1854   xxv

4. The Hell Ride (1): position of the Russian forces and the Light and Heavy Brigades at 11.10 a.m., 25 October 1854   xxvi

5. The Hell Ride (2): the Light Brigade passes through the first field of fire   xxvii

6. The Hell Ride (3): the Light Brigade charges the guns   xxviii

7. The Hell Ride (4): the pursuit and the Russian trap   xxix

8. The Hell Ride (5): the breakout and the return   xxx

Acknowledgements

A number of organizations and individuals have helped in the preparation of this book. I would like to thank the staff of the Reading Room at the National Army Museum, without whom most research into the Victorian soldier would prove impossible, the Ministry of Defence Information and Library Service and the Public Record Office (now the National Archive) at Kew. The present regimental museums of the original Light Brigade regiments have given their assistance and support: The King's Royal Hussars, the Light Dragoons, The Queen's Royal Hussars and The Queen's Royal Lancers. I am especially indebted to the several members of the Crimean War Research Society whose advice and comments have been both informed and helpful. My wife Janet spent many hours working on the roll of officers and men who charged at Balaklava.

Special thanks must go to those who read the final manuscript in full and offered their expert advice: Michael Hargreave Mawson, whose encyclopedic knowledge of the Crimean War is unrivalled, and my colleague at The Queen's Royal Lancers Museum, Captain Mick Holtby, who once again placed his specialist knowledge of the cavalry at my disposal. Thanks also go to my agent Luigi Bonomi for making the right decision while I was without a phone in Greece, and to Eleo Gordon at Penguin for her belief and guidance (and for surviving the cannonball).

All of the above have helped to make this a better book than it could otherwise have been, though the opinions expressed and any faults that remain are my own. Finally, it does not seem out of place to acknowledge as my co-authors the twenty or so survivors of the charge who wrote first-hand accounts of their hell ride at Balaklava. No words of mine could conjure up the reality of the charge as surely as theirs, and it is to them that I owe the greatest debt.

Introduction

The truth about war is not found in the politics or in the strategy, or even in the official dispatches of generals, but in the experiences and observations of fighting men. This truth is often missing from the history books, where the need to summarize the countless individual actions that constitute a great battle takes readers ever further from the brute facts as recorded by the original combatants.

The charge of the Light Brigade has suffered greatly from this process. Throughout the English-speaking world and beyond there remains a fascination with the hell ride at Balaklava that far exceeds its military significance. Yet the popular impression of what happened during the charge and in the mêlée behind the Russian guns would hardly be recognized by the men who charged.

My aim in writing *Hell Riders* has been to rediscover the full story of the charge *as the survivors told it*. With the help of the twenty or so men of the Light Brigade who wrote down their experiences I have recreated what really happened and what it was like to ride in history's most famous cavalry charge.

On 27 February 1854, Britain issued an ultimatum to Tsar Nicholas I of Russia, whose troops had crossed the Danube into Turkey. The view of London was that if Russian forces took the Turkish capital Constantinople (now Istanbul) then the Tsar's Black Sea Fleet would gain access to the Mediterranean and from there his warships could dominate the seas. Britain demanded the Tsar withdraw his troops and told him that 'refusal or silence will be equivalent to a declaration of war'. He took no action and had nothing to say.

On 28 March, Britain declared war on Russia. At the time this was known as the Great War with Russia; we know it as the Crimean War because most of the action took place on the Crimean peninsula in the Black Sea, at the southernmost point of the Russian

empire. Britain joined forces with France and Turkey to send a
fleet of sixty-seven warships and several hundred troop transports
carrying a combined army of 64,000 men. In September this force
invaded the Crimea and began bombarding the Russian naval base
of Sevastopol, home of the Black Sea Fleet. If the city could be
taken and its fleet destroyed, the Tsar's expansionist plans would
be foiled.

But on 25 October, with Sevastopol still holding out, the Russian
army struck back, attacking the British base at Balaklava. Just after
11.00 a.m., acting in defence of Balaklava, the Light Brigade of the
British Cavalry Division charged a battery of Russian artillery guns
ranged across the far end of a mile-long valley. As they brought
their mounts to the gallop and headed straight for the muzzles of
the guns ahead, the five regiments that made up the brigade also
came under fire from enemy guns on both flanks. The barrage of
roundshot and shell was constant and deafening. Men and horses
fell dead or mutilated at every stride. The carnage was horrific, yet
still the survivors spurred their mounts on. To those watching from
high ground to the rear as what remained of the Light Brigade
disappeared into the smoke of the Russian guns, it seemed that
these magnificent cavalrymen had charged into hell itself.

The charge down the valley was not what Lord Raglan, commander-in-chief of the British Army in the Crimea, had intended.
His written order had been carried by an aide-de-camp to Lord
Lucan, who commanded the Cavalry Division; Lucan in turn gave
the order orally to Lord Cardigan, commanding the Light Brigade.
Somewhere on its journey from Raglan to Cardigan the meaning
of the order had been misunderstood. It was not clear who was to
blame; the bloody outcome was obvious to all.

That there was also something 'special' about the charge was
evident from the day news of it first broke in England. William
Russell, war correspondent of *The Times*, described both the splendour of the disciplined advance under fire and the terrible loss of
life. For the first time the nation shared (albeit from the breakfast
table and the drawing room) in the experience and suffering of its

soldiers on the battlefield. A sketch in *Punch* magazine showed an excited father wielding a poker while he read out an account of the charge to his enthralled family. It seemed as if every city and town in the land had lost a man and gained a hero.

There was something mythical about a brigade of cavalrymen sent rushing to their deaths by human error, carried at an ever faster pace, not knowing the reason why but held by their courage on that fatal course. Here, condensed into a frantic, seven-minute dash, was the heroic life lived to the full, in stark counterpoint to the daily slog of life in the trenches above Sevastopol and the humdrum existence of those at home, tilling the soil, working the lathe or scribing in the ledger book. When the Poet Laureate Alfred, Lord Tennyson put a rhythm and a beat to it, even the many who could not read heard in his ballad something of the tragic magnificence of the charge.

Later, when the army returned from the Crimea and it was said that a medal and a stirring tale of the charge were worth a free quart of ale in any hostelry in England, some of the survivors realized that a more detailed (and sober) description was required and began writing down their experiences.

The last surviving veteran of Balaklava died in 1927. Long before then the charge of the Light Brigade had been moved by public acclaim from the historical record to the realm of legend. This popular interpretation of the charge owed more to Tennyson – schoolchildren learned his poem by rote – than to the facts recorded in survivors' accounts, which, if they were published at all, had often been privately printed. Tennyson had based his poem on Russell's first report in *The Times*, which contained crucial inaccuracies. Russell soon put the record straight, but by then the poem had caught the public imagination and there was no changing that. In any case the legend was preferred to the facts.

This is the form in which the charge of the Light Brigade comes down to us, an interpretation that for the most part ignores the personal testimony contained in survivors' accounts. In *Hell Riders*

I have put aside the legend and returned to the original evidence. Tennyson immortalized a remarkable tale; the truth is yet more incredible.

Hell Riders concentrates on the story of the charge as the survivors told it. Of course their accounts contain discrepancies and are unlikely to be correct in every detail – it really was hell out there and no one was taking notes. But *these men were there* and their story is as close as we can come to the truth about the charge of the Light Brigade.

Terry Brighton
The Queen's Royal Lancers Regimental Museum, Belvoir Castle

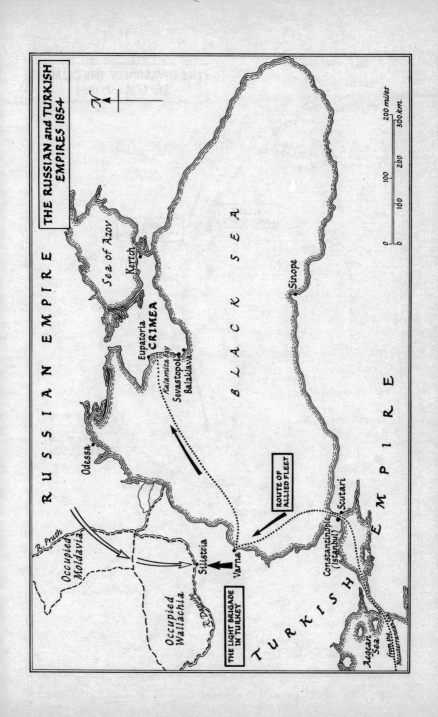

THE RUSSIAN and TURKISH
EMPIRES 1854

N

200 miles
300 km

200

100

100

0
0

RUSSIAN EMPIRE

Sea of Azov

Kertch

CRIMEA

Eupatoria

Kalamita Bay
Sevastopol
Balaklavia

Odessa

BLACK SEA

Sinope

R. Pruth

Occupied
Moldavia

Silistria

Varna

R. Danube

Occupied
Wallachia

THE LIGHT BRIGADE
IN TURKEY

ROUTE OF
ALLIED FLEET

Scutari

Constantinople
(Istanbul)

TURKISH EMPIRE

Aegean
Sea

from the Mediterranean

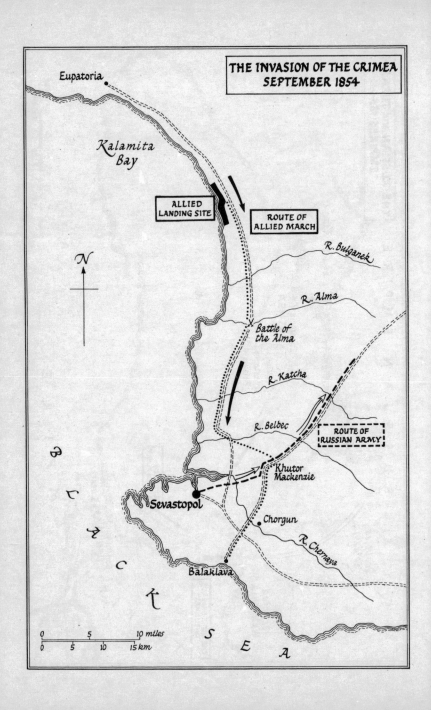

THE INVASION OF THE CRIMEA
SEPTEMBER 1854

Eupatoria

Kalamita Bay

ALLIED LANDING SITE

ROUTE OF ALLIED MARCH

N

R. Bulganek

R. Alma

Battle of the Alma

R. Katcha

R. Belbec

ROUTE OF RUSSIAN ARMY

Khutor Mackenzie

Sevastopol

Chorgun

R. Chernaya

Balaklava

B L A C K   S E A

0   5   10 miles
0 5 10 15 km

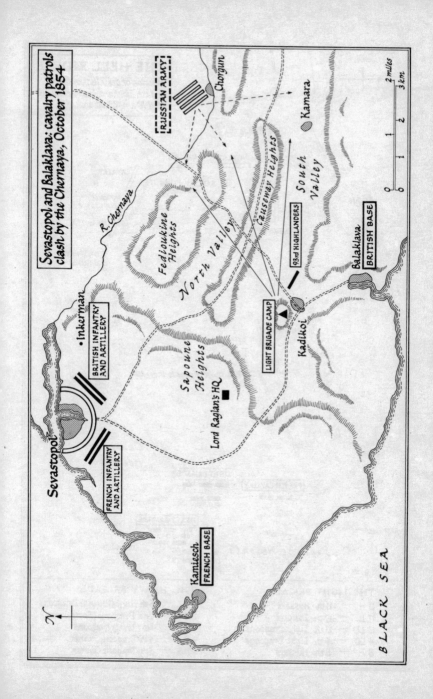

Sevastopol and Balaklava: cavalry patrols clash by the Chernaya, October 1854

RUSSIAN ARMY

Chorgun

Kamara

R. Chernaya

Fedioukine Heights

North Valley

Causeway Heights

South Valley

Inkerman

BRITISH INFANTRY AND ARTILLERY

93rd HIGHLANDERS

Balaklava
BRITISH BASE

Sapoune Heights

Lord Raglan's HQ

LIGHT BRIGADE CAMP

Kadikoi

Sevastopol

FRENCH INFANTRY AND ARTILLERY

Kamiesch
FRENCH BASE

BLACK SEA

N

0   1   2 miles
0   1   2   3 km

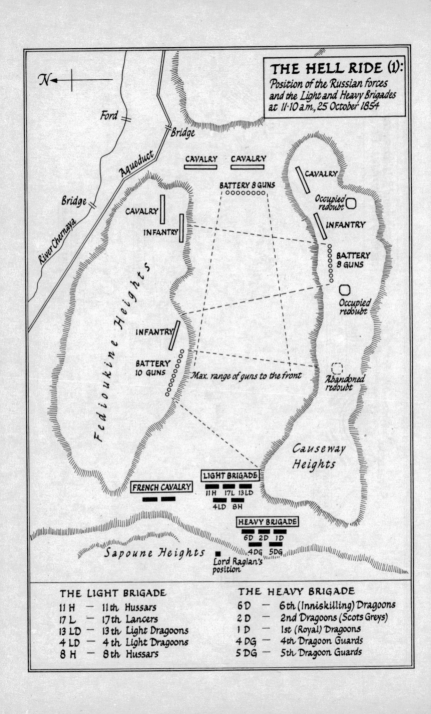

THE HELL RIDE (1):
Position of the Russian forces and the Light and Heavy Brigades at 11·10 a.m., 25 October 1854

N

Ford

Bridge

Aqueduct

Bridge

River Chernaya

CAVALRY   CAVALRY

BATTERY 8 GUNS
○○○○○○○○

CAVALRY

Occupied redoubt

CAVALRY

INFANTRY

INFANTRY

BATTERY 8 GUNS
○○○○○○○○

Occupied redoubt

Fedioukine Heights

INFANTRY

BATTERY 10 GUNS
○○○○○○○○○○

Max. range of guns to the front

Abandoned redoubt

Causeway Heights

LIGHT BRIGADE
11H 17L 13LD
4LD 8H

FRENCH CAVALRY

HEAVY BRIGADE
6D 2D 1D
4DG 5DG

Sapoune Heights

Lord Raglan's position

THE LIGHT BRIGADE		THE HEAVY BRIGADE	
11 H	11th Hussars	6 D	6th (Inniskilling) Dragoons
17 L	17th Lancers	2 D	2nd Dragoons (Scots Greys)
13 LD	13th Light Dragoons	1 D	1st (Royal) Dragoons
4 LD	4th Light Dragoons	4 DG	4th Dragoon Guards
8 H	8th Hussars	5 DG	5th Dragoon Guards

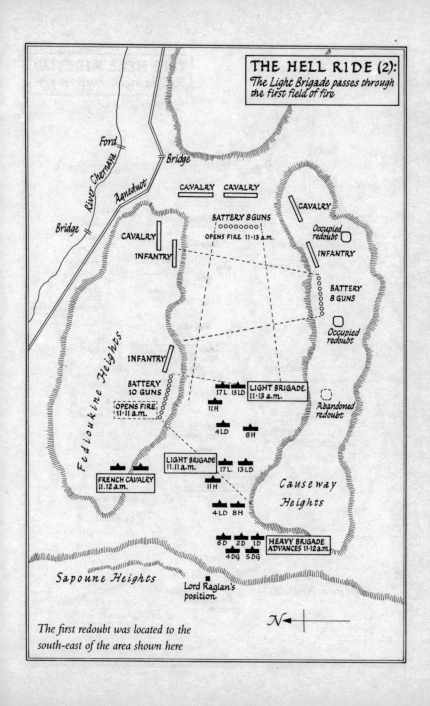

THE HELL RIDE (2):
The Light Brigade passes through the first field of fire

Ford

Bridge

River Chernaya

Aqueduct

Bridge

CAVALRY   CAVALRY

CAVALRY

BATTERY 8 GUNS
○○○○○○○○○
OPENS FIRE 11·13 a.m.

Occupied
redoubt

CAVALRY

INFANTRY

INFANTRY

BATTERY
8 GUNS
○○○○○○○○

Occupied
redoubt

Fedioukine Heights

INFANTRY

BATTERY
10 GUNS
○○○○○○

OPENS FIRE
11·11 a.m.   ○○

17 L   13 LD

LIGHT BRIGADE
11·13 a.m.

11 H

Abandoned
redoubt

4 LD   8 H

LIGHT BRIGADE
11·11 a.m.

17 L   13 LD

FRENCH CAVALRY
11·12 a.m.

11 H

*Causeway
Heights*

4 LD   8 H

6 D   2 D   1 D

HEAVY BRIGADE
ADVANCES 11·12 a.m.

4 DG   5 DG

Sapoune Heights

Lord Raglan's
position

N ←

*The first redoubt was located to the
south-east of the area shown here*

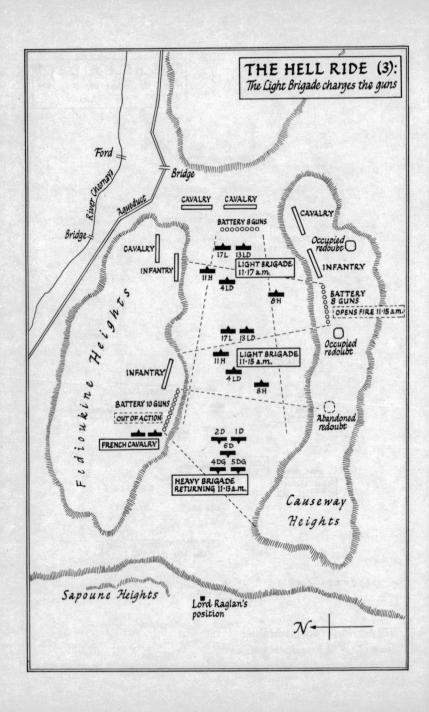

THE HELL RIDE (3):
The Light Brigade charges the guns

Ford

Bridge

River Chernaya

Aqueduct

Bridge

CAVALRY   CAVALRY

BATTERY 8 GUNS
○○○○○○○○

CAVALRY

Occupied
redoubt

CAVALRY

17 L   13 LD

INFANTRY

INFANTRY

LIGHT BRIGADE
11·17 a.m.

11 H

4 LD

8 H

BATTERY
8 GUNS
OPENS FIRE 11·15 a.m.

17 L   13 LD

Occupied
redoubt

11 H

LIGHT BRIGADE
11·15 a.m.

INFANTRY

4 LD

8 H

BATTERY 10 GUNS

OUT OF ACTION

Abandoned
redoubt

FRENCH CAVALRY

2 D   1 D

6 D

4 DG   5 DG

HEAVY BRIGADE
RETURNING 11·13 a.m.

Causeway

Heights

Fedioukine Heights

Sapoune Heights

Lord Raglan's
position

N

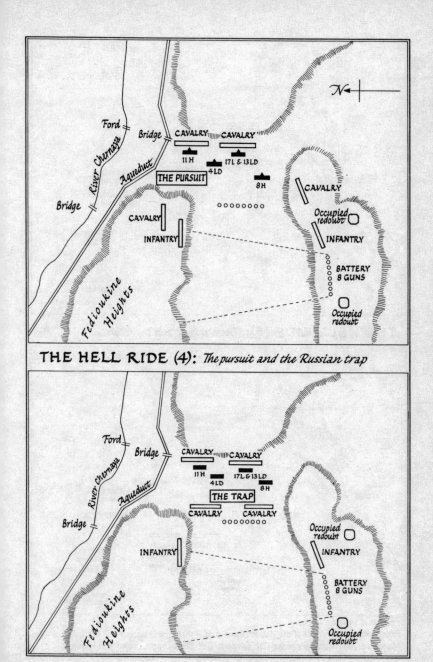

N

Ford
Bridge
River Chernaya
Aqueduct
Bridge

CAVALRY   CAVALRY
11 H   17 L & 13 LD
4 LD
8 H

THE PURSUIT

○○○○○○○○

CAVALRY

CAVALRY
Occupied
redoubt
INFANTRY

INFANTRY

BATTERY
8 GUNS

Occupied
redoubt

Fedioukine Heights

THE HELL RIDE (4): *The pursuit and the Russian trap*

Ford
Bridge
River Chernaya
Aqueduct
Bridge

CAVALRY   CAVALRY
11 H   17 L & 13 LD
4 LD   8 H

THE TRAP

CAVALRY   CAVALRY
○○○○○○○○

Occupied
redoubt
INFANTRY

INFANTRY

BATTERY
8 GUNS

Occupied
redoubt

Fedioukine
Heights

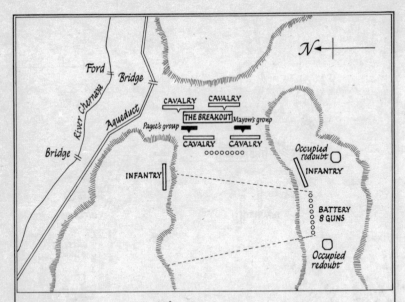

THE HELL RIDE (5): *The breakout and the return*

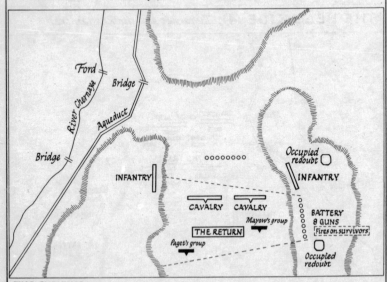

THE SURVIVORS

Paget's group: survivors of the 11th Hussars and 4th Light Dragoons

Mayow's group: survivors of the 17th Lancers, 13th Light Dragoons and 8th Hussars

ONE

The Invasion of the Crimea

Nothing remains but to fight it out with Russia.
The Times, 27 February 1854

1. The Bear Hunt

The Light Brigade prepares for war

On 11 March 1854, more than two weeks before Britain declared war on Russia, the five regiments of light cavalry that were to form the Light Brigade were alerted for foreign service. The first that the cavalrymen in the ranks knew of it was when they were required to hand in their sabres for sharpening.

Troop Sergeant Major George Smith of the 11th Hussars wrote that when the sabres were reissued, 'an order was given that they were not again to be drawn till required, when in the presence of the enemy'. This meant that all sword practice was banned, and for good reason. Each time the sabre was withdrawn from its unlined steel scabbard and each time it was replaced, the blade ran against the steel and lost something of its edge. A sharp blade had to be preserved for the enemy.

Britain declared war on Russia on 28 March. The five regiments were ordered to provide 300 men each, to form a brigade of 1,500. They were to march to their allotted embarkation ports: the 13th Light Dragoons and 17th Lancers to Portsmouth, the 4th Light Dragoons and 8th Hussars to Plymouth, and the 11th Hussars (then stationed in Ireland) to Kingstown. These 1,500 formed one small part of the army being mobilized, which with its infantry and artillery amounted to 27,000 men. The French would send 30,000 and the Turks 7,000.

Within days, throughout Britain, troops were marching south towards the ships waiting to transport them to the Black Sea. Queen Victoria and Prince Albert appeared on the balcony of Buckingham Palace to wave farewell to the regiments leaving London, and wished them a speedy victory. Most of Her Majesty's cavalry officers took that for granted. A cartoon in *Punch* magazine had an elegant young officer, clearly more familiar with the racecourse and the horse paths through London's fashionable parks than with the battlefield, addressing a lady: 'Of course it's rather a bore just at the beginning of the season, and I shall miss the Derby! Wish they could have the Russians over here, because then we could have thrashed them in Hyde Park, and dined at Greenwich afterwards, you know.'

The men, in contrast, exhibited the traditional bravado of soldiers off to war. When one restive mount of the 17th Lancers kicked out and Private Alfred Housden received a blow to the head that drew blood, the commanding officer of the regiment, Lieutenant Colonel Lawrenson, asked him if he was fit to continue. Housden replied that it was nothing to the cuts he expected to get before long.

The war against Russia was certainly popular with the people. The *Morning Advertiser*, much read in public houses, had declared Tsar Nicholas to be 'a fiend in human form' whose aim was to 'achieve an empire in Europe'. Crowds lined the streets of every town the Light Brigade regiments rode through, to shout 'Hurrah!' over the clatter of horseshoes on the cobblestones and the jingle of harness. The colourful uniforms and glinting sabres of the cavalrymen bobbing up and down on magnificently groomed thoroughbreds, and the pennons fluttering from the nine-foot shafts carried by the lancers, compounded the patriotic fervour of the people.

Popular cartoonists portrayed the Tsar as a mad bear about to ravage Turkey first and all Europe next. Englishmen who had never seen the Tsar, but had taunted the great bears exhibited by touring menageries, cried out to the men of the Light Brigade, 'Bring back the Big Bear in a cage.'

The thoughts of the men turned more readily to those they were leaving behind, and the two popular songs on every soldier's lips were 'Oh, Susannah, don't you cry for me' and 'Cheer, boys! Cheer'.

Cheer, boys! Cheer!
No more of idle sorrow.
Courage, true hearts, shall bear us on our way.
Hope points before and shows the bright tomorrow;
Let us forget the darkness of today.

In Russia troops were moving south too, to support those regiments that had already crossed the border into Turkey and to prevent any attempt to thwart the Tsar's plans. Priests travelled with the troops and led the constant chanting of psalms and singing of hymns, and peasant soldiers brought up in obedience to the faith joined in with gusto.

The Russian army was the largest in the world and as far as its officers were concerned their primary problem was not winning the war but getting there: the new railway from St Petersburg stopped at Moscow and from that point the infantry, artillery and cavalry had to travel by macadamized road or, more usually, dirt track. It would take these reinforcements as long to march to the battle zone as it took the British to sail there.

Among the reinforcements on the move were regiments of Don Cossack cavalry, made up entirely of farmers granted land by the Tsar on condition they fought for him when the need arose. While Russian regular troops were splendidly dressed and weighed down with equipment, Cossacks wore what they pleased, often a sheepskin cap and jerkin, and travelled light. Their ponies came from the wild herds that roamed the steppes and there was something wild about the men too. It was said that their own officers feared them.

Attached to the Don Cossack regiments were batteries of light horse artillery, each equipped with eight field guns manned by 200 gunners. It took a draught team of six horses to pull each gun and a team of three horses for each ammunition cart. Peasants working the fields in the great heartland of Russia spotted the dust clouds thrown up by hooves and cart wheels at a distance and stopped to watch the Cossack artillery pass by. When the gleaming brass guns on their bright green carriages accompanied by countless ammunition carts clattered through small towns and villages people left their homes to stare, awe-struck, or handed up vodka and cake to the gun crews.

Two great armies were on the march, thousands of miles apart. The cavalry of one and the artillery of the other had begun a journey that would bring them into bloody conflict at Balaklava, where the British light cavalry would ride hell's mile straight at the muzzles of the Russian guns.

The official cause of the war was a violent squabble between monks in one of the world's most holy places. What would lead eventually to the slaughter of the Light Brigade at Balaklava began with bloodshed and murder in the Church of the Nativity in Bethlehem, which is believed by Christians to stand over the site of the stable in which Jesus was born.

Palestine – the Holy Land – was at that time part of the Turkish empire; Turkish troops patrolled outside the Church of the Nativity to ensure the safety of pilgrims. But the real dangers were inside the building. The church was in the joint care of Greek Orthodox and Roman Catholic monks. The Orthodox monks held the key to the main entrance and, in the opinion of the Roman Catholics, acted as if they had sole ownership of the place. In 1847 the Orthodox monks removed a silver star fixed by the Roman Catholics to the precise spot on which the manger once stood. The Roman Catholics demanded that it be replaced. The Orthodox monks refused and fighting followed. Candlesticks and crucifixes were used as weapons.

Matters further escalated in 1852 when by some means the Roman Catholics acquired the key to the main door and replaced the star, though not without a violent struggle in which several Orthodox monks were killed. This became an international incident when the Orthodox monks asked for help from Tsar Nicholas I of Russia, who saw himself as the protector of Orthodox Christians around the world. The Tsar blamed the Turks for failing to protect the Orthodox monks in Bethlehem and demanded that the keys to the church be returned to them. In addition he required that the

Sultan of Turkey acknowledge the Tsar of Russia as the protector of all Christians on Turkish territory.

The keys were returned, but the Turks scoffed at the Tsar's claim to be the protector of Christians within their empire. In response Nicholas I sent his army into the Turkish provinces of Moldavia and Wallachia. He announced that he was not 'invading Turkey'; he was 'going to the defence of the Orthodox religion'.

No one in Constantinople, London or Paris swallowed that for a minute. For one hundred years the Russian empire had been expanding south into the Ukraine and the Crimea, until the Russian fleet sailing out of the great naval base at Sevastopol near the southern tip of the Crimea controlled the Black Sea. Yet Russia had still not become a world power on the scale of Great Britain and France; Turkey stood in the way of further expansion. The Turkish capital commanded the narrow straits linking the Black Sea to the Mediterranean. If Tsar Nicholas could take Constantinople, his fleet and troops would have access to the Mediterranean and from there the oceans and continents of the world. The occupation of Moldavia and Wallachia took his army as far as the Danube and within striking distance of Constantinople.

Initially the British and French sent their diplomats, not their gunboats. It was thought that Russia could be negotiated away from all-out war. In any case Queen Victoria, the Prime Minister Lord Aberdeen and *The Times* – a formidable threesome – were against military involvement.

In October 1853, after the Tsar had ignored a Turkish ultimatum to withdraw from the two provinces, fighting began between Russian and Turkish troops at Silistria on the Danube. But it was the war at sea that swung opinion in Britain. On 30 November the Russian Black Sea Fleet left its base at Sevastopol, mounted a surprise attack on the Turkish fleet at Sinope, and sank every ship; almost 4,000 Turkish sailors were killed or drowned.

Just as the incident in Bethlehem had given Tsar Nicholas a phoney reason for invading Turkey, so the action at Sinope gave Britain a phoney reason for rushing to Turkey's defence. The British press reported that most of the Turkish sailors had abandoned their sinking ships and been shot by Russian gunners while in the water crying out for mercy. Although there was no real evidence for this, the 'massacre' fuelled British public enthusiasm for war with Russia. Crowds gathered in London to demand that action be taken against Tsar Nicholas. The Queen and the Prime Minister changed their minds in favour of war. *The Times* agreed and on 27 February 1854 – the day Britain issued an ultimatum to the Tsar to withdraw his troops from Moldavia and Wallachia – an editorial attempted to define the war fever that gripped the nation: 'The prevalent feeling is an honourable and a just one. It is that England has bound herself to assist a weak neighbour against the violence of a strong one. It is, in fact, the people's quarrel.'

Tennyson was living on the Isle of Wight and could see the ships of the British fleet gathering at Portsmouth. He began work on a long poem, *Maud*, about a young man torn between fighting for the love of a girl and enlisting for the coming war. The man – and Tennyson – came down on the side of a war that was seen as a moral crusade:

> Let it flame or fade, and the war roll down like a wind,
> We have proved we have hearts in a cause, we are noble still,
> And myself have awakened, as it seems, to the better mind;
> It is better to fight for the good, than to rail at the ill.

This simplistic explanation for British involvement in the Crimea can still be found 150 years later in history books. It is argued that after forty years of peace (since Waterloo) the British sense of goodness and justice 'awakened' to oppose the evil designs of a Russian tyrant on a weak neighbour. Some even suggest that popular opinion ran ahead of political intent and forced a decision in favour of war that might not otherwise have been taken.

This view is naive in the extreme. The politicians in London were not about to fight – from their perspective, fund – a war merely because the British sense of goodness and justice demanded it, however much the press and the public clamoured for action. They needed a much stronger reason than that, and they had one.

Whether it was a massacre or not, the action at Sinope proved the power of the Russian Black Sea Fleet. It was a naval challenge to the British, who supposedly reigned supreme on the seas of the world. The threat was not primarily to Europe, as the popular press trumpeted and the people believed, but to the all-important trade routes to India. When a number of prominent businessmen voiced opposition to the war, the well-connected *Westminster Review* let slip what it was really about: 'Everything hangs upon our conduct in the present crisis. Our passage to India depends upon it. Our commerce with all free nations depends upon it. When the Tsar makes a Russian lake of the Mediterranean, our merchants will rue their blind folly in declining to stop him while it was yet possible. The crisis of the civilised world is upon us.' The brand of civilization under threat was that carried around the world by British trade.

Military thinking in London was that Tsar Nicholas wished to expand his empire into India, and that taking Turkey was merely the first step. The British ambassador in St Petersburg Sir George Seymour had suggested to his political masters in London: 'If Turkey falls, Russia might be expected to revert with increased eagerness to her designs on the Indian possessions of Great Britain.' The First Lord of the Admiralty, Admiral Sir James Graham, wrote to Lord Clarendon, British Foreign Secretary, advising what must be done to prevent this: 'The operation which will be decisive is the capture and destruction of Sevastopol. The eye-tooth of the Bear must be drawn, and his Fleet and Naval Arsenal in the Black Sea destroyed.'

The French too felt that an extension of Russian sea power into the Mediterranean would threaten their overseas possessions. The British ambassador in Paris Lord Cowley, after sounding out Napoleon III, reported to Clarendon that the French would join any move against this common threat, and added a note of his own which confirmed the true objective of the war: 'How I rejoice at your determination about Sevastopol. It was but the other day that I said to the Emperor that if we let slip this occasion to do up the Russian navy in the Black Sea, we should repent it bitterly.

Therefore I say burn and destroy everything, and send double the ships to do it if necessary.'

Four weeks after Britain's ultimatum the Tsar had not withdrawn his troops from Moldavia and Wallachia. On 27 March, Queen Victoria informed Parliament that she felt 'bound to afford active assistance' to Turkey against 'unprovoked aggression'. The following day both Britain and France declared war on Russia. The plan revealed to the press was to send an allied force to Constantinople in support of the Turks fighting to repel Russian troops at Silistria on the Danube. No one mentioned invading the Crimea. But the base chosen for the Anglo-French force was Varna, strategically placed in accord with the declared aims of the campaign between Constantinople and the border with Russia – and directly across the Black Sea from Sevastopol.

The real reason why Britain declared war on Russia had less to do with defending Turkey or any higher battle on behalf of goodness and justice than with giving the Russian bear a beating, preserving the supremacy of the Royal Navy and protecting the trade routes to India. It was a stroke of sheer luck that the Russian 'massacre' of Turkish sailors at Sinope had the British public clamouring for an attack on the naval base of Sevastopol, the true but as yet unacknowledged target of the British and French armies now on the march towards their embarkation ports.

The Cavalry Division embarking for the war with Russia in April 1854 was composed of two brigades: the Heavy Brigade, made up of five heavy cavalry regiments, and the Light Brigade, with five light cavalry regiments. In practice there was little difference between 'Heavies' and 'Lights'. Traditionally, light cavalry (lighter men on swifter horses) was used to patrol ahead of the army, while heavy cavalry (bigger men on more powerful horses) was held back for the final, decisive charge in a battle. But since Waterloo the number of regiments had been reduced and it had become necessary for both types of cavalry to perform both functions. The difference in 1854 was little more than a matter of colour: red uniform jackets for the Heavy Brigade and blue for the Light Brigade.

There were three types of light cavalry: light dragoons, hussars and lancers. The Light Brigade was composed of the 4th and 13th Light Dragoons, the 8th and 11th Hussars, and the 17th Lancers. They performed identical duties and their blue uniform jackets were resplendent with similar gold braid and silver accoutrements, so that when brigaded together they were most easily told apart by their headgear. Light dragoons wore a beaver-skin shako shaped like a tall top hat with a peak; hussars sported a fur busby similar to a shako but without the peak and with a decorative 'bag' hanging to one side; lancers wore a leather chapska – a square-topped cap much like an academic mortar-board with a peak.

When the press mocked the appearance of these 'peacock regiments' and declared their apparel unfit for war, it was not the elaborate jackets or caps that were picked out, but their impractical tight-fitting trousers. Because two regiments wore their trousers in blue, two in grey and the 11th Hussars in cherry red, the latter attracted the greatest ridicule. When ordered to mobilize, the 11th's officers – aware their skin-tight trousers would not withstand the many hours in the saddle required by active service – sent them to their tailors to have black leather patches sewn onto the seats. *Punch* magazine made fun of this reinforcement in verse:

> Oh, pantaloons of cherry!
> Oh, redder than raspberry!
> For men to fight in things so tight
> It must be trying – very.
>
> 'Gainst wear, though fine the weather,
> They would not hold together.
> On saddle-back they'd fly and crack,
> Though seated with black leather.

On 22 April a letter writer to *The Times* who signed himself 'Common-sense' joined in: 'The splendour of these magnificent light horsemen, the shortness of their jackets, the tightness of their cherry-coloured pants, is as utterly unfit for war service as the garb of the female hussars in the ballet of Gustavus, which they so nearly resemble.'

There was however a more serious accusation levelled against the Light Brigade as it prepared for war: that its officers, rather than its uniforms, were most unfit for active service.

Most cavalry officers had attended exclusive schools such as Eton where knowledge of Greek and performance on the sports field mattered most and anything smacking of practical education was considered below those born to command the lower classes. There was no required military training – the Royal Military College at Sandhurst admitted only six students in 1854 – and young men went straight into cavalry regiments as officers. Nothing was asked of them except the purchase price of the commission they were acquiring. The lowest officer rank, that of cornet, could be bought for £840, a sum only the sons of the wealthiest families could hope to raise. Many new officers brought with them some skill in riding and an enthusiasm for hunting the fox, but little else.

Those cavalry officers who were no longer so young wore whalebone corsets to hide unsoldierly bellies and show off their exquisitely tailored and very expensive uniforms to best effect, and were more often to be found in gentlemen's clubs than in barracks. Cartoonists exaggerated their waspish waists and drew them perpetually surrounded by clouds of cigar (not cannon) smoke. A *Punch* cartoon mocking their stilted speech and air of superiority, had one cavalry officer ask of another: 'I say, old Fellah – Do you think it pwobable the infantwy will accompany us to Sevastopol?'

There were exceptions: officers who combined intelligence with experience and held their ranks on merit. Typical of these was Captain William Morris of the 17th Lancers. At thirty-four he was one of very few to have attended the Royal Military College, had fought in three previous campaigns, and while serving with the 16th Lancers had taken part in that regiment's charge against a battery of Sikh guns at Aliwal. Sadly, Morris and officers with similar experience, most of it gained in India, were outnumbered by those whose only qualifications were wealth and social standing and who had nothing but contempt for these 'Indian' officers.

Because officers with the funds to do so invariably went on half-pay to avoid accompanying their regiments to India, those who had served there were considered to have revealed their lower standing and were shunned.

Among the 1,500 private soldiers of the Light Brigade there was a similar mixture of experienced men and raw recruits. Each regiment had its share of long-serving cavalrymen with hard-won experience of battle. Private John Brooks of the 13th Light Dragoons enlisted in 1842 and took part in all the major battles of the Sikh Wars of 1845–6 and 1848–9, while Trumpeter William Smith of the 11th Hussars enlisted in 1836 and fought in the Afghan War of 1839 and the Sikh Wars. Some experienced cavalrymen in regiments not chosen for the Crimea transferred to regiments that were. Corporal John Penn had served in India with the 3rd Light Dragoons, which had only recently returned to England and was bottom of the list for foreign service, and he transferred to the 17th Lancers.

Despite many such transfers each of the five regiments remained under strength. When regimental bands were broken up and the musicians returned to the ranks, not all of the bandsmen were happy about going to war. Two brothers named Deakon, who played first cornet and trombone for the 17th Lancers, deserted and were traced to the orchestra at the Argyle Rooms, a London music hall. They escaped capture by the patrol sent to arrest them and were later rumoured to be working as performers with Wombwell's Travelling Menagerie. Even with their bandsmen the regiments were forced to include among those marching to war raw recruits totally lacking in cavalry experience. Thomas Tomsett, a bricklayer, enlisted in the 4th Light Dragoons on 25 January 1854, and George Wootten, a baker, joined the 11th Hussars on 27 January. Seven weeks later their regiments were mobilized and the two men were marching south for the ships. It is questionable how confident such recruits were in the saddle, let alone how proficient they were with a sabre.

There was a wide age range. Trumpeter Smith of the 11th Hussars joined his regiment in the year that eighteen-year-old

Private Henry George of the 13th Light Dragoons was born. Private William Wilson of the 8th Hussars, the youngest man in the brigade, was only sixteen. Most were in their mid to late twenties. Of those men whose occupation prior to enlisting was recorded, more than one third were land workers, farriers, grooms and others whose work brought them into daily contact with horses. Others had worked as servants, tailors, shoemakers, clerks, carpenters, painters, chemists and weavers. Private James Dies of the 8th Hussars had been an umbrella-frame maker. Most had one thing in common: they had never drawn a sabre in anger or faced enemy guns.

Although the primary weapon of the cavalry other than lancer regiments was the sabre, there was no literal sabre rattling at the prospect of war. The term derived from the metallic clatter produced when the scabbard was shaken with the sabre inside, this done to instil fear in an enemy, though even walking or riding made a similar jangle. The continuous movement of steel against steel had a blunting effect even if the sabre was never drawn, and many experienced cavalrymen stuffed straw down the full length of the scabbard to protect the newly sharpened blade.

The sabre's three-foot blade was slightly curved to ease its passage through flesh and blood. It was a cut and thrust weapon – a sharp edge to cut and a point to thrust – and there was much argument about which of these was better in the mêlée. The cut had to slice deeply enough to disable; drawing blood was not enough. Because the leather helmets and belts and the particularly thick greatcoats worn by Russian soldiers had to be cut through first, if a blade was not razor sharp it might bruise or bloody an opponent without disabling him. Those against the cut described it as 'hacking' because several swipes were often required to cause injury. The thrust was favoured by many cavalrymen because using this action the sabre could penetrate further into the body and was more likely to disable or kill an opponent and to do so in one go. It had one disadvantage: the blade could become 'locked' inside an opponent's body, held by bone or contracting muscle, and prove impossible to withdraw.

The main weapon carried by the 17th Lancers was a nine-foot

ash lance with a pointed steel head, held by a white leather arm strap fixed at the point of balance. Attached just below the point was a swallow-tailed, red-over-white pennon. While on patrol or during an advance the lance was held at the 'Carry' – upright with its base resting in a small leather bucket fixed to the stirrup. When the regiment was ordered to charge, it was removed from the bucket and lowered to the 'Engage', angled slightly downward to target the chest of a dismounted man.

The lance was made for the charge. The sight of lance points hurtling forward could unnerve an enemy; running was useless and the longer reach of the lance meant that a man who stood and fought was pierced long before he could slash at the lancer with his sword. But the lance lost its benefit in the mêlée. With the loss of momentum and distance from an opponent, it became an unwieldy impediment totally without penetrative power. Once an enemy got 'inside' the lance it was the lancer who was left defenceless until he could draw his sabre.

All cavalrymen except lancers carried a percussion carbine; lancers carried a percussion pistol. The carbine, with an unwieldy twenty-one-inch barrel, was of little use to a man mounted and on the move. The pistol's nine-inch barrel made it a more practicable weapon, although its holster was attached to the saddle and covered by the saddlecloth, making it almost inaccessible in action. None of the survivors of the charge record using these weapons. Apart from a few officers who used one of the new Colt or Adams 're-volving pistols' in the mêlée following the charge, the Light Brigade faced the enemy with sabre and lance.

The batteries of Cossack horse artillery travelling south through the heartland of Russia were each equipped with four 6-pounder and four 12-pounder guns. These figures indicate the weight of the ammunition each gun fired, and multiplying the weight by one hundred gives an approximate maximum range in yards, so a 6-pounder could fire up to 600 yards. The guns fired three types of ammunition: roundshot, shell and canister.

A roundshot, or cannonball, was a solid iron ball most effective against compact groups of men. Its weight and momentum were such that it could pass right through a man without losing power, and on through the next, and so on, killing or removing a limb from up to eight men. Nevertheless men who had seen action in India knew that cavalry could successfully charge artillery – the 16th Lancers had done so at Aliwal in 1846 – and sustain bearable losses. Because they charged in a line only two deep, the maximum loss from any one roundshot fired from the front was two men. But roundshot fired from one or both flanks, which came *along* the line, could hit four, six or eight men apiece, and it was a maxim of the cavalry charge that enemy artillery on either flank had to be put out of action before the advance began.

Although roundshot was still extensively used, it was rapidly being replaced by the shell. This was a metal container packed with gunpowder and fitted with a fuse preset to ignite the powder after between five and thirty seconds, according to the distance between the gun and the enemy. If the fuse was set correctly the shell exploded over the heads of the enemy troops, showering them with deadly shards of shell casing.

Both roundshot and shell were used against a distant or middle-range enemy. As an enemy closed on the guns, the crews loaded canister, also known as case shot. This was a thin metal container which broke up as it left the muzzle of the gun and dispersed the pellets it contained over a wide area. At short range, canister had a devastating effect on men and horses alike.

As they journeyed towards their embarkation points the officers and men of the Light Brigade gave little thought to the capabilities of Cossack guns; it was the capabilities of their own commanders that most concerned them. Lord Lucan had been appointed to command the Cavalry Division in February 1854, placing him in overall command of the Heavy and Light Brigades. On 1 April the two brigade commanders were appointed: General Scarlett was given the Heavies and Lord Cardigan the Lights.

This news shocked the Light Brigade. Some of the men thought it an April Fool's jest. All had heard of their lordships Lucan and Cardigan. In barrack rooms and public houses where soldiers gathered there was much talk of them. The newspapers catalogued their ineptness, their scandals and their cruelty to officers and men alike. Moreover these two aristocratic brothers-in-law so hated each other that on the rare occasions when they met, they refused to speak. Now the well-being of the Light Brigade depended on their generalship and their ability to work together.

Few cavalrymen had any real hatred for the Russians they expected to face; most detested and feared their divisional and brigade commanders with a passion far more keenly felt. The officers were just as outspoken and Captain Robert Portal of the 4th Light Dragoons dared to include his opinions in a letter home: 'We are commanded by one of the greatest old women in the British Army, called the Earl of Cardigan. He has as much brains as my boot. He is only equalled in want of intellect by his relation the Earl of Lucan. Without mincing matters two such fools could not be picked out of the British Army to take command.' These sentiments shocked Portal's parents and his father replied with a reprimand.

While officers of the Heavy Brigade regiments applauded the appointment of the popular James Scarlett as their brigade commander, they sympathized with the plight of their Light Brigade comrades. Major William Forrest of the 4th Dragoon Guards wrote: 'We all agree that two greater muffs than Lucan and Cardigan could not be. We call Lucan the cautious ass and Cardigan the dangerous ass.'

2. The Ruling Asses

Their lordships Lucan and Cardigan take command

At 11.00 a.m. on 25 October 1854, on the plain above Balaklava, an aide-de-camp delivered Lord Raglan's order to Lord Lucan. Lucan rode over to Lord Cardigan with the written order in his hand. It took the two men twenty seconds to determine the fate of the Light Brigade.

LUCAN: Lord Cardigan, you are to advance down the valley with the Light Brigade. I will follow in support with the Heavy Brigade.
CARDIGAN: Certainly, sir. But allow me to point out to you that the Russians have a battery in the valley on our front, and batteries and riflemen on both sides.
LUCAN: I know it, but Lord Raglan will have it. We have no choice but to obey.

They did in fact have a choice. Raglan himself said as much that evening after the enormity of the mistake had become clear: 'Lord Lucan, you were a Lieutenant General and should therefore have exercised your discretion, and, not approving of the charge, should not have caused it to be made.' Lucan could and should have discussed the sense of the order with Cardigan. Agreeing that a charge into the muzzles of the Russian guns meant the obliteration of the brigade, he should have sent the aide back to Raglan with this observation, requesting confirmation of the order. The misunderstanding would then have been revealed.

Such a discussion should have come naturally for they were brothers-in-law, yet hardly a civil word had passed between them since Lucan married Cardigan's sister Ann in 1829. At this most critical moment when a frank examination of their options could have saved the Light Brigade, they could not break through the rigid civility of a mutual disgust that had been building for twenty-five years.

And so the Light Brigade advanced.

George Bingham, third Earl of Lucan was fifty-four years old when he took command of the Cavalry Division bound for the Crimea. Long before that he had become one of the most reviled men in Britain.

Born in London in 1800, the eldest son of the second Earl of Lucan, at the age of sixteen George Bingham joined the 6th Regiment of Foot. Ten years later he was commanding officer of the 17th Lancers, one of the most distinguished cavalry regiments in the British army. Such rapid promotion might suggest remarkable skills as a cavalry officer. In truth it indicated only great wealth. The purchase system by which officer ranks could be bought and sold allowed the landed gentry to leapfrog more experienced men. They knew well enough how to work the system – they had been brought up to it and considered a position of command their rightful place – but if some wag had thought to write down the necessary steps, it would have gone something like this:

How to Buy a Cavalry Regiment

1. Purchase the rank of cornet (the lowest officer rank). Any regiment will do, because you will soon be moving on. Cost: £840. This amount is set by an official list, but you may have to pay up to twice as much. Because it is illegal to ask more than the authorized price, the seller will require you to pay £840 for the rank and a second, exorbitant sum for a worn sword or a useless horse.

2. Purchase the rank of lieutenant as soon as a vacancy arises in your own or some more desirable regiment. Cost: £1,190 or more. Remember that you can sell your old rank of cornet and set the proceeds against the cost of your new rank of lieutenant.

3. Purchase the rank of captain. Cost: £3,225 or more, minus what

you receive when you sell the rank of lieutenant. You are not, of course, financially dependent on your pay as an officer; therefore in the case of this and every other rank, the day after purchasing it, go on half-pay. You will then have no duties to perform and will not even have to reside with the regiment while you wait for a vacancy to arise in the next rank.

4. Purchase the rank of major. At this level there may be officers with the rank of captain who have seen many years active service in India and who feel themselves more qualified for promotion, but you have nothing to fear from them – they do not have the wealth to outbid you. Cost: £4,575 or more.

5. You may now wish to spend some time with your regiment. It can be most pleasant parading the men in Hyde Park and the social life of the officers' mess is quite acceptable. Should your regiment be posted to India or some other undesirable foreign quarter, return immediately to half-pay.

6. Purchase the rank of lieutenant colonel. This rank is held only by the commanding officer and the regiment is now yours. Cost: £6,175, but you may have to pay a great deal more for a distinguished cavalry regiment.

Bingham worked the system to perfection, using the twin absurdities of purchase and half-pay to gain promotion without spending time with the regiments he passed through. Thus he became a cornet in the 3rd Foot on 24 December 1818 and went on half-pay the next day. He transferred to the cavalry when an opportunity arose, remaining a lieutenant and then a captain only until a vacancy occurred above him. He purchased the rank of major in the 17th Lancers on 1 December 1825, and less than one year later the rank of lieutenant colonel, for which he paid £25,000, four times the official figure.

The senior major of the 17th Lancers Anthony Bacon was an officer of long experience who had fought against Napoleon at Waterloo and thought himself next in line to command the regiment. But because he did not have sufficient funds to meet the asking price, the command went to Bingham, who had seen no action whatsoever. Bacon, in disgust, resigned from the regiment.

Although the purchase system was clearly absurd – in this instance it meant that the 17th Lancers was commanded by its wealthiest rather than its most experienced officer – it existed for a reason: if the upper class commanded the army, the army could not become a threat to the upper class. The French Revolution had succeeded at least partly because it had gained the support of middle-class army officers, men who had risen to senior positions on merit. English aristocrats were not about to let that situation develop in their own land.

Having bought the 17th Lancers, Bingham lavished more of his money on the regiment, buying smart uniforms for the men and the best horses available. The 17th soon acquired a reputation for elegance and the nickname 'Bingham's Dandies'. What money could not buy – a perfect, regulation-book performance on the parade ground – he sought to achieve by bullying the officers and constantly drilling the men. Officers were publicly abused for the slightest irregularity and soldiers flogged for trivial offences. Lady Lavinia Spencer, his aunt, wrote to him: 'I hear universal criticism of your conduct as Colonel of the 17th, your reputation of great severity and harshness, lack of self control and unpopularity with your officers.' Due to Lady Spencer's intervention or not, he decided to absent himself from his regiment for twelve months, much to the relief of the 17th.

In June 1829, Bingham married Lady Ann Brudenell, daughter of the sixth Earl of Cardigan and sister of James Brudenell. Bingham and Brudenell, who would become the seventh Earl of Cardigan, had always disliked each other and the fact that they were now brothers-in-law magnified that dislike to the point of mutual loathing. Whenever they met they either argued or refused to speak. For the moment the solution was simple enough: they contrived as far as possible never to meet.

Bingham and his wife settled in Ireland, where the 17th Lancers was stationed, and he reassumed command of the regiment. He appeared to have mellowed and there were junior officers who spoke well of him. In 1837 he gave up his command to concentrate on running the family estate at Castlebar in County Mayo, and when his father died in 1839 he became the third Earl of Lucan.

Ireland was a nation of tenant farmers whose plots of land barely produced enough to sustain the families that worked them and lived on their main crop, the potato. If a surplus was produced any money made was needed to pay rent to English landlords. The rent due to Lord Lucan from the tenants on his Castlebar estate should have provided a considerable annual income, but they could not pay it. His solution was to group the smallholdings into larger, more profitable farms and greatly reduce the number of men working the land, so that the remaining few could support themselves *and* pay him rent. It meant turning the majority off the estate and he conducted a campaign against his own tenants, evicting families by force and demolishing the huts in which they lived so that they could not return. He quickly became the most hated man in Ireland.

In 1845 an evil greater even than Lord Lucan spread across the land. Potatoes became diseased with 'the rot' and the whole crop was lost. With no income to buy other food, many families starved. In 1846 the crop failed again and virtually the whole Irish population of eight million was without food.

Lucan's campaign nevertheless continued without pause. He formed 'crowbar brigades' of fifty men each to pull down the huts. If the occupants refused to move out, their homes were demolished over their heads. The Bishop of Meath witnessed a hut pulled down with a family still inside but unable to move out, so weak were they from starvation. Josephine Butler, who was a young girl in Mayo during the harsh winter of 1846, later wrote: 'Sick and aged, little children, and women with child were alike thrust forth into the cold snows of winter, and to prevent their return their cabins were levelled to the ground. The majority rendered penniless by the years of famine, wandered aimlessly about the roads and bogs till they found refuge in the workhouse or the grave.'

As whole villages disappeared from the Irish landscape, the Earl of Lucan was nicknamed 'The Exterminator'. The government in London was by now alarmed, not so much by the heartlessness of

Lucan's campaign, as by its effects on the exchequer. Relief was paid to the starving and homeless in the form of road-building work for the men and food for the women and children, and by January 1847 half a million men were employed on the roads and their two million dependants were receiving food.

Many other English landlords evicted their tenants too, making thousands more homeless, but Lord Brougham, speaking in the House of Lords on 15 February 1847, laid particular blame on the Earl of Lucan: 'The landlord in Mayo had thought it necessary to serve his tenants with notice to quit in the midst of one of the most severe winters that had ever been known, in the midst of the pestilence too which followed in the train of famine. He had turned out these wretched creatures when there was no food in the country and no money to buy it.' Brougham went on to describe the flood of starving Irish families pouring into Liverpool – 5,200 people in the last five days, he said – and every one of them had to be fed at England's expense. Many more fled to the United States.

Hundreds of Irishmen chose to join the British army in prefer-ence to starvation or the workhouse. A large proportion of them had worked horses on the land and joined cavalry regiments if they could. Ironically, many of these would eventually serve in the Crimea under the command of the man who had evicted them from their homes.

Throughout the period that Lucan lived at Castlebar House, Lady Lucan was seldom more than a visitor. She spent most of her time in London and was regularly seen at fashionable dinner parties. She complained to her brother Lord Cardigan that Lucan treated her badly. Cardigan confronted Lucan, who was enraged at such interference, and the animosity between the brothers-in-law further increased. When the commander-in-chief the Duke of Wellington attempted to mediate, he got nowhere and gave up, declaring that his victory at Waterloo was far easier won than any reconciliation between these two feuding earls.

Their mutual hatred might well have gone no further. Lucan was in Castlebar, while Cardigan divided his time between the family estate in Northamptonshire and his London house, and they never met. Two events early in 1854 combined to change that. First, Lady Lucan left her husband, Cardigan blaming Lucan for the failure of the marriage and his sister's 'disgrace'. Second, as the army prepared for war with Russia both men were given senior positions of command in the cavalry.

Lord Lucan had given up command of the 17th Lancers in 1837, and despite having no military service since then on 21 February 1854 he was appointed to command the Cavalry Division. His limited experience as an officer hardly explained the appointment, and some thought his conduct as a landlord – particularly the relentless war he waged against the Irish peasants and the ruthless energy with which he fought it – had won him this promotion from command of the crowbar brigades. Lucan was overjoyed, until command of the Light Brigade was given to the one Englishman he despised more than the lowliest Irish peasant, his brother-in-law. Lord Cardigan would be his subordinate but their animosity, so recently intensified by the breakdown of Lucan's marriage, would make the Cavalry Division an uncomfortable command.

The two appointments shocked London society. It was said that hostilities between the British cavalry and the Russians might be a trifle compared with those expected to break out between their lordships Lucan and Cardigan.

James Brudenell, seventh Earl of Cardigan was fifty-seven when he took command of the Light Brigade. While some considered his brother-in-law the most reviled man in Britain, others thought Cardigan more deserving of the title.

James Brudenell was born in 1797, the eldest son of the sixth Earl, and grew up at the family's ancestral home, Deene Park in Northamptonshire. In May 1824, aged twenty-seven, he purchased the rank of cornet in the 8th Hussars. He bought the rank of lieutenant in January 1825, captain in June 1826 – married Elizabeth Tollemache that same year, a good marriage being second only to a good regiment – and paid for his promotion to major in August 1830. Finally, in 1832 he purchased the lieutenant colonelcy of the 15th Hussars. Brudenell said that it cost him £10,000; *The Times* claimed that he paid between £35,000 and £40,000. It had taken him only eight years to gain command of a distinguished cavalry regiment, though in that time he had seen no action and only been present for regimental duty for a total of three years, having spent five years absent on half-pay.

Experienced and long-serving junior officers of the 15th Hussars without the means to buy promotion hardly welcomed their new commanding officer. Brudenell had no great regard for them either. He habitually shouted at and publicly reprimanded them for trivial offences, and appeared to delight in taunting those who had neither his wealth nor his social position, which was almost everyone.

He picked on Captain Augustus Wathen more than any other. Among Wathen's misdemeanours were purchasing new stable jackets for the men – even though Brudenell himself had ordered the purchase – and speaking discourteously to his commanding officer – when Wathen protested about the former accusation, pointing out that *he* had considered the old stable jackets to be still serviceable. Brudenell brought Wathen to court martial, but when detailed in court the pettiness and trickery behind the accusations became apparent and the captain was acquitted. It was left to *The Times* to ask:

How came Lord Brudenell – an officer of no experience comparable to those of a hundred other gentlemen who had seen and beaten a foreign enemy – how came such an unripe gallant as this to be put over the heads of so many worthier candidates, to be forced into a command for which he has proved himself utterly incompetent? Such a man ought never to have been placed at the head of a regiment.

King William IV agreed and ordered that Brudenell be removed from command of the 15th Hussars. That should have put an end to his military career. But *The Times* knew well enough the answer to its own question – wealth had enabled Brudenell to secure command of the 15th – and only two years later, on 25 March 1836, this same allowed him to purchase the lieutenant colonelcy of the 11th Hussars. It was rumoured that he paid more than

£40,000 for it, and that the King had come under pressure from the Cardigan family not to prevent it, being assured that Brudenell had learned his lesson. That was hardly the point. There were two majors in the 11th Hussars, both with considerable experience, but neither could find the money to outbid Brudenell. A Member of Parliament asked how such men would 'view the advancement over their heads of one who had never heard the sound of a musket'. But Brudenell was working the system and there was nothing to be done.

On the death of his father on 14 August 1837 James Brudenell became the seventh Earl of Cardigan. With the income of the family estates now at his disposal he spent £10,000 a year on his new regiment, purchasing bright new uniforms for the men, including tight, cherry-coloured trousers. These latter earned the 11th Hussars the nickname 'Cherry Bums' (discreetly pronounced 'Cherubims' in drawing rooms and wherever ladies were present). New uniforms, combined with constant drilling, soon won the 11th a reputation as the best-attired and most competent regiment on the parade ground.

On 18 May 1840, Major General Sleigh, inspector general of cavalry, visited the 11th Hussars at Canterbury Barracks and was entertained to dinner in the officers' mess. Although the champagne flowed freely, one member of Sleigh's staff asked if he might be served wine and Captain John Reynolds ordered a bottle to be brought to him. Cardigan, who had ordered only champagne to be served, later reprimanded Reynolds. When the captain replied that he had merely acceded to a guest's request when to refuse might have given offence, he was placed under arrest. From that day Cardigan continued to victimize Reynolds until the captain took the only remedy allowed him and left the regiment.

Cardigan immediately picked on another officer, Captain Richard Reynolds (no relation). Although this man's parents had died, leaving him responsible for ten younger brothers and sisters, Cardigan ordered that 'Richard Reynolds is not to be granted even a day's leave of absence on any pretext whatsoever'. When Reynolds protested, Cardigan shouted at him in front of the regiment, calling him 'insubordinate and insulting'. And when Reynolds wrote to Cardigan in words that appeared to challenge his commanding officer to a duel, he was arrested and held to await court martial.

On 4 September a letter in support of Reynolds appeared in the *Morning Chronicle*, claiming that Lord Cardigan regularly insulted his officers and, when challenged by them, used his position as their commanding officer to avoid a duel. The writer, Captain Harvey Tuckett, had recently left the 11th Hussars, having had enough of Lord Cardigan. Cardigan demanded an apology and, when Tuckett refused, challenged him to a duel.

The two men met at the windmill on Wimbledon Common at 5.00 p.m. on 12 September 1840. It was a poor choice of meeting place for what was an unlawful pursuit because the miller also served as a constable. Cardigan and Tuckett exchanged shots; both missed. Each took up a second pistol and fired again; Tuckett collapsed, wounded in the side. By this time the constable had reached them. He confiscated the pistols and arrested Lord Cardigan. In a brief appearance at the Old Bailey to answer a charge of participating in a duel, Cardigan claimed the right to be tried by his peers in the House of Lords. This was arranged for February the following year.

Meanwhile the court martial of Richard Reynolds took place. In his defence Reynolds described 'the long course of violence, insolence and vindictiveness' by which Cardigan had victimized him. But Cardigan was not on trial and Reynolds, in responding to such provocation in words that appeared to challenge his commanding officer to a duel, had committed an offence. For that he was cashiered: forced to leave the regiment without the right to sell on his rank to another.

The Times asked why Cardigan should 'for the second time be whitewashed from his offences' and there were demonstrations in London demanding that he be removed from command of the 11th Hussars. He was recognized on Brighton station and loudly booed until the crowd gathered round him became so agitated that he had to be protected by railway staff. On 30 October he attended a performance at Brighton Theatre, but when he was noticed in his box those in the stalls hissed and booed, and the commotion continued for so long that the theatre manager asked Cardigan to leave so that the performance might begin.

On 16 February 1841 he appeared in the House of Lords to answer the charge of duelling, for which the penalty was death or transportation, although clearly a peer of the realm was not going to face either of those. *The Times* demanded far more than a reprimand – 'Let his head be cropped, let him be put on an oatmeal diet, let him labour on the treadmill' – and while the thought of such indignities may have delighted the paper's readers, all knew what the verdict must be. Cardigan's defence rested on an absurd legal technicality: that while the constable had taken the name of the wounded man as 'Harvey Tuckett', his full name was Harvey Garnett Phipps Tuckett, and the prosecution had not proven these to be one and the same person. That was enough for the Lords. They unanimously found him not guilty. It was a travesty of justice, and when on the evening of his acquittal Cardigan attended a theatre in Drury Lane, once again those in the stalls shouted and jeered. Some attempted to storm his private box and he had to be ushered out of the theatre by a side door. All of Britain, it seemed, reviled Lord Cardigan.

In April 1843 the 11th Hussars was posted to Dublin. The following winter, when Captain William Forrest obtained leave to escort his pregnant wife to her relatives in England, she gave birth prematurely and on a doctor's advice the captain remained with her. Lord Cardigan reprimanded him severely for extending his period of leave without permission; Forrest protested that he had acted correctly. Even the Duke of Wellington, who had ignored previous calls for Cardigan to be removed from command of the 11th, now wrote to him: 'If the foolish quarrels of the officers of the 11th among themselves continued, the Duke might think it necessary to submit to Her Majesty some plan to relieve the Department from an intolerable nuisance.'

The 11th returned to England in 1846. Cardigan, now separated from his wife Elizabeth, divided his time between Deene Park, his

London mansion in Portman Square and the luxury yacht he kept at Cowes on the Isle of Wight. He was nearly fifty years old and in failing health – he suffered from chronic bronchitis and a recurring bladder complaint – and his military career ought to have been over. Skirmishes with Lord Lucan however continued, and intensified early in 1854 when the Lucans' marriage broke up.

In March that year, when it was clear that war with Russia was inevitable, Cardigan wrote to Lord Raglan – appointed to command the army being assembled for foreign service and an old friend of the family – asking for a senior position with the cavalry. In his thirty years as a cavalry officer the closest Cardigan had come to combat was the discharge of a duelling pistol on Wimbledon Common yet on 1 April he was given command of the Light Brigade. He was overjoyed until he learned that Lucan, commanding the Cavalry Division, would be his immediate superior.

In London's clubs and everywhere that gentlemen gathered the talk was all of these two appointments. Most expected the war with Russia to be short, sharp and over by Christmas but that hostilities between their lordships Lucan and Cardigan would fill more column inches in *The Times* than the beating the British would give the Tsar.

Lord George Paget, whose 4th Light Dragoons was to be one of the Light Brigade regiments, told friends that he doubted Lucan and Cardigan could work together at all. Lieutenant Colonel Hodge, commanding one of the Heavy Brigade regiments, wrote: 'They do not speak. How this will answer on service I do not know.' Lieutenant Somerset Calthorpe, appointed aide-de-camp to Lord Raglan, commented: 'If they do not clash, 'tis passing strange.'

The charge at Balaklava might not have occurred if these two men had been competent cavalry officers and able to talk to each other. That they were neither was well known at the time of their appointments. Everyone in London society knew it. The press gleefully reported it. William Russell, *The Times* war correspondent in the Crimea, was later to write: 'When the Government made

the monstrous choice of Lord Cardigan as Brigadier of the Light
Cavalry Brigade of the Cavalry Division, well knowing the private
relations between the two men, they became responsible for
disaster.'

3. Journey into Hell

Three trials en route to the Crimea

Everything started well enough. When the 17th Lancers arrived in Portsmouth on 18 April 1854, virtually the whole town – its population swelled by Easter holidaymakers – turned out to watch and cheer. D. H. Parry, the regimental historian, interviewed some of those present and described the scene:

About a mile out, the head of the blue column came in sight, and to the strains of 'Cheer, boys! Cheer!' and 'Oh, Susannah, don't you cry for me', the gallant lads, with their red and white pennons fluttering gaily from the lance shafts, rode in through the streets thronged with onlookers, who cheered them to the echo, and dismounted near the quay somewhere about ten o'clock. The mounts were very restive and the process of 'slinging' them on board the *Pride of the Ocean* was an exciting one.

Further down the coast the men and horses of the 8th Hussars were boarding ships at Plymouth while a band on the quay played 'God Save the Queen'. The officers intended their journey to the East to be as comfortable as possible, and cases of wine and hampers of delicacies from Fortnum's were strewn about the decks. Among the personal items these gentlemen took with them were hunting rifles (there was said to be some excellent duck shooting in Turkey), silver tableware especially teapots, and tin bathtubs. Many took their servants. Some took their wives, and their wives in turn took their maids. Captain Henry Duberly took his wife, his servant, his wife's maid and their five horses.

The original plan had been for the Light Brigade to cross the English Channel by ship and march down through France to Marseille, re-embarking there to continue the voyage by sea. But it was decided that English regiments might not be welcomed in the French countryside, where ageing veterans of Waterloo remained village heroes and the English rather than the Russians were the enemy. Instead the cavalry embarked at Portsmouth, Plymouth and Kingstown, bound via Gibraltar and the Mediterranean for Turkey, a sea journey of some 3,400 miles.

It was well known that horses suffered badly at sea, tethered in dark, cramped holds. As sailing ships would take up to five weeks to reach Turkey and the new steam ships could complete the journey in half the time, the Light Brigade regiments expected to be put on steamers. There is no record of their reaction when it was decided to transport them by sail. The *Daily News* protested on the cavalry's behalf, pointing out that the horses would not be able to lie down or move about for up to six weeks, and when they were finally put ashore their legs would be cramped and useless.

It took five vessels to accommodate the 300 men and the horses of a single regiment. Private Albert Mitchell of the 13th Light Dragoons described how the troop horses ('troopers') were swung aboard at Portsmouth:

Each horse was led up to the ship's side (which lay close alongside the quay); a sling was placed beneath the horse's belly, and fastened to the tackling on the main-yard. The word was given to 'hoist away', when about a hundred convicts manned a large rope, and running away with it, the poor trooper was soon high in the air, quite helpless. He was then gradually lowered down the main hatchway (which was well padded round to prevent accidents) until he arrived at the hold which was fitted up as a stable, each horse being provided with a separate stall. They were placed with their heels towards the ship's side, and heads towards each other, with a passage between them. There were strong mangers fixed beneath their heads, to which they were fastened, so that there was no chance of lying down while they were on board.

The 17th Lancers left Portsmouth on 25 April, followed two days later by the 8th Hussars sailing from Plymouth. The 11th Hussars left Kingstown on 10 May and the 13th Light Dragoons sailed from Portsmouth on 12 May. The 4th Light Dragoons was the last of the Light Brigade regiments to leave and Lord Paget, aboard the *Simla* as it sailed out of Plymouth, wrote: 'On weighing anchor I assembled the men on deck and gave the signal for three cheers for the Queen, for a glorious war and happy return, which was warmly responded to.'

As these regiments set sail for the Black Sea, a rumour spread among the men that the Russians had a secret weapon of terrifying capability that could destroy them while they were still aboard the ships of the fleet. The 'Boulet Asphyxiant' was said to be a liquid fire that exploded beneath the water's surface to produce a gas that suffocated all within a certain distance. If that worried the cavalrymen, who at the best of times were unnerved by lengthy sea journeys, they perhaps took comfort from rumours of their own navy's secret device: 'MacIntosh's Portable Buoyant Wave Repressor' was claimed to have the quite remarkable effect of subduing storm waves at sea.

Neither the asphyxiant nor the wave repressor made an appearance and the ships duly reached Turkey. Yet all was not well. Before a single cavalryman had set foot on Russian territory or engaged the enemy, the brigade had suffered severely. More than a hundred men had died or been hospitalized, several hundred horses were unfit for duty and morale was so low that some officers thought their men no longer capable of taking the field.

Three factors combined to virtually defeat the Light Brigade before the war had even begun: the cruelties inflicted on the horses by the sea; the cruelties inflicted on the men by cholera; the cruelties inflicted on both by their lordships Lucan and Cardigan.

From the outset the horses reacted badly. Private Mitchell told how the men spent all of their free time in the hold, 'coaxing their horses to eat, bathing the face and nostrils with vinegar and water'. The troop horses were tethered only by tie ropes, and the narrowness of their stalls supported them as the vessel pitched. Officers' horses ('chargers') were allowed greater space and had to be supported by slings to prevent them being thrown from side to side. Despite these precautions they suffered too. On 4 May, when the *Star of the South* had been at sea for one week, Captain Duberly's wife Fanny wrote in her diary:

A fourth horse died last night. They tell me he went absolutely mad, and raved himself to death. The hold where our horses are stored, although considered large and airy, appears to me horrible beyond words. The slings begin to gall the horses under the shoulder and breastbone; and the heat and bad atmosphere must be felt to be understood. Every effort to alleviate their suffering is made; their nostrils are sponged with vinegar, which is also scattered in the hold.

That was on a relatively calm sea. On 12 May they reached the Bay of Biscay and sailed into a violent storm. Cornet George Clowes of the 8th Hussars said in a letter home that although 'everybody was dreadfully sick in all directions', the first concern of the men was for their horses. Lieutenant Edward Seager of the same regiment described what happened:

We had all the men standing at the horses' heads, although some were so sick they could hardly stand. As the vessel rolled from one side to the other, it pitched all the horses forward off their feet against the manger; they were absolutely frantic, the stamping of their feet on the boards, their screams together with the shouts of the men trying to pacify them, were something awful. Horse after horse got down, and as soon as one was, with great difficulty and danger, got up, others went down. Some were lying under the other horses who were kicking and plunging upon them. Such a fearful scene I never wish to witness again, 85 horses all mad with fright, trying to break loose from their fastenings and I am surprised they did not succeed, for when the vessel rose on one side, all the horses on that side dashed forward simultaneously against their mangers with all their force, and this occurred every five minutes throughout the night.

Several horses broke their legs; these were shot and thrown overboard.

Storms seemed to hang permanently over the Bay of Biscay, for the 4th Light Dragoons, passing through much later, suffered just as badly. Private Robert Farquharson reported hearing the captain of the ship tell Lord George Paget that 'if the storm did not abate in a quarter of an hour, he would be obliged to throw the horses overboard', to which Paget replied, 'Do what you like with the horses, but save my men.' Luckily this extreme remedy proved not to be necessary.

Because the 4th had left England much later than the other regiments, all 300 men and horses had been put aboard the *Simla*, a steamer, in order to make time over the sailing ships. Once they had passed through the Bay of Biscay the heat increased and added to the discomfort of the horses tied below decks where steam from the engines entered the hold. Captain Robert Portal wrote: 'Two horses got perfectly mad from the heat, and at last became so dangerous that they had to be destroyed. I am afraid that we shall lose many more from the intense heat. Those poor beasts that stand below close to the engines are in perfect steam all day and night too. We ought not to have any horses there at all.'

The 17th Lancers and 8th Hussars arrived off Constantinople on 20 May. Their lordships Lucan and Cardigan were waiting and these first two regiments of the Light Brigade now came under their command. Lucan was quick to comment on the state of the light cavalry. Far from sympathizing with the men after such a long and troubled sea passage, he issued an order expressing his dissatisfaction with their appearance:

The Major General finds it necessary to observe on the hair and beard of both officers and men. Long hair on the head is most objectionable; on service the hair cannot be kept too short. Moustachios and whiskers are to be allowed to grow, but no officer or private will be allowed to wear a beard. Below the mouth there is to be no hair whatever, and the whisker is not to be worn more forward on the chin than the corner of the mouth.

The regiments set up camp outside Constantinople and Cardigan now joined them. He had chosen not to make the long sea journey with them, preferring to travel overland with his servants and baggage, the latter including a spring bed and two large tents – so that he could dine in one and sleep in the other.

The Light Brigade lost fifty-seven horses during the journey from England – twenty-six of these by the 17th Lancers – and had to declare most of the rest 'unserviceable', meaning they were unfit for the very duties required of light cavalry: reconnaissance and patrol. Although the obvious remedy was to purchase fresh mounts locally, Captain Louis Nolan, aide-de-camp to General Airey and an expert on horses, described the Turkish specimens as 'ponies too weak to resist an attack of Russian cavalry, or to be of use in the field in any way'. Lord Raglan sent him to Syria to see if he could purchase 500 suitable horses there. The cavalry was crucial to the campaign, but without a proper supply of fit horses it would be of no use whatsoever.

After only one week in Constantinople the 8th Hussars received orders to continue on by sea to Varna on the coast of the Black Sea, a further 160 miles. The Russians had crossed the Danube at Silistria, fifty miles north of Varna, and the British cavalry was urgently required to support Turkish forces. The 17th Lancers followed four days later.

Lord Cardigan felt that although only two of his five regiments were proceeding to Varna, as brigade commander he should go with them. Instead of applying for permission to his immediate superior Lord Lucan, he applied over Lucan's head, direct to Lord Raglan. Raglan made matters worse by granting permission without discussing the request with Lucan, possibly because he thought that putting 160 miles between the two earls was quite a good idea. Unfortunately this reinforced Cardigan's belief that he should be allowed to act independently of Lucan. It also led Lucan to fire off his first shot of the campaign (against his brother-in-law), writing to Cardigan: 'It is obvious that the service cannot be carried out as it should be, if a subordinate officer is allowed to pass over his immediate superior.' Cardigan did not reply.

The 8th Hussars reached Varna on 31 May to find that there was insufficient depth of water for the ships to berth beside the quay.

Fanny Duberly was worried about the horses: 'Here the disembarkation of the horses was dangerous and awkward, for they were obliged to lower them into boats, and row them ashore. All were frightened – some very restive. One troop horse kicked two men, bit a third, and sent a fourth flying overboard.' Lest this conjure up a comical image of horses sitting in rowing boats, it should be noted that the normal method of disembarking horses in such circumstances was to lower them from the ships onto large rafts constructed by fixing planks crossways across two rowing boats lashed together, which were then towed ashore by other boats – an altogether more satisfactory procedure.

The 17th Lancers arrived in Varna on 4 June, and by the time the 13th Light Dragoons joined them, a cavalry camp had been established outside the port. Lucan, although supposedly in command of the cavalry, was left in Constantinople. He attempted to exert his authority from a distance by writing to Cardigan on 11 June requiring that all brigade reports be sent to him – the correct procedure – and not direct to Raglan, as Cardigan was doing. Replying on 15 June, Cardigan refused: 'I consider that being sent forward in advance of the Army, and not being very far distant at the present moment from the enemy, that my command may be considered as a separate and detached command.'

Varna lay 300 miles across the Black Sea from the Crimea and the Russian naval base of Sevastopol. At this stage no final decision had been made to invade Russian territory or attack Sevastopol. The cavalry was to remain at Varna, ready to move rapidly north towards Silistria if as was expected Turkish forces failed to stop the Russian advance.

The British and French infantry had by now arrived at Constantinople and soon followed the cavalry to Varna, until over 50,000 men were camped there. The heat was relentless, the town's narrow streets were crowded with troops and the open drains overflowed with raw sewage. Dysentery spread among the men and the first cases of cholera appeared.

Then came surprising news from Silistria. The Turks had pressed the Russians back across the Danube without assistance from the Light Brigade or any other part of the British army. If this was not merely a strategic withdrawal but a full retreat then the war might be over. 'Might be' because, courtesy of *The Times*, it was common knowledge that the government in London would not consider Russia beaten while its fleet was free to operate out of Sevastopol.

During the first week of July the Light Brigade regiments at Varna were inspected by Omar Pasha, the Turkish commander. Uncertain now whether they would see action or not, they were determined to put on a fine display and fielded a sufficient number of fit horses to mount a charge in line against a mock enemy. Fanny Duberly was watching: 'He complimented all our troops, and insisted on heading the Light Cavalry charge, which made me laugh, for he was on a small Turkish horse, and had to scramble, with the spurs well in, to get out of the way of our long-striding English horses.'

Omar Pasha was apparently impressed. 'Nothing in the world could stand against the English cavalry,' he told them. Perhaps he was just as struck by Fanny – she was a voluptuous, blue-eyed blonde and had already caught the eye of many a young cavalry officer – for he later told Lieutenant Calthorpe that after the war with Russia he would travel to England and marry 'une Miss Anglais'.

Whatever the truth of Omar Pasha's views on the diminished English cavalry, it was certain that nothing in the world could stop the spread of cholera through a closely packed army of 50,000 men, and as the number of the dead and dying soared with the midsummer temperatures, it was decided to break up the camp. The Light Brigade regiments were moved nineteen miles inland in the direction of Silistria – to whose relief they might still be ordered if the Russians counter-attacked in force – to establish a new camp at Devna.

Meanwhile, back in Constantinople Lord Lucan was finally authorized to proceed to Varna, where he expected to catch up with the Light Brigade and exercise full authority over Lord Cardigan. On reaching the port he was livid to find that Cardigan and the Light Brigade were no longer there. He complained to Raglan and demanded that he be allowed to continue on to Devna immediately. Raglan refused on the grounds that the five Heavy Brigade regiments and the 4th Light Dragoons of the Light Brigade had not yet reached Varna and Lucan as divisional commander should be there to receive and inspect them. Lucan was further incensed; he felt that Cardigan had for the moment got the better of him. The feud between the brothers-in-law was simmering nicely in the heat but Lord Raglan was cleverly keeping the two men apart.

At Devna, as the Light Brigade settled into its new camp, none of the men could understand why the picturesque dale with a small river running through it was known by the local Turks as Death Valley. Troop Sergeant Major Smith of the 11th Hussars thought it a splendid place after the open sewers of Varna and commented on its 'romantic appearance'. Too late they discovered it had been named after its permanent resident: cholera. The 17th Lancers had appointed Corporal James Nunnerley as regimental grave digger and possibly for that reason he remembered the first man to die: 'He partook very freely of a plum tree, up which he had climbed. This brought on the cholera and, before night, the regiment had lost a good man.' Perhaps the disease was endemic in the valley as the locals claimed, although it seems just as likely the men carried it with them from Varna.

After the first deaths, in an attempt to outpace an epidemic the Light Brigade moved twenty-four miles from Devna to Yeni Bazaar, arriving there on 28 July. This took the cavalry far in advance of the army and brought them virtually to the rear of the Turkish army at Silistria, and only seven miles from the Danube.

Yeni Bazaar was extremely hot and the only shade was provided by a small oasis — a group of trees and a spring — where Cardigan had his two tents pitched. His first order was to declare the spring for his use only; the men were forbidden to take water for themselves or their horses. Private Mitchell was none too happy about it: 'At the fountain there was a good supply of water, quite enough to have supplied the whole brigade, had we been permitted to use it; but a sentry was posted on it night and day to prevent any man taking any. Instead of being able to get water at about 100 yards, we had to go upwards of a mile, and climb a steep hill on our return loaded.'

If Cardigan was selfish in asserting the privilege of his rank, he was also obsessive in applying the minutiae of cavalry regulations to the men. Fanny Duberly noted in her diary: 'Our tents were not quite in a line, though I confess it was barely perceptible; but at evening we had to strike and move all our tents about a foot and a half further back.' The men grumbled, but a much greater affliction soon struck. The cholera had travelled to Yeni Bazaar with them. Private Mitchell watched the situation grow daily worse:

At first we had regular funeral parties, with trumpets sounding in front of the procession, but as it soon became an everyday occurrence, and the number of men in hospital increased daily, the 'Dead March' was ordered to be discontinued; for to say the least of it, it was a most doleful noise, and must have had a depressing effect on the sick, some of whom were hourly expecting to go the same road.

The worst among the sick were sent back by bullock cart to the general hospital at Varna; no one expected to see them again. On 12 August, Lieutenant Clement Heneage of the 8th Hussars complained that a quarter of his men were there, and seemed genuinely sorry for the rest: 'Every man has to look after two horses, and it seems quite a shame to get them up in the morning, they look so tired and wretched.'

In some cases this wretchedness might have been due to a hangover. A rumour had spread that cholera could be prevented by the particularly strong brandy available from local travelling tradesmen at 3*s*. 6*d*. for a large bottle. Many of the men, seeing the terrible suffering of the dying, thought this preventative worth a try, and some reasoned that if a little might stop the disease, then a great deal more would surely do so. As a result drunken soldiers were often found lying around the camp, and officers who would normally have placed these men under arrest left them where they lay.

When the latrines filled up a sufficient number of men could not be found with the energy to dig out new ditches. Many of the horses had not fully recovered from the sea voyage and were finished off by the heat, but because the men were also incapable of excavating the large pits required to bury them, these had to be dragged a distance away from the camp and left. Cornet George Wombwell of the 17th Lancers wrote: 'In less than twelve hours he is a perfect skeleton, being entirely eaten up by vultures, dogs and other carnivorous animals, with which this country abounds. You can see as many as thirty vultures standing on a horse at one time.'

Those who still hoped for orders to take Sevastopol were no longer confident that the Light Brigade was up to the task. Captain Portal told his father: 'The men and officers are daily more dispirited and more disgusted with their fate. They do nothing but bury their comrades. There is nothing to do but listen to growls and grumbling from all sides, from the highest to the lowest. I wish I could believe that we are, in our present state, strong enough for this tremendous undertaking.'

Others no longer cared about the war. Lieutenant Heneage was startlingly candid about their lack of interest: 'Such is the state of apathy that we are reduced to, that no one seems to care whether we go to Sevastopol or South America or stay as we are or do nothing.'

If later, in the Crimea, Lucan and Cardigan would betray the full extent of their incompetence, in Turkey they gave a fair indication of what was to come. It was as if they competed in this as in all else, each attempting to prove himself the more inept.

During the time that Lord Lucan had any part of his division with him in Varna he drilled the men using the words of command he knew from seventeen years earlier when he had last commanded cavalry. Because the drill book had since then been rewritten and the commands changed, neither officers nor men understood what manoeuvres were required and the result was an embarrassing shambles. When the Heavy Brigade regiments arrived, Major William Forrest quickly took stock of the situation and displayed a staggering premonition of the tragedy to come. He wrote home:

Lord Lucan is a very clever sharp fellow, but he has been so long on the shelf he does not even know the words of command. If he is shown by the drill book that he is wrong, he says, 'Ah, I'd like to know who wrote that book, some Farrier I suppose'. Officers who drill under him are puzzled to know what he means when he gives a word of command. I write all this to you in order that if any mishap should occur to the cavalry, you may be able to form a correct idea how it happened.

A wise commander might have set about learning the new words of command, but not Lucan. The 4th Light Dragoons was the last of the Light Brigade regiments to reach Varna and Lord Paget did not appreciate Lucan's attempt to re-educate his men: 'Instead of bending to the new order of things, he sought to unteach the troops the drill which they had been taught, and to substitute for this the drill which in his time was in vogue.' Paget was on familiar terms with Lucan from the House of Lords and convinced him that it was impossible to teach the officers and men the old commands in the time available. Lucan grudgingly agreed to learn the new commands.

It might be thought difficult for Lord Cardigan to have beaten such a display of ineptness but he was more than up to the task. When Lord Raglan received news of the Russian withdrawal across the Danube, he was sceptical about the unexpected Turkish success and ordered Cardigan to take a patrol north to 'ascertain the movements of the enemy'. Cardigan led 120 men from the 8th Hussars and 75 from the 13th Light Dragoons out from Varna with minimum rations and no tents – though *he* took a tent and a spring bed. They reached the Danube in four days and found the Russians gone. Captain Soames Jenyns of the 13th Light Dragoons wrote in a letter: 'The whole country is deserted, not a soul to be seen, and the villages burned down and battered. We had only salt beef and biscuits and what we had on. No tents, of course, which in this hot weather on plains is no joke.'

His mission achieved, Cardigan should have returned to camp. Instead he led the patrol along the banks of the Danube, taking a detour that extended an eight-day reconnaissance into a seventeen-day trek. When Cardigan's return was overdue, Raglan sent out another patrol to search for him. This reported that there was no sign of his lordship or the 195 men, and all were feared lost.

When the 'lost' patrol returned, both men and horses were exhausted and starving. The horses were too weak to carry their riders and the men had to lead them in on foot. Fanny Duberly watched them:

The reconnaissance under Lord Cardigan came in this morning. They have lived for five days on water and salt pork; have shot five horses, which dropped from exhaustion on the road, brought back a cart full of disabled men, and seventy-five horses which will be unfit for work for many months, and some of them will never work again. A piteous sight it was, men on foot driving and goading the wretched, wretched horses, three or four of which could hardly stir. There seems to have been much unnecessary suffering, a cruel parade of death.

The loss of horses virtually cancelled out the number of remounts Captain Nolan had managed to bring back from Syria and left the Light Brigade still deficient in the number available for duty. While the patrol had gathered valuable intelligence – the Russians truly had withdrawn – no one thought that it had been properly organized or led, and most felt that no competent officer would have taken an unnecessary detour and put both men and horses through such agony. Captain Shakespear of the Royal Horse Artillery, attached to the Light Brigade, wrote: 'Lord Cardigan is the most impracticable and most inefficient cavalry officer in the service. We are all greatly disgusted with him.'

Fanny Duberly put it more graphically: 'I hope that Cardigan, whom all abhor, will get his head in such a jolly bag he will never get it out again.'

The retreat of the Russian forces attempting to take Silistria had achieved the British government's declared object of the campaign without the involvement of the British or French armies, and the more naive among the cavalrymen expected that soon they would be ordered to break camp and head back to Varna for the ships home. However, instead of an order recalling the troops, Lord Raglan received a dispatch from the Secretary for War the Duke of Newcastle instructing him to invade the Crimea, take Sevastopol and destroy Russia's Black Sea Fleet. Newcastle added: 'There is no prospect of a safe and honourable peace until the fortress is reduced and the fleet taken or destroyed. Nothing but insuperable impediments should be allowed to prevent the early decision to undertake these operations.'

Raglan felt that there were indeed 'insuperable impediments': his army was severely diminished and weakened by disease; no proper maps of the Crimea were available; and he had no reliable knowledge of the strength of Russian forces defending Sevastopol – estimates ranged from 20,000 to 100,000. Nevertheless he had no choice, as General Sir George Brown, who commanded one of his infantry divisions, pointed out to him: 'It is clear to me from the tenor of the Duke of Newcastle's letter that they have made up their minds to it at home, and that if you decline to accept the responsibility, they will send someone else out to command the Army.'

Raglan gave orders for the invasion and his instructions reached the Light Brigade at Yeni Bazaar on 25 August: the regiments were to return immediately to Varna and embark for the Crimea. When they left England the crowds had cheered and the cavalrymen had waved back and sung lustily. Now, Fanny Duberly observed, 'the order was heard silently; not a single cheer'. As they struck camp and set off, Private Mitchell was in a solemn mood: 'The sick, of whom there were many, were placed in wagons drawn by two bullocks or water buffaloes. There were a few poor fellows who were past recovery, yet not dead. These were left behind to die, a party of hospital orderlies being left with them to see the last of them and bury them.'

The able-bodied and the sick arrived in Varna after a four-day march. On 30 August those fit enough to form up on parade were inspected by Lord Lucan, at last reunited with his light cavalry. He expected to see the same pristine uniforms and proud appearance they presented in England, and was shocked by what he found:

The men are not cleanly in their appearance or in their persons. Their clothes are unnecessarily dirty and stained, their weapons are not as clean as they ought to be; their belts, leathers and appointments, both of man and horse, are rusty and dirty; it would appear as if the object were that every soldier on service should look as unsoldierlike and dirty as possible.

There were not enough vessels for the whole Cavalry Division to sail with the invasion fleet, so the Light Brigade was embarked and the Heavy Brigade left behind to follow when the ships returned for them. The fleet left Varna on 7 September, its troopships packed with the infantry, cavalry and artillery of the British, French and Turkish armies. They were entering enemy waters and the speed of the ships could not be left to the wind, as Troop Sergeant Major Smith observed: 'We sailed and joined the fleet. We then formed six lines, each line consisting of sailing transports towed by a steamer; we were then covered and flanked by the line of battleships.'

The Crimea lay 300 miles across the Black Sea and they were unlikely to take the Russians by surprise. On 15 June – almost three months earlier – an editorial in *The Times* had informed its readers, among the most eager of whom were the Tsar's advisers in St Petersburg: 'The taking of Sevastopol and the occupation of the Crimea are objects which would repay the costs of the present war, and would permanently settle in our favour the principal questions of the day.'

Despite that advance warning, few thought the Russians would put up more than a token resistance. Cornet Fisher-Rowe declared with all the confidence of a young officer off on his first campaign: 'Hurrah for the Crimea; take Sevastopol in a week or two, and then into winter quarters.'

4. The Invasion of the Crimea

From Kalamita Bay to Balaklava

On 13 September 1854 the British and French fleets reached Kalamita Bay, thirty-three miles north of Sevastopol. A line of warships dropped anchor between the coast and the transport ships, their 32-pounder guns ready to fire on any attempt by the Russians to interfere with the landing.

The Crimean peninsula protruded from the south coast of the Tsar's burgeoning empire into the Black Sea, with the city and naval base of Sevastopol near its southern tip. Massive stone forts festooned with gun emplacements protected the harbour and the Russian warships that had taken refuge there, making it impossible even for the combined British and French fleets to take the city from the sea. Lord Raglan, in consultation with the commander of the French army Marshal St Arnaud, decided to disembark the 64,000 allied troops to the north, at such a distance from Sevastopol that the enemy was unlikely to be present in force, and make a land attack on the city.

The invasion began at first light on 14 September. The sea was calm and although observers on the ships spotted a number of Cossacks on the hills above the beach, the riders merely watched while their officer studied the fleet and wrote in a notebook. The infantry was put ashore first, ferried in rowing boats that moved constantly between the ships and the stony beach, while the cavalry, whose task it would be to send patrols inland to scout for the enemy, was left waiting.

By mid-afternoon a gathering storm had roughened the waters of the bay and the disembarkation of the cavalry had to be put off to the following day. As a result the 46,000 infantrymen who had been put ashore so far spent their first night on the beach and the hills above without any mounted pickets – cavalrymen positioned forward of the camp – to provide advance warning of an attack and delay the enemy. Luckily the Russians had sent only scouts to watch and report on the allied landing, having chosen to make a stand at the river Alma, fifteen miles to the south and approximately midway between Kalamita Bay and Sevastopol.

The first cavalry horses went ashore the following morning. These were lowered in slings onto horse rafts which were then towed ashore. The 11th Hussars went first. It was a tricky operation and Troop Sergeant Major Smith told how it was done:

Now commenced the slinging and drawing the horses out of the hold by the sailors. Each man, as his horse came up, descended into the boat. As the horses were lowered into the boat, they were placed side by side, their masters standing to their heads. Each boat contained about 16 horses. When ready we were towed to the beach. When near it, the sailors turned their boat from in front of us and the impetus with which we were going carried the boat on to the beach. The horses readily jumped one after another on to the shore.

It did not all go quite that easily. The tremendous weight of the horses combined with the impetus that carried the rafts to the beach often holed the rowing boats supporting them. Those rafts that survived and returned to take on more horses were therefore no longer beached. Instead the horses were pushed overboard and left to swim the final twenty yards. It was a slow process and was still under way on the 16th when Lord Paget described the scene: 'It is distressing to see the poor horses, as they are upset out of the boats, swimming about in all directions. They swim so peacefully, but look rather unhappy with their heads in the air and the surf driving into their poor mouths. Only one has drowned yet.'

Each of the Light Brigade regiments was divided into two squadrons, and each squadron into two troops. The brigade was landed one troop at a time, each consisting of up to seventy-five men. As each troop formed up on the beach, the men were marched up to the plain above and several miles inland to bivouac in front of the infantry. Mounted pickets were sent out immediately.

The cavalrymen had been put ashore with three days' water, rum and rations of salt pork and biscuit for themselves and three days' corn for their horses. The most urgent task was to find fresh water for the horses. Cornet Wombwell had to lead his troop of the 17th Lancers on a six-mile ride to find the nearest source, although he does not record whether this was a stream or one of the many farm wells in the area.

As darkness fell it began to rain and the officers and men of the Light Brigade looked for their tents among the supplies put ashore. There were none. When the tents had been loaded at Varna they had gone into the holds first and a great deal of less important equipment stacked on top of them. With no shelter of any kind on the open plain the men lay on the ground in their uniforms with only their cavalry cloaks and blankets to cover them. Each slept with his sabre at his side and his horse left saddled, for no one knew how far or near the Cossacks might be. It rained heavily throughout the night – some men described it as a deluge – and by morning they were drenched to the skin. Their ornate uniform jackets were bedraggled, and their skin-tight trousers clung tighter still.

Raglan now sent Lord Cardigan inland with a patrol of 250 cavalrymen to identify the strength and location of any enemy force in the area. A secondary but crucial aim of this reconnaissance was to locate sources of fresh water and to search farms in order to requisition carts for transport, fresh food for the men, and corn and hay for the horses. Cardigan returned, having seen no evidence of the Russians, located no fresh water and secured only a few carts. It is difficult to reconcile the relative ease with which Cornet Wombwell found fresh water for his horses with Cardigan's inability to locate any after a thirty-mile reconnaissance, although some reports indicate that Cossack patrols were by this time poisoning the wells.

While Cardigan may not have seen the enemy or discovered food and forage, later patrols sent out by the 13th Light Dragoons witnessed Cossacks setting fire to barns full of corn. Others brought in supplies of fresh food that included cattle and poultry. Local farmers were given no choice as to whether or not they supplied these goods, and were in no position to argue about the price offered. Captain Portal of the 4th Light Dragoons observed: 'The cavalry have been busy driving in bullocks, sheep and ponies, etc., all of which we pay for at our price, which is a very fair one.'

Once Cossack patrols had been spotted there was considerable nervousness among the less experienced men, particularly when on picket duty. On the evening of 17 September a picket of the 11th Hussars came under fire and galloped into camp, shouting the alarm. The brigade was ordered to mount and form line to meet the attack, but none came. It transpired that a British infantry picket had glimpsed the hussars in the dark and opened fire, mistaking them for the enemy. The cavalrymen in turn assumed that Cossacks had crept in between their position and the camp, and raised the alarm. The confusion must have been considerable, for the only casualty, a man of the 11th Hussars, was shot in the thigh by a young officer, Cornet Annersley, of his own regiment.

Thirty-three miles and four rivers separated Kalamita Bay from Sevastopol and the march south began on 19 September. The Light Brigade, reduced by cholera and dysentery to less than 1,000 men fit for duty, was given the task of protecting the front, left flank and rear of this great army, which had the Black Sea and the warships of the fleet on its right flank. Lord Cardigan went ahead with the 11th Hussars and 13th Light Dragoons; Lord Lucan rode out on the left flank with the 8th Hussars and 17th Lancers; Lord Paget brought up the rear with the 4th Light Dragoons. The open plain reminded many cavalrymen of Salisbury Plain in England, where they trained, and for the moment it seemed just as peaceful.

The first day's march had to take them ten miles to the river Bulganek, the next source of fresh water. After seven miles, infantrymen began to drop. Many had still not recovered from the sea voyage; some were suffering the first pains of cholera, which had travelled with them from Varna; and the scorching midday sun took a heavy toll on the rest once their water bottles had been emptied. To stop would only have compounded the problem. Lord Paget, bringing up the rear with the 4th Light Dragoons, was well placed to describe the scene as they marched on: 'The stragglers were lying thick on the ground, and it is no exaggeration to say that the last two miles resembled a battlefield.' At 2.00 p.m. the infantry came within sight of the Bulganek and the most desperate broke ranks to run into the water and drink their fill, ignoring the most profane threats bawled by their sergeant majors.

When a Cossack patrol was spotted on the crest of the hill that rose from the southern bank of the Bulganek, Lord Raglan sent Cardigan and the front guard across the river to reconnoitre the area ahead. The enemy patrol pulled back as Cardigan and his two regiments advanced. Troop Sergeant Major Smith was riding with the 11th Hussars: 'On gaining the crest of the hill, we came in sight of the main body of the Cossacks, spread out in skirmishing order in a beautiful valley about a mile across. As we descended the hill, the two regiments in line, we lost sight of our Army.'

Although Cardigan with only 400 men at his back was advancing on a body of 1,500 Russian cavalrymen, he appeared eager to engage them, and put out skirmishers from the 13th Light Dragoons. The Cossacks facing him were keener still, according to Smith: 'It was now that the first shot of the campaign was fired. A Cossack directly in front of the 11th Hussars raised his carbine and fired. It was instantly taken up by the whole line. Our trumpets now sounded the "Fire".' This exchange of carbine fire took place at maximum range and had little effect on either side, as if each were throwing taunts at the other with powder and ball. At this point Lord Lucan galloped up to join the two Light Brigade regiments and took command, much to Cardigan's chagrin, although Lucan was just as intent on a scrap.

Unknown to their lordships, who had moved over the crest of the hill and lost visual contact with the main army, an even larger enemy force of 6,000 infantrymen with accompanying artillery lay in wait for them, concealed below the crest of the next hill. If the two regiments charged, a deadly trap would be sprung and a good part of the brigade wiped out. Lord Raglan had by now taken up a new position on high ground to one side and had spotted this force. He sent an urgent order for Lucan to withdraw. According to Smith it arrived with only seconds to spare: 'The crest of the hill in front suddenly became lit up with the glitter of swords and lances. Lord Cardigan now gave the order, "Draw Swords – Skirmishers In – Trot". The ground in front of us was uphill. We had not proceeded far, when an aide-de-camp galloped up with an order from Lord Raglan that we were to retire.'

The ADC seen by Smith was Captain Nolan, although it was General Richard Airey who brought the order. Raglan had surmised that only an officer with great authority could recall Lucan and Cardigan from an action they seemed set on. Airey was the quartermaster general and in effect acted as Raglan's second-in-command; Nolan, as Airey's ADC, merely accompanied him. Because it was too dangerous for Lucan's regiments to turn and trot away – as enemy cavalry was moving across their left and appeared ready to take them in the flank – Airey informed Lucan that the 8th Hussars, 17th Lancers and a troop of the Royal Horse Artillery had been ordered up to support their withdrawal, and that meanwhile he must sit and wait.

While Lucan waited with the 11th Hussars and 13th Light Dragoons for their supports to arrive, a Russian battery opened fire. The expectation of officers that their men should not even flinch was too much for many of the young, inexperienced recruits, who ducked as the roundshot came flying towards them and the shells burst overhead. Private William Pennington was twenty-one years old and had enlisted in the 11th Hussars only six months earlier: 'I shall never forget the sensation of sitting perfectly inert on my horse. I recall how when some of us more nervous fellows bowed our heads down to our horses' manes, how angry and indignant was the tone of Major Peel's remonstrance: "What the hell are you bobbing your heads at?"'

None of the men would dare answer back but a moment later they were 'bobbing' their heads more vigorously still. Private Mitchell of the 13th Light Dragoons described what happened: 'Several shells burst close to us. One struck a troop horse in the side, and bursting inside the horse, cleaned him out as though a butcher had done it. Our Horse Artillery now galloped up and quickly came into action.'

The 8th Hussars and 17th Lancers arrived too, and as the artillery opened up on the enemy Cardigan ordered the retreat. Five cavalrymen had been injured by Russian fire. A private of the 11th Hussars lost a foot and a sergeant of the 13th Light Dragoons lost his right hand. These two men disputed the dubious privilege of being the first of the Light Brigade to be wounded by the enemy. The 13th claimed that it was Sergeant Joseph Priestly. The 11th countered that it was Private James Williamson, who at least deserves credit for one of the most memorable lines of the war. According to the report of his troop commander, Lieutenant Roger Palmer: 'Williamson rode out of the ranks, his leg shot off and hanging by his overall. Coming up to me he said, quite calmly, "I am hit, may I fall out?"'

More keenly felt by most officers and men of the two regiments was the injury to their pride. The Russians jeered them as they fell back and that they could take. But the British infantry down at the Bulganek river laughed at them too – none had seen the 6,000 enemy infantrymen and artillery waiting in ambush which made the withdrawal essential – and that was too much. A private of the 41st Foot shouted out that they were 'silly peacock bastards'. The humiliation of the Light Brigade had begun.

The encounter at the Bulganek left everyone nursing a grievance. Lord Lucan felt that Raglan, in recalling him, had interfered with the proper exercise of a divisional commander's authority in the face of the enemy – never mind that two regiments might have been lost. Lord Cardigan felt that Lucan's earlier arrival and assumption of command had interfered with *his* authority as brigade commander. And every regimental officer and cavalryman felt humiliated at being recalled from an advance that had already begun. An inglorious retreat having replaced the charge they had anticipated, most of them – quite unfairly in this instance – blamed Lucan for the burden of shame they now carried into the campaign.

*

At first light the next day, 20 September, the horses were watered in the Bulganek. This took priority and it was only afterwards that the men could collect water to make tea. The river had been so stirred up that after drinking their tea most men found a thick layer of mud at the bottom of their tin mugs.

The army continued south towards Sevastopol with a march of six miles to the Alma, the second of the four rivers. Captain George Maude of the Royal Horse Artillery, riding ahead of the infantry divisions with the advance guard, soon discovered that this was where the Russians planned to make a stand:

After advancing about six miles we came to a very strong position, where the Russians had entrenched themselves on the banks of the River Alma where the south side rises steeply to about 300 feet. Up the side of the steep slope the enemy had entrenched batteries with some very heavy guns. They began a tremendous cannonade on us when we came within 2,000 yards.

Lord Raglan's unsophisticated grasp of battlefield tactics favoured the straight line over any other approach and he ordered the infantry to make a frontal attack. They were required to march downhill, cross the river, then march uphill straight at the muzzles of the guns, all of it under heavy fire – the foot soldiers' Balaklava – to take the Russian batteries that defended the road to Sevastopol. The Light Brigade regiments were held on the left to protect against a flank attack by Russian cavalry. They dismounted in a melon field to watch the assault, until Russian artillerymen spotted them and dropped a few roundshot among them, at which they hastily remounted and moved out of range.

Meanwhile the infantrymen were marching *into* range, shoulder to shoulder and in perfect line. At first the roundshot fell some distance ahead, bounced, and came towards them at a reduced pace. Private Timothy Gowing of the 7th Fusiliers noted that it was sometimes expedient for the line to part: 'As soon as the enemy's roundshot came hopping along, we simply did the polite thing – opened up and allowed them to pass. As we kept advancing, we had to move our pins to get out of their way. Presently they began to pitch their shot and shell right amongst us, and our men began to fall. I know that I felt horribly sick.'

Soon there were heavy losses on both sides. Private Henry Blishen of the Rifle Brigade, one of the units equipped with the new Minié rifle, saw its devastating effect on the Russian musketeers who came forward to oppose them, and the effect of the Russian batteries on his comrades: 'We shot and made dreadful havoc amongst them, for as we advanced we stumbled over their dead and wounded, and I am sorry to say that our poor fellows fell like grass before a scythe.'

The Russians had expected to decimate the allied armies with artillery fire and finish them off with the bayonet. Their artillery certainly told, but their infantry was unable to close on the survivors. The Minié was accurate at a range of 500 yards, which none of the Russian muskets could match. Russian infantrymen fell dead or wounded and others looked about in confusion unable to understand where the shots were coming from, the enemy in front of them being so far distant.

Despite heavy losses, British infantry divisions took the batteries commanding the Sevastopol road. At the same time the French gained control of the heights between the road and the coast. The battle was won.

It was an established principle that when an enemy was pressed to retreat, cavalry took up the pursuit in order to prevent the enemy rallying or even counter-attacking. An effective pursuit by cavalry might even turn a retreat into a rout. To the Light Brigade, watching the Russians throw away their weapons and equipment as they dashed south in the direction of Sevastopol, a rout seemed likely and all expected to receive the order to pursue at any moment. Officers and men tightened their grips on the hilts of their cavalry sabres and the staves of their lances, ready for the off. They waited and waited, and then finally an order came – they watched Lord Lucan become red-faced and speechless with anger.

Raglan did not wish to risk his cavalry by sending them in pursuit. A body of Russian cavalry estimated at 3,000 men was known to be in the area and had taken no part in the battle. If the Light Brigade, numbering less than 1,000 men, was sent in pursuit and found itself confronted by and outnumbered three times over by this Russian force, Raglan guessed that Lucan might consider these odds acceptable and order the charge. The commander-in-chief wished to preserve his cavalry to fight another day. Which fine thought mattered not at all to Lucan as he struggled to comprehend the order. Raglan wished the cavalry to advance, but only to escort the guns of the horse artillery to a point within range of the fleeing Russians, from where shot and shell could help them on their way. The cavalry was specifically instructed not to attack.

Somehow Lucan interpreted this order as allowing him to go forward with one troop of the 17th Lancers and another from the 11th Hussars – given that both were under strength, about a hundred men in total – to capture stragglers. He must have known that he was acting contrary to Raglan's meaning. Cornet Wombwell clearly saw it as a pursuit:

We went forward at a gallop, cheering and holloaing as loud as we could. We could see the enemy running as hard as they could go, throwing away their knapsacks, arms and even coats to assist them in their flight. Morgan's Troop of my regiment were sent out to pursue and bring in prisoners, in which they succeeded very well, bringing in a good many. On coming up with the poor fellows they dropped on their knees and begged for mercy.

Not all of them. One Russian infantryman pretended to surrender to Sergeant Seth Bond of the 11th Hussars, then slashed at his face with a bayonet. It seemed to Bond that some extreme reprisal was in order and only the arrival of an officer prevented him from cutting the man down with his sabre. Private James Wightman of the 17th Lancers had a similar experience. A Russian officer made as if to surrender then pulled out a pistol and fired at him. It missed and Wightman knocked the man to the ground with the butt of his lance. Colonel Lawrenson, unaware of the pistol shot and seeing what appeared to be a private mishandling a prisoner (and an officer at that), rebuked Wightman and called him a coward. Wightman wisely held his tongue but later wrote that he thought Lawrenson 'a little too dainty for the rough and ready business of warfare'.

Lord Raglan had seen these men of the Light Brigade go forward and sent a second order recalling them. Lucan 'delayed' giving the order; put plainly, he ignored it. When Raglan sent a third order, repeating the second, Lucan saw that he had pushed his luck as far as he could and stopped the pursuit. In a fit of pure pique he ordered that the prisoners be released. The hussars·and lancers were confused, and their Russian captives hardly less so. The watching British infantry pointed and laughed as the cavalry rode back empty-handed. And again the officers and men of the Light Brigade, not party to Raglan's communications, blamed Lucan for humiliating them in front of both the enemy and their own army. Captain Portal wrote home to say that the cavalry was commanded by 'old women' who 'would have been better in their drawing rooms'.

Although the Russian cavalry had been seen in the area during the battle, by this point it had withdrawn. An opportunity to use the Light Brigade to great effect had been missed and Captain Nolan's passionate outburst at the time was later revealed by William Russell of *The Times*: 'There was one thousand British Cavalry looking on at a beaten army retreating, within a ten minutes' gallop of them – enough to drive one mad! It is too disgraceful, too infamous. They ought to be damned!' 'They' were their lordships Raglan, Lucan and Cardigan, for although Nolan considered the two cavalry commanders to be particularly inept, as General Airey's ADC he knew more than the regimental officers of Raglan's involvement.

Lord Paget, a level-headed man and often critical of Lucan and Cardigan, also believed that on this occasion it was Raglan who got it wrong: 'When I asked Lord Raglan whether the cavalry might not have been of more use, he replied that his object all day had been to – what he called – "shut them up" (those were his words), the enemy's cavalry being so superior in numbers.'

The grievance felt by the cavalry, born at the Bulganek, was compounded at the Alma. Lord Lucan now realized that although he was divisional commander Raglan would not allow him the slightest initiative in exercising that command. The officers and men felt yet again humiliated; a campaign that they had expected to reveal the dash and esprit de corps of the light cavalry regiments was rapidly making a laughing stock of them.

That night the men watered their horses in the Alma and bivouacked on the heights where the worst of the infantry fight had taken place, lest the Russians regroup and attack at first light. They were issued with fresh meat, which was boiled in pots over the campfires and consumed with their rum. It was not until they had settled down to sleep between the horse lines, each man lying adjacent to his horse so that he could mount up in an instant, that many experienced for the first time the terrible aftermath of a great battle. Private Mitchell was among those who could not sleep:

Then it was that we heard around us the groans of the wounded and the dying; some calling for the love of God for a drop of water. Others were praying most devoutly, well knowing this to be their last night in this life. We had already seen sufficient to harden our feelings, and make us callous to human suffering, but I lay some time thinking very seriously and praying to God for protection from all dangers.

The next two days were spent doing what little was possible for the wounded and burying the dead. On 23 September the march south was resumed and continued as far as the third river, the Katcha. While the army set up camp there, Raglan – nervous that the Russians might by this time have recovered sufficiently to mount an attack – ordered the Light Brigade forward to scout ahead without allowing time for the horses to be watered.

The following day the army crossed the Belbec, the fourth and final river on the route to Sevastopol. The horses were by this time desperate for water. Troop Sergeant Major Smith, no slouch when it came to imposing discipline on the men, was shocked by what took place:

Opposite the part we were fording sat Lord Lucan, storming and threatening that he would flog any man who attempted to water his horse, so that the men who passed over directly opposite him had great difficulty in forcing their horses through the water, as they plunged their heads into it eager to drink, not having been watered since we left the Alma. What could have been Lord Lucan's reason for this I never could make out, for a greater piece of cruelty I never witnessed. Lord Cardigan sat some little distance from him, lower down the stream, evidently indignant for he rendered no assistance in enforcing the order.

Cardigan was more than indignant. Wrapped up in his own battle with Lucan, he had already written to Raglan to complain that Lucan always rode with the Light Brigade and took away his rightful command. However, in fairness to Lucan the Heavy Brigade had not yet arrived in the Crimea and his division consisted of only one brigade; he could do no other than ride with that. Raglan had previously allowed Cardigan to act as if he was independent of his divisional commander, but now he supported Lucan: 'A General of Division may interfere little or much with the duties of a General of Brigade; all his orders and suggestions claim obedience and attention.' Cardigan had been told, most politely, to shut up and do as his divisional commander told him.

As the army neared Sevastopol, Troop Sergeant Major Smith was one of the first to glimpse the city: 'I happened to look to my right, when to my surprise through an opening in the trees I had a full view of Sevastopol. I called out involuntarily, "Sevastopol". All within hearing halted and for a few moments sat gazing at the beautiful town with its church spires and white buildings reflected in the sun. This was our first view of the prize we hoped soon to seize.' Raglan and his generals surveyed the city through telescopic lenses. The ships of the Black Sea Fleet anchored in the harbour and the naval facilities that served them were now within striking distance. Officers and men alike expected to be in Sevastopol within twenty-four hours.

The Russians looked back fearfully and expected much the same. Still reeling from their defeat at the Alma, they believed the

British and French would quickly overcome their defences and sack the city.

Only one man seemed to think otherwise. Sir John Burgoyne, Raglan's engineering adviser, argued that because the Russians had always anticipated an attack from the north they would have prepared well for it, and that an attack from the south might succeed with fewer casualties. Although none of the generals who studied Sevastopol could see evidence of any such preparations, Burgoyne convinced the French commander, Marshal St Arnaud. Lord Raglan, under orders from London to maintain the alliance at all costs, then felt he had to agree.

An attack from the south required the army to break with the fleet, which had been moving down the coast parallel with the land force, and make a flank march inland, moving in a great semicircle round the city to take the small fishing village of Balaklava. Once there, contact with the fleet could be re-established. Balaklava, six miles south of Sevastopol, would provide a safe harbour and act as the supply base for the army during its assault on the city.

Taking Balaklava would be easy enough. Getting there presented far greater risks. Once inland the great marching columns of cavalry, infantry and artillery would lose contact with their supplies and their only means of escape from the Crimea if things went badly wrong.

The flank march began on 25 September. Almost immediately the army entered a thick forest criss-crossed by narrow tracks. According to the only map available, one track cut straight through the forest and came out onto the Sevastopol–Simpheropol road at Khutor Mackenzie (Mackenzie's Farm, named after a previous owner who was a Scottish settler) seven miles north-east of Sevastopol.

Lucan, Cardigan and the Light Brigade went ahead, accompanied by Captain Wetherall, an officer from Raglan's staff, acting as path-finder, though none knew why this young officer's sense of direction was preferred to their own. Raglan and the artillery followed some distance behind the cavalry along the same track. The infantry had to make their way through the forest on either side, marching by compass bearing. The cavalry was to occupy Khutor Mackenzie, ascertain that the road was free of the enemy, and send a report back to Raglan that it was safe for him to come up.

Prince Alexander Menshikov, commander-in-chief of the Russian army, had meanwhile decided that rather than allow his forces to be attacked or besieged in Sevastopol he would lead them out along the Simpheropol road through Khutor Mackenzie. This then was the march of the two armies, a comic opera in which the Light Brigade played its part with gusto and for which William Russell later set the scene most wittily: 'The English General, in order to take Sevastopol, was marching round it! The Russian General, anxious to save Sevastopol, was marching away from it!'

Captain Wetherall and the Light Brigade followed the forest track until it reached a fork that was not marked on the map. Wetherall decided that the left track led to Khutor Mackenzie and took that one. The last mounts of the cavalry were out of sight when Raglan and his staff officers reached the same point. Judging that the right fork led to Khutor Mackenzie, he went that way.

Raglan was correct; he was also now ahead of his own advance guard and riding straight towards the enemy. Prince Menshikov and his army had already moved through Khutor Mackenzie, but his baggage carts and their escorts bringing up the rear had stopped to rest at precisely the point where the forest track joined the road. General Airey was riding a little ahead of Raglan and was the first to emerge from the trees. Spotting Russian soldiers resting and drinking by the carts, he backed his horse beneath the heavy foliage and hurriedly explained the situation to Raglan, who sent one rider to look for the cavalry and another to call up the artillery.

Raglan was furious and with good reason: he could have been killed or captured by the enemy. Luckily the Russian soldiers in charge of the baggage train were not elite troops, took their time investigating the sudden appearance and disappearance of a strangely uniformed officer, and fled at the approach of British artillery guns, abandoning their carts. By the time an ADC found

Lucan and the cavalry and led them to Khutor Mackenzie, the enemy was some distance away. A rapid pursuit at the gallop was cut short by order of Lord Raglan, eager perhaps not to lose sight of the Light Brigade again, but not before Sergeant John Berryman of the 17th Lancers had taken three prisoners.

Raglan was reported to have raised his voice in anger, a rare event for such a softly spoken man: 'Lord Lucan, you are late!' He felt that Lucan and the cavalry had let him down. Lucan in turn felt that Raglan was unfair in blaming him, as it was the staff officer Raglan himself had attached to the cavalry who had advised on which track they should take. Cardigan on this occasion was content to remind Raglan that *he* was not in command of the cavalry. The officers and men of the Light Brigade felt that once more they had been humiliated and their ability to perform the most basic role of mounted troops – that of an advance guard – put in question.

Having marched inland, the army now turned south and continued as far as the Chernaya river, bivouacking there within striking distance of Balaklava. The baggage carts abandoned by the enemy had been taken as booty of war and could now be inspected, though there was a protocol even to pillage: officers took what they wanted first, then gave permission to the men to rummage through what was left, which in this case was quite a lot, perhaps because the officers had been interested only in the silver plate and had already filled their saddlebags. The carts contained the property of Russian officers and William Russell saw what the jubilant infantrymen pulled out first: 'Plenty of Champagne was discovered among the baggage, and served to cheer the captors during their cold bivouac that night. This plunder put the soldiers in great humour.'

Unusually for a newspaper correspondent, Russell understated the facts. The drink dispelled all soldierly inhibition and, ladies' underwear and pornographic novels being found too, there seems to have been something of a party, which the officers most wisely permitted. Lieutenant Somerset Calthorpe of the 8th Hussars watched his men:

The troops were allowed to pillage. In a few moments the ground was strewed with every sort of thing – handsome Hussar uniforms, rich fur cloaks, every kind of undergarment, male and female. Several wigs I saw being offered for sale, amidst the laughter of the men. French books and novels of an improper kind were not infrequently met with in the baggage of the Russian officers.

It is unlikely that any of the men could read French – a good proportion could not read English – and it must be assumed that Lieutenant Calthorpe had already made a close examination of the books and novels 'of an improper kind'.

While the infantrymen made merry, the cavalry had acquired a quantity of tobacco and cigarettes from the carts and stood around smoking sombrely. On the march from Kalamita Bay they had been humiliated at the Bulganek, at the Alma and at Khutor Mackenzie. They had been held in check, been recalled whenever they advanced on the enemy, got themselves lost, and been laughed at by both the enemy and their own infantry. They wanted desperately to prove themselves.

The opportunity would come, but the lessons learned by their commanders would then come fatefully into play. Lord Lucan had discovered that he was not allowed to exercise the initiative proper to a divisional commander in the field and must do as Raglan required without question. Lord Cardigan had been told that he must obey his divisional commander however ludicrous an order might seem. Their lordships Lucan and Cardigan, and the Light Brigade, were ready for Balaklava.

5. Reconnaissance and the Cossacks

*The secret intelligence that could have saved
the Light Brigade*

On the morning of 26 September the Light Brigade provided the advance and rear guards for the army on its final, four-mile march from the Chernaya river to the Black Sea coast and Balaklava. The area between the river and the coast was a wide, open plain crossed by two parallel valleys. As the officers and men descended at a trot into the first of these, they could no longer hear the tread of the great army coming up behind, leaving only the constant jingle of harness and the occasional neighing of horses. Troop Sergeant Major Smith later wrote of this moment: 'How little did many a fine fellow of our brigade think that, that day the following month, he would be lying dead, unburied on that very ground. Many a man this day rode over his own grave.'

Families fled from the hamlet of Kadikoi at the edge of the plain as the army approached and halted nearby. A small force with Raglan at its head descended the steep track to Balaklava. The small fishing village was taken without opposition, apart from a couple of token shells fired from a ruined fort by the Balaklava militia, a 'Dad's Army' of elderly men who, having 'resisted', promptly raised a white flag.

Most of the inhabitants were of Greek descent and had no particular loyalty to the Tsar. As Lord Raglan entered the village the men came out of their cottages to welcome him, though more in hope that they and their womenfolk would not be maltreated than in genuine friendship. Through an interpreter he assured them that they would come to no harm. His only proviso was ruthlessly put: they must immediately evacuate the village, taking only what they could carry.

The British fleet, or as much of it as the small harbour could accommodate, sailed in. The village and its simple cottages would not be used to house the troops, for once the transports began unloading supplies and ammunition the area would become one huge supply depot. The infantry divisions left waiting at Kadikoi now turned north and marched a further four miles up the coast to occupy the hills overlooking Sevastopol.

The sudden appearance of enemy troops on the southern heights shocked the people of the city. When the allied armies approached from the north and then promptly disappeared, some had dared to hope that Sevastopol's northern defences had convinced them the city could not be taken by a land assault. Yet now the British and French prepared to swarm down from the hills to the south where the defences had still not been completed. The British on the heights, from generals to private soldiers, certainly expected the assault to be ordered within a day or two. General Sir George Cathcart, commanding the 4th Infantry Division, surveyed the city while his men set up camp. It seemed to him that the southern defences could be easily overcome and he wrote a private note to Raglan: 'The place is only enclosed by a thing like a low park wall, not in good repair. I am sure I could walk into it with scarcely the loss of a man at night or an hour before daybreak. We could run into it even in open daylight, only risking a few shots. We see people walking about the streets in great consternation.'

Raglan rode up to the heights to personally inform General Cathcart that an assault was not to be made. Instead heavy siege guns were to be brought up from the ships at Balaklava – a task that would take at least two weeks – in order to first bombard the defences. Cathcart's reaction was recorded by Alexander Kinglake, a gentleman traveller and historian who had followed the army out to the Crimea: 'Land the siege train! But, my dear Lord Raglan, what the devil is there to knock down?'

Raglan himself had wanted to attack Sevastopol right away, but again he allowed an alliance of Sir John Burgoyne and the French to persuade him otherwise. Most British officers who inspected Sevastopol believed that an immediate assault would take the city.

After the campaign senior Russian officers admitted that they had thought so too. Burgoyne disagreed, and the French were reluctant to send in their infantry before the 'defences' had been reduced by bombardment.

That decision made, the infantry became fully occupied in moving up the siege guns from the harbour to the heights and digging out gun emplacements. Meanwhile Balaklava had to be defended against a possible Russian counter-attack. Raglan established a defensive screen on the plain above Balaklava, centred on the hamlet of Kadikoi, comprising the Light Brigade, the 93rd Highlanders and 2,000 Turkish troops.

The Light Brigade set up camp beside Kadikoi and sent out pickets to watch for the enemy. Patrols went out to search local farms and returned with forage for the horses. Some of the men brought back ducks and chickens, but their greatest prize was a fat bullock. The regimental butchers got to work and soon fresh beef was boiling in countless pots over bivouac fires. To accompany the cooked meat there was an ample supply of grapes taken from nearby vineyards. The temper of the men improved, although they were still without their tents and had to sleep on the grassy plain. One man of the 11th Hussars had brought back an empty wine barrel and crawled inside it for the night; when he was asleep, some of his comrades rolled it about the camp while he shouted oaths from inside, much to the amusement of all.

During the first four days of October the Heavy Brigade regiments – the 1st (Royal), 2nd and 6th Dragoons, and the 4th and 5th Dragoon Guards – arrived at Balaklava and encamped beside the Light Brigade at Kadikoi. For the first time during the campaign Lord Lucan had the complete Cavalry Division present with him. The two brigades now shared the daily picket and patrol duties.

The location of Prince Menshikov's army was unknown and the cavalry had to be continually alert. Lieutenant Richard Temple Godman of the 5th Dragoon Guards had been in the Crimea for less than forty-eight hours when he wrote to his father on 3 October: 'We are harassed night and day with pickets and patrols. Our inlying picket has just turned out in a great hurry after two squadrons of Cossacks, but the latter know better than to stand a charge of even a dozen of our men. They come near and shoot at us.'

Godman refers to pickets – of which there were two kinds, inlying and outlying – and patrols, and it is important to note the differences between them. An outlying picket consisted of an officer and between thirty and forty men positioned four to five miles ahead of the line to be defended, to watch for the enemy, to raise the alarm if any approach was observed and if possible to fight a delaying action. An inlying picket was a body of men that remained within the lines but with its mounts saddled up, ready to give immediate support to the outlying picket when an alarm was raised. A patrol consisted of an officer and a variable number of men from ten upwards sent forward to reconnoitre the area ahead and actively seek out – to report on, not attack – the enemy. Essentially then a picket was a stationary force watching for the enemy to appear, while a patrol was a mobile force sent out in search of the enemy beyond the positions occupied by pickets.

The patrols that rode out constantly across the Chernaya river often encountered Cossacks, as Lieutenant Godman told his father: 'We have daily skirmishes with the Cossacks; they nearly surrounded our patrol yesterday and drove them in before they saw them, but tho' supported by a considerable body of cavalry they did not even fire at us, though we were only about a dozen strong. Today our patrol was fired on, some shot and shell.' The 'shot and shell' is significant. A routine enemy patrol would not be accompanied by artillery and this suggests a reconnaissance in force – a larger body of cavalry and horse artillery sent forward of the main army.

At this stage there is no evidence that Russian patrols were crossing or even approaching the Chernaya, and in order to come under fire from the enemy, British patrols must have been doing so in the opposite direction. It is likely that a line of pickets was established on the high ground overlooking the river four miles from Balaklava, and that patrols went ahead of this line, crossing the river in an attempt to locate the position and gauge the strength of Russian forces. Raglan knew that Prince Menshikov's army had

1. Assistant Surgeon Henry Wilkin, 11th Hussars. As a surgeon, Wilkin was not required to ride with his regiment in the charge, but chose to do so. He is seen here in full dress uniform and fur busby. Both man and horse survived unscathed

17. *The Thin Red Line*. During the Russian attempt to retake Balaklava, their cavalry charged the 93rd Highlanders. Standing in line only two deep, the Highlanders turned back the Russians with volleys of rifle and musket fire

18. *The Charge of the Heavy Brigade*. A second body of Russian cavalry advanced and was pressed back by the Heavy Brigade. The enemy reformed at the far end of the North Valley on the Balaklava plain. The scene was set for the Light Brigade to advance

left Sevastopol, and he urgently wanted to know where it was now.

While the officers and men of both cavalry brigades were constantly on picket or patrol duty, Lord Cardigan described himself as 'very unwell with diarrhoea'. He was examined by the principal medical officer on 5 October and ordered on board ship to rest. He was provided with a cabin on the *Star of the South*, the ship on which Fanny Duberly was living while her husband was encamped with the 8th Hussars at Kadikoi. In Varna, Fanny had hoped to see Cardigan get his head in such a bag that he would never get it out again. Since then the two had struck up an unlikely friendship. There were soon whispers of an affair, although Fanny's reputation was such that an officer barely had to be seen in her presence for the rumour mongers to have him in her bed. There is however no proof that she was anything more than a most sociable flirt.

In a more significant development enemy patrols were for the first time observed riding along the far bank of the Chernaya. The Russians were closing in. Lord Raglan ordered that British patrols were no longer to cross the river, considering the risk too great. When Captain John Oldham of the 13th Light Dragoons spotted movement on the far bank and sent a sergeant across to investigate, the man did not return and Lucan had the captain placed under arrest for disobeying orders. As patrols could not now advance further than their own picket line established on the heights overlooking the river, they were effectively stripped of their reconnoitring role.

During this crucial phase of the campaign when enemy patrols were beginning to probe British defences, Light Brigade pickets took on an intelligence-gathering role alongside their normal tripwire function. Officers wrote down detailed descriptions of the uniforms worn by the enemy and passed this information to Charles Cattley, a civilian interpreter attached to Lord Raglan's staff. Cattley had an encyclopedic knowledge of Russian regiments and, given accurate reports of uniforms or cap badges, could inform Raglan which troops were in the area, estimate their strength, and suggest what their purpose might be.

What the officers of the Light Brigade did not know, though some may have guessed, was that Cattley was head of Lord Raglan's Secret Intelligence Department. The SID did not appear on the official list of British units in the Crimea and its existence was known only to a small circle of high-ranking officers in Balaklava and senior politicians in London. Colonel Lloyd, the first head of the SID, died of cholera shortly after the Battle of the Alma and Raglan appointed Cattley to succeed him.

Charles Cattley had worked for several years in St Petersburg, and had been British vice-consul at Kertch in the Crimea when Britain and France declared war on Russia and Tsar Nicholas ordered all British diplomats out of the country. He returned to London and was immediately sent back with the invasion force. Few of Cattley's intelligence reports have survived, as might be expected of paperwork generated by a clandestine organization, but those preserved among the Raglan Papers in the National Army Museum in London indicate that he reported directly to Lord Raglan.

When first made head of the SID, Cattley expected to make much use of Light Brigade patrols for forward reconnaissance and intelligence-gathering but Raglan required the cavalry to concentrate on defending the approaches to Balaklava. There was clearly a conflict between the tripwire function demanded by Raglan and the intelligence-gathering required by Cattley. Raglan allowed patrols to be sent across the Chernaya until the enemy showed itself in force in that area, and then forbade them. In order to maintain the flow of information Cattley had to send spies – Turks, or locals of Greek descent – across the river to seek out Prince Menshikov's army.

At first light on 7 October, Cornet Edward Fisher-Rowe and a patrol of ten men of the 4th Dragoon Guards moving along the British side of the Chernaya found themselves suddenly confronted by a large number of Russian lancers and were, as Fisher-Rowe put it, 'obliged to retire'. The enemy gave chase. Three men were cut off and 'speared in the most merciless manner' as the patrol galloped back to camp and raised the alarm.

Lord Lucan, fearing an attack in force on Balaklava, led the Cavalry Division out; Cardigan was still recovering from his diarrhoea on the *Star of the South* and was not present. Captain Nolan was eager to be part of any action that might result and went too. They reached the hills overlooking the river to find a sizeable Russian force manoeuvring in the valley below.

Lucan noted that the enemy's movements to and fro showed no sign of any advance uphill towards him, as if inviting him to lead his cavalry down. That was exactly what Captain Nolan, who sat watching the Russians with the 17th Lancers, thought Lucan should do. But Lucan did not believe he had any choice in the matter; Lord Raglan had given strict orders that the cavalry was to deploy defensively and under no circumstances be drawn into an unnecessary engagement. Lucan held his two brigades in position between the Russians and Balaklava, but made no move towards the enemy.

Light Brigade officers protested that they should be allowed to charge. Lucan refused. The encounter at the Bulganek when they were ordered to retire in the face of the enemy was still fresh in their minds and they protested more strongly. Again Lucan refused. After some time Captain Maude came up with the guns of the horse artillery and it took only a few shells to force the enemy to withdraw. Captain Shakespear, second-in-command to Maude, felt that: 'The finest opportunity for thrashing the Russian cavalry had been thrown away.'

Most officers and men of the Light Brigade thought so too. They had little doubt who was responsible and were naming him openly, according to Lieutenant Calthorpe: 'I heard great blame given to Lord Lucan for not ordering the Light Cavalry to advance and charge the Cossacks.'

It was following this incident that Lord Lucan was given the nickname 'Lord Look-on'. There is no record of who first used the name, though the obvious suspect is Captain Nolan, already outspoken about what he considered to be Lucan's preference for sitting and watching rather than leading the cavalry into action. It was thought such an apt play on the man's name that it spread quickly. Unfortunately the witticism rebounded against the Light Brigade. Infantrymen who had laughed at the cavalry's failure to charge at the Bulganek and the fiasco at the Alma now adopted the name 'Look-ons' for the cavalry as a whole.

George Evelyn, an ex-officer of the Rifle Brigade who was following the army as a gentleman traveller, wrote in his diary: 'Our cavalry is the most inefficient in Europe. They certainly have not done as much as was expected of them.' Such taunts and criticisms might have been unfair, given the restrictions imposed on the divisional commander by Lord Raglan, but the infantrymen who had won a major battle at the Alma and believed themselves poised to take Sevastopol felt that as yet the cavalry had done nothing.

Lord Lucan earned his nickname on 7 October. One week later Lord Cardigan was granted his by the disgruntled men under his command. He had returned from sick leave on 12 October. The following day his luxury yacht, the *Dryad*, arrived from England and anchored in Balaklava harbour. After only one night back with his brigade at Kadikoi, Cardigan announced that he had received Lord Raglan's permission to sleep on the *Dryad*. With the yacht came his French chef and stocks of champagne, so he dined aboard too. Men of the Light Brigade sleeping on the windswept Balaklava plain, surviving on meagre rations of salt pork and biscuit now that the local supply of fresh meat had been used up, and with only sarcasm left to express their opinion, named him the 'Noble Yachtsman'.

Lucan felt as dissatisfied as the men about this arrangement. He was the divisional commander and he lived in camp with his regiments and inspected them when they paraded each morning before dawn. Meanwhile Cardigan, one of his brigade commanders, was sleeping and breakfasting on a luxury yacht and, because of the journey up from the harbour to the cavalry camp, was not normally present until 10.00 a.m.

That was one irritation among many. Their lordships were still squabbling over every trifle and even Lord Raglan had heard enough of them. When he ordered the Light Brigade camp to be moved, while retaining the Heavy Brigade at Kadikoi, Lord Paget could see no strategic reason for it and believed this was done merely to separate the divisional and brigade commanders: 'There are Lucan and Cardigan again hard at it, and it is found desirable to separate them. Cardigan must needs be ordered up here to command regiments which are usefully placed with their divisional general, and all this must needs be upset to part these spoilt children.'

Raglan had bigger problems on his mind. Although the Russian advance of 7 October had come to nothing, it confirmed a growing fear that the enemy might attempt an attack in force on Balaklava from the direction of the Chernaya. Between the river and the village, two valleys – the British named them the North Valley and the South Valley – cut across the plain, and the Russian army would have to cross them to reach Balaklava. As an additional defence Raglan ordered a line of redoubts to be constructed along the high ground – the Causeway Heights – that ran between the two valleys. Four redoubts were hurriedly built at intervals of 500 yards. These were forts constructed out of earth, the soil dug out from the centre being used to build a parapet around the perimeter, with occasional breaks left for the muzzles of artillery guns. None of them was formidable. Each contained two or three 12-pounder guns and between 200 and 600 Turkish infantrymen. They might delay an advancing army, but they would not stop it.

The redoubts now became Balaklava's first line of defence. Behind them the second line consisted of the 93rd Highlanders and the remainder of the Turkish infantrymen. Lord Lucan's Cavalry Division with Captain Maud's attached troop of Royal Horse Artillery formed a mobile defence, able to move as required between the first and second lines.

Lucan had previously been in charge of the defence of Balaklava, but on 14 October Raglan put Sir Colin Campbell, commanding officer of the 93rd Highlanders, in overall command of the defences although Lucan retained independent command of the cavalry. This was a tremendous humiliation for Lucan, who outranked

Campbell, and while many must have drawn the obvious conclusion, Captain Maude put it in writing: 'Lord Raglan would not trust Lord Lucan to defend Balaklava, so sent down Sir Colin Campbell.' The reputation of the cavalry within its own army had never been lower. This was not what the Light Brigade had expected.

On 17 October the siege guns were finally in position on the heights overlooking Sevastopol and the bombardment of the city began. Most of the British and a good many among the Russians took this to be the beginning of the end. The artillery would require two or three days to reduce the defences to rubble and then the infantry would storm in. There was no obvious role for the cavalry.

Although the first day's bombardment appeared to seriously damage Sevastopol's walls and forts, at first light on the following morning the British were shocked to see that during the night the Russians had rebuilt everything and left it stronger than before. This pattern repeated itself on the second day, and again on the third. On the evening of 19 October, Colonel Charles Windham, one of the officers detailed to lead the infantry assault, wrote in his diary: 'The pounding match went on as usual, without our gaining the slightest advantage, and I am convinced that we shall lose double the men in taking the place (if we do succeed) than we should have done had we attacked it twenty-four days ago. This long range firing is all nonsense. Our present attack is an absurdity.'

Sevastopol's fortunes had been changed by two men: Lord Raglan, who had allowed himself to be persuaded against an immediate assault, and Lieutenant Colonel Franz Todleben, a Russian army engineer. Granted time by the enemy, Todleben supervised the building of earthworks to complete and strengthen the southern defences, and fortified them with naval guns from the fleet. He put the whole population of men, women and children to work in shifts so that construction and repair continued by day and night, and incredibly their work outpaced the destructive efforts of the British and French siege guns.

Meanwhile tensions were rising in the cavalry camp. Cossack

patrols were regularly encountered on the near side of the Chernaya and everyone expected the Russians to attempt something soon to divert the allies from the bombardment of Sevastopol. Regular patrols rode out across the South Valley, over the Causeway Heights and across the North Valley as far as the river. Pickets needed no bawling sergeant to keep their eyes and ears alert for the first sign of an advance, especially at night, and Lord Paget felt that some of the men had become too jumpy: 'We are now regularly turned out about midnight. Every fool at the outposts, who fancies he hears something, has only to make a row, and there we all are, generals and all. Well, I suppose 500 false alarms are better than one surprise.' During one alert a stray cow was mistaken for a Cossack and shot dead.

Not all of the officers were as philosophical about the situation as Paget. Cornet Wombwell wrote to his father: 'The way they keep turning us out is ridiculous. If a heavy dragoon or any other thick-headed individual sees a Cossack, he comes galloping into camp and instantly magnifies the Cossack to 500. So of course out we all go and by the time we all get there, not a soul is to be seen.'

On being turned out, whether the enemy was then in evidence or not, the cavalry remained in the saddle until first light. The nights were bitterly cold and Cornet Fisher-Rowe wore 'two pairs of drawers, two pairs socks, two jerseys, a red flannel under stable jacket, and thick stable jacket'. Often on returning to camp, before the men had time to boil water and brew tea, another alert was sounded and out they went again. It was tiring work and Private Robert Farquharson of the 4th Light Dragoons was clearly dispirited:

The nights were awfully cold, and the heavy dews would almost drench us, till the blood felt like ice, and what with 'outlying' and 'inlying' pickets, almost always in the saddle, and never undressed, sickness, want of food – and I've gone entire three days without food – we were very queer indeed. Every day now the Russians loitering or moving in great masses about the Chernaya, keep us on the alert morning, noon and night. If we came in from picket fagged, cold and hungry, we might hear the trumpet sound 'boot and saddle' at any moment.

The men were living on biscuit and small amounts of salt pork. Many were ordered to the sick tents, placing an additional burden on those still available for duty. Some who mounted the pickets and patrols were completely exhausted. Lieutenant Roger Palmer of the 11th Hussars, sitting out through the night with his picket, found Private Gregory Jowett asleep in the saddle. Although the man should have been put under arrest Palmer let him off with a few severe words. It was perhaps deliberate policy on the part of the Russians to keep the British guessing and to weaken the cavalry. Major Forrest suggested as much: 'They worry us a great deal by constantly making believe that they mean to attack us.'

They did not appear to be 'making believe' on the evening of 21 October when a spy came in with a report of 20,000 Russian infantrymen and 5,000 cavalry advancing on Balaklava from the direction of the Chernaya. Lord Lucan took this to be the expected attack and led his two brigades out, while Lord Raglan ordered an infantry division down from the Sevastopol heights to reinforce the Balaklava defences. The cavalry stood out all night – the coldest of the campaign so far – without sighting a single Cossack. At first light the infantry marched back to the heights and the cavalry returned to camp. All were tired and despondent.

There was one casualty. Major Augustus Willett, who had taken command of the 17th Lancers when Colonel Lawrenson became ill after the Alma, died the next day of 'cholera brought on by exposure'. Willett considered the cavalry cloak an unnecessary article of clothing – or took his lead from Cardigan, who thought it 'effeminate'. He had no use for such a thing and refused his men permission to wear theirs, however cold the weather. The lancers suffered badly through the bitter night of 21 October and when Private Wightman wrote that 'Willett was a corpse before sundown of the following day', it was with a hint that some kind of natural justice had worked its course.

There was another alert on the afternoon of 22 October, and

that evening the cavalry was turned out again and remained out all night. When they returned to camp at first light the men were utterly exhausted. Lord Raglan now decided that unnecessary alerts were being called and that they were taking the possibility of a Russian advance on Balaklava too seriously.

Meanwhile, across the Chernaya, the Russians had finalized their plan of attack. Prince Menshikov had assembled his army at Chorgun, north of the river, from where he could hit the flank of any British infantry assault on Sevastopol. The city was holding out longer than expected and the British infantry divisions were sitting on the heights, waiting. As the reinforcements Menshikov requested had arrived, he decided that he could now go on the offensive. Reconnaissance patrols sent out on 18 and 19 October reported that the British outer defences – the redoubts on the Causeway Heights – were weak and the British cavalry exhausted.

By 24 October, Menshikov had gathered an attack force at Chorgun under the command of Lieutenant General Pavel Liprandi comprising 25,000 infantry, 3,400 cavalry and 2,300 artillerymen manning seventy-eight guns. He gave orders for the assault to begin at first light the next day.

The precise objective of the Russian attack has always been disputed. British historians represent it as an attempt to take Balaklava and for that reason the engagement is known in Britain as the Battle of Balaklava although all the action took place on the plain above the village. Russian historians claim that Menshikov intended to take the area around Kadikoi and cut off the British army besieging Sevastopol from its supply base, and they describe the battle of 25 October as the Battle of Kadikoi.

On the morning of 22 October Charles Cattley delivered his most crucial intelligence report of the campaign to Lord Raglan. It was based on the interrogation of two Polish sailors who had deserted from Sevastopol, and contained useful information: British shells were inflicting heavy damage; food stocks were low but the supply of roundshot was ample. Most significant of all, the sailors told Cattley that large numbers of fresh troops were arriving in the

Crimea to reinforce the Russian army, and that Prince Menshikov planned to attack 'with great force and attack us in the rear and deliver the Town'.

Here was specific information about an attempt to relieve Sevastopol ('the Town') through a major attack ('with great force') behind the British army on the heights ('in the rear'). This does suggest that the objective of the attack was in fact the area around Kadikoi, but because the British had established their defences in order to protect Balaklava, there was a predisposition to assume that Balaklava must be the target of any enemy advance. In practice it made little difference, for in order to take Kadikoi Menshikov would have to defeat the forces that Raglan had put there to defend Balaklava: the Heavy and Light Cavalry Brigades, the Highlanders and the Turkish troops.

Lord Raglan ignored Cattley's intelligence report. He had two reasons. First, it was based on the interrogation of men from Sevastopol as opposed to a source within the Russian army. Second, it came from Polish sailors, who were unlikely to be party to Menshikov's intentions; it could be a rumour deliberately circulated in the city to shore up the failing morale of those besieged there. But if Raglan had linked this report with an earlier piece of intelligence supplied by Cattley, he might have taken it more seriously. The captain of HMS *Retribution* had been told some weeks previously by the master of an Austrian ship that 40,000 Russian troops had left Odessa en route to the Crimea. Here was independent verification of the Polish sailors' assertion that large numbers of fresh troops were arriving. If Menshikov had been waiting for these reinforcements to join him before he attacked, then that attack must now be imminent.

As if all this was not enough, on the evening of 24 October a Turkish spy sent out to locate the position of the Russian army returned to report that enemy forces were massed beyond the Chernaya and would attack the following morning. The intelligence was considered sound and the spy was taken before Lord Lucan, who wrote an urgent letter informing Lord Raglan and sent it immediately by galloper to headquarters. Raglan read it, said,

'Very well,' and did nothing. There had been a considerable number of false alarms during the previous week. He believed these were needlessly exhausting his men and gambled that this too would prove of no consequence.

Cattley's report of 22 October, taken together with the earlier intelligence received from HMS *Retribution* and the report of the Turkish spy on 24 October, clearly indicated a major Russian attack to be launched on 25 October. If Raglan had acted on this – by ordering infantry divisions down from the heights above Sevastopol onto the Balaklava plain – then the battle would have taken a different course.

Moreover the 'secret intelligence' that could have saved the Light Brigade was virtually public knowledge. William Russell of *The Times* visited the cavalry camp on the evening of 24 October:

I was told that 'the Russkies were very strong all over the place', that reports had been sent to headquarters that an attack was imminent, and that Sir Colin Campbell was uneasy about Balaklava. As I was leaving Nolan overtook me. The evening was chilly. He remarked that I ought to have something warmer than my thin frock coat, and insisted on my taking his cloak – 'Mind you send it back to me tomorrow; I shall not want it tonight.' Nor did he next day or ever after! All the way back he 'let out' at the Cavalry Generals, and did not spare those in high places. 'We are in a very bad way I can tell you.'

At 5.00 the next morning the Russian attack began.

TWO

The Charge of the Light Brigade

The charge must be decided promptly and executed vigorously.
Captain Louis Nolan

On 25 October 1854 on the plain above Balaklava there occurred not one but four cavalry charges.

The battle began with a Russian artillery and infantry attack on the redoubts that formed the allies' first line of defence. When the Turks manning them abandoned the redoubts, the Russian cavalry charged the British infantry forming the second line of defence, which held firm and later became known as the thin red line.

The second charge took place when an additional body of Russian cavalry advanced on Balaklava, but was met and charged by the Heavy Brigade of the British Cavalry Division, and turned back.

With the Russians forced onto the defensive, the Light Brigade of the British Cavalry Division charged an enemy artillery position at the far end of a mile-long valley; it immediately came under fire from Russian artillery on high ground to the left.

French cavalry charged and silenced the enemy guns to the left, but nothing could be done about the Russian guns about to open fire on the Light Brigade from the high ground to the right, or the guns directly ahead . . .

6. Towards the Valley of Death

The Russian attack, the thin red line and the Heavy Brigade

We groomed and saddled our horses as well as we could, wiped the dews off our swords and scabbards, which were red and rusty despite all our care, got our cloaks, equipments, and so on, in order, and moved up the brow of the hill.

It was bitterly cold and still dark at 5.00 on the morning of 25 October when this anonymous private of the 8th Hussars stood to his horse with the Cavalry Division. Turning out one hour before daybreak in anticipation of a Russian attack had become routine, but it was sapping the spirit of the men, as Private William Pennington of the 11th Hussars suggested: 'The coldest hour in all the twenty-four is that before the dawn; and fasting even from the meagre allowance of the coarsest ration, standing drowsily at our horses' heads in the bleak morning air sweeping fitfully across the plain, are not conditions favourable to the most hopeful and heroic frame of mind.'

In the minutes before sunrise, officers and men alike kept their eyes on the Causeway Heights between the North and South Valleys, waiting to catch first sight of the cavalry vedettes stationed there. A vedette consisted of two mounted sentries, and it was normal practice for the officer in charge of a picket to place a line of vedettes forward of his position. Vedettes used a system of signalling manoeuvres to communicate with the picket. On seeing an enemy approach, the two men would ride in a circle: if they saw cavalry, they circled clockwise; if they saw infantry, they circled anticlockwise; if they saw both cavalry and infantry, one man rode clockwise while the other rode anticlockwise. Each vedette was positioned within sight of the next, so that immediately one vedette began signalling, this was taken up by the next to left and right, and so on along the line. The system worked well by daylight, but until the sun was up it was no system at all.

First to discover that the Russians had moved up under cover of night was Captain Alexander Low of the 4th Light Dragoons. He was duty field officer of the day and it was his task to check the outlying pickets. Just after 5.30 a.m. he approached the most distant picket at Kamara, about two miles from the Chernaya, and glimpsed a party of Cossacks stealing up on the village. The picket had not seen them – there is some suggestion that the men might have been dozing – and it was only Low's timely arrival and his shouts that enabled them to scuttle away and escape capture or worse. Low and the picket made for the Causeway Heights and took refuge in the nearest redoubt.

The massive Russian forces advancing behind them were heading for the same point, and next to spot the enemy were the vedettes on the heights. At first light – a little before 6.00 a.m. – the most keenly sighted men of the Light Brigade saw the vedettes signalling. Private Robert Farquharson of the 4th Light Dragoons knew now that an engagement of some kind was likely: 'The vedettes were circling to right, and also to left, some of them being at a trot. These combined movements signalled to us that the enemy were showing with both infantry and cavalry.' Troop Sergeant Major George Smith of the 11th Hussars noted that the vedettes were circling 'rapidly', and this was significant, for the size of the enemy force observed was communicated by the speed with which the vedettes circled.

Last to realize what was happening was Lord Lucan, who had gone forward as he did before daybreak each morning to inspect the redoubts. With him were Lord George Paget, Lord William Paulet and Major Thomas McMahon. Their position close in beneath the Causeway Heights made it impossible for them to see the cavalry vedettes circling just above them. Another signalling system using flags had been agreed for the Turks manning the redoubts, although none of these four gentlemen seemed too sure what it was. Paget described what happened:

'Hello,' said Lord William, 'there are two flags flying; what does that mean?'

'Why, that surely is the signal that the enemy is approaching,' said Major McMahon.

'Are you quite sure?' we replied.

Hardly were the words out of McMahon's mouth, when bang went a cannon from the redoubt in question. I turned round and galloped back 'best pace' to my brigade, which I at once mounted.

The Lights were not of course Paget's brigade, but he took command when Lord Cardigan was absent, and, it being only 6.00 a.m., he was still in his bed on the *Dryad*. The commanding officers of the regiments yelled instructions to their men as they settled in the saddle. Lieutenant Colonel John Douglas turned his horse to face the officers and men of the 11th Hussars and shouted: 'Eleventh, attention. Now men, in all probability we shall meet the enemy today. When you do, don't cut but give them the point, and they will never face you again.'

Seconds later the sound of heavy artillery fire reached them as the Russian artillery began bombarding the redoubts on the Causeway Heights. The Battle of Balaklava had begun. Captain Henry Duberly of the 8th Hussars sent his servant down to the harbour with a note and a spare horse for his wife Fanny, who had insisted that if any general action took place she wished to see it. He told her: 'The battle has begun and promises to be a hot one. I send you the horse. Lose no time, but come up as quickly as you can. Do not wait for breakfast.'

Lord Lucan rode quickly back towards Kadikoi in search of Sir Colin Campbell, in overall command of the Balaklava defences, and found Campbell riding out to seek him. They spoke briefly and agreed that this was not another Russian feint but an attack in force with the intention of taking the British base. A message to that effect was sent to Lord Raglan. Campbell turned back to prepare the 93rd Highlanders to meet the enemy and Lucan returned to the cavalry.

Leaving the Light Brigade where it stood, Lucan led the Heavy Brigade out towards the redoubts. He had no intention of engaging such a huge enemy force or advancing up onto the heights in support of the Turks, but hoped that by manoeuvring within sight of the Russians he might discourage any further advance towards Balaklava. Although the Russian artillery was firing only on the Turkish redoubts, Lucan somehow managed to position the brigade directly in the line of fire and ammunition that overshot its target found the Heavies instead. Lieutenant Colonel John Yorke, commanding officer of the 1st Dragoons, was unhappy about the unnecessary casualties his regiment sustained:

All the very large shot that over-crowned the heights naturally bowled like cricket balls into our ranks. The officers could easily escape; we had only to move our horses a few yards to let the shot pass, which movement I effected frequently, but when a shot came opposite the closely packed squadron it generally took a front and rear rank horse. In this foolish manner we lost seven horses and two men.

Deciding that the Russians would not be put off by his presence, Lucan led the Heavy Brigade back to its original position beside the Light Brigade. The Turks manning the guns in the redoubts, who had taken the presence of the British cavalry nearby as an indication that support was on its way, now saw the Heavies retreating. The British too had thought they were merely waiting for further support to come up. Lord Paget had been left watching with the Light Brigade and wrote that all were 'straining our eyes in vain round the hills in our rear for indications of support'. None came. It would take at least two hours to march an infantry division down from the heights overlooking Sevastopol and the Russians had calculated that they could take the redoubts in less time than that. The Turks were left to face the full force of the Russian assault alone.

British accounts of this action have traditionally portrayed the Turks as abandoning their guns and running away very soon after the redoubts came under attack. One much-retold anecdote has the wife of a British infantryman beating the fleeing Turks with her hands in an attempt to prevent their cowardly race towards their only means of escape, the ships at Balaklava. Yet the Russian attack began before 6.00 and the first redoubt did not fall until after 7.30 a.m. During that time the 500 Turks defending this most exposed position suffered a heavy artillery bombardment – Russian 18-pounder guns were firing from 1,800 yards, while the 12-pounders in the redoubt had a maximum range of 1,200 yards – followed by an infantry assault by a force that at the lowest recorded estimate numbered 2,500 and some observers thought twice that. The Russians bayoneted 170 of the men inside before the rest ran for their lives.

The Light Brigade had to sit and watch. Among the men who found this distressing was Troop Sergeant Major Smith, as eager as the rest to go out in aid of the Turks:

As the last of them came over the parapet, I noticed the Russians were hard at their heels. As they gained the plain, a number of Cossacks swept round the foot of the hill, killing and wounding many of them. Some of them being unharmed raised their hands imploringly, but it was only to have them severed from their bodies. Had a dozen or two of us been sent out, numbers of these poor fellows might have been saved.

The cavalry blamed Lord Lucan for yet again looking-on when he should have led them out. Lucan in turn blamed Lord Raglan:

Lord Raglan not having acted on the communication sent him the day previous informing him of the approach of a considerable Russian Army, and leaving us altogether without support, we considered it our first duty to defend the approach to the town of Balaklava; and as this defence would depend chiefly upon the cavalry it was necessary to reserve them for the purpose.

The Turks were outgunned and outnumbered. Those manning the second, third and fourth redoubts, seeing the Russian infantry take the first and realizing that the British were not coming to their assistance, fled back towards Balaklava pursued by Cossacks. British infantrymen had no liking for the Turks and, being far from the action, thought this a cowardly retreat. British historians have made it so, often in counterpoint to the heroic stand made later by the 93rd Highlanders, taking as their evidence a single line in William Russell's first report of the action for *The Times* in which he wrote that the Turks 'received a few shots and shell and then bolted'.

Russell afterwards admitted that he had not witnessed the start of the battle. Like any good correspondent he filled in what he had missed with snippets overheard from others who had not seen it either. He wrote: 'Our treatment of the Turks was unfair; but I confess that I at the time shared the disgust which was expressed by everyone, ignorant as we were that the Turks in No. 1 redoubt had lost more than a fourth of their number ere they abandoned it to the enemy.'

The cavalry was positioned closer to the redoubts and saw what really happened. One incident recorded by Private Albert Mitchell of the 13th Light Dragoons demonstrates how the Turks (all known as Johnny because of their unpronounceable names) fleeing on foot nevertheless took every opportunity to fight back:

Two Cossacks came over the ridge together. One of them lanced a Turk in the back, who uttered a loud scream and fell. Another Turk being a short distance ahead, they both made for him, but before they could reach him, Johnny, who had his piece loaded and bayonet fixed, turned suddenly and fired at the foremost, knocking him off his horse. The other coming up made a point, but whether it touched the Turk I cannot say; but in an instant he had bayoneted the Cossack in the body, and he also fell from his horse. Johnny resumed his journey at a walk.

Immediately the Turks abandoned their positions the Russians occupied the redoubts and took possession of the British 12-pounder guns. The Russian artillery then turned its attention onto the only enemy force within range, the British cavalry. Lord Paget was still in command of the Light Brigade in Cardigan's absence and soon found himself under fire:

I was standing clear of the front of the brigade, when all sorts of gesticulations and cries of 'Look out, Lord George!' met my ears. Bewildered, I moved my horse two or three paces, which had the effect of bringing me into the line of the roundshot, which they saw coming, and which bounded actually between my horse's fore and hind legs, bursting a cloud of dust up into my face. The first knowledge I had of the danger I had passed was a laugh from my rollicking orderly, 'Ah, ha! It went right between your horse's legs;' responded to by me, 'Well, you seem to think it a good joke; I don't see anything to laugh at.'

Nor did anyone moments later when a man in the front line of the 4th Light Dragoons was hit. It was the first time Paget heard a sound which was soon to become all too familiar: 'The roundshot completely whizzed him round, and I can well remember the slosh that sounded as it went through the centre of his belly.'

Around this time – approximately 7.45 a.m. – three latecomers arrived. Lord Cardigan reached the cavalry after riding up from his yacht and took command of the Light Brigade. Lord Raglan took up his position on the Sapoune Heights, 650 feet above the Balaklava plain, from where he was to command the battle. And Fanny Duberly appeared there too.

William Russell was already on the heights with his pencil and notebook. He thought that the commander-in-chief had not taken the first report of an attack seriously and had not hurried: 'I could never understand why they were so long in turning out at Headquarters. The advance of the Russians was detected as soon as it was daylight. A quiet canter would have taken one from headquarters to the edge of the plateau in twenty minutes.'

Fanny Duberly had made her way up as quickly as possible from the *Star of the South* after receiving her husband's note:

I was hardly clear of the town, before I met a commissariat officer, who told me that the Turks had abandoned all their batteries, and were running towards the town. He begged me to keep as much to the left as possible, and to lose no time in getting amongst our own men, as the Russian force was pouring on us; adding, 'For God's sake, ride fast, or you may not reach the camp alive.'

Fanny joined Lord Raglan on the heights from where they could clearly see the two valleys that cut across the plain below and the deployment of the British forces. Lieutenant Somerset Calthorpe and Captain Louis Nolan were among the several staff officers and ADCs mounted and standing ready to act as gallopers carrying Raglan's orders at speed to the commanders down below.

Raglan had at first thought the Russian advance reported by Sir Colin Campbell a feint, possibly designed to occupy him while the enemy stormed out from Sevastopol to attack his army on the heights overlooking the city. Now he saw that he had been wrong. An enormous Russian force had already taken the redoubts on the Causeway Heights and all that protected Balaklava were the 93rd Highlanders and some Turks, reinforced by many of their countrymen from the redoubts, who had rallied and formed up alongside them, supported by Lord Lucan's Cavalry Division. It was only now that Raglan sent orders for two infantry divisions to march down from the heights above Sevastopol to the plain. It would take them over two hours to arrive. The Russians appeared to have both the intention and the forces to take Balaklava in a much shorter time.

Lord Raglan's obsession with preserving his cavalry, in evidence throughout the campaign so far, shaped his first order of the day to Lucan – who had, with for him rare tactical insight, positioned the cavalry to one side of the line of advance the Russians must take if they were to attack the line formed by the 93rd Highlanders and the Turks. From this position he could charge the enemy flank. Raglan did not want to risk his cavalry in any such action before the infantry divisions arrived, and although he was not so indiscreet as to use the word 'withdraw', that is what the movement required by his order amounted to.

8.00 a.m.
Lord Raglan's first order to the Cavalry Division

Cavalry to take ground to the left of the second line of redoubts occupied by Turks.

It took a rider twenty minutes to reach the cavalry with this order. Lord Lucan received it angrily. Again the cavalry was to be withdrawn, and this left Campbell's 550 Highlanders and the Turks to meet the full onslaught of the Russian army without cavalry support. Suspecting that he might be blamed if these men were overrun and Balaklava taken, Lucan ordered the staff officer who had brought the order to remain with him while the required movement was carried out, and to confirm that this was precisely as ordered and not a misunderstanding on his part. At this early point in the battle Lucan was displaying a remarkable degree of good sense. At the same time he was demonstrating that he had learned to obey Lord Raglan's orders whether they appeared reasonable or not.

Raglan's lackadaisical wording was a harbinger of worse to come. By 'redoubts occupied by Turks' he meant those previously occupied and now abandoned. It is impossible to be certain what he meant by 'the second line of redoubts' as there was only one line. If he saw the Highlanders as the first line of defence – that is, the line nearest to him – he might then have referred to the redoubts as the second line of defence, but 'the second line of redoubts' makes no literal sense. More seriously, military orders required movements by the compass – east or west, for example – because the meaning of the terms 'left' and 'right' depends on which way the recipient is facing. On this occasion Lucan interpreted 'take ground to the left' correctly and moved the cavalry to the west from where it could not be seen by or engage the Russians. This new position placed the Light Brigade near the mouth of the North Valley.

Raglan expected the enemy to advance directly on Balaklava by cutting diagonally across the two valleys. Some of the cavalrymen feared that instead the Russians might move unseen up the full length of the North Valley and then turn towards Balaklava. Because the Light Brigade was standing near but to one side of the valley mouth, enemy troops would not be seen until they reached the opening, at which point they would be barely fifty yards away. This possibility made the cavalry's new position more precarious than its former place on the open plain. Troop Sergeant Major Smith was one of those concerned: 'We took up a position facing the opening at the top of the valley through which it was thought the enemy cavalry would come. We were out of sight of the enemy, but expected every moment to see them.'

As Lord Raglan watched the cavalry 'take ground' – it was now thirty minutes after he issued the order – he changed his mind. Earlier the Turks in the redoubts had held steady until they saw the cavalry fall back and only then abandon the guns. He now decided that the Turks formed up beside the Highlanders, having seen the cavalry again withdraw, might once more turn and run if approached by the enemy. He therefore sent an order for part of the cavalry to return to the position just vacated.

8.30 a.m.
Lord Raglan's second order to the Cavalry Division

Eight squadrons of heavy Dragoons to be detached towards Balaklava to support the Turks who are wavering.

There is no evidence that the Turks were wavering, but Raglan thought they were or might soon do so. As each regiment comprised two squadrons, Lord Lucan was required to move four of his five Heavy Brigade regiments back to the defensive line at Kadikoi.

Lucan received this second order about twenty minutes after taking up his new position and became angrier still. Lord Raglan's instructions made no sense. Moving four regiments back onto the open plain while leaving five regiments of Lights and one regiment of Heavies where they stood merely divided the cavalry – by about one mile – and reduced the effectiveness of each part. However, doing precisely as Raglan wished, he ordered General James Scarlett in command of the Heavy Brigade to lead four regiments back to where they had just come from.

Although it is clearer to describe the two actions known as the thin red line and the charge of the Heavy Brigade as if they were separate events, they resulted from the two forks of a single Russian cavalry attack and occurred virtually simultaneously at about 9.15 a.m. The enemy cavalry had advanced unseen part-way along the North Valley, then separated into two groups and turned up over the Causeway Heights to advance directly on Balaklava. The first group, a relatively small force of 400, headed straight for the 93rd Highlanders and the Turks. The main body advanced a little further before turning to attack this line too, but at the crest of the heights saw below them the four Heavy Brigade regiments passing by on their return to the position ordered by Lord Raglan.

Sir Colin Campbell's 550 Highlanders and the Turks to either side of them were prepared for an attack. If musket and rifle fire failed to stop the assault, their bayonets were fixed and ready. A few artillery guns were also drawn up on both flanks. As the Russian cavalry came on at the gallop, Campbell rode quickly along the line formed two men deep, shouting, 'Men, remember there is no retreat from here. You must die where you stand.' Private John Scott broke both regimental etiquette and the tension of the men by calling back, 'Aye, aye, Sir Colin, and needs be we'll do that.'

Lord Raglan and those with him on the Sapoune Heights had a grandstand view. Fanny Duberly watched intently and William Russell wrote furiously in his notebook: 'The Russians dash at the Highlanders. The ground flies beneath their horses' feet; gathering speed at every stride, they dash on towards that thin red streak topped with a line of steel.' To receive cavalry, infantry normally formed squares or a line four men deep, and a line only two deep was unheard of – thus Russell's description of a 'thin red streak', which only in later accounts became the 'thin red line'.

Captain Shakespear of the Royal Horse Artillery described what happened in the words of a soldier rather than the prose of a correspondent:

The whole plain swarmed with cavalry. The left column charged the 93rd Highlanders, who, under Sir Colin, stood on some rising ground with Turkish infantry on both flanks, the whole flanked by guns on the right and on the left. The Highlanders ruined the charge in line, the guns worked them with grape and case; the enemy fled in great confusion.

From the viewpoint of the Highlanders facing the charge it was not quite such an easy affair. It is possible that Campbell ordered his men to fire too early, for their first volley failed to fell a single Russian. Private Donald Cameron of the 93rd wrote that although the enemy cavalrymen then wheeled away, they were far from done:

The Russians coming again towards us, we opened fire on them the second time and turned them. They seemed to be going away. We ceased firing and cheered. They wheeled about and made a dash at us again. We opened fire on them the third time. They came to a stand, wheeled about and rode off at a canter. We ceased firing and cheered. Our heavy guns fired after them. They were soon back over the hill the way they came.

The Highlanders threw their bonnets in the air and cheered as the Russian cavalry disappeared, pursued by roundshot from the artillery. The first charge of the day – the only one made by the enemy – had been repulsed by an infantry line a mere two men deep.

While this action was going on, the second fork of the attack had topped the Causeway Heights and found four regiments of the Heavy Brigade trotting across their path.

It is questionable whether the Russians or the British were most surprised by their meeting. General Scarlett was short-sighted and it was his ADC Lieutenant Elliot who pointed out the lance points

above the crest of the heights on their left flank. As the helmets of
the enemy appeared, Scarlett gave the order 'Left wheel into line',
which turned the two advance regiments into a single line facing
the enemy. The two regiments coming up behind then moved
forward and turned to form a second line behind the first.

Some estimates put the number of Russians as high as 3,500.
Lieutenant Richard Godman of the 5th Dragoon Guards thought
it less than that: 'A large mass of cavalry came over the hill, and
would in a few minutes have been in our line, when we got the
order to advance. Their front must have been composed of three
regiments, and a very strong column in their rear, in all I suppose
about 1,500 or 2,000, while we were not more than 800.'

Although outnumbering the British by two or three to one and
having the advantage of high ground, the Russians seemed so
shaken by the unexpected presence of British cavalry that they
froze. This hesitation gave Scarlett time to bring his men into line
and order the advance. Captain Henry Clifford of the Rifle Brigade
watched the foremost regiments of the Heavies move uphill: 'The
Scots Greys [2nd Dragoons] and the Enniskillen [6th] Dragoons
advanced in a slow, steady trot towards them, the Russians looked
at them as if fascinated, unable to move. The distance between the
two Cavalries at last decreased to about 50 yards, and the shrill
sound of the trumpet, ordering the charge, first broke the awful
silence.'

Lord Lucan had by this time left Cardigan in command of the
Light Brigade and galloped across to be with the Heavies. There is
some discrepancy about whether he or General Scarlett ordered
the charge. Lucan later claimed that he had done so. He certainly
ordered his duty trumpeter, Trumpet Major Joy of the 17th Lancers,
to sound the charge, and the notes were blown – but nothing
happened. Scarlett was still bringing his squadrons into proper
alignment and his officers would not move until he gave the order.
When Scarlett was satisfied that his men were ready he ordered *his*
trumpeter, Trumpet Major Monks of the 5th Dragoon Guards, to
sound the charge and the Heavies spurred their mounts uphill.

Technically it was not a charge at all, properly defined in terms of the pace of the horses, for the short distance between the two forces and the fact that the Heavies were riding uphill hardly allowed their horses to reach the trot, let alone the gallop. Moreover, the Russians had by this time overcome their initial shock and were moving downhill to meet them.

From within his regiment moving up in support of the front line, Lieutenant Godman saw both sides brought quickly to a standstill:

The charge sounded and at them went the first line; Scarlett and his ADC well in front. The enemy seemed quite astonished and drew into a walk and then a halt; as soon as they met, all I saw was swords in the air in every direction, the pistols going off, and everyone hacking away right and left. In a moment the Greys were surrounded and hemmed completely in; there they were fighting back in the middle, the great bearskin caps high above the enemy.

This was the work of a moment; as soon as we saw it, the 5th advanced and in they charged, yelling and shouting as hard as they could split, the row was tremendous, and for about five minutes neither would give way, and their column was so deep we could not cut through it.

Vastly outnumbered and with the disadvantage of having to fight their way uphill, the Heavies swung their sabres viciously. When several Russians surrounded an officer, Sergeant Major Grieve spurred his horse into them and decapitated the first with a single swipe, at which the rest backed away. Troop Sergeant Major Henry Franks thought that it was the greater stature of both the men and their mounts that soon told against the enemy:

Some of the Russians seemed to be rather astonished at the way our men used their swords. It was rather hot work for a few minutes; there was no time to look about you. We soon became a struggling mass of half frenzied and desperate men, doing our level best to kill each other. Both men and horses on our side were heavier than the enemy, and we were able to cut our way through them, in fact a good many of them soon began to give us room for our arms.

However, if a man became dismounted he was at the mercy of the enemy, as Corporal Gough discovered:

My horse was shot and fell. He got up again and I was entangled in the saddle. My head and one leg were on the ground. He tried to gallop on but fell again and I managed to get loose. A Russian lancer was going to run me through; Macnamara came up and nearly severed his head from his body so, thank God, I did not get a scratch.

Some commentators have suggested that as these regiments were outnumbered and engaged in an uphill struggle they could not possibly have routed the Russians and that it was only when British artillery opened fire that the enemy retreated. But no artillery fire was directed into the mêlée – it would have hit as many British as Russians – and if the Heavies had deliberately retired downhill to allow such a bombardment the Russians would merely have moved down with them. In a letter home Lieutenant Godman described how the Russians were pressed back:

At length they turned and well they might, and the whole ran as hard as they could pelt back up the hill, our men after them all broken up, and cutting them down right and left. We pursued about 300 yards, and then called off with much difficulty, the gunners then opened on them, and gave them a fine peppering.

The enemy being gone, and we all right, had time to look round, the ground was covered with dead and dying men and horses. I am happy to say our brigade lost but seven dead, but had a considerable number wounded, some mortally. The ground was strewn with swords, broken and whole, trumpets, helmets, carbines, etc. There must have been some forty or fifty of the enemy dead, besides wounded.

An Englishman to the core, Godman concluded his graphic account of the charge and its aftermath with: 'The weather continues fine and cool, in fact most delightful.'

The guns that he saw open up on the Russians were from a troop of the Royal Horse Artillery under Captain Brandling. Russian officers had been rallying their men at the top of the heights with some success, but when Brandling's 24-pounders fired roundshot and shell into them over the heads of the Heavies, they quickly withdrew.

Watching from the Sapoune Heights with Lord Raglan, Fanny Duberly and all, William Russell wrote that they were 'spectators of the scene as though looking down on the stage from the boxes of the theatre', and now as these observers applauded enthusiastically so too did the Heavies below them: 'A cheer burst from every lip – in the enthusiasm, officers and men took off their caps and shouted with delight – and they clapped their hands again and again.'

As Godman related, there were surprisingly few casualties inflicted by either side during this fierce, five-minute mêlée, and survivors told Lieutenant Fox Strangways of the Royal Horse Artillery why they thought that was: 'It was stated that they could make no impression on the Russians, owing to the thick overcoat they wore; but it is believed our men's swords were not sufficiently sharp, and as for the Russians no attempt whatever had been made to sharpen theirs. The few picked up on the ground were as blunt as could be.'

That view was supported by the body of one of the Heavies described to Colonel Whinyates by Lieutenant Strangways: 'A dead soldier of the 4th Dragoon Guards had red or fine hair, which was cut as close as possible, and therefore well suited to show any wounds. His helmet had come off in the fight, and he had about fifteen cuts on his head, not one of which had more than parted the skin. His death wound was a thrust below the armpit, which had bled profusely.' Luckier than this man was Lieutenant Elliot, who presented himself before the surgeons with fourteen sabre wounds and was recorded as 'slightly wounded' because only one of them, a cut across his face, had opened the flesh.

Assistant Surgeon William Cattell went onto the battlefield immediately to treat the wounded and claimed that unknown to their officers several men of the Light Brigade had taken part in the charge of the Heavy Brigade. He particularly noted two privates of the 11th Hussars who 'must have been doing a bit on their own hook'. Their names were not recorded and other than Cattell's account there is nothing to substantiate this. It is highly unlikely that two men could have left the Light Brigade unnoticed; they may however have come out from the sick tents in the nearby camp and rushed to join in.

There were certainly many among the five Light Brigade regiments waiting dismounted 500 yards away who wanted to be involved. Every officer and man watching the Russians withdraw in disorder after the artillery had done its work expected Lord Cardigan to lead a pursuit and finish them off. When Cardigan sat still in front of the brigade and gave no such order, Captain William Morris, commanding the 17th Lancers since the death of Major Willett three days earlier, rode up to him and suggested that they pursue the enemy. The men in the front line of the 17th were near enough to hear what was said and according to Private James Wightman the exchange went like this:

MORRIS: My Lord, are you not going to charge the flying enemy?
CARDIGAN: No. We have orders to remain here.
MORRIS: But, my Lord, it is our positive duty to follow up this advantage.
CARDIGAN: No. We must remain here.
MORRIS: Do, my Lord, do allow me to charge them with the 17th. Sir, my Lord, they are in disorder.
CARDIGAN: No, no, sir. We must not stir from here.

Wightman adds that when Captain Morris returned to his position in front of the 17th Lancers he slapped his leg angrily with his sabre and, probably within Cardigan's hearing, shouted, 'My God, my God, what a chance we are losing!'

Morris had pressed Cardigan as hard as a captain dared press a brigade commander and with good reason. A man of great experience – he had fought in the Sikh Wars and charged with the 16th Lancers at Aliwal – he saw that if the Light Brigade could get among the fleeing Russians the Battle of Balaklava might be ended within minutes. Private Mitchell and the men of the 13th Light Dragoons saw it too: 'All this time we were expecting an order to pursue, but no order came, and soon the opportunity was lost. We all felt certain that if we had been sent in pursuit we should have cut up many of them, besides capturing many prisoners.'

Cardigan claimed that he held the brigade where it was because Lord Lucan had told him to: 'I had been ordered into a particular position by my superior officer, with orders on no account to leave it, and to defend it against any attack of the Russians; they did not however approach the position.'

Predictably, Lucan gave a different version, confirming that he ordered Cardigan to defend the position but insisting that he added: 'My instructions to you are to attack anything and everything that shall come within your reach.'

The fleeing Russian cavalry had certainly been within reach of the Light Brigade. An opportunity had been lost. The Light Brigade was left frustrated and bitter. The Heavy Brigade had made a charge and turned back a far larger enemy force; even Lord Raglan sent an ADC to say, 'Well done the Heavies.' The Light Brigade had yet again done nothing but look on. That was about to change.

It was now 9.30 a.m. The stand made by the Highlanders and the charge of the Heavy Brigade had repulsed an enemy cavalry attack intended to reach Kadikoi. The British successes opened up the possibility of a counter-attack on the Causeway Heights where the redoubts were situated – the only area lost to the Russians – re-taking the lost ground and bringing the day's proceedings to a satisfactory end.

Lord Raglan had sent orders for the two infantry divisions commanded by the Duke of Cambridge and General Sir George Cathcart to march down from their positions overlooking Sevastopol. The infantry had to cover between three and four miles to reach the Balaklava plain and had been expected to appear at about 9.30, yet there was no sign of them. Captain Ewart, the ADC sent to Sir George Cathcart with Raglan's order, had reached him at 8.00 a.m., but his message had not been treated with the urgency it deserved:

EWART: Lord Raglan requests you, Sir George, to move your division immediately to the assistance of the Turks.

CATHCART: It's quite impossible, sir, for the 4th Division to move.

EWART: The Russians are advancing on Balaklava!

CATHCART: I can't help that. The best thing you can do, sir, is to sit down and have some breakfast.

Fanny Duberly had done without her breakfast to ride to the scene of battle; General Cathcart was determined to finish his. In fairness part of his division had been in the trenches around Sevastopol through the night and had only just returned to camp. Nevertheless he must have been aware of the frailty of the Balaklava defences and that without infantry support the British base could fall. It was 8.30 a.m. before he gave the order for the 4th Division to move and a valuable thirty minutes had been lost. If the Highlanders and the Heavies had failed to turn back the Russian cavalry, Balaklava might have been lost.

By 9.45 Lord Raglan could not understand why the infantry divisions had still not arrived. He sent General Airey to hurry them on and to tell Cambridge and Cathcart that their immediate task was to retake the Causeway Heights and the redoubts occupied by the enemy. Every minute that passed gave the Russians more time to organize their defences for the British counter-attack they surely anticipated. The Russian cavalry had reformed at the far end of the North Valley protected by eight Don Cossack artillery guns drawn up across their front and additional guns on the high ground to each side of the valley.

Raglan had hitherto refused to risk his cavalry in any action not supported by infantry or artillery, but contradicting his previous caution he now decided to use the cavalry in advance of the infantry's arrival. He did not at this point order Lord Lucan to attack but to 'advance' towards the enemy. Raglan believed that the Russians had retreated in such disorder that this show of force would without further fighting persuade them to abandon the Causeway Heights. Unfortunately the wording of his order was sufficiently ambiguous for Lucan to misunderstand what was required.

10.00 a.m.
Lord Raglan's third order to the Cavalry Division

Cavalry to advance and take advantage of any opportunity to recover the Heights. They will be supported by infantry which have been ordered. Advance on two fronts.

Raglan wished the cavalry to advance immediately; the infantry would arrive later. However, Lucan understood that he was to wait until the infantry arrived and then advance the cavalry with them.

As the Causeway Heights ran between the two valleys, Lucan moved the Light Brigade into the entrance to the North Valley and held the Heavy Brigade at the entrance to the South Valley. This suggests that he planned a simultaneous advance down the two valleys to take the objective from both sides at once, perhaps in response to Raglan's instruction to 'Advance on two fronts.' He now believed that he had complied with the order as far as he could until the infantry arrived to support him. He positioned himself midway between the two brigades and waited.

It is difficult to fault Lucan's interpretation. The wording of the order allows it. Both that morning and during the campaign as a whole Raglan had refused to allow the cavalry to move forward of immediate support. Lucan could not have been expected to guess that the commander-in-chief had suddenly changed his methods and required the cavalry to advance on a heavily defended enemy position with merely the promise that the infantry had been ordered and would arrive some time.

Lord Cardigan waited ahead of the Light Brigade. The North Valley sloped gently down from his position towards the Chernaya, and apart from an area of ploughed ground immediately in front of them it was open grassland with no trees or vineyards to obstruct the movement of cavalry. The valley turned slightly at its far end so that the river could not be seen, but the enemy battery was just visible one and a quarter miles away. Private Mitchell was more concerned about the appearance of guns on the heights to both sides: 'We were now dismounted, and soon we could see the enemy had placed a number of guns across the lower part of the valley. At the same time a field battery ascended a hill on our left front, where it was placed in a position facing us. They also placed a field battery on the slope on our right.'

Meanwhile Lord Raglan was staring down from his grandstand position on the Sapoune Heights with growing impatience. General Airey had returned to say that the infantry divisions were nearby and would arrive and deploy in about twenty minutes. Now Raglan was exasperated to see his cavalry lingering. He had ordered Lord Lucan to advance and yet nothing appeared to be happening. The men had even been dismounted.

The Light Brigade was making good use of this pause. It was a cold morning and the officers were sharing flasks of rum. Some of the men were peeling and eating hard-boiled eggs. Others teased Jemmy, a rough-haired terrier, originally the pet of an officer of the 8th Hussars and now adopted by the whole regiment, or played with Boxer, who ran with the 11th Hussars. A few ribald comments were flung in the direction of the French cavalrymen of the Chasseurs d'Afrique as they rode by to form up on the left of the brigade. Private John Doyle was among several men of the 8th Hussars who stuffed and lit their pipes. He soon discovered that this was not to the liking of Lieutenant Colonel Frederick Shewell, their commanding officer:

I saw as he passed in front of us, that all at once his face expressed the greatest astonishment, and even anger, and walking on he broke out with, 'What's this? What's this? One, two, four, six, seven men smoking! Sergeant! Sergeant Pickworth!'

The truth is we were warming our noses each with a short black pipe, and thinking no harm of the matter.

'Sergeant, advance and take these men's names.'

It might not be quite according to regulation to be smoking sword in hand, when the charge might be sounded at any moment. The Colonel comes up to another now, that hadn't heard what had been said, and he sings out, 'Sergeant Williams!'

'Yes, sir,' replies the sergeant.

'Did you not hear what I said about smoking just now?'

'I've not lit my pipe yet, sir,' answered the sergeant.

'Fall back to the rear, and take off your belts. Why, here's another! To the rear, fall back. I'll have this breach of discipline punished.'

Lord Paget had just cut and lit a fresh cigar when he heard Colonel Shewell's reaction to the men smoking pipes: 'The question then arose in my mind, "Am I to set this bad example (in the Colonel's opinion at least) or should I throw away a good cigar?" Well, the cigar carried the day.'

As the officers and men stared down the valley at the enemy, all expected that some deadly action would soon be ordered and many found comfort in the personal items they carried with them. Lieutenant Edward Seager of the 8th Hussars later wrote to his wife:

I suppose you would like to know what I had about me through all this danger. In my sabretache [a flat leather satchel on long straps worn by some cavalry] was yours and the darling children's picture, my dear mother's present of Prayer Book and Testament, and in the pocket of my jacket was your letter containing dear little Emily's hair which has been there since I received it. In my haversack was some biscuit and a bottle with some whisky and water in it, and around my neck was the dear locket you gave me in Exeter.

Lord Raglan was by now furious with his cavalry, which was sitting and watching the enemy when it should have been carrying out his order to 'advance and take advantage of any opportunity to recover the Heights'. It was at this point that a staff officer whose identity has never been established shouted out that the Russians in the redoubts on the Causeway Heights were dragging away the

British guns. This triggered the fourth and final order to Lord Lucan.

The redoubts lay at such a distance from Raglan's position that even through a telescopic glass it is unlikely anything more specific than the movement of horse teams could have been seen. It is by no means certain that these movements indicated an attempt to drag away the guns, and Russian historians assert that no such operation was taking place at that time. The material loss involved, even if the Russians did remove every gun from the redoubts they occupied, was negligible. It was the psychological blow that taxed Raglan. Losing artillery guns to the enemy was considered a sign of defeat and he knew that Wellington, his military mentor and perhaps idol, had never lost a single gun.

The infantry divisions were only minutes away, but only one force could move quickly enough to prevent the Russians taking away the guns: the cavalry. It seemed to Raglan that if Lord Lucan had acted on his third order, the two brigades would already be moving up onto the heights and in position to interfere with the enemy's actions. Raglan now dictated a new order. General Airey copied it down in pencil on a piece of paper resting on his sabretache and signed it. This fourth order was to be understood in conjunction with the third, as an instruction to do immediately what had previously been ordered.

10.45 a.m.
Lord Raglan's fourth order to the Cavalry Division

*Lord Raglan wishes the Cavalry to advance rapidly to the front –
follow the Enemy and try to prevent the Enemy carrying away the guns
– Troop Horse Artillery may accompany – French cavalry is on
your left.*
R Airey
Immediate.

Lieutenant Somerset Calthorpe was next in line for duty and nudged his horse forward to take the order as Airey held it out to him. 'No,' Raglan said. 'Send Nolan.'

Captain Nolan was one of the army's most accomplished horse-men. The direct route from the Sapoune Heights to the cavalry on the Balaklava plain 650 feet below was by a precipitous track and Raglan wanted the order to reach Lucan as quickly as possible. Nolan was also a leading advocate of the view that Lucan was mishandling the cavalry by continually looking on when he should have been leading an advance, although there is no evidence that Raglan himself knew the extent of his galloper's grudge against the commander of the Cavalry Division.

It was normal practice for an ADC carrying an order to be allowed to read it and request any further elucidation he might require. If its meaning was not clear to Lucan, Nolan would be expected to explain it on Raglan's behalf. Lieutenant Calthorpe was still nearby and observed what took place: 'This order was entrusted to Captain Nolan, aide-de-camp to General Airey, a cavalry officer of great experience. Previous to his departure he received careful instruction from both Lord Raglan and the Quartermaster-General.'

Calthorpe was Raglan's ADC and nephew. It is not certain that Raglan, eager to see his order on its way, did give Nolan 'careful instruction'. Nor is it certain that Nolan, in the excitement and rush of the moment, was paying attention.

As Nolan turned his horse to dash away, Raglan called after him, 'Tell Lord Lucan the cavalry is to attack immediately.' How Nolan must have relished those words. The young officer who had in all probability originated the name Lord Look-on was now entrusted with Raglan's specific order to Lucan that the cavalry 'attack immediately'.

7. The Charge

Seven minutes into hell with the Light Brigade

It took Captain Nolan fifteen minutes to reach the Light Brigade, and it was just after 11.00 a.m. when he approached the regiments from behind and raced through the gap between the 17th Lancers and the 13th Light Dragoons to the front. There he spotted Captain William Morris waiting ahead of the 17th.

Nolan shouted, 'Where is Lord Lucan?'
  'There,' replied Morris, pointing, 'there on the right front!' He then added, 'What's it to be, Nolan? Are we going to charge?'
  To which Nolan yelled over his shoulder, 'You'll see! You'll see!'
            Private James Wightman, 17th Lancers

Captain Nolan came galloping down and handed a paper to Lord Lucan. We now felt certain there was something cut out for us.
            Private Albert Mitchell, 13th Light Dragoons

Lucan read the order. Although as yet uncertain exactly what Lord Raglan required, he told his duty trumpeter to mount the division and Trumpet Major Joy sounded the order. To left and to right, officers and men of the two brigades climbed into their saddles, certain now that they were off.

Lucan read the order again. As there was no mention of the heights – it referred instead to 'the front' – and no word of the infantry he had been waiting for, he treated this as a fresh instruction not connected with the previous order. He was told to 'follow the Enemy', but he could not see any Russian unit on the move. He must then 'try to prevent the Enemy carrying away the guns', but from his position he could not see any guns being carried away. Which enemy and which guns were meant?

The guns on the Causeway Heights, although out of sight from the valley floor, had been the subject of Raglan's previous order and Lucan should have made this connection or at least queried Nolan as to whether that might have been Raglan's meaning. Yet this was not a calm discussion between the two men and their animosity at this crucial point was most evident to an ADC waiting nearby.

An order was brought by an officer personally hostile to him, and received without the discretion fitting an officer of high rank. Lord Lucan, instead of taking the order and exercising his own judgement as to how he carried it out, asked Captain Nolan what he was to attack, and was answered by his pointing to the Russians drawn up across the valley, with the words: 'There, my Lord, is your enemy, there are the guns.'

Captain Walker, ADC to Lord Lucan

Some of the staff officers present thought that Lucan attempted to discuss the order and was cut short by Nolan. Others noted the abruptness with which both men conducted this exchange:

Nolan: 'Lord Raglan's orders are that the cavalry should attack immediately.'
Lucan: 'Attack, sir! Attack what? What guns, sir? Where and what to do?'
Nolan: 'There, my Lord! There is your enemy! There are your guns!'

Recorded by Alexander Kinglake

I saw Lucan's evident astonishment at the message; Nolan pointed right down the valley.

Captain Arthur Tremayne, 13th Light Dragoons

Surprised and irritated at the impetuous and disrespectful attitude and tone of Captain Nolan, Lord Lucan looked at him sternly, but made no answer.

Sir John Blunt, interpreter to Lord Lucan

More should have been said. Nolan, seeing Lucan's confusion, should have explained precisely what was intended, perhaps making the link between the present order and the previous one – though this assumes that he himself understood the two to be linked; he may not have done so. Lucan, being unsure of Raglan's intent and required by military protocol to obey Nolan's instructions as if they were spoken directly by Raglan himself, should have questioned the ADC at greater length. The hostility between the two men prevented this and allowed a terrible misconstruction.

As it was, in the thrill and agitation of the moment Nolan could bring to mind no more than Raglan's final, shouted order to 'Tell Lord Lucan the cavalry is to attack immediately.' He certainly did that, and in indicating a direction for the attack he did more, by implication adding to the written order. Lucan had said angrily, 'Attack what?' and Nolan had responded impulsively to what he took to be an idiotic question. Whether or not he intended the arm he flung out across a landscape that had the enemy on three sides to point 'right down the valley', Lucan and the staff officers present saw it that way. It appeared that Nolan – and thus Raglan himself by proxy – had indicated that the enemy and the guns referred to in the order were those visible at the far end of the valley.

Although Nolan should then have returned to Raglan's position on the Sapoune Heights he had no intention of missing out on the action to come. He rode over to Captain Morris in front of the 17th Lancers and asked permission to ride with that regiment, which Morris gave. Morris and Nolan, both Indian officers, had become close friends and had exchanged letters to their next of kin lest the worst should happen. Morris carried a letter addressed to Nolan's mother, while Nolan kept a letter written by Morris to his wife. It is often assumed that the two men began the advance together, but it is more likely that because Nolan was not an officer of the 17th he moved to one side of the regiment.

The crucial exchange between Lucan and Nolan was quickly followed by a second between their lordships Lucan and Cardigan. This was no warmer than the first, though the loathing the two brothers-in-law felt for each other was cloaked by the formality of rank. Lucan rode across to Cardigan. Both men recorded their brief conversation:

With General Airey's order in my hand I trotted up to Lord Cardigan, and gave him distinctly its contents so far as they concerned him. I would not say on my oath that I did not read the order to him. He at once objected, on the grounds that he would be exposed to a flanking battery. I told him that I was aware of it. 'I know it,' but that 'Lord Raglan would have it,' and that we had no choice but to obey. I then said that I wished him to advance very steadily and quietly, and that I would narrow his front by removing the 11th Hussars from the first to the second line. This he strenuously opposed; but I moved across his front and directed Colonel Douglas not to advance with the rest of the line.

Lord Lucan (recorded by Alexander Kinglake)

Lucan came in front of my brigade and said, 'Lord Cardigan, you will attack the Russians in the valley.' I said, 'Certainly, my lord,' dropping my sword at the same time; 'but allow me to point out to you that there is a battery in front, a battery on each flank, and the ground is covered with Russian riflemen.'

Lord Lucan answered: 'I cannot help that; it is Lord Raglan's positive order that the Light Brigade is to attack the enemy;' upon which he ordered the 11th Hussars back to support the 17th Lancers.

Lord Cardigan (recorded by Alexander Kinglake)

Although Lucan said he told Cardigan 'to *advance* very steadily' and Cardigan claimed the order was 'you will *attack*', this is not the significant difference it might appear to be. Both men believed the guns in Raglan's order to be those one and a quarter miles to the front, and the horses could not sustain the pace of a charge over such a distance. The Light Brigade would have to advance at a steady rate and only when near the guns would the pace be increased to the charge. The advance and charge taken together would constitute the attack.

Both Lucan and Cardigan realized what was involved – the

certainty of heavy casualties and perhaps even the total annihilation of the cavalry – but the campaign had taught Lucan that he must carry out Lord Raglan's orders, however senseless they might seem, and Raglan himself had told Cardigan that in turn he must do as Lucan ordered. This unbreakable hierarchy of command was about to break the Light Brigade.

The brigade had formed up in two lines, with the 11th Hussars, 17th Lancers and 13th Light Dragoons in the first line and the 4th Light Dragoons and the 8th Hussars in the second. Lucan had now reduced the width of the front line by ordering the 11th Hussars to fall back and ride behind the 17th Lancers. It has been assumed this was because at three regiments – a total width of 200 yards – the line was wider than the battery to be attacked – eight guns at twenty-yard intervals, making 140 yards – and men riding on the left and right flanks would have charged into empty space. Yet at the time Lucan believed there to be twelve guns, giving a width of 220 yards. He later explained the true reason for the change: 'I carefully divided the Light Brigade into three lines, to expose as few men as possible in the first line, and that the first line should be efficiently supported.'

Lucan thus chose to remove Cardigan's own regiment from the front line while leaving the 17th Lancers – *his* former regiment – in place, which explains Cardigan's strenuous opposition. Lucan's choice of the 11th may not have had the ulterior motive Cardigan supposed. The 17th was the only lancer regiment present and because the lance when dropped to the 'Engage infantry' position was known to terrify opponents, lancers always rode in the front line.

Lord Cardigan rode back to Lord George Paget, commanding officer of the 4th Light Dragoons, waiting ahead of the second line and told him: 'You will take command of the second line, and I expect your best support – mind, your best support.' Cardigan then returned to the front. The formation of the brigade was as yet unchanged; the 11th Hussars would not fall back behind the 17th Lancers until the brigade moved off. Each regiment was formed up in two ranks, the second rank only half a horse's length behind the first. The men in each rank sat knee to knee. Cavalry regulations were nothing if not precise and required the right knee of each man to be six inches from the left knee of the next.

Although as the cavalrymen waited for the off they could see the enemy battery at the far end of the valley, it was impossible to clearly distinguish one gun from another and the exact number of guns has always been disputed. The British reported twelve while Russian historians insist that there were eight – the number of guns to be expected in a Don Cossack battery.* What is certain is that in the eyes of men who knew already what Lord Cardigan's next order must be, the number of guns multiplied alarmingly:

The thirty guns which we had to take were stretched right across the valley.

Private John Richardson, 11th Hussars

The men were also aware of enemy guns on the heights to both sides and the black mass of cavalry and infantry gathered behind the guns at the end of the valley. In the absence of precise information many assumed that they were facing the whole Russian army:

Lord Cardigan received the order from Lord Lucan to attack the battery of guns which was placed across the valley immediately in our front about a mile off. There was likewise a battery on the Fedioukine Hills on our left and the enemy had possession of the Redoubts on our right, where another battery and riflemen were posted. This army in position numbered about 24,000 and we, the Light Brigade, not quite 700.

Troop Sergeant Major George Smith, 11th Hussars

Cardigan gave his first order: 'Draw swords'. The men of the light dragoon and hussar regiments and all the officers advanced with their swords held upright while the lancers held their lances vertical at the 'Carry' with the red-over-white pennons fluttering high overhead. Several men tied the hilts of their sabres to their

* This is the number assumed to be correct here.

right hands with twisted handkerchiefs so as not to lose them in the gallop or the mêlée that might follow.

Most had guessed; now with this order they knew for sure. Private Farquharson overheard a man state the obvious: 'Many of us will not get back to the lines again.' Private Pennington admitted that he 'had no hope of life'. They knew all too well what was happening:

A child might have seen the trap that was laid for us, every private dragoon did.

Captain Thomas Hutton, 4th Light Dragoons

Despite that, these men would follow Cardigan into hell itself. Tennyson's 'theirs not to reason why' was the motto of the common soldier long before the Poet Laureate found the words for it:

Every private soldier could see what a mistake was being made; but all we had to do was obey orders.

Private John Richardson, 11th Hussars

Lord Cardigan could see it too but he was determined to set an example. Private James Wightman of the 17th Lancers, sitting almost immediately behind the brigade commander, was impressed by his bearing during these tense seconds: 'Calm as on parade – calmer indeed than usual on parade – stately, square and erect, with his stern face and soldierly bearing, master of himself, his brigade and his charger, Lord Cardigan looked the ideal cavalry leader.'

Cardigan gave his second order: 'The brigade will advance. First squadron of the 17th Lancers direct.' Wightman described his voice as strong and hoarse.

This order was for information only; no move would be made until the bugles sounded. The crucial fact imparted was that the first squadron of the 17th Lancers – that commanded by Captain Robert White – would act as the 'squadron of direction'. The front line of two regiments would have a width of 140 yards, with 125 men in the forward rank. It was important that during the advance these men moved in the same direction so that no part of the line diverged from the rest, and at the same pace so that they reached the enemy together. To ensure this, all would take their direction and pace from Captain White's squadron. White in turn would take his direction and pace from Lord Cardigan, and maintain the proper interval of fifteen yards between the brigade commander and the front line.

This was to be an advance of the whole Cavalry Division and not just the Light Brigade. Once Cardigan and the Lights had moved off and an interval had been allowed to develop, Lord Lucan would follow with the Heavies in support. As he sat waiting Lucan must have realized that if the advance was the catastrophe he expected and he survived it, he might well be blamed. Lucan still had Raglan's written order in his hand; he gave it to Sir John Blunt his civilian interpreter, who would not be required to go forward with them, and asked him to keep it safe.

11.10 A.M.

Those watching with Lord Raglan on the Sapoune Heights could distinguish the cavalry in the valley below by the colour of the uniform jackets: the two blue lines of the Light Brigade and the two red lines of the Heavy Brigade. The sound of the bugles now carried up to them and they saw the first blue line move steadily forward.

At ten minutes past eleven, our Light Cavalry Brigade advanced.
William Russell, The Times

The word was given to 'charge guns to the front'. We advanced at a gallop to these guns.
Private William Pennington, 11th Hussars

Occasionally those observing from the heights record what happened more accurately than those in the valley. Russell realized that he was witnessing a big story and had as least as much reason as the military men involved to check his pocket watch, so the time he noted down is likely to be accurate. Both of Pennington's statements are misleading: there was at this point no order to charge and there was certainly no immediate spurring of the horses to the gallop. Cardigan hardly required Lucan's advice to 'advance very steadily and quietly'. The Russian guns were over a mile away and a steady advance was essential, both to preserve the horses for the final dash and to maintain the line for the shock effect of hitting the enemy as a single, compact force.

Lord Cardigan ordered his duty trumpeter, Billy Brittain of the 17th Lancers, who rode at the front beside and a little behind him, to sound the 'Walk'. Cardigan sat stiffly upright as he urged his chestnut thoroughbred Ronald forward ahead of his men. He expected to be killed and later told William Russell that at this time he said aloud, though only to himself, 'Here goes the last of the Brudenells.' He had no children.

An order given by an officer was sounded first by that officer's trumpeter and immediately taken up by the regimental trumpeters to right and left, so that it could be heard by the whole body of cavalry under his command. As the order sounded along the line, two of the front-line regiments, the 17th Lancers and 13th Light Dragoons, moved forward behind Cardigan. The 11th Hussars for the moment remained still. The advance of the Light Brigade began at a pace of four miles per hour.

When the first line was well clear of the second, Cardigan gave the order, 'Trot'. The bugles sounded again and the two regiments following him increased their pace to about eight miles per hour. The 11th Hussars waited until an interval of a hundred yards had developed and then set off too, falling in behind the 17th Lancers.

The men were silent and the only sound was the constant jingle of collar chains and the occasional whinnying of horses – at this point they were moving over ploughed ground so there was no beat of hooves. The more experienced cavalrymen were adept at judging distance and pace, and without being conscious of the calculation they knew that at the trot it would take them at least seven minutes to reach the enemy. Many a man with an eye on the still-silent guns hoped that the next increase in pace would come sooner than regulations required.

They were to be disappointed. Lord Cardigan commanded his cavalry by the rule book; he knew no other way. He led at the trot and intended to hold that pace until only 250 yards from the enemy line. The paces to be observed by the cavalry were contained in the *Regulations For The Instruction, Formations, and Movements of The Cavalry*, issued in May 1851, and were as follows:

Walk:	not to exceed four miles per hour
Trot:	not to exceed eight and a half miles per hour
Gallop:	eleven miles per hour
Charge:	not to exceed the utmost speed of the slowest horse

The regulations also included the instruction: 'Whatever distance a Line has to go over, it should move at a brisk trot, till within 250 yards of the enemy, and then gallop, till within 40 or 50 yards of the point of attack, when the word 'Charge' will be given, and the gallop made with as much rapidity as the body can bear in good order.'

Many later accounts of the charge suggest that immediately the brigade came under fire regulation paces were ignored and officers and men in their eagerness to be out of it dug in their spurs and brought their horses to the gallop, forcing the pace and allowing Cardigan no choice but to increase his pace too. That could not have been so. The distance they were to ride was too great to sustain the gallop throughout.

Survivors' accounts generally agree that the distance from the Light Brigade's starting position to the Russian guns was one and a quarter miles – one man made it a quarter mile less, another a quarter mile more – and that the advance and charge took seven minutes. A body of cavalry making an advance and charge over that distance, keeping to the paces and distances laid down in regulations, would take precisely seven minutes. There is evidence that some of the front-line officers, particularly Captains White and

Morris of the 17th Lancers, attempted to force the pace but that Cardigan kept them at the trot.

Throughout the advance, in describing this or that incident the survivors record their position in the valley in terms of distance either from their starting position or from the Russian guns, and because we know the pace they were held to we can translate these positions into times. The distances quoted under such circumstances were rough estimates made in haste and the times extracted from them must be considered approximations too.

11.11 A.M.

The Russian view. On the Fedioukine Heights, directly across the valley from the Causeway Heights, a battery of the 16th Artillery Brigade had positioned its ten guns to fire into the flank of any British force foolhardy enough to advance on Russian forces reforming by the Chernaya. For forty minutes the British light cavalry had stood at the entrance to the valley, about 1,000 yards away and just within range of the 12-pounder guns, but there was no question of opening fire while they presented no threat. Immediately they moved into the valley the order was given, the gun teams went into action, and in less than a minute the men stood back ready. The British advanced at a trot as if unconcerned. The guns boomed and leapt, and battery officers peered through the powder smoke to see what damage had been done.

We had not gone many yards before we were under fire, I think from a heavy battery on our left.

> *Captain Godfrey Morgan, 17th Lancers*

As we moved off, the Russians opened fire from all their batteries. The round shot passed through us and the shells burst over and amongst us, causing great havoc.

> *Troop Sergeant Major George Smith, 11th Hussars*

It must have sounded as if all the Russian guns opened fire at once, but Captain Morgan was correct: at this point only the ten guns of the enemy battery on the Fedioukine Heights to their left could reach them and only the first-line regiments were under fire. Behind them the 11th Hussars had just set off and the second-line regiments had not yet moved.

Survivors differ about how far the front line had advanced before the Russians opened fire. According to Troop Sergeant Major Smith the first shells exploded as the 11th began to move, which would put the first line about a hundred yards down the valley. Private Wightman of the 17th Lancers thought that his regiment had covered nearly 200 yards. All agree on the precise damage done:

Captain Nolan should have gone back to Lord Raglan; but I suppose he wanted to be in the fight, and he charged in front of the Brigade. He was the first man killed. He was done for by a round shot.

Private John Richardson, 11th Hussars

The first shot killed poor Nolan, a splinter going through his heart, and his horse carried him back to us. He was riding about twenty yards in front of us.

Captain Godfrey Morgan, 17th Lancers

We had ridden barely 200 yards, and were still at the trot, when poor Nolan's fate came to him. I saw the shell explode of which a fragment struck him. From his raised sword-hand dropped the sword. The arm remained upraised and rigid, but all the other limbs so curled in on the contorted trunk as by a spasm, that we wondered how for the moment the huddled form kept the saddle. The weird shriek and the awful face haunt me now to this day, the first horror of that ride of horrors.

Private James Wightman, 17th Lancers

A shell fell within reach of my horse's feet and [of] Captain Nolan, who was riding across the front retreating with his arms up through the interval of the brigade.

Lord Cardigan

The first shell burst and killed poor Captain Nolan. I shall never forget the shriek that he gave; it rung in my ears above the roaring of the cannon.
Private Henry Naylor, 13th Light Dragoons

Richardson assumed that Nolan was hit by a roundshot, but other survivors agree with Wightman, Cardigan and Naylor that a shell exploded in the air ahead of the front line and a burning fragment pierced the ADC's chest.

Controversy has raged ever since about this first casualty of the charge. Some survivors claim that Nolan was hit while riding with the 17th Lancers and only then did his mount race out ahead of Cardigan, the ADC screaming with his arms raised, dying in the saddle. Others are certain that he moved far ahead of the front line shouting and waving his sabre in the air *before* the shell exploded, and there are good reasons for believing them to be correct. First, if he had been struck by a fragment of shell casing while riding in the line, others nearby should have been hit at the same time, but he was the only casualty. Second, Captain Morris saw Nolan dash forward and shouted out to him, 'That won't do, Nolan; we've a long way to go and must be steady!' These are hardly the words he would have chosen had his friend's sudden move been the result of serious injury. Third, and most crucially, Cardigan himself testified that Nolan was 'riding across the front' at the time he was hit. This confirms Captain Morgan's belief that Nolan was 'twenty yards in front of us' when the shell exploded, a distance that puts him not merely ahead of the line but five yards ahead of Cardigan too.

The question then arises of why Nolan dashed forward. Denied the opportunity to account for himself, survivors who saw what happened came up with two explanations. Some thought that he was dissatisfied with the trot and attempting to force the pace, his eagerness to reach the guns at the end of the valley getting the better of him. Others believed he suddenly realized the terrible mistake that had been made and his part in it, and was attempting to change the direction of the charge away from the guns to the front and towards Raglan's intended objective, the guns on the Causeway Heights to the right. These two explanations have been taken up by later writers and the argument about which is correct – for they cannot both be – continues 150 years after the event.

Cardigan admitted that when Nolan rode out and crossed his front, his first thought was that the ADC was attempting to take command of his brigade. He then described the wounded officer as 'riding to the rear and screaming like a woman', and if that seems to imply something unsavoury, Cardigan surely intended it so.

Nolan's wound was so severe that some claimed it exposed the heart. His horse sensed the free reins:

The horse, finding the rider had no control over it, turned sharply to the right – the way home – throwing the lifeless body head-first to the ground.

Corporal Thomas Morley, 17th Lancers

This first Russian volley had exploded twenty yards ahead of the front line and was either misdirected or a deliberate attempt to kill or wound the most senior officer near that spot: Lord Cardigan. The silence that fell while the Russian gunners reloaded and redirected their guns was hardly reassuring to those who rode on.

Lord Paget and the second-line regiments, the 4th Light Dragoons and the 8th Hussars, had sat and watched as the first line advanced, and seen the enemy open fire before they set off:

The second line (under me) formed up in rear of the first line, (under Lord Cardigan). The first line started off (down somewhat of a decline) at a brisk trot, the second line following though at rather a decreased pace, to rectify the proper distance of 200 yards. When I gave the command to my line to advance, I added the caution, 'The 4th Light Dragoons will direct.'

Lord George Paget, 4th Light Dragoons

Lucan's last-minute order for the 11th to fall back from the first line caused some confusion because he had not thought to tell Paget this was to happen. Paget now saw the 11th hold back, but he did not know whether that regiment was to ride between the first and second lines, or join the second line. He guessed correctly that Lucan intended the 11th to ride between the two lines, and maintained his distance.★

Now 200 yards ahead of Paget, the first line trotted steadily forward. Only Nolan would have disagreed that these men had had a lucky escape from the first enemy shells. Then the second volley exploded directly overhead.

11.12 A.M.

Neither Lord Raglan nor any of those looking down with him from the Sapoune Heights had been surprised when the Russians opened fire. They expected the Light Brigade to advance a short distance along the valley before turning to its right and climbing the slopes of the Causeway Heights towards the guns in the redoubts; during that initial stage the regiments would briefly come under fire from enemy guns on the Fedioukine Heights. But now there were horrified gasps of disbelief. Instead of turning, Cardigan was continuing straight on towards the Don Cossack guns at the far end of the valley – a long ride that would bring his regiments under intense and sustained artillery fire.

We all saw at once that a lamentable mistake had been made – by whose fault it was then impossible to say.

Lieutenant Somerset Calthorpe

Down in the valley, those few men who had harboured the same hope – that the brigade was heading somewhere other than straight ahead – now knew the truth too.

The men on the right and left of me were old Indian soldiers, they had seen many a hard fought field in India. They did not believe that we were

★ Although the Light Brigade regiments were now in effect advancing in three lines, in 2–1–2 formation, survivors without exception refer in their written accounts to the first line and the second line, and describe the 11th Hussars independently as riding between these two. That practice has been maintained in this present work.

going to attack the enemy in front of us, but they soon found out that we were; poor fellows, for that was their last field. Both were killed.

Private Henry Naylor, 13th Light Dragoons

The next discharge tore wide gaps through our ranks and many a trooper fell.

Private James Lamb, 13th Light Dragoons

In the interval between one volley and the next, once the boom of the guns and its echo had faded, a new sound was added to the familiar neighing of horses and jingle of harness:

Oaths and imprecations might be heard between the reports of the guns and the bursting shells as the men crowded and jostled each other in their endeavour to close to the centre. This was unavoidable at times, especially when a shell burst in the ranks, sometimes bringing down three or four men and horses, which made it difficult to avoid an unpleasant crush in the ranks.

Private Albert Mitchell, 13th Light Dragoons

Men swore at one another as they egged on their comrades and perhaps struggled to hold fast to their own courage. As shells opened up gaps in the line, the men closed up to maintain a solid front and the width of each regiment contracted. If the two front-line regiments could reach the guns still in a compact line, they would hit the enemy with a devastating shock. The integrity of the line was an abiding concern of the sergeants and it was they who were most vocal in calling to the men to close up.

The cornets, lieutenants and captains who rode slightly ahead of the line were less aware of the effect of the shells on their men. Officers were more intent on setting a good example, and if they shouted out at all it was to urge the survivors forward. One officer could do no more than that: Lieutenant Percy Smith of the 13th Light Dragoons was disabled, his right hand left useless by a shooting accident, and although he normally wore an iron arm-guard he had mislaid it that morning and rode without it, controlling his horse with his left hand. He carried neither pistol nor sabre, yet rode on anyway, calling out to the men behind and cursing the enemy.

The 11th Hussars coming up behind the 17th Lancers now came under fire too:

The first man of my troop that was struck was Private Young, a cannon ball taking off his right arm. I, being close on his right rear, fancied I felt the wind from it as it passed me. I afterwards found I was bespattered with his flesh. Private Turner's left arm was also struck off close to the shoulder and Private Ward was struck full in the chest. A shell too burst over us, a piece of which struck Cornet Houghton in the forehead and mortally wounded him.

When Private Young lost his arm, he coolly fell back and asked me what he was to do. I replied: 'Turn your horse about and get to the rear as fast as you can.' I had scarcely done speaking to him when Private Turner fell back, calling out to me for help. I told him too to go to the rear.

Troop Sergeant Major George Smith, 11th Hussars

Men in the second-line regiments under Lord Paget saw the effect of the guns on their comrades and knew as they advanced that it was their turn next. One of them described his feelings in the seconds before he came under fire:

At that moment I felt my blood thicken and crawl, as if my heart grew still like a lump of stone within me. I was for a moment paralysed, but then with the snorting of the horse, the wild gallop, the sight of the Russians becoming more distinct, and the first horrible discharge with its still more horrible effects, my heart began to warm, to become hot, to dance again, and I had neither fear nor pity! I longed to be at the guns. I'm sure I set my teeth together as if I could have bitten a piece out of one.

Anonymous, 8th Hussars

As the second line moved further on, the men of the Heavy Brigade still waiting at the starting position saw that a proper interval had developed and gripped the hilts of their sabres tightly, ready before the order was given. Seconds later Lord Lucan told his duty trumpeter, Trumpet Major Henry Joy, to sound the 'Walk'. The bugle call was taken up to right and to left, as Lucan set off ahead of the brigade. His officers and men had no greater hopes of surviving this ride than their fellows among the Light Brigade. Captain Walter Charteris, Lucan's ADC and nephew, had asked Sir John Blunt for the loan of a handkerchief and used it to bind his wrist to the hilt of his sabre. He flourished the weapon in the air to test that the fastening was secure: 'This will do, Blunt. But I doubt if I shall ever return it to you.'

Charteris moved off with the staff officers grouped behind Lord Lucan. The divisional commander and his staff would ride some distance ahead of the Heavy Brigade, to act as a link between the Lights in front and the Heavies behind. General Scarlett, the brigade commander, allowed Lucan to gain this interval and then led his regiments forward.

Moments later, as Joy sounded the 'Trot' and their pace increased, they met the first wounded men returning to the British lines, and soon came under fire themselves:

In a few moments we were in the hottest fire that was probably ever witnessed. The Regiments were beautifully steady. I never had a better line in a Field Day, the only swerving was to let through the ranks the wounded and dead men and horses of the Light Brigade, which were even then thickly scattered over the plain. It was a fearful sight, and the appearance of all who retired was as if they had passed through a heavy shower of blood, positively dripping and saturated, and shattered arms blowing back like empty sleeves, as the poor fellows ran to the rear. Another moment and my horse was shot on the right flank. A few fatal paces further and my left leg was shattered.

Lieutenant Colonel John Yorke, 1st (Royal) Dragoons

I would not live over that moment for a kingdom. I hope I shall not soon again get such a pelting. Luckily a great many of their shells burst too high.

Captain Walker, ADC to Lord Lucan

Colonel Edward Hodge of the 4th Dragoon Guards glanced back at his men and saw that the guns were 'cutting us up terribly'. Captain Walker saw eight men and their horses felled by a single shell. One man had an incredible escape: a shell entered the chest of Troop Sergeant Major Russell's horse before exploding and blowing the animal to pieces; Russell was thrown over its head, picked himself up unhurt, and caught a riderless horse to rejoin the advance. Lord Lucan was slightly wounded in the leg and his horse hit twice. Captain Charteris, true to his prediction, was killed.

The Heavy Brigade would have suffered even more severely if it had not been for the fourth charge of the day, by the French cavalry. Before the advance began a regiment of the Chasseurs d'Afrique had formed up to the left of the British position. When the Frenchmen saw the Light Brigade come under fire from Russian guns on the Fedioukine Heights, Major Abdelal led an attack up through tall shrubs that concealed them during the early part of their approach. Immediately they were spotted they charged the flank of the battery, from where the gunners could reply only with musket fire. The Russians were forced to hitch up their guns and drag them away – too late for the Lights, but the French charge undoubtedly saved lives among the men of the Heavy Brigade.

Yet it was now, controversially, that Lucan decided to turn the Heavy Brigade back. During this manoeuvre there was further confusion. Lucan was riding 100 yards ahead of General Scarlett when he ordered his trumpeter to sound the order for the brigade to retire. As the regiments swung about, General Scarlett ordered *his* trumpeter to turn them again to the advance. Lucan rode back to Scarlett and after a few hot words that were not recorded the retreat was once again sounded.

The incident was later explained as a misunderstanding; Scarlett had not heard Lucan's trumpeter sound the initial order to turn back. Yet Scarlett's regiments, riding behind him, heard the call clearly enough. This discrepancy has led some to suggest that he disagreed with Lucan's decision and only when confronted by Lucan in person did he obey the order. That is unlikely; military men did not so easily break the shackles of command. It is more likely that given the distance between Lucan and the brigade, and the commotion of the guns, he sent Trumpeter Joy back to the line to sound the order among the men. As Joy would then be behind Scarlett, the general might not have heard the call. Alexander Kinglake estimated that Scarlett was sixty yards ahead of his men when he saw them withdrawing and 'sent back his trumpeter with orders to sound the halt'.

Whatever Scarlett thought of the decision to retire, many of his men were scandalized. For these hardy cavalrymen the one prospect worse than advancing into the fire ahead was turning back and deserting their comrades in the Light Brigade. In retiring the Heavies Lucan left the Light Brigade without the support Cardigan and his regiments assumed was coming up behind them.

The French had put the guns on Lucan's left out of action. If he considered it possible that the Light Brigade would reach and silence the guns to the front, then the Heavies would have only the battery on the right to contend with, and his turning back does him no credit. While there remained any possibility that some part of the Light Brigade might reach the Russian guns, he was obliged to follow up with the supports. Only the obliteration of the regiments ahead of him could render the continued advance of the regiments behind him unnecessary.

At the moment he decided to turn back, Lucan turned to Lord William Paulet and said, 'They have sacrificed the Light Brigade; they shall not have the Heavy, if I can help it.' His words reveal that although the Light Brigade still had far to ride, he had already concluded that it would be wiped out before reaching the guns. He then determined to at least preserve half of his division. He did not turn back because of what had already happened to the Heavy Brigade, but because of what he believed was about to happen to the Light Brigade.

Lucan seems to have chosen his words carefully: 'They have sacrificed the Light Brigade . . .' He must already have been aware that after it was all over there would be many who thought *he* had sacrificed the Light Brigade.

11.13 A.M.

*The Russian view. General Ryzhov, commanding the Russian cavalry's
6th Hussar Brigade, smiled as he sat on horseback at the end of the valley.
Immediately in front of him stood the eight guns of the Don Cossack battery
attached to his brigade. All along the line the men prepared the guns, and
then stood back, ready.*

*Only minutes earlier he had decided that the day's fighting was done –
Prince Menshikov's attack had failed – and had ridden over to speak with
the officer in command of the battery, Colonel Obolensky. While they were
talking their attention was attracted by a murmuring among the gun crews:*

*The sharp eyes of the Don gunners noted the distant cloud of dust raised by enemy
cavalry coming down the valley. Two minutes later it was clear that the enemy
was coming along the valley into the attack.*

General I. Ryzhov

*The gunners cheered as they realized that these insane cavalrymen were
riding straight at the muzzles of their guns. As the enemy came within
range, the order to fire was given.*

At that instant, the Russian Artillery in position across the valley, fired a
volley into the 17th, which seemed to paralyse it, killing and wounding
a number of officers and men. It seemed to me a troop of horses fell,
myself and horse knocked down with them. I remounted and followed
the shattered line.

Corporal Thomas Morley, 17th Lancers

My right-hand man, Walter Brooks, was shot. He was my comrade for
over three years. We got a bit further, when my left-hand man fell. My
blood was up, and I began to wish to get near the enemy.

Private William Butler, 17th Lancers

By this time the guns on our front were playing on us with round-shot
and shell, so the number of men and horses falling increased every
moment. I rode near the right of the line. A corporal who rode on the
right was struck by a shot or shell full in the face, completely smashing it,

his blood and brains bespattering us who rode near. His horse still went on with us.

Private Albert Mitchell, 13th Light Dragoons

The first line had now travelled almost halfway down the valley and entered the extreme range of the battery to the front. Further back, Lord George Paget was having difficulty keeping the two regiments of the second line together:

The 4th Light Dragoons and 8th Hussars composed the second line, under my command. I led in front of the 4th (the directing regiment). I began to observe that the 8th were inclining away from us. At the top of my voice I kept shouting, '8th Hussars, close in to your left', but all to no purpose. Gradually, my attention being occupied with what was going on in my front, I lost sight of the 8th.

Cornet Fiennes Martin was riding on the left of the hussars and when he heard Paget shouting he rode across to Colonel Shewell, who commanded the 8th, to pass on the order. Shewell replied: 'I know it, I hear him, and am doing my best.' However, the 8th moved further to the right until the distance was such that Paget gave up attempting to hold the second line together.

11.14 A.M.

It was now, in their agony, that officers and men in the front line and particularly in the 17th Lancers attempted to force the pace.

Every man felt convinced that the quicker he rode, the better chance he would have of escaping unhurt.

Cornet George Wombwell, 17th Lancers

There is a natural instinct to dodge cannon balls. In such fire as we were under it changed to an impulse to hurry. There was no time to look right or left, and the guns in front were what I looked out for. They were visible as streaks of fire about two feet long and a foot thick in the centre of a gush of thick white smoke, marking about every three hundred yards of the way, as they would reload in 30 or 40 seconds.

Corporal Thomas Morley, 17th Lancers

Captain Morris, whether on his own part or compelled by the pace of the line behind him, at one point came within a horse's length of Cardigan.

Lord Cardigan, almost directly behind whom I rode, turned his head leftwards toward Captain Morris and shouted hoarsely, 'Steady, steady Captain Morris!'

Private James Wightman, 17th Lancers

Captain White, leading the first squadron of the 17th – the squadron of direction – seems to have drawn virtually level with the brigade commander, and considering that he was responsible for preserving the proper interval of fifteen yards must have been under severe pressure from behind. Cardigan laid his outstretched sabre across White's chest, ordering him angrily not to force the pace or ride alongside his superior officer.

The 11th Hussars, coming up behind the 17th Lancers, were by now level with Russian infantrymen massed on the Fedioukine Heights. Although the men of the 11th were to some extent sheltered from the fire of the guns to the front by the line of the 17th, this fact caused the enemy infantry to concentrate a withering fire on them. They also had to contend with the many riderless horses falling back from the line ahead.

We now came under a terrific fire, for the infantry in and about the redoubts kept up a continual fusillade as we came opposite to them, but the men hung well together, keeping their line and closing in as their comrades fell wounded or killed. Many riderless horses were now galloping along with us, forcing their way into the ranks and keeping their places as well as though their masters had been on their backs. Many of these horses belonged to the first line, for we now frequently met with their lifeless bodies. I was particularly struck with one of the 17th Lancers lying on his face with his arms stretched out and a short distance from his right hand was his lance with the pole broken.

Troop Sergeant Major George Smith, 11th Hussars

To see a forearm torn by shot or shell, bleeding and dangling by the tendons which still held it to the upper joint, or brains protruding from a shattered skull, would in cool moments have been a soul-moving and a sickening sight.

Private William Pennington, 11th Hussars

Coming up behind the front line and the 11th Hussars, the second line had now fully divided. The 8th Hussars, still veering to the right, were nearest to the Causeway Heights and became the target of choice for Russian infantrymen on the slopes:

The fire was tremendous, shells bursting amongst us. Cannon balls tearing the earth up and musket balls coming like hail, still we went on never altering our pace.

Lieutenant Edward Seager, 8th Hussars

Lord Paget, supposedly in command of the second line, now led only the 4th Light Dragoons. He too was troubled by riderless horses falling back from the front line:

Bewildered horses from the first line, riderless, rushed in upon our ranks in every state of mutilation, some with a limping gait that told too truly of their state. One was guiding one's own horse (as willing as oneself in such benevolent precautions) so as to avoid trampling on the bleeding objects in one's path – sometimes a man, sometimes a horse – and so we went on. 'Right flank, keep up. Close in to your centre.' The smoke, the noise, the cheers, the groans, the 'ping, ping' whizzing past one's head; the 'whirr' of the fragments of shells; the well-known 'slush' of that unwelcome intruder on one's ears! – what a sublime confusion it was!

Lord George Paget, 4th Light Dragoons

11.15 A.M.

The Russian view. On the Causeway Heights a battery of the 12th Artillery Brigade with eight guns had been positioned facing into the South Valley to target any British force that might attempt to retake the heights from that direction. Immediately the officer in charge heard the Russian guns on the Fedioukine Heights open fire he realized that the attack was coming along the North Valley and ordered his guns to be moved so that he could finish off the enemy if any survivors reached him. This operation took four minutes, and as it took as long for the British to come within range he lost nothing because of it. At 11.15 a.m. his guns opened fire on the right flank of the enemy light cavalry.

We were now fully exposed to the fire from all three batteries, front, right, and left, as also from the infantry on our right. As we drew near, the guns in the front plied us liberally with grape and canister, which brought down men and horses in heaps. Up to this time I was going on all right, but missed my left-hand man from my side, and thinking it might soon be my turn, I offered up a short prayer: 'O Lord, protect me and watch over my poor mother.'

Private Albert Mitchell, 13th Light Dragoons

We advanced at a gallop, amidst a fearful fire from the front, with ditto on the left and right flanks, of grape, shell and canister, and infantry also pouring in a tremendous fire. The effect was that horses and men fell thick and fast, but even this did not check our onward rush.

Private William Pennington, 11th Hussars

Mitchell and Pennington believed that they were under fire from the Russian battery to the front and the batteries to the left and right simultaneously. Since then this 'fire from all three batteries' has become part of the legend of the charge, though it owes more to Tennyson than to the facts. Due to the position, range and angle of fire of the batteries, it was impossible for any of the Light Brigade regiments to come under fire from all three at once. In any case by the time the guns on the Causeway Heights opened fire, the French cavalry had already silenced the guns on the Fedioukine Heights.

That is not to ignore the deeper truth in Mitchell's and Pennington's accounts: to the men in the valley it undoubtedly felt like every artillery gun in the Russian arsenal was firing at them, and all at once.

The front line was now more than halfway down the valley and for the next 400 yards the men would be under fire from two batteries, one to their right on the Causeway Heights and the other to their front.

The Russian gunners were well drilled. There was none of that crackling sound I have often heard, where one gun goes off a little ahead and the others follow, having the effect of a bunch of fire-crackers popping in quick succession. In such cases the smoke of the first gun obscures the aim of the rest.

The Russian Artillery went off at the word of command, all together. One tremendous volley was heard with flashes of flame through the rolling smoke. While they reloaded the smoke lifted so that they could see to take aim again. There were probably twenty cannon at our right firing at us, and two batteries – twelve guns – in front. If we had been moving over uneven ground we should have had some slight protection in the necessary uncertainty of aim of the guns, but moving as we did in compact bodies on smooth ground directly in range, the gunners had an admirable target and every volley came with terrible effect.

Corporal Thomas Morley, 17th Lancers

We had not broken into the charging pace when poor old John Lee, my right-hand man on the flank of the regiment, was all but smashed by a shell; he gave my arm a twitch, as with a strange smile on his worn old face he quietly said, 'Domino, chum', and fell out of the saddle. His old grey mare kept alongside of me for some distance, treading on and tearing out her entrails as she galloped, till at length she dropped with a strange shriek. Peter Marsh was my left-hand man; next beyond him was Private Dudley. The explosion of a shell had swept down four or five men on Dudley's left, and I heard him ask Marsh if he had noticed 'what a hole that bloody shell had made' on his left front. 'Hold your foul-mouthed tongue,' answered Peter, 'swearing like a blackguard, when you may be knocked into eternity next minute!'

Just then I got a musket-bullet through my right knee, and another in the shin, and my horse had three bullet wounds in the neck. Man and horse were bleeding so fast that Marsh begged me to fall out; but I would not, pointing out that in a few minutes we must be into them, and so I sent my spurs well home, and faced it out with my comrades.

Private James Wightman, 17th Lancers

The men in the left division of my squadron were nearly all cut down, including a sergeant, who had his head blown off, but afterwards rode about thirty yards before he fell. Every shot from the enemy's guns now came with the most deadly accuracy.

Corporal James Nunnerley, 17th Lancers

It was about this time that Sergeant Talbot had his head clean carried off by a round shot, yet for about thirty yards further the head-less body kept the saddle. My narrative may seem barren of incidents, but amid the crash of shells and the whistle of bullets, the cheers and the dying cries of comrades, the sense of personal danger, the pain of wounds, and the consuming passion to reach an enemy, he must be an exceptional man who is cool enough and curious enough to be looking serenely about him for what painters call 'local colour'. I had a good deal of 'local colour' myself, but it was running down the leg of my overalls from my wounded knee.

Private James Wightman, 17th Lancers

Shells fell like hail all round us, to say nothing of 18 lb shot, which whistled through our ranks, dealing death and destruction.

Captain Robert Portal, 4th Light Dragoons

11.16 A.M.

On the Sapoune Heights there was the greatest consternation. The commander-in-chief stared down in disbelief that his order had led to this. A French general muttered. Someone sobbed but it was not the English lady, who stared in fascination at the carnage – the men had already nicknamed her the 'Vulture' because of her undue interest in the dead. The war reporter scribbled frantically:

A more fearful spectacle was never witnessed than by those who, without the power to aid, beheld their heroic countrymen rushing to the arms of death.

William Russell, The Times

When the first line was about 250 yards from the guns, Lord Cardigan shouted an order to his trumpeter and immediately a bugle sounded the 'Gallop' – eleven miles per hour. Those who had previously attempted to force the pace now pressed their spurs home. The powder smoke that billowed from each gun as it fired thinned sufficiently before the next volley for Cardigan to spot what he thought to be the gun at the centre of the line and head for that. This would maximize the chances of the remnants of the two regiments behind him hitting the full length of the battery.

My horse was seriously wounded by a ball received in the animal's neck and this had the effect of covering me with a shower of blood from the wound. After this I felt my chance of returning alive was hopeless.

Cornet John Chadwick, 17th Lancers

The shot and shell flew like hail about us, our line began to get terribly thin. My horse began to limp and I could not manage him. My off reins were cut in two. I managed to tie them; my curb was gone likewise. I received a stinging sensation from a wound about my left shoulder.

Private Henry Naylor, 13th Light Dragoons

There were shouts from the lancers of, 'Come on, Deaths! Come on!', a reference to the regimental motto of the 17th and the skull and crossed thighbones on the badge. Some men of the 13th Light Dragoons thought that the lancers to their left were pulling ahead, and even in the midst of the most dreadful carnage, regimental rivalries still mattered:

The last thing I heard before I went down was one man saying to his neighbour, 'Come on; don't let those bastards get ahead of us'.

Captain Arthur Tremayne, 13th Light Dragoons

Officers of the 17th, eager to advance from the gallop to the charge or pressed by the men behind, were once more gaining on Lord Cardigan. He would not allow the pace to be forced:

When we were in the midst of our torture and mad to be out of it, I heard again, high above the turmoil and din, Cardigan's sonorous command, 'Steady, steady the 17th Lancers'.

Private James Wightman, 17th Lancers

The shower of grape shot and round shot was awful, besides the flash fire of artillery and the flames which swept down the ranks every moment. I considered it certain death, but I led straight and no man flinched.

Lord Cardigan

The men may have been in control of their fears, but it was at this moment that the mount of Captain John Oldham bolted, mad with panic, and carried him forward of the 13th Light Dragoons. Two or three men riding immediately behind him misunderstood and went too. Unfortunately this accidental charge carried them directly into the path of a shell:

Oldham I saw killed by a shell which burst under his horse and knocked over two or three others. It blew his mare's hind-legs off, and he jumped up himself not hit, when next minute he threw up his hands and fell dead on his face.

Captain Soames Jenyns, 13th Light Dragoons

As more men fell, so the number of riderless mounts increased. Among them were badly wounded horses which nevertheless galloped on, though at a reduced pace, and sought refuge with Lord Paget's second line coming up behind.

One incident struck me forcibly – the bearing of riderless horses in such circumstances. I was of course riding by myself and clear of the line, and for that reason was a marked object for the poor dumb brutes, who were by this time galloping about in numbers like mad wild beasts. They consequently made dashes at me, some advancing with me a considerable distance, at one time as many as five on my right and two on my left, cringing in on me, and positively squeezing me, as the round shot came bounding by them, tearing up the earth under their noses, my overalls being a mass of blood from their gory flanks (they nearly upset me several times, and I had to use my sword to rid myself of them). I remarked their eyes, betokening as keen a sense of the perils around them as we human beings experienced.

And so, on we went through this scene of carnage, wondering each moment which would be our last. 'Keep back, Private So-and-so. Left squadron, close in to your centre.' It required a deal of closing in, by this time, to fill up the vacant gaps.

Lord George Paget, 4th Light Dragoons

Their mounts were by now tiring. Captain Thomas Hutton of the 4th thought that 'it was awful work on a blown horse'. He soon had greater worries: his right leg was hit with such force that he imagined a roundshot had taken it off at the thigh but, on inspecting it, found that he had been struck by a musket ball. He shouted across to Captain Alexander Low, asking what he should do. Low told him that if he could keep to the saddle it would be better to carry on with the rest, adding: 'There's no use going back now – you'll only be killed.'

For those who had their horses shot beneath them, there was certainly no going on unless they could catch another mount. Russian infantrymen, especially the sharpshooters equipped with Minié rifles, attempted to pick off dismounted men. Some took shelter behind their dead mounts:

I lost my poor horse in the Charge, a shell caught her in the chest and killed her instantly, I shot right over her head on to my face but I thank God that the only harm that happened to me was that the bridge of my nose was broken. I lay behind my poor horse.

Private John Whitehead, 4th Light Dragoons

11.17 A.M.

The Russian view. The Don Cossack gun crews were loading and firing every thirty seconds. A thick bank of smoke rolled over the battery at each volley and for a time the gunners lost sight of the target, then just before they fired again there the British were – the roundshot and shell was wreaking havoc among them and sometimes there appeared to be more empty saddles than cavalrymen, but the madmen who survived were coming on still.

If any of the gunners felt a first twinge of fear – the first doubt that they could stop the enemy charge – they knew also that as the enemy came closer the effect of the canister rounds they were firing increased. At close range the deadly contents of the shot from each gun would have a spread of ten yards, and every man and horse within that arc would be hit. The enemy light cavalry could not possibly survive it.

Some of the gun crews had an extra trick of their own. It was not in the artillery manual, but by loading a roundshot on top of the canister it was possible to fire double-shotted. No force of cavalry could ride through such an iron storm and live to tell of it.

The fire was terrific, it seemed impossible to escape. We were well within range of grapeshot from the barkers in front of us.

Captain Edwin Cook, 11th Hussars

When about a hundred yards from the guns I noticed just in front of me a gunner apply his fuse to the gun at which I appeared to be riding. I shut my eyes for I thought that settled the question as far as I was concerned, but the shot missed me and struck the man on my right full on the chest.

Captain Godfrey Morgan, 17th Lancers

Experienced cavalrymen who had been under artillery fire before knew that as the line came close to the guns, which were twenty yards apart, men approaching the gaps between the guns stood a greater chance of survival than men riding directly at the muzzles, and that therefore closing up was no longer such a good idea:

Here a discharge from the battery in our front, whose guns were double shotted first with shot or shell, and then with case, swept away Captain Winter and the whole division on my right. The gap was noticed by Captain Morris, who gave the order 'Right Incline', but a warning came from my coverer in the rear rank, Corporal John Penn, 'Keep straight on, Jack.' He saw what I did not, that we were opposite the intervals of the guns and thus we escaped, for the next round must have swept us into eternity.

Sergeant John Berryman, 17th Lancers

We were now very close to the guns, for we were entering the smoke which hung in clouds in front. I could see some of the gunners running from the guns to the rear, when just at that moment a shell from the battery on the right struck my horse, carrying away the shoulder and part of the chest, and exploding a few yards off. Fortunately I was on the ground when it exploded, or some of the fragments would most likely have reached me.

Private Albert Mitchell, 13th Light Dragoons

Before we reached the guns every officer of my squadron, the second, was either killed or wounded, leaving no one to command us.

Corporal Thomas Morley, 17th Lancers

Cardigan was still straight in front of me, steady as a church, but now his sword was in the air; he turned in his saddle for an instant, and shouted his final command, 'Steady! Steady! Close in!'

Private James Wightman, 17th Lancers

The Russian view. Colonel Obolensky knew that he should now order his crews to hitch up their guns to the horse teams and withdraw. The enemy front line was less than thirty seconds from them and it took a full thirty seconds to reload. But by ordering his men to ignore safety precautions – that is, to not swab out the barrel, with the risk that hot fragments from the previous shot might ignite the fresh powder charge immediately it was pressed home and kill several among the gun crew – this time could be cut to twenty seconds. That meant a final volley of canister could be fired when the enemy was only twenty or so yards away, and that would surely stop them at the last.

He yelled the order to his men. At the same time he ordered the horse teams to stand ready.

Lord Cardigan shouted his final command and his trumpeter blew the 'Charge', though few could have heard it over the roar of the guns and the constant rattle of musket and rifle fire. In fact neither the command nor the bugle call was required; constant drilling and mock charges had taught every man to know by instinct the regulation distance at which their galloping mounts could be finally spurred to the utmost speed – about seventeen miles per hour – for the final dash. Lances and sabres were brought down to the 'Engage'.

We like Bull dogs who had been tied up all day, were too glad to be let loose and off we went at a thundering gallop, cheering more like mad men than like men with common sense – excitement was great – fear was banished from every mind – on, on we went.

Lieutenant William Gordon, 17th Lancers

On we went, the pace increasing amidst the thickest shower of shell, shot, grape and canister and Minié, from front and flanks, horses and men dropping by scores every yard. The whistling and crackling of shells was beyond all description, the enemy's guns firing in front of us till we were within a yard and a half of them.

Captain Godfrey Morgan, 17th Lancers

The Russian view. As they worked frantically, some among the gun crews now doubted their ability to stop the enemy cavalry. They could see there were lancers in the front line and even as they watched these men lowered their poles – the red and white pennons fluttering madly at the tips were clearly visible. That meant the charge had been called; the horses would be spurred to their utmost and the enemy would be among the guns within seconds. As the gunners stood back ready, panic gripped them. When the guns thundered for the final time, the bravest drew their sabres, though many another dived beneath the gun carriages, not so much seeking shelter from the hooves of any horses that might reach the gun line as safety from the steel tips of any lances that came with them. Only a few of the youngest men turned to run, offering their backs to the lancers and inviting the point.

We reached the battery in a very good line, and at the regular charging pace; and here many officers and men were killed. On leading into the battery a gun was fired close by my horse's head. I rode straight forward at the same pace.

Lord Cardigan

Just as Lord Cardigan got close up to a gun, it went off, luckily without touching him, and not being able to see from the smoke he rode right up against the gun.

Cornet George Wombwell, 17th Lancers

There crashed into us a regular volley from the Russian cannon. I saw Captain White go down and Cardigan disappear into the smoke.

Private James Wightman, 17th Lancers

My attention here was attracted to Private Melrose, a Shakespearian reciter, calling out, 'What man here would ask another man from England?' Poor fellow, they were the last words he spoke, for the next round from the guns killed him and many others. We were then so close to the guns that the report rang through my head, and I was quite deaf for a time. It was this round that broke my mare's off-hind leg, and caused her to stop instantly.

Sergeant John Berryman, 17th Lancers

Just as I came close to a gun, it went off, and, naturally, round went my horse. I turned him round, and put him at it again, and got through.

Captain Godfrey Morgan, 17th Lancers

When I was within a few yards of the Russian guns my horse was shot under me and fell on its head. I endeavoured to pull it up in order to dash at the gunners but found it was unable to move, its foreleg having been blown off. I left it and forced my way on foot.

Corporal James Nunnerley, 17th Lancers

The last volley went off when we were close on them. The flame, the smoke, the roar were in our faces. It is not an exaggeration to compare the sensation to that of riding into the mouth of a volcano.

Corporal Thomas Morley, 17th Lancers

Behind the first line came the 11th Hussars. The Russian guns had by this time been silenced by the arrival of the 17th Lancers and 13th Light Dragoons, and the mêlée in the smoke had begun. The 11th had veered close to the Fedioukine Heights on the left, and once again Russian infantry gathered there poured heavy fire into the cavalry as they charged through the final yards.

At each volley of the Cossack guns the bank of smoke forming about them had drifted further outwards towards the heights on the left and right until it presented an apparent gun line much wider than the actual battery. While the guns had been in action, flashes from the muzzles had indicated their positions. Now that they were silent it was impossible to judge precisely where the hidden battery began and ended. Because the 11th Hussars had drifted to the left, the greater part of the regiment missed the battery altogether and charged into the empty bank of smoke where it had spread towards the Fedioukine Heights. Only those men on the extreme right went in among the guns.

As we neared the battery, a square of infantry that had been placed a little in advance of the guns, gave us a volley in flank. The very air hissed as the shower of bullets passed through us; many men were now killed or wounded. I, at this moment, felt that something had touched my left wrist. On looking down I saw that a bullet, which must have passed close in front of my body, had blackened and cut the lace on my cuff. Private Glanister had his lower jaw shattered, and a bullet passed through the back of Private Humphries' neck just missing the spinal cord. At this time we were at a sweeping gallop. In another moment we passed the guns, our right flank brushing them.

Troop Sergeant Major George Smith, 11th Hussars

As the 11th followed the 17th and 13th into the smoke and disappeared too, officers and men who had been wounded and unhorsed by the final volley faced another danger: the second line, which in effect consisted of the 4th Light Dragoons alone, coming up at the charge was likely to trample them.

On my recovery from the shock, I found my horse was lying on his near side, my left leg was beneath him, and my right above him. I tried to move, but just at that moment I heard the second line come galloping on to where I lay, and fully expecting to be trampled on I looked up and saw it was the 4th Light Dragoons quite close. I called out, 'For God's sake, don't ride over me.'

Private Albert Mitchell, 13th Light Dragoons

Lord Paget and the 4th reached the guns just after the 11th Hussars. Over the final forty yards the ground lay thick with dead and dying men and horses, and although every attempt was made to avoid them some suffered beneath the hooves. The battery had been put out of action by the first line so the second was spared a close-range volley with canister. The cigar that Paget had cut and lit moments before the order to advance still smouldered between his tightly clamped teeth as he led his men into the mêlée.

Dismounted men of the first line who were unhurt caught riderless horses racing along with the 4th Light Dragoons and continued their charge:

I got up to the guns when unfortunately my horse was shot under me, and came down leaving me dismounted. My first act was to get another horse, and seeing a trooper minus his rider I made for him and caught him and jumped on his back and went down again with the second line.

Cornet George Wombwell, 17th Lancers

The 8th Hussars, which should have kept its alignment with the 4th Light Dragoons, had veered consistently away to the right and fallen behind. By the time the 8th reached the battery it was so far to the right that it charged into the smoke drifting out towards the Causeway Heights and missed the guns altogether, apart from a few men on the left flank. One of these, Troop Sergeant Major Henry Harrison, stopped to help a wounded man stranded in front of the guns. Private Pennington had already attracted the attention of Russian riflemen and would not have lasted long:

A musket ball struck my mare's hind leg and lamed her so badly that she became quite useless. But I felt a strange reluctance to dismount. 'Black Bess' had been the fastest mare in all the troop; high-bred and hardy, she had borne campaigning well. With no soul in sight, for the regiments in front had passed away obscured by dust and smoke, I made a good mark for musketry fire. A ball passed through my right leg, a shot from the left tilted my busby over my right ear, while 'Bess' received the *coup de grâce* which brought us both to earth, though I was still astride the mare. I had some half-formed plan of hobbling to the rear, when to my great surprise I heard the thud of hooves behind. Great was my relief and joy as Sergeant Major Harrison, seeing my plight, halted and bade me mount a grey mare he led.

Private William Pennington, 11th Hussars

Harrison and Pennington followed the rear rank of the 8th Hussars into the smoke. They were probably the last mounted men to cross the gun line. Both rescuer and rescued felt elation at reaching the battery alive but neither man could have imagined what lay in store for the survivors of the Light Brigade behind the Russian guns.

All those watching from the Sapoune Heights had their eyes fixed on the bank of smoke that still hung over the silent guns and into which the remains of the Light Brigade had charged and disappeared as if into hell itself. Lord Raglan, staff officers, William Russell – his eyes flitting between the valley and his notebook – and Fanny Duberly looked down from the heights as if from the graveside. No one spoke. No one had any expectation that a single man would return.

8. Behind the Guns

The Light Brigade pursues the Russian cavalry

At the end of their ride the surviving officers and men of the first line dashed through a dense veil – the bank of smoke that lay over the guns as these stilled from the final volley – into the deepest horror:

My horse made a tremendous leap into the air, though I know not what at. The smoke was so dense that I could not even see my arm before me. Then suddenly I was in the battery, and in the darkness there were sounds of fighting and slaughter. In this gloom we cut and thrust and hacked like demons.

Private James Wightman, 17th Lancers

The smoke had also drifted down the valley in the direction of the river, so that by now it lay eighty yards deep, reaching from the gun line almost to the Russian cavalry formed up a hundred yards to the rear. It was into this smoke bank packed with gunners and horse teams that the remnants of the 17th Lancers and 13th Light Dragoons had ridden at the charge. Whatever distance it took them to bring their mounts to a stop they were still inside the smoke.

The nearest Russian gunners – and only the nearest could see them and be seen – slashed out with sabres or aimed carbines as the fight became a series of individual conflicts. It was a desperate struggle in which the low visibility meant that lancers and light dragoons who had been kept going during the advance by their sense of regimental pride – the famous esprit de corps of the cavalry – suddenly had no collective view of what was happening. This abrupt isolation, with the smell and the sharp taste of the powder smoke that enveloped them, and the muffled cries of men cut down that reached them from all sides, increased the sense that they had charged into hell itself.

Because the smoke had also spread outwards from the ends of the gun line Captain Morris and twenty lancers charged in, missed the guns to the left, and raced on through. The rest, as they dragged their mounts to a halt, found themselves among or immediately behind the guns.

What few reached the guns, and I amongst them, cut away like madmen.
Private William Butler, 17th Lancers

Those who did not fall were through the guns in an instant and full of fight. Our arrival at the battery silenced it instantly, and the gunners began to try to move the cannon away. The gospel of Russian fighting was always to save the guns.
Corporal Thomas Morley, 17th Lancers

Save the guns, perhaps, but a good many reasoned that they had to save themselves first. Because Colonel Obolensky's gamble that a final, close-range volley with canister would stop the enemy had not paid off, there was no time left between the firing of the guns and the arrival of the Light Brigade to hitch up the horse teams and drag the guns to safety. The bravest of the gunners tried frantically to hitch up while the fighting went on around them and two of the eight guns were actually moved towards the rear. Most crews thought it better to finish off the enemy cavalrymen with sabre and carbine and so save their guns without the need for horse teams. Men on foot knew the consequences of turning their backs on cavalry.

To the survivors of the Light Brigade the 200 men who made up the eight gun crews were responsible for the terrible carnage inflicted on their fallen comrades, and now they took a terrible revenge. Men of the 17th Lancers, if they spotted Russians before their troopers could be brought to a halt, used their momentum to run them right through. Even gunners who took refuge beneath the guns could not escape the long reach of the lances jabbed after them. But the lance was not made for the mêlée and once they had come to a stop many men of the 17th abandoned this weapon. Corporal John Penn left his lance in a gunner, equal lengths of the ash pole protruding from the front and back of the man's body, and next drew his sabre. He rode at a Cossack officer and with one swing of the blade virtually decapitated the man.

The survivors of the first line did not have it all their own way. The 17th Lancers and 13th Light Dragoons had begun the advance with a total of 250 men; less than half reached the guns and these were outnumbered by the gunners. Survival in the mêlée required a cavalryman to keep his horse 'on the turn'. In order to have the best use of his right (sabre) arm a man had to keep an enemy on that side, which meant continually pulling the horse around with his left (reins) hand to foil an opponent who knew the advantage of coming at him from the left or from behind. A disabling wound in the left arm could leave him almost as defenceless as a wound in the right. Significantly there is no report of cavalrymen forming pairs – a common reaction in a mêlée because by moving together knee-to-knee each man had only one side to protect. Pairing was a defensive manoeuvre and these men were still very much on the offensive.

Many men who had reached the guns uninjured were now handicapped by exhausted or wounded mounts. Cornet John Chadwick of the 17th Lancers found himself stranded on a useless horse. He fought off the gunners who attacked him until he was cut across the neck and fell from the saddle, and was taken prisoner. Cornet George Wombwell, also of the 17th, riding as ADC to Cardigan, lost his mount at the final volley, caught a riderless horse and continued in among the guns, but when this second horse was shot he was quickly surrounded. Rank mattered even in such circumstances – officers were more likely to be taken prisoner, private soldiers more likely to be killed:

I heard a fearful yell, and about 5 or 7 Cossacks came up flourishing their swords, I expected to be cut down, and desiring me to throw down my sword which seeing resistance was useless I did, when I was instantly surrounded, my pistols seized, and was rather roughly helped off my beaten horse. A Russian officer came up and asked me if I spoke French, I told him yes and requested him not to let the savages by whom I was surrounded knock me about, he was uncommonly civil, told me not to be alarmed, they were only rather rough in their manners, so away I was marched off on foot between 2 of them and 3 more behind.

Cornet George Wombwell, 17th Lancers

Two men spotted the first gun being dragged away and attempted to capture it. Troop Sergeant Majors John Linkon and George Smith, both of the 13th Light Dragoons, stopped the team by shooting the lead horse, and inadvertently endangered an officer of the 17th Lancers who was nearby. To add to the irony, this officer's life was then accidentally saved by a Cossack:

I was by the gun and the leading Russian horse, shot I suppose with a pistol by someone on my right, fell across my horse, dragging it over with him and pinning me between the gun and himself. A Russian gunner on foot at once covered me with his carbine. He was just within reach of my sword and I struck at him, which disconcerted his aim. At the same moment a mounted gunner struck my horse with his sabre and the animal bolted.

Captain Godfrey Morgan, 17th Lancers

During these early seconds among the guns when there were no formed groups, some junior officers looked for Lord Cardigan. They had as ordered charged the guns, but what now? The front line had broken up and it was expected that Cardigan or some other senior officer would rally the survivors and tell them what to do next.

Cardigan had charged through the battery ahead of the first line and alone. His ADCs and trumpeter had been hit or unhorsed and left behind, and he had lost contact with Lieutenant Colonel Mayow, his second-in-command. Instead of pulling up at or just beyond the guns, as every other man did, Cardigan rode on through the full eighty yards of the smoke bank and out its far side – to find himself facing a mass of enemy cavalry:

I led into the battery and through the Russian gun limber carriages and ammunition wagons in the rear. I rode within twenty yards of the line of the Russian cavalry. I was attacked by two Cossacks, slightly wounded by their lances, and with difficulty got away from them.

Lord Cardigan

As Cardigan moved back towards the battery a number of men saw and ignored him:

My first thought after we were through the line was to look for an officer to see what we were to do. I saw Lord Cardigan at first but I had no impulse to join him. I think no British soldier ever had. He led 670 and none rallied on him. I saw troopers riding past him to the right and left. He was about 50 yards beyond the guns on their extreme left.

Corporal Thomas Morley, 17th Lancers

Lieutenant Henry Maxse, the second of Cardigan's ADCs to lose his horse in the final volley, stumbled on foot through the smoke and was almost run down by Private Wightman. After crying out, 'For God's sake, Lancer, don't ride over me,' he pointed towards Cardigan and said, 'Rally on him.' Once ordered, Wightman would have done so, but at that point a mounted Russian appeared from the smoke to cut him in the thigh, and then made the mistake of fleeing. Wightman was still armed with his lance; his revenge was quick and final:

I went for him, but he bolted; I overtook him, drove my lance into his back and unhorsed him.

Private James Wightman, 17th Lancers

After this sighting of Cardigan by Morley, Wightman and Maxse, the brigade commander 'disappeared' – he moved back towards the guns where the smoke was still dense and from that moment gave no orders and played no further part in the action. Some among both the officers and the men believed that he deserted his brigade at the guns and retired early.

19. Lord Cardigan, resplendent in the full dress uniform of the 11th Hussars, leads the charge of the Light Brigade on his favourite charger, Ronald. Behind him the 13th Light Dragoons can be seen on the left and the 17th Lancers on the right

20. *Sir Briggs*, the horse used in the charge by Captain Godfrey Morgan (later Lord Tredegar) of the 17th Lancers, pictured here at the cavalry camp at Kadikoi

21. *The Midnight Alarm*. The cavalry turns out after pickets have raced into the camp at Kadikoi to raise the alarm. Russian patrols continually tested the defences around Balaklava and, once called out, the cavalry had to remain in the saddle until first light

22. *The Charge of the Light Brigade.* A panoramic view of the charge as it would have been seen by the Russians on the Fedioukine Heights. Long before they reached the enemy guns the regiments had lost the perfect formation depicted here

23. *The Charge of the Light Brigade.* As they approach the guns, men and officers of the 17th Lancers spur their horses to the charge and almost come level with Lord Cardigan. The figure in the foreground is Private James Wightman, who was later wounded and taken prisoner

24. *The 17th Lancers at Balaklava.* The 17th, in the front line of the Light Brigade, pass through the Russian battery. Gunners are pierced through by lances or fight back with sabres. The gunner in the foreground holds a sponge staff used to swab out a gun before reloading

25. *The Relief of the Light Brigade.* The 11th Hussars, riding behind the front line, reach the battery and relieve those survivors of the 17th Lancers still engaged in combat among the guns

26. *The rescue of Captain Augustus Webb, 17th Lancers.* Webb fell near the
Russian guns with a shattered leg and was carried out of range of enemy fire by
Sergeants John Berryman and John Farrell of his own regiment and Corporal
Malone of the 13th Light Dragoons. All three men received the Victoria Cross
for this action

27. *Balaklava: the Return.* The survivors of the charge make their way back towards the British lines. Several men sat for Lady Butler during the painting of this scene. The figure on the left is Private Pennington, 11th Hussars. Behind him Corporal James Nunnerley, 17th Lancers, is shown mounted and bringing in the mortally wounded Trumpeter Billy Brittain

28. *Florence Nightingale in the Military Hospital at Scutari*. Inside the hospital where the most seriously wounded survivors of the charge were taken, Florence Nightingale is making her evening round of the wards. Although shown here carrying an oil lamp, she normally used a candle lantern

29. *Our Cavalry, December 1854*. Many of the horses that survived the charge died of exhaustion and starvation during the harsh winter that followed. With insufficient fit men available to bury them, the carcasses were left to be consumed by vultures

After each man's first, instinctive reaction to whatever confronted him in the smoke – some dispatching an enemy, others forced to defend themselves – the survivors took stock of their situation. Their training taught them to rally on a senior officer, but for most neither Cardigan nor any senior regimental officers could be seen, and no bugle or voice called out to them. In the absence of any command to rally or withdraw they applied themselves to the one task that followed logically from the charge, and attempted to take the guns and return with them to the British lines. This effort was organized by a junior officer, Lieutenant Edward Jervis of the 13th Light Dragoons.

Corporal Morley was among the men who joined Lieutenant Jervis, although he did so only by mistake; in the smoke he mistook Jervis for an officer of his own regiment, the uniforms of the 17th and 13th being similar. Jervis had seen the second gun being dragged to safety by the Cossacks and was so intent on stopping it that when Morley told him Lord Cardigan was nearby, he chose to go after the gun in preference to seeking out his brigade commander:

Lieutenant Jervis was riding towards a cannon that was retreating to the rear. I galloped up to him and informed him that Lord Cardigan was above, pointing my sword to the place, my lance having been shot away at the last volley as we charged the guns. He replied, 'Never mind, let's capture that gun!' We raced towards it. He said, 'Cut down the gunners!' He shot one of the horses in the head bringing it to a sudden stop. The gunners disappeared between the horses and the gun-carriage as we slashed at them. We both dismounted and took out the dead horse while more of the Brigade gathered about to assist us. Private John Smith mounted one of the horses attached to the gun, and another soldier mounted another horse of the gun. We started back off the field at a gallop with the mounted cannon.

Corporal Thomas Morley, 17th Lancers

Jervis was informed of Cardigan's location but, like the men who glimpsed their commander through the smoke, did not rally to him. Colonel Mayow, second-in-command of the brigade, spent this first frantic minute at the guns searching for Cardigan, but could not find him. Deciding that Cardigan must have been killed or taken prisoner, Mayow finally decided that command of the brigade fell to him and called out to the men. He was shocked by how few rallied to him: fifteen men of the 17th Lancers and twelve men of the 13th Light Dragoons. Those still attempting to take the guns neither saw nor heard him and he had no trumpeter.

Mayow's search for Cardigan must have taken him to the far edge of the smoke where it was thinning, for he became aware of the mass of Russian cavalrymen formed up in line a hundred yards behind the guns. He knew that once the survivors of the Light Brigade set off back up the valley, with or without captured guns, this cavalry was certain to pursue with devastating results. The only alternative was to attack them. He began to organize his small group, placing those men of the 17th Lancers who had not discarded their lances in favour of the sabre in the front rank.

Within a minute of reaching the battery the survivors of the two front-line regiments had divided between those reforming under Mayow and preparing to charge the Russian cavalry, and those continuing the fight on the gun line and attempting to capture the guns. Each of these groups was unaware of the other and neither knew of the group led by Captain Morris, commanding officer of the 17th Lancers, which had missed the battery altogether and charged by to the left, unwittingly becoming the first to pursue the enemy beyond the gun line.

The momentum of the charge carried Captain Morris deep into the bank of smoke drifting out from the gun line towards the Fedioukine Heights, and because he encountered neither guns nor gunners he carried right on through. When he finally pulled his mount to a halt on the far side of the smoke, a mere twenty men behind him stood in place of the regiment he had started out with seven minutes earlier. Worse still, a complete regiment of Russian hussars was lined up in front of him.

The Russians were just as shocked by the abrupt appearance of this band of survivors from a ride no man should have lived through, and in those first crucial seconds it was Morris who took the initiative. Turning to yell to his men, 'Remember what I have told you, and keep together,' he led them straight at the enemy. The effect of the impact of these twenty lancers was far out of proportion to their number and must have been primarily psychological. Remarkably, the Russians scattered in disorder, all the more so because these were hussars – regular cavalry rather than the less disciplined Cossacks.

Morris made for an officer he took to be the Russian commander, charging with his sabre arm held straight out and the point of his blade targeting the chest; it slid in up to the hilt so that half of its length protruded from the man's back. The blade locked in muscle and bone, and as the body slumped back in the saddle Morris was almost pulled from his horse. While struggling to withdraw his sabre, two of the enemy closed on him. He was hit by the swing of a blade above the left ear, and a second blow came down across his skull. As he fell his sabre came free.

Captain Morris was one of the most experienced cavalry officers on the field and admitted later that he did not know how he came to use the thrust in preference to the cut, but vowed never to do so again. At the time his wounds were such that he seemed unlikely to get the chance:

Morris received a sabre cut on the left side of the head which carried away a large piece of bone above the ear, and a deep, clean cut passing down through the acorn of his forage cap, which penetrated both plates of the skull.

Alexander Kinglake

Having taken command of the 17th Lancers only days earlier, Morris was still wearing the frail forage cap of a staff officer. If his head had been protected by the high, square-topped, leather chapska – shaped to deflect a blade – he might not have been so badly wounded. Yet despite these injuries he was back on his feet within seconds.

The hussars now thought it an easy task to finish off a wounded man on foot, partly blinded by his own blood:

Morris sought to defend himself by the almost ceaseless 'moulinet' or circling whirl of his sword and from time to time he found means to deliver some sabre cuts upon the thighs of his assailants. Soon however he was pierced in the temple, which splintered up a piece of bone and forced it in under the scalp. This wound gave him great pain and he believed that his life must be nearly at its end.

Alexander Kinglake

So it would have been had not a Russian officer called off the hussars and demanded in English that the wounded man surrender. Morris reversed his sabre and handed it up to the officer.

By now the shouts of officers had rallied the hussars, and their courage returned when they saw how few the British were and that the lancers were trapped in their midst. Most of the twenty were attacked from all sides and cut down.

Meanwhile, Colonel Mayow rode in front of the twenty-seven men of the 17th Lancers and 13th Light Dragoons he had rallied among the guns, heading straight at the Russian cavalry formed up directly behind the battery. Everyone following him must have known that if the enemy stood firm they were dashing to their deaths. They had one hope: the second line must come crashing through the guns to their support at any moment, and the Heavy Brigade behind them. None knew that Lord Lucan had long since turned back with the Heavies.

No adequate explanation has ever been given as to why the several Russian cavalry regiments behind the guns, with an over-whelming numerical advantage, fell back when charged by Mayow and his men. It is possible that they too believed a considerable force was rushing up in support of these few, and withdrew because of the enemy they anticipated rather than the enemy they saw. Yet they had sat contentedly in the saddle a mere hundred yards behind the guns throughout the advance, certain that *no* enemy force could survive the shells and trouble them. It is more likely that panic was triggered by the same psychological factor that caused the enemy to flee Captain Morris and his twenty men. The Russians had not expected a single Englishman to survive the guns, and the sudden appearance of these bloodied figures from the smoke – who fought like demons and by now looked the part – must have unnerved them.

Whatever the cause, they turned and fled in disorder. Mayow's group pressed them a further 500 yards back towards the Chernaya. Most of the Russian cavalry, which included both Cossacks and hussars, were eager to reach the river and had no inclination to fight back, but any who stood firm were quickly dealt with:

When pursuing the Cossacks, I noticed Colonel Mayow deal very cleverly with a big Russian cavalry officer. He tipped off his shako with the point of his sword and then laid his head right open with the old cut seven.

Private James Wightman, 17th Lancers

The Russian view. General Ryzhov had expected the hussars and Cossacks drawn up behind the guns to mop up any British survivors. The hussars were regular cavalry and considered the Cossacks uncouth and unreliable. Ryzhov knew that the Cossacks were not noted for their discipline under threat, but there were a great many of them and they faced only the smallest possibility that any of the enemy would live to reach them.

An officer of the regular cavalry saw what happened and blamed the Cossacks. It seemed to him that they panicked and fled, forcing the hussars to fall back too, although the latter put up a fight by the river:

The Englishmen charged the guns and not even the canister fire could stop them; they kept on racing forward. The Don Cossack gunners saw that there was no time to save their guns, and withdrew in order to save themselves. But the enemy rode on at their backs and cut them down without mercy.

When the Cossack cavalry saw the discipline by which the enemy cavalry kept a line as it bore down upon them, they panicked and wheeled to their left to escape. Some of the men fired on their own comrades to clear a passage for themselves. In *their flight the Cossacks rode straight into the regiment that was supporting the guns, and caused great mayhem, and this regiment fell back on the next, and soon all of our cavalry in the valley was withdrawing in disorder. The bravest among the officers called out to stop it, and when the men would not listen, these few dashed forward alone against the enemy and so lost their lives.*

Our hussars were pressed as far as the Chernaya river where there was only one bridge by which they could escape. All of the cavalry and the artillery wished to cross the bridge at once. The Cossack gunners were so afraid of the enemy that they urged on their horse teams and forced a way through, leaving the hussars to the fight. Sabres clashed as the English came on and the hussars fell back, as many as could do so crossing the bridge.

Lieutenant Koribut Kubitovich

Another Russian observer thought that the hussars had been the first to break and that the retreat was not the fault of the Cossacks alone:

Once through our guns the enemy moved quickly and bravely at a gallop towards our cavalry. was so unexpected that before anyone realized it our cavalry had broken. First of all the hussars showed themselves unready to stand against the enemy cavalry, and after them the Cossacks, so that all of our cavalry was soon retreating in disorder.

It was chaos. Our cavalry outnumbered the enemy five times over, and yet it fell back in total disorder to the Chernaya, with the English coming hotly forward at the hooves of our horses. Then it became impossible for our regiments to escape and both bodies of cavalry came to a stop. In this tight space at the end of the valley, were packed four regiments of our Cossacks and hussars, and here and there inside this great mass, were the English, probably as surprised as ourselves at this unexpected circumstance.

Lieutenant Stefan Kozhukhov

The official reports of this debacle were written by officers of the regular cavalry and predictably these blamed the Cossacks.

Evidence from Light Brigade survivors suggests that while the whole of the Russian cavalry fled, it was the Cossacks who put up most resistance. Certainly it was Cossacks who advanced to attack the men left among the guns. Lieutenant Jervis and his group had captured one gun and were leading it away:

A large body of Cossacks charged and surrounded our group. I was riding on the right of the gun, the direction in which the Cossacks attacked us. In the mêleé I got through the wrong end and had to ride back again down the valley. I was pursued by seven of them until they fairly chased me into a body of Russian Cavalry with its back to me. There was no alternative but to ride through or surrender to the Cossacks. I put spurs to my horse and bolted into the line. I got through with a knock on the head from a Russian officer, that would have wounded me but for my dress cap. More members of the Light Brigade were riding about – some of them wounded – fighting as best they could.

Corporal Hall, of my own troop, had his lance trailing about and covered with blood. I told him to throw it away and wanted to pick it up myself, as I needed one, but there was no time. I ordered Private Clifford of my own troop to halt, instead of which he charged into the Russians and was cut and pierced to death before my eyes.

Corporal Thomas Morley, 17th Lancers

Of the survivors of the two first-line regiments, Mayow's group had pursued the Russian cavalry to the Chernaya and the remainder still fought among the guns. All still expected the three regiments coming up in support to arrive at any moment.

As we have seen, the 11th Hussars had set off between the first and second lines, behind the 17th Lancers, and should have hit the guns soon after the 17th. Unfortunately Colonel Douglas and his regiment had veered to the left – even more so than Captain Morris – so that most of the hussars missed the battery completely. Only those riding on the extreme right went in among the guns:

There was a lot of smoke about, and I couldn't see much. I remember after we got among the artillery and came to hand-to-hand work, my horse was killed and fell with me under him.

Private John Richardson, 11th Hussars

Troop Sergeant Major Smith was riding to the rear and looked to his right as they drew level with the battery:

I saw one of the guns some distance to our right being taken away; it was a large brass gun, with carriage painted green, drawn by six horses, there were only three men and a driver with it. Feeling that it had escaped from the battery, I at once formed the resolution to retake it, so seeing three men riding independently in the rear, I called to them to follow me, saying, 'Let us take this gun.' I at once galloped off, supposing they were following me, when within a short distance of it I saw a Hussar Officer and three Cossacks, who had detached themselves from the main body for its protection, and were coming rapidly between me and my regiment. On looking round I found I was alone, that the three men had not followed me as I had expected. Feeling it would be madness to attempt the capture single-handed, I instantly halted, turned about and galloped off in the direction of my regiment.

Troop Sergeant Major George Smith, 11th Hussars

The main body of the 11th had rushed on through the smoke and found their route blocked by the same Russian hussars who had seconds earlier taken Morris prisoner and cut down most of his group. Colonel Douglas halted the men – he had lost fifty during the advance and had eighty with him now – and called to them urgently to 'Close in on the centre.' There were many gaps and forming a solid line was crucial if they were to withstand an attack by enemy cavalry. Yet once more the Russians hesitated and lost the initiative. Douglas decided, like Morris and Mayow before him, that to turn his back would prove fatal and that his only option was to charge.

Again the Russians reacted badly to the challenge and fell back with their comrades already fleeing the gun line:

As we came upon them they got into confusion and very loose order. My men got greatly excited, and we pursued at our best pace, they sweeping round the base of the hills to our left front, forming the end of the valley.

Lieutenant Colonel John Douglas, 11th Hussars

We were now nearing the extreme end of the valley, about a mile and a half from our position, still pursuing this body of Cavalry. In their confusion I saw one of their leading Cossacks fall from the bridge, there being no parapet. Near the bridge was a moderately steep hill which formed the end of the valley, up which they rode a short distance, their rear being at the foot, close to us.

Troop Sergeant Major George Smith, 11th Hussars

There were now two formed groups of survivors behind the Russian guns: Colonel Mayow with the remnants of the 17th Lancers and 13th Light Dragoons to the right, and Colonel Douglas with eighty men of the 11th Hussars to the left. Both groups had pursued the Russian cavalry as far as the Chernaya, and both knew that they were holding the enemy back not by force of arms but by the promise of support coming up from behind. In addition, those left fighting the Russian gunners at the gun line had now been joined by a small number of men separated from the 11th. All looked desperately for the two regiments of the second line to come thundering in, and the five regiments of Heavies behind them.

There was in effect no second line. The 4th Light Dragoons had advanced straight down the valley, while the 8th Hussars had fallen behind and veered ever further to the right. As a result the 4th reached the battery alone. Lord Paget arrived at the centre of the gun line and so led the full width of his regiment in among the guns, though more by chance than by judgement:

This battery, owing to the dust and confusion that reigned, had not been perceived by us (by me at least) until we got close upon it, though we had of course been suffering from its fire on our onward course. The first objects that caught my eyes were some of these guns, in the act of endeavouring to get away from us, who had by this time got close upon them. The men were dragging them away, some by lasso-harness, but others with their horses still attached. Then came a 'Holloa!' and a sort of simultaneous rush upon them by the remnants of the 4th and cut and thrust was the order of the day.

To some of the guns, however, horses were attached, and some of the drivers of these, in the mêlée, tried to let themselves fall off between the horses. There were some fierce hand-to-hand encounters, and our fellows, in the excitement of the moment, lost sight I fear of the chief power of their sabres, and for the point substituted the muscle of their arms, in the indiscriminate appliance of the cut, which generally fell harmlessly on the thick greatcoats of the Russians.

Lord George Paget, 4th Light Dragoons

The debate between cutting and thrusting was here continued on the battlefield. Morris had used the thrust and survived (just) to regret it; Paget was angry with his men for favouring the cut. One man attempting to halt the Russian driver of a horse team dragging a gun to safety found the cut most effective:

He struck me across the eyes with his whip, which almost blinded me, but as my horse flew past, I made a cut and caught him in the mouth, so that his teeth all rattled together as he fell. I can hear the horrible sound now.

Private Joseph Grigg, 4th Light Dragoons

Private Robert Farquharson saw one man take on five or six mounted Cossacks and unhorse every one of them, while Captain Alexander Low, carrying a sabre of considerably more than regulation length, dispatched eleven Russians. These numbers should not perhaps be taken literally, but they do indicate that despite the efforts of the first line there were many gunners still alive, and that the 4th Light Dragoons went at them with a vengeance. When Lord Paget noticed a straggler of the 17th Lancers jabbing frantically with his lance at a disarmed man cowering beneath a gun carriage, and ordered him to stop, the lancer appeared not to hear. There was among the survivors a blood lust that we might not condone but should strive to understand.

One young officer decided to capture a Russian gun. Paget thought it a greater priority to put the gunners out of action first and called him away:

Cornet Hunt was close to my right, when he returned his sword, jumped off his horse, and began trying to unhook the traces from a gun! The only acknowledgment of this act of devotion being, I fear, a sharp rebuke, and an order to remount. He thus disarmed himself in the mêlée, amid hand-to-hand encounters, and the act which he attempted would have been a most useful one, had support been near to retain possession of the gun which he was trying to dismember, though under the circumstances it was a useless attempt.

Lord George Paget, 4th Light Dragoons

The gunners were fighting back. Private Samuel Parkes had his horse shot under him, rolled safely away from the falling horseflesh and continued to fight on foot. Nearby, Trumpeter Hugh Crawford fell from his mount too and struggled up with difficulty. Seeing the trumpeter wounded and disarmed, two Cossacks closed on this easy prey. Parkes immediately put himself between Crawford and the Cossacks and slashed at them with his sabre until they stepped back.

Parkes now supported Crawford with his left arm – he could not walk unaided – while keeping the Cossacks at bay with his sabre arm, and together they headed slowly away from the gun line. There was no place of safety and once out of the smoke they were surrounded by Russian cavalrymen. Although Parkes swung his sabre viciously at them, a cut across the right arm disabled him, and both he and Crawford were taken prisoner.

Victoria Cross citation
Private Samuel Parkes, 4th Light Dragoons

His horse having been shot, he went to the aid of Trumpeter Crawford, who was dismounted and disarmed, and placed himself between the trumpeter and two Cossacks, and drove them away with his sword. They were attacked by a further six Russians, whom Parkes kept at bay until he was deprived of his sword.

Lord Paget now decided that the gunners had been beaten and correctly interpreted the absence of the two first-line regiments and the 11th Hussars as indicating that they had continued the advance in pursuit of the enemy. He led the 4th Light Dragoons after them:

When those guns had been disposed of, which did not occupy a long space of time, the 4th (by this time resembling more a party of skirmishers than a regiment), leaving the disabled guns behind them, pursued their onward course in support of the first line.

Lord George Paget, 4th Light Dragoons

Not all of the gunners had been beaten – one man swung a sabre at Private Farquharson and missed, but the blade as it fell slit open the breast of the cavalryman's horse. As the animal dropped to the ground, Farquharson managed to cut down the gunner. By this time his regiment had galloped away and he was left on foot among the guns.

The 4th soon engaged the fleeing Russian cavalry and again it was the Cossacks who put up the strongest resistance:

Beyond the guns, we went at the Russian cavalry with a rush. I selected a Cossack, who was making for me with his lance pointed at my breast. I knocked it upwards with my sword, pulled up quickly and cut him down across the face. I tried to get hold of his lance but he dropped it. As he was falling, I noticed that he was strapped on to the saddle, so that he did not come to the ground, and the horse rushed away with him.

Private Joseph Grigg, 4th Light Dragoons

Last to reach the still-lingering bank of smoke were Colonel Shewell and the 8th Hussars. The regiment missed the battery altogether except for a few men on the extreme left who went in among the guns. The last of the Russian gunners made a stand against the last of the Light Brigade, and again the cut proved itself against any unprotected part of the body put in its way:

The first thing I did, once within the guns, was to cut clean off the hand of a Russian gunner who was holding up his sponge-staff against me. He fell across the gun-carriage glaring savagely, but I cared little for that. I had seen too much. Bodies and limbs scattered in fragments, or smashed and kneaded together, and blood splashed into my face.

Anonymous, 8th Hussars

It was almost dark with smoke and fog, and you did not know where you were until you ran against a Cossack. You know your blood soon gets warm when you are fighting, and it didn't take us long to find out that we had nothing to do but give them a point as good as their cut. I got a cut with a sword on the forehead at the guns. We were cut and shot at in all directions, and it was each man for himself. I gave the Cossacks a great deal more than I got.

Private Anthony Sheridan, 8th Hussars

Those of the 8th Hussars involved in the mêlée in the gun line included Sergeant Williams, who just prior to the advance had been found with a pipe in his mouth and was ordered by Colonel Shewell to give up his sabre. Unarmed and surrounded by Russian gunners he was easily killed.

Shewell and the main body of the 8th charged by to the right. When they emerged on the far side of the smoke without encountering guns or gunners, he halted the regiment. Despite the storm of shot and shell they had come through and their losses the men closed up and formed line as if on the parade ground – except Sergeant Michael Reilly, who sat stiffly upright but refused to move. Shewell spotted the man out of position and shouted at him angrily, then saw that his eyes were fixed and staring and his face was 'as white as a flagstone'. Reilly must have been dead in the saddle for some time and carried along by his horse.

All mounted survivors of the Light Brigade were now behind the gun line. Three groups – led by Mayow, Douglas and Paget – had pursued vastly superior forces of Russian cavalry further down the valley to the Chernaya. A fourth group under Shewell had come to a stop on the far right between these groups and the guns. The turning point of the action was the recognition by both sides that these men were alone – the Heavy Brigade was not coming up behind.

To our horror the Heavy Brigade had not followed in support.
Captain Edwin Cook, 11th Hussars

That sounds like a sudden realization, but it came slowly. At first it was impossible to be sure because the bank of smoke still lay like a barrier from the Fedioukine Heights on the left to the Causeway Heights on the right and concealed the full length of the valley, but every passing second confirmed it.

Russian cavalry officers managed to halt their retreat, and once the men turned to face the enemy it dawned on them how superior their numbers were. They began to edge forward. Colonel Mayow and his men of the 17th Lancers and 13th Light Dragoons withdrew reluctantly towards the gun line. Colonel Shewell, waiting further back with the 8th Hussars, saw them and moved his regiment across to reinforce them, and this again brought the Russians to a standstill. Mayow's first words to Shewell were: 'Where is Lord Cardigan?' Shewell had hoped that Mayow knew. The two officers sat trying to decide what to do next. They wondered where Cardigan was; the men were asking far less politely where Lord Lucan was.

Across the valley to their left, Colonel Douglas and his eighty men of the 11th Hussars knew they could not drive the enemy cavalry back indefinitely and had expected the Heavy Brigade to arrive by now.

The Russians now halted, but remained for a few moments with their backs to us, looking over their shoulders. Seeing there were so few of us, and without supports, they turned about, and we sat face to face, our horses' heads close to theirs. The stillness and suspense during these moments was terrible; at last it was broken by their officers calling out to their men to follow them, and break through us, which they attempted to do by driving their horses at our front rank, but our men showed a firm front, keeping close together, and bringing their swords down to the right front guard, kept them at bay.

Many of them now took out their pistols and fired into us, and the Cossacks began to double round our flanks and get in our rear. Our position became every moment more critical, for we were in danger of being surrounded, overwhelmed and killed to a man. But, had a few more of our squadrons come up at this time, I am of the opinion that this body of cavalry would have surrendered to us.

Troop Sergeant Major George Smith, 11th Hussars

Colonel Douglas too thought that the Russians could have been beaten. Having seen how poorly they reacted when challenged he briefly considered charging them without the Heavies, though his men were outnumbered twenty times over:

My first impulse was to charge; the word was almost out, but at the instant I saw how fruitless such a proceeding would be. I halted the regiment within forty yards of them, and gave the order to retire.

Lieutenant Colonel John Douglas, 11th Hussars

The Russians now pressed forward and Douglas was forced to fall back. Lord Paget and the survivors of the 4th Light Dragoons were still advancing from the gun line, but seeing the 11th withdrawing the 4th turned to do so too. However, Paget felt that once they turned their backs on the enemy they would be quickly overrun and slaughtered, and ordered his men to face the Russian cavalry.

The 11th had by this time been compelled to retire, and we consequently soon met their compact little knot retreating. When we met, the 4th hesitated, stopped, and without word of command 'went about', joining themselves to the retiring 11th. Masses of the enemy's cavalry were pursuing the latter, the more forward of them being close upon us. It now appeared to me that the moment was critical, and I shouted at the top of my voice, 'Halt, front; if you don't front, my boys, we are done!'

and this they did, and for a few minutes both regiments showed a front
to the advancing enemy.

Lord George Paget, 4th Light Dragoons

Paget's first words to Douglas were: 'Where is Lord Cardigan?'
Douglas had no idea. Exactly what else was said between them was
not recorded, but they decided to continue the withdrawal. It is
uncertain whether they actually joined to form a single group under
the command of the senior officer, Lord Paget, which is what Paget
says happened, or whether they fell back as separate regiments with
Paget commanding the 4th and Douglas still in command of the
11th, which is how Douglas describes it. It hardly matters. As one
force or two groups moving side by side, they fell back towards the
battery with the Russian cavalry just behind, apparently content
for the moment to follow and not to pounce. Meanwhile, to the
right of the valley the survivors of the 17th Lancers and 13th Light
Dragoons under Colonel Mayow had joined forces with Colonel
Shewell's 8th Hussars and were now at a standstill, face to face with
the enemy. The tension felt by both sides was immense as all
realized that the stand-off had to break soon.

*The Russian view. The hussars and Cossacks by the river had reformed
and were pressing the survivors of the enemy cavalry back towards the gun
line without the necessity of engaging them. Russian lancer regiments
waiting in reserve on the heights were now ordered down into the valley to
form a line behind the British, to block their route of escape and finish them
off. Pressed from behind by the sabres of the hussars and confronted by the
points of the lancers, the enemy must surrender or be cut down and pierced
to the last man.*

*The enemy came back down the valley and to give them their due they moved at
a trot and in perfect order as if this were nothing but an exercise. My regiment then
began to deploy. No. 1 Squadron advanced to the right and then to the front, and
dashed at the foe. My squadron was next and I led it straight forward. No. 3
Squadron turned left and came on next. Brave Cornet Astafev of my squadron,
spurred ahead of us and charged into the enemy. This was a breach of discipline,*

but his bravery heartened our many recruits. I ordered my squadron to attack and even as I did so the men of Astafev's platoon flew forward ahead of us, following their commander.

Lieutenant Koribut Kubitovich

The uhlan lancers were ordered to attack the enemy cavalry as they returned up the valley, so that these men who had been made drunk by their generals to give them the courage for what they must do, were nevertheless trapped between our lances and our sabres. Even the enemy's supporting force, seeing how things must end, had turned back from the attempt to save their comrades. The battle was thus concluded to our satisfaction. The pure truth runs with the ink from my pen.

General I. Ryzhov

The 'pure truth'? Not exactly. The survivors of the Light Brigade were undoubtedly trapped and that should have been the end of them. It was not:

Everyone thought that there was only one way out of the valley for the English – they had no choice now but to surrender. We watched for them to lay down their sabres and lances. But that is not what happened. The English chose to do what we had not considered because no one imagined it possible – they chose to charge our cavalry once again, this time heading back along the same ground. These mad cavalrymen were intent on doing what no one thought could be done.

Lieutenant Stefan Kozhukhov

The first of the survivors to realize that the Russian cavalry had sprung a trap were the men of the 13th Light Dragoons, 17th Lancers and 8th Hussars who had come together under Colonels Mayow and Shewell, now at a standstill facing the enemy. A man of the 11th Hussars, who had become separated from his regiment and joined them, heard the alarm called:

We numbered only some seventy well-mounted men. It was now discovered that some squadrons of Russian lancers had ranged themselves across the valley to our rear, thus interposed between us and the British lines. 'Cut off' was the excited cry.

Private William Pennington, 11th Hussars

Colonel Shewell, according to the official version of what occurred next – which drew on his account – immediately saw that the only chance of escape was to break through the uhlans and ordered his men to wheel round and charge them. Lieutenant Seager may however have had something to do with the decision:

They afterwards gave us great credit for wheeling about and attacking the lancers. The Colonel gets the credit for it but Lieutenant Phillips, who was riding next to me, could tell you who it was that called to the Colonel to let us wheel about and attack them.

Lieutenant Edward Seager, 8th Hussars

Whether Shewell gave the order first or only after Seager's suggestion, he was clearly flustered and required Seager's help to order the manoeuvre:

Colonel Shewell shouted, 'Threes about!' His able subordinate Seager interposed, 'Excuse me, sir; 'tis right about wheel.' The Colonel then cried, '8th right about wheel!' The 8th responded as if on home parade, and thus we faced the strong squadrons to our rear.

Private William Pennington, 11th Hussars

We dashed at them. They were three deep with lances levelled. I parried the first fellow's lance, the one behind him I cut over the head which no doubt he will remember for some time, and as I was recovering my sword I found the third fellow making a tremendous point at my body. I just had time to receive his lance point with the hilt of my sword; it got through the bars, knocked off the skin of the top knuckle of my second finger, and the point entered between the second and top joint of my little finger, coming out the other side.

After I found myself through the Russians, I saw the Colonel and the Major a long distance ahead going as fast as their horses would carry them, the batteries and rifles peppering them in grand style. On looking to see what had become of my men, I found they had got through and scattered to the left.

Lieutenant Edward Seager, 8th Hussars

We were obliged to pass through a strong body of the enemy's cavalry. Of course with our handful, it was life or death; so we rushed at them to break through them. With five or six fellows at my rear, I galloped on, passing with the determination of one who would not lose his life, breaking the lances of the cowards who attacked us in the proportion of three or four to one, occasionally catching one a slap with the sword across his teeth, and giving another the point on his arm or breast.

Private William Pennington, 11th Hussars

As this action was taking place on the right of the valley, far to the left the second group of survivors – Colonel Douglas's 11th Hussars and Lord Paget's 4th Light Dragoons, withdrawing side by side and followed by the enemy – also discovered that fresh units of the Russian cavalry had come between them and the British lines. This took a moment to dawn on Colonel Douglas, who at first thought that the line of uhlans across their front was the 17th Lancers:

I saw two squadrons of Lancers drawn up. I instantly proclaimed, 'They're the 17th. Let us rally on them.' At this moment Lieutenant Roger Palmer rode up and said, 'I beg your pardon, Colonel, that is not the 17th, that is the enemy.' 'Well,' I exclaimed, 'we must only retire and go through them.' So with the 4th Light Dragoons we charged the Russian Lancers.

Lieutenant Colonel John Douglas, 11th Hussars

Colonel Douglas, seeing that there was no time to lose, and expecting every moment that we should be charged by this body of Cavalry in our front, called out, 'Give them another charge men, Hurrah.' Waving our swords over our heads, on we galloped, expecting the next minute to be amongst them.

Troop Sergeant Major George Smith, 11th Hussars

Lord George Paget, leading the 4th Light Dragoons, had seen the lancers too. He had no doubt they were the enemy and shouted out, 'We must do the best we can for ourselves.' Captain Low was not so certain and said, 'I say, Colonel, are you sure those are not the 17th?' Paget pointed out their yellow and white lance pennons and ordered the charge. Even as the light dragoons and hussars spurred their horses forward they saw the Russian lancers swing back to form a line at right angles to the route they must take to break free:

Helter-skelter then we went at these Lancers as fast as our poor tired horses could carry us. As we approached them I remarked the regular manner in which they executed the movement of throwing their right half back, thus seemingly taking up a position that would enable them to charge down obliquely upon our right flank, as we passed them. Well, as we neared them, down they came upon us at a sort of trot (their advance not being more than twenty or thirty yards).

Lord George Paget, 4th Light Dragoons

Paget and his men rushed on, though all expected the uhlans to take them in the flank and knew they had no defence against the long reach of the lances. Yet for no discernible reason the Russians advanced slowly to within a few yards of them and halted:

Strange as it may sound, they did nothing, and actually allowed us to shuffle, to edge away, by them, at a distance of hardly a horse's length. I can only say that if the point of my sword crossed the ends of three or four of their lances, it was as much as it did, and I judge of the rest by my own case, for there was not a man, at that moment, more disadvantageously placed than myself (being behind and on the right rear). Well, we got by them without, I believe, the loss of a single man. How, I know not! It is a mystery to me! Had that force been composed of English ladies, I don't think one of us could have escaped!

Lord George Paget, 4th Light Dragoons

Paget thought himself the most disadvantaged of the group, but that position was held by Sergeant William Bentley of the 11th Hussars. Wounded by an enemy lancer he had fallen behind the rest and the Russians in pursuit were closing on him. Lieutenant Alexander Dunn saw his predicament and turned back to help.

Dunn carried one of the new revolving pistols and emptied the gun into the pack threatening Bentley – no one recording whether these shots hit or missed – and then attacked them with his sabre:

I noticed the gallant bearing of Lieutenant Dunn; he was a fine young fellow, 6 feet 3 inches, and mounted on a powerful horse, and wielding a terrific sword, many inches longer than the regulation; he saved the life of Sergeant Bentley, when surrounded by Russians, by cutting them down right and left.

> *Troop Sergeant Major George Smith, 11th Hussars*

I was attacked by an officer and several men, and received a wound from a lance. I was pursued by them, and cut the officer across the face. Lieutenant Dunn came to my assistance. I saw him cleave one almost to the saddle.

> *Sergeant William Bentley, 11th Hussars*

Victoria Cross citation
Lieutenant Alexander Dunn, 11th Hussars

For having saved the life of Sergeant Bentley, 11th Hussars, by cutting down two or three Russian lancers who were attacking him from the rear, and afterwards cutting down a Russian hussar, who was attacking Private Levett, 11th Hussars.

The Russian view. General Ryzhov reported that the Russian trap had been 'a brilliant success'. Most of his officers and men knew that it had failed miserably:

These mad British cavalrymen raced along the valley floor littered with their dead and wounded from the advance, and now more of them were felled at every step, yet with a kind of desperate heroism they forced a path through our cavalry and rushed away, and not a single man surrendered.

General Ryzhov called the Uhlan attack 'brilliant'. Those of us who watched the lancers noticed no brilliance at all. We did not even see a real attack. If General

Ryzhov is correct, how do we explain the fact an exhausted enemy raced through our fresh cavalry and escaped us?

Lieutenant Stefan Kozhukhov

The two groups of survivors had broken through, one on the right of the valley and the other on the left. The Russians now turned their attention to the few mounted men left on the gun line, thinking they would be easy to pick off one by one.

One man of the 17th Lancers left among the guns still expected support to come up, and when he looked back towards the British end of the valley, that is what he thought he saw:

I turned my horse and saw a line of Lancers marching down the valley and instantly thought they were the French Lancers, as they carried flags on their lances. I rode to them, and when within 30 yards they fired at me. I then saw their long grey cloaks and knew they were Russians, formed in close line across the valley, cutting off our retreat. I turned back to my scattered comrades, who were riding about like myself in all directions, not seeing which way to go. I raised my sword and shouted to them to fall in. They galloped to me from all directions.

Corporal Thomas Morley, 17th Lancers

Some of the men had become detached from their regiments as these moved through the battery on the advance, while others had become separated during the retreat. Morley believed that their only chance was to band together and kept on yelling until all within earshot rode to him:

We heard the familiar voice of Corporal Morley, of our regiment, a great, rough, bellowing Nottingham man. He had lost his lance hat, and his long hair was flying out in the wind as he roared, 'Coom 'ere! Coom 'ere! Fall in lads, fall in!' Well, with shouts and oaths he had collected some twenty troopers of various regiments. We fell in with the handful this man of the hour had rallied, and there joined us also under his leadership Private [Corporal] John Penn of the 17th, who had killed a

Russian officer, dismounted, and with great deliberation accoutred himself with the belt and sword of the defunct, in which he made a great show.

Private James Wightman, 17th Lancers

I hastily formed them in lines, putting those with lances in front. I believe there were eight of the 17th Lancers in the front rank, with members of other regiments forming a second line. The Russian Lancers were not more than 40 yards from us when I ordered them to cheer and charge. The Brigade of Russian Hussars were marching up the valley about 50 yards behind and there were Cossacks on each flank. The Russians must have thought we were assembling to surrender, and when we yelled and charged into the centre of their line, they seemed to be paralysed.

The point of a lance through my sword hilt tore the flesh off my middle finger, and this trifling wound was the only injury I received in that immortal fight. Three of the men in my group fell in the charge but I seemed to have more when I got through the line, other stragglers having rushed through the opening we made or rode round the flanks. We galloped off on our way back, pursued by some of the Cossacks, firing at us.

Corporal Thomas Morley, 17th Lancers

So it was that the final group of survivors broke through the Russian cavalry, but their ordeal was far from over. All three groups were one mile from safety; many of the men and horses were exhausted, wounded or both; there were Cossacks at their backs; and the enemy artillery on the Causeway Heights was waiting to have a second go at them as they crossed the muzzles on their way back. Many were yet to fall.

9. The Return

The survivors fight their way back

Those watching from the Sapoune Heights who had seen the Light Brigade disappear regiment by regiment into the smoke at first failed to recognize as its remnants the men who reappeared one by one on their way back:

What can those skirmishers be doing? Good God! It is the Light Brigade!
Fanny Duberly

Officers waiting in front of the Heavy Brigade formed up at the British end of the valley could just distinguish the men returning over the bodies of their comrades:

It was a terrible sight to see them walking back one by one and the valley strewn with them.

Lieutenant Richard Godman, 5th Dragoon Guards

The first to reappear from the smoke were those men on foot who had been dismounted before or at the guns. Unable to take part in the pursuit of the Russian cavalry because they were wounded or could not catch a riderless horse, they began making their way back as their regiments advanced further down the valley. The sight of this scattering of men walking or hobbling towards the British lines convinced the observers that their worst fears were proven – the Light Brigade had been annihilated.

The cavalrymen had a long walk ahead of them. The return was slightly uphill, a gradient they had hardly noticed as they dashed down on horseback but which told now. Many were nursing injuries or helping wounded comrades. They would eventually be overtaken on their journey back by returning mounted men so that while those on foot were first to reappear from the smoke, those still on horseback were first to reach the safety of the British lines.

Private Mitchell rode in the first line of the advance and reached the muzzles of the guns, where his horse fell at the final volley. Pinned by one leg beneath his dead mount, he still lay there when the second line charged in and was lucky not to be trampled. Once all of the Light Brigade regiments had entered the smoke that lay over the battery, Russian sharpshooters on the slopes of the Causeway Heights began picking off the wounded and dismounted men left behind:

After the second line had passed I tried to extricate my leg, which after a short time I succeeded in doing and stood upright, finding myself unhurt, except my leg, which was a little painful from the crush. I still had my sword in my hand, and soon found there were numberless bullets flying around me, which came from the infantry on the flank of their battery, who fired at any of us who were dismounted. Just at this moment a man of my troop named Pollard came to me, and throwing himself down beside the carcass of my horse for shelter from the bullets, called to me saying: 'Come here, Mitchell, this is good cover.' I said: 'We had better make our way back as quick as possible, or we shall soon be taken prisoners, if not killed, if we remain here.' Upon this he jumped up, and we both started to get back.

Private Albert Mitchell, 13th Light Dragoons

Cossack cavalrymen rode down to assist the Russian gunners in the mêlée and when survivors on foot stumbled from the smoke to head back up the valley some of the Cossacks followed them. These horsemen roamed the area forward of the guns, cutting down any dismounted men they found there, although they appeared easily intimidated:

I fought my way from among the guns, and then set out to return on foot. It was all over ploughed fields, and the Russians kept on firing at us all the time. A couple of Cossacks intercepted me on the way and I settled both with my carbine. You only had to point a gun at them, and whether it was loaded or not, they would run.

Private John Richardson, 11th Hussars

There is some evidence that the Cossacks moving about ahead of the guns were more intent on looting than engaging any man who had the energy to fight back. Cornet Denzil Chamberlayne of the 13th Light Dragoons sat by the mutilated body of his horse, stunned and uncertain what to do. Lieutenant Percy Smith told him to remove the saddle and carry it back to the British lines – peculiar advice for a dazed man with more than a mile to travel, but it probably saved his life. Chamberlayne walked back with the saddle across his shoulders and none of the Cossacks paid him any attention. It is assumed that in the confusion they took him to be one of their own, looting a British saddle. Later that day the Cossacks opened a 'market' to sell saddles, sabres and helmets taken from the valley to Russian infantrymen who had not had the opportunity to loot for themselves.

A few Cossacks were seeking lone, unhorsed men with a more sinister motive. Cornet George Clowes of the 8th Hussars was on the ground, wounded and bleeding badly, when he noticed several Russians riding nearby. He thought it a good idea to pretend to be dead until they moved on, but then saw them jabbing their lances into every dismounted man, dead or wounded, and realized he must run for his life. Those unable to get to their feet had no chance. Captain Thomas Goad of the 13th Light Dragoons was last seen sitting on the ground, wounded and holding his revolver in his right hand, clearly determined to fight to the end. The circumstances of his death are unknown.

Dead and wounded lancers, light dragoons and hussars lay scattered about the valley floor. The wounded called out for water or moaned quietly in a private agony. Many of the uninjured men walking back stopped to help those who had been hit, knowing that any left behind were unlikely to survive. Some were beyond saving. Mitchell and Pollard stopped to comfort a man lying on his back. From the gurgling noises in his throat he appeared to be choking on his own blood:

I could see death in his countenance, but turned him over and placed his arm under his forehead, thinking he would be better able to relieve himself of the blood than by lying on his back.

Private Albert Mitchell, 13th Light Dragoons

They had not gone many yards further when a man trapped beneath his fallen horse shouted out for help:

I took him beneath the arms, and Pollard raised the horse's forepart a little, so that I managed to draw his leg from under the horse; but his thigh was broken, and besides, he had a severe wound on his head which covered him with blood. On seeing his injuries we laid him gently down. He said: 'You can do no more for me. Look out for yourselves!' The smoke had cleared away, so that we could see a number of men making their way back the same as ourselves. The number of horses lying about was something fearful.

Private Albert Mitchell, 13th Light Dragoons

Many riderless mounts galloped about, wounded or mad with fear, and these offered a rapid escape. Private Robert Farquharson of the 4th Light Dragoons caught a horse of the 17th Lancers. This too was hit, and while Farquharson was down a passing Russian stabbed a lance at him, which went through his trousers without as much as grazing the flesh. He next caught a Cossack pony and raced up the valley. A second Russian gave chase and swung a sword at him; Farquharson parried the blow and slashed back, cutting open the man's right cheek and making him yell.

Another survivor on foot fought off the Cossacks only to be run down by crazed horses:

I was attacked by Russian cavalry through whom I cut my way, my more than ordinary height combined with a powerful frame proving most advantageous to me. I had no sooner got clear than I was knocked down and ridden over by riderless horses.

Corporal James Nunnerley, 17th Lancers

While it was no easy matter for men on foot to catch horses gripped by sheer fright, occasionally it was the horses that sought out the men, although these were often the most badly wounded:

Three riderless horses were wandering up the valley a little distance from each other. The first, seeing me and knowing the uniform, halted close to me. On looking round him, I found he was badly wounded, the blood flowing in several places, so I gave him a pat and said, 'Go on, poor fellow.' The second then came up, he too was wounded, so I said, 'Go on.' When the third came, I found on looking round him that he was not wounded. I mounted and rode on.

Troop Sergeant Major George Smith, 11th Hussars

Private Mitchell had no such luck. No horse came to him and he could not stop one of those racing about:

There were several riderless horses galloping about the plain. I tried very hard to get one, but could not. I saw two officers' horses belonging to my own regiment. I could tell them by the binding of the sheepskins on the saddles. They appeared almost mad. I would have given a trifle just then to have had my legs across one of them, for I was getting tired, and had nothing to eat since the day before, and to make it still worse there was a piece of ground that lay in my way which had been cultivated, which made it heavy travelling.

I could now see some Cossacks showing themselves in swarms on our right, thinking to cut some of us dismounted men off. As soon as I saw them approaching, I bore more away to my left front.

Private Albert Mitchell, 13th Light Dragoons

To avoid the Cossacks some men moved close in beneath the heights and came within range of the infantry. The dead lying about marked the enemy's reach and one exhausted man, discovering that he had walked within range, had an idea:

I now lost my breath and began to give up all hopes of escaping when the thought occurred to me that, by throwing myself down and pretending to be dead, I might recover myself. Then again, I thought, some of the Russian infantry on my left might come and, on finding me alive, bayonet me, so I decided to keep on the move.

Troop Sergeant Major George Smith, 11th Hussars

It was essential to keep moving. Private Mitchell came across a wounded man standing still and turning as if uncertain which direction to walk in:

As I came along he heard me, and calling out, said: 'Is that an Englishman?' I answered: 'Yes,' and on going to him found he had been wounded by a piece of shell just between the eyes, which had blinded him. He had bled very much, and was still bleeding. I had a handkerchief in my breast, which I bound round his wound, and taking him by the arm, led him along.

Private Albert Mitchell, 13th Light Dragoons

While the Cossacks and infantry sharpshooters continued to harry dismounted men, behind them the uhlan lancers were moving down from the Causeway and Fedioukine Heights to cut off those still on horseback returning from the pursuit.

When those watching with Lord Raglan saw the Russian cavalry trot down into the valley and form a line to cut off any survivors who had not yet reappeared from the thinning smoke about the gun line, they thought the Light Brigade lost. Then quite unexpectedly two formed groups of mounted men burst through the enemy blockade. A Frenchman described the moment:

A cloud of dust, from which came a chorus of British 'hurrahs', advanced towards us; it was the unfortunate cavalry who were returning mutilated and decimated. The Russian artillery on the heights opened fire on this noble debris.

Vicomte de Noé

Those returning on foot had moved some way up the valley but were quickly overtaken by the mounted men. All were still far from the British lines, and the guns on the Causeway Heights that had fired on them during the advance now reopened fire as they returned:

A ride of a mile or more was before us, every step of which was to bring us more under the fire from the heights. And what a scene of havoc was this last mile strewn with the dead and dying, and all friends, some running, some limping, some crawling! Horses in every position of agony, struggling to get up, then floundering again on their mutilated riders!

Lord George Paget, 4th Light Dragoons

At first the mounted men were clustered together in the two groups that charged through the uhlan lancers and offered easy targets for the artillery. Seeing this, some men broke away to avoid the bursting shells overhead, thinking they might fare better on their own, but then attracted the attention of Cossacks:

Riding back I was attacked by two Cossacks. I engaged the one on my right, and dispatched him at the time the other made a cut at me which just caught my nose, chin and bridle hand. But he never cut another, for I left him on the ground. Going a little further my horse was shot beneath me and I lay weltering in blood and swooned.

Private William Butler, 17th Lancers

I thought I heard a rattle behind, and I was only just in time, on looking behind a Muscovite had his sword up just in my range and in the act of cutting down. I showed him the point of my sword instantly close to his throat, and he pulled his horse backwards.

Captain Edwin Cook, 11th Hussars

I had only got a few yards when I saw two Russian lancers coming towards me with clenched teeth and staring like savages. The first one made a thrust at me with his lance. It is a heavy weapon and easily struck down, which I did with my sword, thrusting it at the same time through the fellow's neck. He fell from his horse with a groan. The other fellow wheeled round his dying comrade and made a thrust at me. I had not the strength to strike down the blow for my sword fell from my grasp, but one of our lancers came to my assistance, thrusting his lance through the fellow's body.

Private Edward Firkins, 13th Light Dragoons

I bore well to the left, quite losing touch with the 8th. Thus separated from all aid, Russian lancers pursued me up the valley; but I kept them on my right and rear, my sword arm free to sweep around. With many a feint at cut and thrust (for I feared to check the gallant grey) I kept them at arm's length, foiled their attempts to get upon my left, where they might strike across my bridle-hand, and the grey mare gradually drew ahead. Balls from the causeway ridge raised up the dust around my mare's hoofs, but happily their force was spent.

Private William Pennington, 11th Hussars

Pennington's 'gallant grey' saved him. But most of the horses had carried their riders through the advance and charge, the pursuit of the Russian cavalry to the Chernaya and the charge to break through the uhlans, and were virtually blown. Many were also wounded:

My wounded horse at every step got more jaded, and I therefore saw those in my front gradually increasing the distance between us, and I made more use of my sword in this return ride than I had done in the whole affair.

Lord George Paget, 4th Light Dragoons

Russian infantrymen firing from the Causeway Heights aimed at the horses, which offered much larger targets than the men crouched in their saddles. As Captain Thomas Hutton of the 4th

Light Dragoons raced back he was hit once in the thigh, while his horse was hit eleven times. Any rider who came close to the heights was likely to have his horse brought down and to be killed or taken prisoner, though some escaped on foot:

I cleared myself of the saddle and my poor dying horse and succeeded – through a field of blood, and scrambling over dead and dying men and horses – in getting out of gunshot.

Private Edward Firkins, 13th Light Dragoons

A little after the first two groups broke through the line of uhlan lancers, a third appeared. Corporal Morley's small band made a frantic dash and most of the men got through, but they then unwittingly veered towards the side of the valley and up onto the lower slopes of the Causeway Heights:

We came to a square of infantry on rising ground with muskets and fixed bayonets pointing at us. They yelled something in Russian, I suppose calling us to surrender. When they saw that we were not going to surrender, they fired a volley point blank at us and at the shortest range. This was fearfully destructive, and only a few of my little squad were left. Wightman and Marshall together with others of the 17th were captured here, one with 13 wounds and the other with 9.

Corporal Thomas Morley, 17th Lancers

My horse was shot dead, riddled with bullets. One bullet struck me on the forehead, another passed through the top of my shoulder. While struggling out from under my dead horse a Cossack standing over me stabbed me with his lance once in the neck near the jugular, again above the collar bone, several times in the back, and once under the short rib; and when, having regained my feet, I was trying to draw my sword, he sent his lance through the palm of my hand. I believe he would have succeeded in killing me, clumsy as he was, if I had not blinded him for the moment with a handful of sand.

Private James Wightman, 17th Lancers

The Russian view. The survivors of the Light Brigade were pursued up the valley by hussars and Cossacks, and many British cavalrymen were cut down. Some of the Russians were killed by their own artillery firing indiscriminately from the Causeway Heights:

There was much frantic slashing, and it was then that our artillery and infantry reopened fire. The truth must be told, that this fire hit us just as it did the enemy, with as many men killed and wounded, and even more of our horses killed. The English fought with astounding bravery, and when we approached their dismounted and wounded men, even these refused to surrender and continued to fight till the ground was soaked with their blood.

Lieutenant Koribut Kubitovich

Wightman and several others in Morley's group were taken prisoner and marched away with the butts of Cossack lances prodding them from behind. Most were wounded and Wightman found himself beside Private Thomas Fletcher of the 4th Light Dragoons:

With my shattered knee and the other bullet wound on the shin of the same leg, I could barely limp, and good old Fletcher said, 'Get on my back, chum!' I did so, and then found that he had been shot through the back of the head. When I told him of this, his only answer was, 'Oh, never mind that, it's not much, I don't think.' But it was that much that he died of the wound a few days later; and here he was, a doomed man himself, making light of a mortal wound, and carrying a chance comrade of another regiment on his back. I can write this, but I could not tell of it in speech, because I know I should play the woman.

Private James Wightman, 17th Lancers

These men were marched back to the area of the gun line, where they joined the officers and men captured earlier during the mêlée. Not all of those taken prisoner were still there. The Russians had been thrown into confusion when the formed groups rushed back through the battery and among the captives who took this opportunity to escape was Cornet George Wombwell:

I saw the 11th and 4th Light Dragoons coming back from the Charge, and set off as hard as I could, luckily caught a loose horse, jumped on his back, and looking round to see what my friends who had charge of me were about, and there they were in a great state but did not dare follow me (as if they had done so they would have run up against our troops) and then rode off as hard as I could. Thank God I escaped without a wound, only a little bruise on the arm.

Cornet George Wombwell, 17th Lancers

Captain William Morris had escaped too. With blood still flowing from a severe scalp wound he ran after a riderless horse, caught hold of the saddle and was dragged along for some distance, then lost his grip and fell while the horse galloped away. A mounted Cossack gave chase and closed on him. Morris had given up his sabre and was unarmed. At that moment another horse came by. He managed to pull himself into the saddle and race away. He outpaced the Cossack, but just when he thought that he was safe, his horse was hit and fell, and he found himself on the ground with one leg trapped beneath it. After some time and effort he freed his leg and set off up the valley on foot. Troop Sergeant Major Smith caught sight of him and reported that 'his face was covered in blood and he had a very wild appearance'. Soon after, Morris fell to the ground exhausted. He had lost a great deal of blood and expected the end.

Sergeant John Berryman of the 17th Lancers became stranded when his horse came to a halt and refused to move. He dismounted and discovered that one of the mare's hind legs was broken:

I debated in my mind whether to shoot her or not, when Captain Webb came up to me, and asked me, was I wounded? I replied, 'Only slightly, in the leg, but my horse was done.' I then asked, 'Are you hurt, sir?' He said that he was, and in the leg too; what had he better do? 'Keep to your horse, sir, and get back as far as you can.' He turned and rode back. I now caught a loose horse, and got onto his back, but he fell directly, the brass of the breastplate having been driven into his chest.

Sergeant John Berryman, 17th Lancers

Captain Augustus Webb, also of the lancers, took the sergeant's advice and headed back up the valley, but after only a short distance he pulled his charger to a stop. A fragment of shell had shattered his lower leg and the pain of the wound, intensified by every jolt, was too much to bear. He sat still in the saddle, an easy target for the Cossacks roaming the valley and the riflemen on the heights.

As Berryman picked himself up after losing his second horse, he noticed that Captain Webb had come to a halt. He went to him and finding Webb unable to dismount by his own efforts helped him from the saddle. Seeing Sergeant John Farrell of the 17th nearby, Berryman called out to him for assistance. Farrell's horse had been shot and he was heading back on foot. Corporal Malone of the 13th Light Dragoons heard the call and came to help too.

Berryman and Farrell then set off up the valley, carrying Webb and accompanied by Malone – whose sword hand was free to deter the Cossacks. Artillery on the Causeway Heights may have targeted these four men, for a roundshot took off Farrell's chapska, but without harming him. Seeing they were making slow progress and putting their own lives at risk, Webb told them to leave him and save themselves, but they refused to do so.

At some point on this perilous journey, the escaping Cornet Wombwell spotted them. He knew Webb by his nickname, 'Peck', and while the roundshot flew and the Cossacks prowled about them, this very English exchange took place:

WOMBWELL: What's the matter, Peck?
WEBB: Hit in the leg, old fellow.

Victoria Cross citation
Sergeant John Berryman, 17th Lancers

His horse being shot under him, he stopped on the field with a wounded officer, Captain Webb, amidst a shower of shot and shell, although repeatedly told by that officer to consult his own safety and leave him, but he refused to do so, and on Sergeant John Farrell coming by, with his assistance carried Captain Webb out of range of the guns.

Victoria Cross citation
Sergeant John Farrell, 17th Lancers

For having remained amidst a shower of shot and shell with Captain Webb, who was severely wounded and whom he and Sergeant Berryman had carried as far as the pain of his wounds would allow, until a stretcher was procured, when he assisted Berryman to carry that officer off the field.

Victoria Cross citation
Corporal Joseph Malone, 13th Light Dragoons

For having stopped under a very heavy fire to take charge of Captain Webb, 17th Lancers, until others arrived to assist him in removing that officer, who was mortally wounded. Malone performed this act of bravery while returning on foot from the charge, in which his horse had been shot.

By this time the first of the mounted men had reached the safety of the British lines and one of them called out to Captain Ewart, aide-de-camp to Lord Raglan, that a badly wounded staff officer was lying some distance back. Ewart had been sent down with a message from Raglan to Sir George Cathcart, who had belatedly arrived with his infantry division. Ewart received Cathcart's permission to go in search of this officer.

Riding down the valley at a gallop he soon came across the body of Captain Nolan. Further on – it is unclear whether this was a few yards or some considerable distance – he found Captain Morris. Ewart recognized him easily because he and Morris had worked together as staff officers at Raglan's headquarters before Morris took command of the 17th Lancers.

Ewart spoke to Morris and found him 'almost insensible' and covered in the blood still running freely from a terrible head wound. He found it impossible to lift the wounded man by himself, and on the way back to get help he shouted to a mounted man of the 17th, Private George Smith, to send stretcher bearers out to recover the regiment's commanding officer.

The staff surgeon was sent with Sergeant Wooden to bring Morris in. They found a trooper trying to arrest the bleeding from the scalp. Presently some Cossacks attacked the party and the doctor, Mouat, said he had to draw his sword, which he described as 'a novel experience'.

Assistant Surgeon William Cattell, attached 5th Dragoon Guards

Surgeon James Mouat roughly bandaged Morris's head. They then wrapped him in a cavalry cloak and carried him, Sergeant Charles Wooden taking his shoulders and Mouat his feet, with Private George Mansell of the 17th standing by to fend off the Cossacks. The fact that two men were able to carry Morris back to the British lines in this fashion suggests that they cannot have had too far to travel, and lends credence to the supposition that he fell not far from Captain Nolan's body. Nolan's letter to his mother was found on Morris; the letter written by Morris to his wife was discovered in Nolan's sabretache. So serious were Morris's wounds that both letters were forwarded to England and for a time Amelia Morris believed that her husband had been killed when in fact he survived.

Lord Lucan's interpreter Sir John Blunt saw Morris being carried in by Mouat and Wooden. Morris was semi-conscious and Blunt heard him cry out, 'Lord have mercy on my soul.'

Victoria Cross citation
Surgeon James Mouat

He went to the assistance of Captain Morris of the 17th Lancers, who was lying seriously wounded in an exposed position, and dressed this officer's wounds under heavy fire from the enemy, and by stopping a severe haemorrhage, helped to save his life.

_____

Victoria Cross citation
Sergeant Charles Wooden, 17th Lancers

For being instrumental, together with Doctor James Mouat, in saving the life of Captain Morris of the 17th Lancers, by proceeding under a heavy fire to his assistance when he was lying very dangerously wounded in an exposed position.

_____

While Morris was safely returned to the British lines, a party of men went out to Nolan, but not to recover his body. The first man to be killed was – with undue haste – the first to be buried. The official reason was that he had been killed closer to the British lines than any other officer and his was the only body easily found. There may have been another, less acceptable explanation. One anonymous account claims that when Lord Lucan heard men were going out to recover Nolan's corpse, he said, 'No, he met his deserts – a dog's death – and like a dog, let him be buried in a ditch.'

Captain Brandling of the Royal Horse Artillery supervised the burial on the lower slopes of the Causeway Heights. The precise spot was not recorded and the grave has never been located:

Brandling took with him Bombardier Ormes and four gunners with spades to bury Nolan's body. The bombardier, on his return, said that the poor fellow's chest had been quite broken away, and that the gold lace and cloth of his jacket very much burnt by the shell which killed him, and which must have burst close by. The body was laid in the earth as it was, there was no time to dig a deep grave, as occasional shots were being fired.

Lieutenant Fox Strangways, Royal Horse Artillery

All of the mounted survivors had by now reached the British lines. The Heavy Brigade regiments cheered as they came in. Some of the men were wounded. Most of the horses were wounded and almost all were blown:

With the continual application of the flat of my sabre against my horse's flank and the liberal use of both spurs, I at last got home, after having overtaken Hutton, who had been shot through both thighs, and who was exerting the little vigour left in him in urging on his wounded horse, as I was mine.

Well, there is an end to all things, and at last we got home, the shouts of welcome that greeted every fresh officer or group as they came struggling up the incline, telling us of our safety.

Lord George Paget, 4th Light Dragoons

I found that I could not dismount from the wound in my right leg, and so was lifted off, and then how I caressed the noble horse that brought me safely out.

Private William Pennington, 11th Hussars

I then said to Lord Cardigan, 'I am afraid there are no such regiments left as the 13th and 17th, for I can give no account of them,' but before I had finished the sentence, I caught sight of a cluster of them standing by their horses, on the brow of the hill, in my front.

Lord George Paget, 4th Light Dragoons

The survivors reformed on approximately the position from which the Light Brigade had set off and a first roll was called. The point of the roll was not to establish how many men had survived, but how many were still mounted and fit for duty, lest they be required for further action that day: ·

The whole affair, from the moment we moved off until we reformed on the ground from which we started, did not occupy more than 20 minutes. On the troops forming up, I had them counted by my Brigade-Major, and found that there were 195 mounted men out of about 670.

Lord Cardigan

Many men on foot, some badly wounded or supporting wounded comrades, were still less than halfway back. These arrived much later and in ones and twos. When the first of them was spotted, help was sent out. Private Mitchell was still leading the blinded man:

We met our commissary officer, Mr Cruickshank, mounted on a pony with saddle bags filled with bottles of rum. He was making his way to meet any of the men returning from the charge. He very kindly gave us a good drop each, which helped us along nicely. I could see a couple of ambulance wagons, and several surgeons hard at work dressing wounds. After seeing the poor fellow's wound dressed, and assisting him into the wagon, I bade him goodbye.

Private Albert Mitchell, 13th Light Dragoons

The injured were left with the surgeons. Uninjured but dismounted men were dismissed and sent back to camp, which was nearby:

Going to my tent, I found near it my comrade, the orderly-room clerk; he shook hands with me, saying, 'How glad I am you have escaped, George'. I told him I had lost my horse, and how fearfully the regiment had been cut up. He then said, 'What is this on your busby and jacket?' and on picking it off I found it to be small pieces of flesh that had flown over me when Private Young's arm had been shot off. I now sat down, and the feelings that came over me are not easy to describe, I was moved to tears when I thought of the havoc I had witnessed, and that I had lost my beautiful horse; she was a light bay, nearly thoroughbred, I became her master three years before. It was now about twelve noon, and I had eaten nothing since the day before, so my comrade made me some tea, which was very acceptable.

Troop Sergeant Major George Smith, 11th Hussars

I went down to our camp which was close by, and finding my own tent soon dived into the biscuit bag, and putting two or three handfuls into my haversack, began to make up for lost time, for I was hungry indeed, so, eating as I went, made my way over the ridge again to the ground from whence we had started, and joined the remnant of the brigade, who had by this time nearly all straggled back. I counted thirteen mounted men of my own regiment, but I think there was very little difference, each regiment's losses then appearing to be about equal. I don't mean to say that thirteen was all that came back, but that was all that were mounted and fit for duty.

Private Albert Mitchell, 13th Light Dragoons

Pistol fire could be heard as the farriers destroyed badly wounded horses, of which there were many. The two dogs – Jemmy, who ran the charge with the 8th Hussars, and Boxer, with the 11th – returned with the first mounted men of their regiments. Jemmy had a slight neck wound and Boxer was unscratched.

The men experienced a curious mixture of elation and anger. They felt that they had done everything asked of them and much more besides, yet so many of their comrades had been left behind in the valley. It would be later that severe questions were asked about why the charge was ordered; on the afternoon and evening of that day what the survivors of the Light Brigade most wanted to know was why the Heavy Brigade had not come up to support them at the guns:

And who, I ask, was answerable for all this? The same man who ordered Lord Cardigan to charge with 670 men an army in position, and then left them to their fate – it was not unlike leaving the forlorn hope, after storming a town, to fight their own way out again, instead of pushing on the supports. We cut their army completely in two, taking their principal battery, driving their cavalry far to the rear. What more could 670 men do?

Troop Sergeant Major George Smith, 11th Hussars

That night the men were ordered not to light campfires or make any noise. The Russians still occupied the Causeway Heights and might not be done. Most of the cavalrymen had not eaten for twenty-four hours. All were exhausted yet few could sleep. Many stood about the camp in small groups, talking over every incident. Others sat alone in silent contemplation. Some began their most difficult letter home:

I want to see no more fighting, it has pleased God to keep me safe through what I have seen, and I am now anxious to get home.

Cornet George Wombwell, 17th Lancers

While the men thought over the battle that had passed, the first shots in the battle to come were already being exchanged. William Russell reported that Lord Raglan was 'much moved with anger', that he had 'given it hot to Lord Lucan' and had 'given Lord Cardigan a tremendous wigging'. Cardigan said the blunder was all Lucan's fault; Lucan pointed an accusing finger at Raglan; Raglan blamed them both. The battle of the lords had begun.

For the moment the generals had to tell their political masters in St Petersburg and London what had been won or lost at Balaklava:

The English Cavalry under Lord Cardigan charged 3 Don Battery, sabring some of the gunners, and attacked the hussar brigade of 6 Cavalry Division, with unexpected recklessness. The enemy was taken in the flank by the Uhlan Regiment and the crossfire of riflemen and the artillery. Enemy losses are reckoned to be heavy.

Prince Menshikov

Lord Cardigan charged with the utmost vigour, attacked a battery which was firing on the advancing squadrons, and, having passed beyond it, engaged the Russian cavalry in its rear; but then his troops were assailed by artillery and infantry, as well as cavalry, and necessarily retired. The loss they have sustained has, I deeply lament, been very severe in officers, men and horses.

Lord Raglan

While Prince Menshikov and Lord Raglan penned their dispatches, Corporal James Nunnerley of the 17th Lancers returned to the tent he had shared with nine other men. He spent that night alone.

10. Experience and Observation

Death in the valley and glory on the heights

The charge was over and most of the survivors back at the British lines by 12.00 noon. It would be nightfall before any of them had the opportunity to note down their experiences in a diary entry or a rushed letter home, and some waited many years before they wrote a full account of their ride down hell's mile. But those who had observed the charge from the Sapoune Heights were already at work. Lord Raglan sat down to write an official dispatch to his political masters in London, choosing his words carefully, and William Russell was furiously scribbling out the first report for *The Times*.

The two types of account, one describing the experience of those in the valley and the second based on the observations of those on the heights, are very different in what they report and the words and phrases they use. Yet both are important if we want to know the truth about the charge and understand why it quickly achieved legendary status.

The most remarkable account by a survivor was dictated by an illiterate cavalryman, Private John Vahey of the 17th Lancers. He began the advance 'deucedly muzzy' and 'fully half-seas over' (half-drunk on rum), in the charge he 'went stark mad', on reaching the enemy battery he 'with one blow of my axe brained a Russian gunner', and he came out of the mêlée 'as sober as a bishop'. Many survivors wrote their accounts after thinking it over and with half a mind on the eventual reader; Vahey's words tumble out without a care, much as the tale might have done when told in an alehouse, with a laugh and a jibe at his own state before the graphic details and the heart-wrenching sob, and the vindication that came with the medal at the end. It is very much a soldier's tale, yet so much of it is confirmed by other survivors that there remains little room for elaboration.

While only those in the valley could capture the immediacy of the experience, only those on the heights could see the 'big picture', and they claimed to have seen something that the survivors missed – the glory and the magnificence. A Frenchman, General Bosquet, famously said: '*C'est magnifique, mais ce n'est pas la guerre!*'

Bosquet is remembered now but was unknown at the time. It was William Russell who, in his first report of the charge, written in almost biblical English and intended to impress, did most to create the legend. His description caused a sensation among readers at home. While revealing to a shocked nation that the action was a blunder and the losses severe, he suggested that despite this – and perhaps because of it – the charge was in some way special. The urgency of Russell's report – it was written on the afternoon of the charge – carried with it some inaccuracies. His first estimates of the number of men who charged in each regiment added up to '607 sabres'. Tennyson, reading this, penned the most famous description of the charge: 'Into the valley of Death / Rode the six hundred.' He was upset when later reports revealed the true number to be nearer 700, but by then the poem was in print.

Neither Vahey nor Russell could tell the full truth: the soldier was too close to the action; the correspondent was too far away. Both the experience of survivors in the valley and the observation of those on the heights are part of the truth about the charge of the Light Brigade. The two accounts reproduced here, read one after the other, are as close as we can get to the experience and the observation, and it is perhaps only when in our minds we hold them side by side that we can approach the full truth.

Private John Vahey of the 17th Lancers enlisted in 1838, and as one of the older and more experienced men in the Crimea it was surprising that he was still a private – except to those who knew him. Vahey was a heavy drinker. He earned extra money by always volunteering to act as the regimental butcher, and so gained the nickname 'Butcher Jack'. In regimental records his surname is variously recorded as Vahey, Fahey and Veigh; he could neither write not tell another how his name should be spelt, so those recording it made their own guesses.

The night before the charge he had been discovered drunk, still in his butcher's overalls, and put under guard in the prison tent. He awoke on the morning of 25 October still the worse for the rum and still imprisoned. None of that would stop him taking part in the charge of the Light Brigade.

Vahey 'spoke' his account of the charge for publication in a Victorian magazine, *Soldiering and Scribbling*. Much of the prose is not that of the spoken word and must have been reworked by the correspondent, yet here more than in any other account the expressions and raw experience of the uncouth cavalryman break forcefully through the text.

It was in the autumn of 1854 that the English and French armies were lying lovingly enough together in front of Sevastopol, that nut which it took them such a time to crack. Our cavalry had a camp of their own upon the hill-side near Kadikoi, and the old 'Death's head and Cross-bones', to which I belonged, were there amongst the rest, forming part of the Light Brigade. We had a separate commissary of our own, and handy men were told off from the various corps to act as butchers. I never was backward when there was any work to do and, when some fellows were moping helplessly in the tents, or going sick to hospital every morning, I was knocking about as jolly as a sandboy, doing a job here and one there, and always contriving to get more or less tipsy before nightfall. If you ever drop across any of the old Crimean Light Brigade, just you ask them if they remember 'Butcher Jack' of the Lancers, and see what the answer will be. I was as well known in the Brigade as old Cardigan himself, and in my rough-and-tumble way got to be quite a popular character. Indeed, had it not been for my inordinate fondness for the drink, I might have got promotion over and over again. But I used to find my way shoulder-high into the guard-tent pretty regularly once a week, and more than once I only saved the skin of my back by being known as a willing, useful fellow when sober.

One slaughtering day at the Commissary we had killed, flayed and cut up our number of beasts, and there was a lot of rum knocking about, for the Commissary Guard knew how to get at the grog, and were free enough with it among the butchers, for the sake of a nice tender steak. Paddy Heffernan, of the Royals, and I, managed to get as drunk as lords before we found time for a wash, and one of the Commissary officers came across us while in this state, and clapped us in the guard-tent before you could say 'knife'. One place was as good as another to us, so we lay there contented enough all night, taking an occasional tot out of a bottle which Paddy managed to smuggle into the tent where we were confined. It was getting on for morning before we dropped off into a heavy, drunken sleep, out of which the Commander-in-Chief himself would have had a tough job to have roused us. We must have had a long snooze, for it was broad daylight before we were wakened by the loud thundering of a tremendous cannonade close by, making the very tent-poles quiver again.

I still felt deucedly muzzy, for Commissary rum, as you would know if you ever got tight on it, is hard stuff to get sober off, yet I managed to pull myself together enough to know where I was, and could give a shrewd guess what all the row was. I sat up, with the intention of hearing more about it from some of the guard, but to my surprise there was not a soul in the tent but Paddy and myself, and there was not even a sentry upon the door. So we both got up on end and had a stretch, and then walked coolly out of the guard-tent, only to find the camp utterly deserted, not a man being apparently left in it.

Turning into our own tent, we sat down, and over a refresher out of the inexhaustible rum bottle, we tried, in a boozy sort of way, to argue out the position. From where the camp was we could not see what was going on down in the valley by reason of a low ridge which intercepted the view; but we could tell it must be pretty warm work, from the hot and continuous firing which was being kept up. At last I says to Paddy, 'Why the devil should we be out of the fun? Let's go up to the sick horse lines, and see if there be anything left there to put one leg in front of another.' 'Agreed,' cries he, heartily enough; so I got hold of a butcher's axe for a weapon, and he a sword, and, half-drunk as we were, and just in the condition we had left off killing the night before, we started off for the sick horses. But it was no go for a moment here, for there were but two brutes left, and one of them had a leg like a pillar letter-box, while the other was down on his side, and did not look much like rising again. Determined not to be beaten, we started off on foot, and making our way round by the rear of the staff, who were on the edge of the little ridge, we dodged down into the valley just in the rear of the position of the heavy cavalry.

It was Balaklava morning, and the heavies had already charged the Russian cavalry, and emptied a good many saddles. Russian horses were galloping about riderless, and Paddy and myself parted company to give chase to a couple of these. With some trouble I captured my one, a tidy little iron-grey nag, which I judged from the saddle and accoutrements must have been an officer's charger. It was easy to see from the state of the saddle that the former rider had been desperately wounded, and the reins too were bloodier than a dainty man would have liked; but I was noways squeamish, and mounted the little horse in a twinkling. The moment I had got my seat, I galloped up to the Heavy Brigade, and formed up coolly on the left flank of the old Royals. They laughed at me as if I had been a clown in a pantomime; and I had not been in position a couple of minutes when up came Johnny Lee, their adjutant, on his old bay mare, at a tearing gallop, and roared to me to 'Go to Hell out of that.' There's no mistake, I was not much of a credit to them. I was bare-headed, and my hair was like a birch-broom in a fit. I was minus a coat, with my shirt-sleeves turned up to the shoulder, and my shirt, face, and bare hairy arms were all splashed and darkened with blood, which I had picked up at the butchering the day before, and had never wiped off. A pair of long, greasy jack-boots came up to the thigh, and instead of a sword I had the axe over my shoulder at the slope as regimental as you please. The Russian must have ridden very short, for my knees were up to my nose in his stirrups, and so you may imagine that, taking me all in all, I was a hot-looking member, especially if you remember that I was fully half-seas over.

The heavies were in position to support the Light Brigade, which had just got the word to advance. So when the adjutant of the Royals ordered me off, I looked straight before me, and saw the light bobs going out to the front at an easy trot, and on the right of the front rank I caught sight of the lance hats of my own corps, the old seventeenth. My mind was made up on the instant. Ramming my spurless heels into the ribs of the little Russian horse, I started off in pursuit of the Light Brigade as fast as I could make him go, with shouts of laughter from the heavies ringing behind me, and chased, unsuccessfully, by a couple of officers of the Greys, who tried to stop me for decency's sake.

As the light bobs were only advancing at the trot, I wasn't long before I ranged up alongside their right flank, and there was old Nosey, as we used to call Cardigan, well out to the front, and in front of him again was young Nolan of the 15th, with his sword down at the 'Right engage' already, although we were a long way off any enemy. Just as I came up in line with the flank sergeant of the front rank, who looked sideways at me as if I had been a ghost, Cardigan turned round in his saddle to say a word to the field trumpeter riding at his heels, and then with a wave of his sword went off at a score out to the front. In another second, all the trumpets of the brigade sounded the 'Charge', and sitting down on our saddles and setting our teeth hard, off we went pellmell across the valley as hard as ever horse could lay foot to ground. Presently we got within range of the devilish Russian battery which was playing right into our teeth, and I saw Nolan, who was a long way out to the front, galloping as if for a wager, toss up his arms, and with a wild shriek fall from his horse. On still, on we went, faster and faster as our horses got excited and warmed to their work, heedless of the torrent of shot that came tearing through us, and stopping for ever many a bold rider. As for myself, what with the drink in me, and the wild excitement of the headlong charge, I went stark mad, and sent the plucky Russian horse ahead at a pace which kept me in line with the very foremost.

Nearer and nearer we came to the dreadful battery, which kept vomiting death on us like a volcano, till I seemed to feel on my cheek the hot air from the cannon's mouth. At last we were on it. Half a dozen of us leaped in among the guns at once, and I with one blow of my axe brained a Russian gunner just as he was clapping the linstock to the touch-hole of his piece. With another I split open the head of an officer who was trying to rally the artillery detachment in the rear; and then what of us were left went smack through the stragglers, cutting and slashing like fiends, right straight at the column of cavalry drawn up behind the battery. What happened then, say you? I can't tell you much more than this, that they were round us like a stream of bees, and we, not more seemingly than a couple of dozen of us to the fore, were hacking and hewing away our hardest, each individual man the centre of a separate mêlée. I know I never troubled about guards myself, but kept whirling the axe about me, every now and then bringing it down to some purpose; and ever as it fell, the Ruskies gave ground a bit, only to crush denser round me a minute after. Still nothing seemed to touch me. They dursn't come to close quarters with the sword, for the axe had a devil of a long reach; and they dursn't use pistols, for they were too thick themselves.

I'm hanged if I don't half think I should have been there till now, had I not chanced to hear above the din a trumpet from somewhere far in the rear sound 'Threes about'. Round I wheeled, still thrashing about me like a windmill, slap through the heart of the battery again, knocking over an artilleryman or two as I passed, and presently overtook a small batch of men of various regiments, who under Colonel Shewell of the 8th Hussars, were trying to retreat in some kind of order. I was as sober as a bishop by this time, take my word for it, and I joined them right cheerfully; but the chances of getting back again to our own side of the valley looked very blue. The Russian cavalry were hard on our heels, and we suffered sorely from the devilish battery in our rear, which kept pelting into the thick of us, without much discrimination between friend and foe. The guns on those forts on our left, out of which the cowardly Turks had sneaked, and which had been pounced upon by the Russians, were not doing us much good neither, I assure you, and it was for all the world like being between the devil and the deep sea. Soon what little formation we had got was knocked to pieces, and then the word was, 'Every man for himself, and God help the hindmost.' A young fellow of the 11th Hussars and myself hung together for a while, both of us trying to make the most of our blown and jaded horses; but at last down he went, his horse shot under him, and himself wounded. As the lad's busby rolled off when his head touched the ground, he gave a look up at me which went to my heart, rough as I was. God pity him, he was little more than a boy, and I had a mother myself once. I was out of the saddle in a twinkling, and had him across the holsters and myself in the seat again only just in time, for the damnable Cossacks were down upon us like so many wolves. Oh! he was a good plucky one, was that little Russian horse; right gamely did he struggle with the double load on his back, and hurrah! here were the heavies at last, and we were safe.

As I was riding to the rear to give the wounded man up to the doctor, I passed close under the staff, who were on the brow of the hill above me, but there was no notice taken of me that I perceived. I rode up to our own camp, and by and by a sergeant came and made a prisoner of me, for the crime of breaking out of the guard-tent when confined thereto – a serious military offence, I can tell you. I wasn't shot for it, though; for next day I was brought in front of Lord Lucan, who was in command of the cavalry, and who told me, that although he had a good mind to try me by court-martial, as, he said, I certainly deserved, he would let me off this time, in consideration of the use I had made of the liberty I had taken, and perhaps he would do more for me if I kept sober. And that's how, sir, I came by this little medal, which is Britain's reward for distinguished conduct in the field.

Several officers and men report seeing Butcher Jack in the charge. One of them, Private Anthony Sheridan of the 8th Hussars, described him for the *Illustrated London News*:

I remember a man of the 17th Lancers riding to the charge in a curious dress, he was a butcher. Attired in a blood-bespattered smock-frock, he ran after and caught a stray horse, and then took his place in the ranks, and, amidst the laughter and jeers of his comrades, dashed ahead. He was a big, powerful fellow. I have forgotten his name, but he was seen doing good service amongst the Russians, who were puzzled to understand to what corps he belonged.

Sheridan and others confirm the details of Butcher Jack's story, except that no one other than Vahey himself records that he used an axe in place of a sabre. Of particular interest is an account written by Sergeant Joseph Pardoe of the 1st (Royal) Dragoons, one of the Heavies formed up behind the Light Brigade, who claims to correct some of the details and add the final part of the story that Vahey chose for good reason to leave out:

The Light Brigade advanced and we the support followed them for some distance down the valley. I can at this point retell the true story of Butcher Jack. He came up between the two squadrons of the 1st Dragoons and joined us as we advanced, in fact he was on my right hand. Colonel Yorke looked round and said to me, Sergeant, that man does not belong to my regiment, who is he? The man answered, I belong to the 17th Lancers, sir. Colonel Yorke replied, I admire your spirit my man, but you had better join your own regiment. He replied, All right, sir, and galloped away. That was the last I saw of him that day. He was not mounted on a grey horse, nor had an axe in his hand, he had no coat on and his shirt sleeves were turned up. He had one sword in his hand and one in a scabbard buckled round his waist. He had been made a prisoner the night before, having taken too much rum. I was told by one of the 17th that he was not seen or heard of for three days and it was thought he was killed, but when he found out by some means that he would be pardoned for breaking his arrest, he turned up.

If Pardoe is correct, then Vahey's claim that he was taken before Lord Lucan on 26 October conveniently loses the three days during which he was 'not seen or heard of'.

In 1857, Vahey went to India with the 17th Lancers. He remained a heavy drinker and dug graves to earn extra money. In 1860, on the march from Gwalior to Secunderabad, the regiment was struck by cholera. Vahey was among the seven men who died. He was buried in a grave he himself had dug. He had served in the regiment for twenty-two years.

William Howard Russell was war correspondent for *The Times* throughout the Crimean War. He watched the charge from Lord Raglan's position on the Sapoune Heights, overlooking the valley. His report was written at or soon after 2.00 p.m. on 25 October, only three hours after the charge, and was the very first written account by one who was there. The sights and sounds were still fresh in his mind, as were his own reactions to what he had seen. He interviewed survivors, but instead of quoting them absorbed their impressions into his own as if all was observed from the heights. Some of the men felt that they had charged thirty guns, and this was one of the inaccuracies that crept into the correspondent's account.

Russell had previously reported on the inadequacies of the army and the hardships suffered by the men because of poor organization. As a result senior officers snubbed him and one said he ought to be hanged for treason. He was denied the facilities normally given to journalists but that did not stop him reporting what he saw, and in the charge at Balaklava he saw much that the public at home needed to be told before it was 'explained' in official dispatches.

His eyewitness account of the charge was published in *The Times* on Tuesday 14 November 1854. Part of Russell's initial scene-setting before he gets to the news has been cut here – his newspaper may have 'thundered' but its correspondents were allowed to be long-winded in the literary style of the day. Nevertheless his report thrills with its expressive and bountiful language.

This is how the British people first learned of the charge of the Light Brigade:

THE CAVALRY ACTION AT BALAKLAVA
October 25

If the exhibition of the most brilliant valour, of the excess of courage, and of a daring which would have reflected lustre on the best days of chivalry can afford full consolation for the disaster of today, we can have no reason to regret the melancholy loss which we sustained in a contest with a savage and barbarian enemy.

I shall proceed to describe, to the best of my powers, what occurred under my own eyes, and to state the facts which I have heard from men whose veracity is unimpeachable. Before I proceed to my narrative, I must premise that a certain feeling existed in some quarters that our cavalry had not been properly handled since they landed in the Crimea, and that they had lost golden opportunities from the indecision and excessive caution of their leaders.

And now occurred the melancholy catastrophe which fills us all with sorrow. It appears that the Quartermaster-General, Brigadier Airey gave an order in writing to Captain Nolan to take to Lord Lucan, directing his Lordship 'to advance' his cavalry.

A braver soldier than Captain Nolan the army did not possess. He rode off with his orders to Lord Lucan. He is now dead and gone. God forbid I should cast a shade on the brightness of his honour, but I am bound to state what I am told occurred when he reached his Lordship. I should premise that the Russian cavalry retired, leaving men in three of the redoubts they had taken. They had also placed some guns on the heights over their position, and about 30 guns were drawn up along their line. Our cavalry had moved up to the ridge across the valley. When Lord Lucan received the order from Captain Nolan and had read it, he asked, we are told, 'Where are we to advance to?' Captain Nolan pointed with his finger to the line of the Russians, and said, 'There are the enemy, and there are the guns, sir, before them; it is your duty to take them,' or words to that effect, according to the statements made since his death.

Lord Lucan, with reluctance, gave the order to Lord Cardigan to advance upon the guns, conceiving that his orders compelled him to do so. The noble Earl, though he did not shrink, also saw the fearful odds against him. Don Quixote in his tilt against the windmill was not near so rash and reckless as the gallant fellows who prepared without a thought to rush on almost certain death. It is a maxim of war, that 'cavalry never act without a support,' that 'infantry should be close at hand when cavalry carry guns,' and that it is necessary to have on the flank of a line of cavalry some squadrons in column, the attack on the flank being most dangerous. The only support our light cavalry had was the reserve of heavy cavalry at a great distance behind them, the infantry and guns being far in the rear. There was a plain to charge over, before the enemy's guns were reached, of a mile and a half in length. At 11.10 our Light Cavalry Brigade rushed to the front. They numbered as follows, as well as I can ascertain: 4th Light Dragoons 118 men; 8th Hussars 104 men; 11th Hussars 110 men; 13th Light Dragoons 130 men; 17th Lancers 145 men; Total 607 sabres.

As they passed towards the front, the Russians opened on them from the guns in the redoubt on the right, with volleys of musketry and rifles. They swept proudly past, glittering in the morning sun in all the pride and splendour of war. We could scarcely believe the evidence of our senses! Surely that handful of men are not going to charge an army in position? Alas! it was but too true – their desperate valour knew no bounds, and far indeed was it removed from its so-called better part – discretion.

They advanced in two lines, quickening their pace as they closed towards the enemy. A more fearful spectacle was never witnessed than by those who, without the power to aid, beheld their heroic countrymen rushing to the arms of death. At the distance of 1,200 yards the whole line of the enemy belched forth, from 30 iron mouths, a flood of smoke and flame, through which hissed the deadly balls. Their flight was marked by instant gaps in our ranks, by dead men and horses, by steeds flying wounded or riderless across the plain. The first line is broken, it is joined by the second, they never halt or check their speed an instant; with diminished ranks, thinned by those 30 guns, which the Russians had laid with the most deadly accuracy, with a halo of flashing steel above their heads, and with a cheer which was many a noble fellow's death-cry, they flew into the smoke of the batteries, but ere they were lost from view the plain was strewed with their bodies and with the carcasses of horses. They were exposed to an oblique fire from the batteries on the hills on both sides, as well as to a direct fire of musketry. Through the clouds of smoke we could see their sabres flashing as they rode up to the guns and dashed between them, cutting down the gunners as they stood.

We saw them riding through the guns, as I have said; to our delight we saw them returning, after breaking through a column of Russian infantry, and scattering them like chaff, when the flank fire of the battery on the hill swept them down, scattered and broken as they were. Wounded men and dismounted troopers flying towards us told the sad tale – demi-gods could not have done what we had failed to do. At the very moment when they were about to retreat an enormous mass of Lancers was hurled on their flank. Colonel Shewell, of the 8th Hussars, saw the danger, and rode his few men straight at them, cutting his way through with fearful loss. The other regiments turned and engaged in a fearful encounter.

With courage too great almost for credence, they were breaking their way through the columns which enveloped them, when there took place an act of atrocity without parallel in the modern warfare of civilised nations. The Russian gunners, when the storm of cavalry passed, returned to their guns. They saw their own cavalry mingled with the troopers who had just ridden over them, and, to the eternal disgrace of the Russian name, the miscreants poured a murderous volley of grape and canister on the mass of struggling men and horses, mingling friend and foe in one common ruin. It was as much as our Heavy Cavalry Brigade could do to cover the retreat of the miserable remnants of that band of heroes as they returned to the place they had so lately quitted in all the pride of life. At 11.35 not a British soldier, except the dead and dying, was left in front of these bloody Muscovite guns. Our loss, as far as it could be ascertained, in killed, wounded, and missing at 2 o'clock today, was as follows: 4th Light Dragoons 79 lost; 8th Hussars 66 lost; 11th Hussars 85 lost; 13th Light Dragoons 69 lost; 17th Lancers 110 lost; Total lost 409. The ground was left covered with our men and with hundreds of Russians, and we could see the Cossacks busy searching the dead.

All our operations in the trenches were lost sight of in the interest of this melancholy day, in which our Light Brigade was annihilated by their own rashness, and by the brutality of a ferocious enemy.

Russell's reports from the Crimea made him a household name in Britain and were the main source by which the public learned the horrifying truth about the cavalry action at Balaklava. His brilliant prose joined forces with the simple beat of Tennyson's ballad to win for the charge of the Light Brigade a special place in the minds of Englishmen, which persists to this day.

After the Crimean War, Russell went on to report for *The Times* on the Indian Mutiny, the American Civil War and the Zulu War, before retiring in 1882. He died in London in 1907 and there is a memorial to him in St Paul's Cathedral in London.

While written descriptions of the charge can be divided between the accounts of those who took part and those who looked on, the artist William Simpson attempted to combine the two perspectives on canvas. He arrived in the Crimea soon after 25 October, interviewed those who watched from the heights and several of the survivors who fought in the valley, and used what they told him to make a sketch of the charge. He took this to Cardigan, who said, 'It is all wrong.' If Simpson's sketch was to be accepted in England as an authentic representation of the charge it had to gain Cardigan's approval. Simpson spoke to the observers and survivors again, made a few corrections to his picture and returned to Cardigan. Once more he was told that it was wrong. Simpson produced a third sketch without speaking to anyone, certain that this time he would get it right, and indeed Cardigan praised it warmly. Simpson later wrote: 'The real truth was that in the last sketch I had taken greater care than in the first two to make His Lordship conspicuous in the front of the Brigade.'

In this case, the experience of one of those involved was not properly reflected by the observations of those watching from the heights. The reverse is equally true. A survivor's experience, while true to his own appreciation of what happened around him, might misrepresent the larger picture, which can only be seen from afar.

Part of the big picture was the 'magnificence' observed from the Sapoune Heights by General Bosquet and William Russell. The men in the valley could hardly have been expected to see *that*, and yet it was that which in the minds of the English at home set the charge apart from all previous cavalry actions and made of it a legend.

THREE

The Last of the Light Brigade

Here comes one of the miserable remains of the Light Brigade.
Which most is to be pitied, the man or the horse?
Captain Henry Clifford

11. The Miserable Remains

The Light Brigade in winter

The wounded men of the Light Brigade received their first treatment in the small Orthodox church at Kadikoi, which was used as a field hospital. The more serious cases were then transported on carts down to the general hospital at Balaklava, where Lord Cardigan visited them and spent some time comforting his trumpeter Billy Brittain. The hospital could not cope with the number of injured men or the severity of their wounds, and a troopship, the *Australia*, left Balaklava on 26 October with more than a hundred of the most critically hurt for the four-day journey across the Black Sea to the barrack hospital at Scutari, a suburb of Constantinople.

The conditions inside the Scutari hospital, a dilapidated three-storey building once used as a barracks by the Turkish army, were horrific, from the algae-covered walls to the rats that roamed the rotting floorboards. There were no beds, no bandages and no nurses; Florence Nightingale and her nurses had not yet arrived. These men had survived the valley of death. It seemed unlikely that any would survive the barrack hospital.

Those still in the Crimea who had escaped injury or suffered only minor wounds expected *their* conditions to improve, and at first it seemed that the Russians themselves might unwittingly help the Light Brigade to recover after the charge. During the night of 26 October about a hundred Russian horses got loose, galloped across the plain and came to a stop in the British cavalry camp near Kadikoi. The sound of approaching hooves had triggered an alert and the men were mounted and had their swords drawn. Anxiety turned to delight when they saw the empty saddles. Among the

Russian horses was the mount of Trumpeter Lovelock of the 4th Light Dragoons, who had been killed in the charge, and it was supposed that this horse had led the others into the camp. The large number of uninjured Light Brigade cavalrymen counted as non-effectual because their horses had been killed could now be remounted courtesy of the enemy.

The Russians had helped; Lord Raglan did not. On 27 October, two days after the charge, he visited the cavalry camp to speak with their lordships Lucan and Cardigan. Lord Paget thought it a great pity that he did not also speak to the men: 'How I longed for him to do so as I walked by his horse's head. One little word. "Well, my boys, you have done well!" or something of the sort, would have cheered us all up.' But Raglan had other things on his mind. He had come to consult Lucan and Cardigan on a matter regarding the Light Brigade. General Canrobert, who had succeeded St Arnaud as commander of the French Army in the Crimea, believed that as the Russian attack on Balaklava had failed the enemy would next try an assault on allied positions on the heights overlooking Sevastopol, where the French were particularly vulnerable. He had asked Raglan to move what was left of the brigade up onto the heights, close to the French positions, to protect against any such Russian move.

When Raglan put this to Lucan and Cardigan, the latter immediately pointed out that the move would place the brigade in an exposed position seven miles from Balaklava, the only source of supplies. If with the onset of winter the road became impassable, the supply of forage would cease and the horses would starve to death. Raglan then revealed that he had already made up his mind. He acknowledged Cardigan's warning but ordered the Light Brigade to move camp anyway. This order would prove more disastrous than that received on the morning of 25 October.

On 28 October the Light Brigade moved up onto the heights and made camp by the Inkerman windmill, between the French and the direction from which a Russian attack might come. Pickets were placed forward of this position to watch for the enemy.

The new camp was exposed to the bitter winds that swept across the Crimean peninsula and two days later the first snow fell. Officers and men alike had only the shelter of their tents, with the exception of Lord Cardigan, who dined each evening on his yacht and slept there, then rode up to his brigade after breakfast. He now appeared each morning wearing an additional garment shaped like a woollen jacket and buttoning down the front, which being unfamiliar to the men became known as a 'cardigan'.

All forage arrived by ship at Balaklava. Each day a train of horses selected from those still fit enough to make the fourteen-mile return journey went down to the harbour and carried a meagre supply of barley and hay back to the brigade on the heights. The condition of the road and of the horses worsened daily. Officers and men alike thought Raglan's order absurd and knew it would be impossible to survive the winter there; the difficulty of supply and the weather formed an alliance against them more powerful even than the Russian army.

In fairness to Raglan he judged that Sevastopol would soon be taken and that the Light Brigade would not be left on the heights for long. No one seriously contemplated the campaign continuing beyond the end of the year. What happened on 5 November changed all that.

The presence of the Light Brigade by the Inkerman windmill might have deterred an enemy patrol, but the Russians had something larger in mind. At 5.00 a.m. on the misty morning of Sunday 5 November an estimated 60,000 Russians attacked uphill, and so outnumbered the British infantry camped on the heights over-looking the city that these troops initially fell back with heavy losses. During the hours that followed reinforcements were brought up. Although this was an infantry battle involving such huge numbers that the weakened regiments of the Light Brigade could play no effective role, they were ordered to stand ready just behind the front line.

Lord Cardigan had not yet come up from his yacht and Lord Paget had taken command of the brigade in his place. Paget formed up the regiments out of sight of the enemy artillery. Troop Sergeant

Major Smith described how despite this precaution they still suffered casualties:

The enemy must have known where we were, for they dropped their cannonballs just over the brow of the hill so that they passed through us about breast high. One struck a horse's head, knocking it to pieces, then took off Sergeant Breese's arm. It then struck Private Wright full in the chest, passing through him. He fell out of the saddle close to my horse's feet. Another cannonball struck a man's leg just above the knee, taking it clean off, and passing through his horse.

Cardigan arrived at about 9.00 a.m. and immediately ordered the brigade to move back several hundred yards, taking it out of range of the Russian guns. In this instance the normally inept Cardigan gave a sensible order, when the normally astute Paget had failed to do so.

By 1.00 p.m. the Russian attack had been repulsed. It was a hollow victory. British losses were so high that Raglan no longer considered his army strong enough to storm Sevastopol. The siege would continue through the winter.

Cardigan's fears for the Light Brigade were proving well founded. At this point the road down to Balaklava was still open and the remounts inadvertently provided by the Russians were fit enough to make the return journey each day to bring up forage and supplies. But the artillery had lost many of its transport ponies and on 8 November the cavalry was ordered to hand over its Russian horses to carry ammunition from the ships up to the guns on the heights. The brigade was left to depend on the fittest among its own horses to make the daily return journey. Exhausted and fit horses alike had to stand out all night with no shelter and suffered dreadfully from the icy winds that howled across the heights.

The cavalrymen were suffering from the cold too and even before the loss of the Russian horses the brigade did not have sufficient fit men to mount them. Then the winter arrived with a vengeance.

★

A mighty gale – some called it a hurricane – hit the southern tip of the Crimea on 14 November. The cavalry camp had its tents and stores blown away, and men and horses were bowled over. Twenty-one ships waiting on the open sea to enter Balaklava harbour were sunk with the supplies they carried, including much-needed winter clothing for the men, wood for campfires, and three weeks' supply of hay for the horses. The storm was followed by heavy sleet and snow. Boots and hooves soon turned the camp into a morass of slush and mud, and it became impossible for the officers and men, traditionally proud of their appearance, to keep clean. Captain Robert Portal of the 4th Light Dragoons described the cavalrymen on 17 November:

Clothes all in patches, of every colour and size, all begrimed with mud; few have straps, and some no boots; these wear hay bands round their feet. Such is the present appearance of the once smart, clean Lancer, Hussar, and Light Dragoon. The horses are thin, miserable-looking brutes, covered all over with mud and dirt, the saddlery the same, a mass of mud.

The men were constantly cold and survived on reduced rations of biscuit and salt pork. Their stock of wood was quickly used up, so there were no campfires and no boiling water to brew tea. The loss of three weeks' hay meant that each horse was restricted to three pounds of barley per day, and soon this was cut even further. Exhausted and underfed before the storm, they were now starving. Lieutenant Edward Phillips of the 8th Hussars wrote: 'The last two weeks have been wet and cold. They have told severely on the horses; having had no hay the poor brutes are desperately hungry, and at least ten horses have lost their tails in consequence: they have literally been eaten off. Some horses have lost their manes also.'

By the end of November additional supplies had arrived at Balaklava but the constant rain and snow had transformed the track from the cavalry camp to the harbour into a quagmire, and the Light Brigade had very few horses still fit enough to make the return journey with even a half-load. Cornet George Wombwell of the 17th Lancers wrote to his father:

The weather here is dreadful, nothing but rain, rain, rain which nearly washed us out of our tents, and we have not a dry corner to put a thing in, the ground is over one's ankles in mud, and the poor horses are standing up to their knees in wet mud and dying as fast as they can from cold, wet and starvation. Where we are now encamped is near seven miles from Balaklava where the forage is all loaded, but the roads are in such a state, that it is impossible to get it up from there to our camp, so the consequence is when it does come it is in very small quantities and the wretched animals do not get more than 2 handfuls a piece all day, hay we scarcely ever get, so you can easily imagine our horses are nearly starved.

Lucan had ordered that no horse, however exhausted, starved or sick, was to be killed except those with glanders or broken legs. Horses that collapsed on the track between the camp and Balaklava were left where they fell and died horribly, savaged by wild dogs. Even those that died in camp could not be buried, as the ground was frozen solid and it was impossible to dig graves. Those pitiful creatures still alive would eat anything, as Private Mitchell of the 13th Light Dragoons discovered: 'When a horse dropped dead in the lines, the others that could reach it would gnaw the hair off its skin. Saddlery, blankets, ropes, and picket pegs all were eaten by them, and we had to be careful on going near them, or they would seize us by the beard and whiskers for the same purpose.'

It was painful for cavalrymen who had for years devoted much of their time to stable duties, feeding and grooming these once magnificent mounts, to see them reduced to such a state. On 1 December, Lieutenant Phillips noted: 'They actually come, when loose of a night, and gnaw our tent ropes. These tail-less, maneless, skinny brutes would never be recognised as the remains of five as fine regiments as ever left England.'

On that same day Lord Lucan reported to Raglan that for all military purposes the Cavalry Division had to be considered extinct:

the weather had beaten them when the hell ride could not. Raglan ordered the Light Brigade down from the heights to its original camp near Kadikoi, only two miles from Balaklava.

The move took place on 3 December. Lieutenant Colonel Charles Doherty recorded that the horses were too weak to be ridden and were led down by the men, and that even so 'about seventeen fell dead on the road from sheer exhaustion'. The Light Brigade now had only ten per cent of the horses it had brought from England. Worst hit was the 13th Light Dragoons with only twelve of its original 250 horses.

Many of the men were sick and exhausted too, and even at Kadikoi there was no escaping the cold. Camp duties such as watering the horses twice daily and shovelling dung away from the horse lines were all that most could cope with. Several of those fit enough to be sent out on picket duty returned with frostbite and lost all or part of their earlobes; after that, light dragoons, hussars and lancers alike dispensed with their ornate headgear in favour of sheepskin caps that could be pulled down to cover the ears.

Cardigan now decided to escape not only the cold but also the Crimea. William Russell reported that, 'Lord Cardigan is almost unable to leave his yacht owing to his indisposition.' In fact Cardigan had already applied to Lord Raglan for permission to return to England, and perhaps because of the embarrassing nature of his 'indisposition', he asked to be allowed to go 'without having to explain my ailments in detail before a Medical Board'. Raglan replied that he must go before a medical examiner, though this could take place on his yacht. The examiner recommended that Cardigan be allowed to return to England. He was reported as suffering from diarrhoea so severe that at times it 'assumed a dysenteric form', and also 'pains and difficulty in voiding his urine'. Cardigan left Balaklava on 8 December to sail home; few among the survivors of the Light Brigade were sad to see him go. One he left behind was described by Captain Henry Clifford of the Rifle Brigade on 16 December:

Here comes one of the miserable remains of the Light Brigade. Which is most to be pitied, the man or the horse? He can only get what forage it can carry up on its back, to keep it alive. It has been tied up in all weathers without any covering but its saddle, which has not been taken off for days because that reopens the dreadful sore back under it. He will soon have no further trouble with it. He says he wishes he had been cut up in the Charge of the Light Brigade, and then all would have been over.

The return to Kadikoi had relieved the cavalry of the fourteen-mile return journey to bring up supplies, and all had expected their situation to improve. Their hopes were quickly dashed. Many of the mules, ponies and Russian horses used to transport supplies from Balaklava up to the artillery and infantry on the heights had by now died or were too exhausted to continue. The cavalry was ordered to assist with this transport, making the same return journey as before. Each day a train of the most able horses had to go down to Balaklava, load provisions, carry these up to the heights, and tramp back again. Initially they were required to carry up ammunition for the artillery. Colonel Whinyates explained why that proved impossible:

They placed the shot and shell in sacks, two or four in each, according to size, and tied up the mouth; then the sack was lifted across the saddle seat, and the men walked on foot, leading their horses from Balaklava to the Siege Depots before Sevastopol. This very soon told on the horses' backs, for they were in such poor condition that the wooden arch of the saddle-tree was quite down on the backbone and withers; so after a time it had to be discontinued.

Next they carried meat for the infantry. Cavalrymen had always thought themselves superior to foot soldiers; now they were reduced to transporting provisions for them. Captain Portal, writing on 21 December, clearly found this humiliating: 'All the cavalry is used for now is to carry meat to the army on the heights. We call ourselves "the Butcher Boys".'

They soon became grocer boys too, for on 8 January 1855 Cornet

Wombwell wrote home: 'It took 58 horses loaded with biscuit from 9 a.m. till half past 3 p.m. to get there and back, a distance of nearly six miles. It was most wretched to see the poor troop horses, so weak from cold and starvation. We had to leave several on the road unable to move.'

Troop Sergeant Major Smith described the macabre memorial to the dead horses that grew up in the centre of the cavalry camp:

It was a common occurrence for men to come to me carrying their saddles to report that their horses had fallen down dead, or that they had left them on the road dying. Wild dogs prowled about living on the dead horses. The saddles, as the horses died, were placed in the centre of the encampment, frozen together and covered with snow.

Lord Lucan sent a note to Raglan on 17 January protesting that the cavalry was being destroyed by these 'duties so totally foreign to their profession'. He added: 'Feelings of dissatisfaction are felt by the officers, and this army is losing a cavalry it will be difficult to replace. Since the 12th December, no less than 426 horses have died.'

It was not only the horses that were dying en route. On the return journey to Balaklava they carried sick infantrymen down from the heights to the general hospital. Not all of these survived the ride, as Lieutenant Heneage of the 8th Hussars recorded on 19 January:

Half-dying men have no other conveyance than a trooper to come seven miles to Balaklava in the bitter frost and snow. Constantly they die on the road, either frozen to death or exhausted by the exertion of sitting up on a hard saddle with no covering but a tattered coat and a thin blanket which they have not the strength to hold over their heads.

Sickness, exhaustion and cases of severe frostbite were increasing among the cavalrymen too. In the Balaklava hospital the sick lay closely packed side by side on the bare floor with their cavalry cloaks rolled up as pillows. There was no medicine and the only

food was rice and biscuit boiled to produce a thick soup. Elizabeth
Davis, a Welsh nurse, described her work there:

I began to open some of their wounds. The first that I touched was a case
of frost bite. The toes of both the man's feet fell off with the bandages.
The hand of another fell off at the wrist. It was a fortnight, or from that
to six weeks, since the wounds of many of those men had been looked at
and dressed. One wound had not been dressed for five weeks, and I took
at least a quart of maggots from it. From many of the other patients I
removed them in handfuls.

Back at the cavalry camp the men were still sleeping in tents
in freezing conditions and the horses still standing out overnight
on the open plain. Wooden huts had been ordered and the first
consignment had already arrived at Balaklava. A single hut could
accommodate twenty-five men or ten horses, but because of picket
and transport duties the Light Brigade had neither the manpower
nor the time to carry the several sections of each hut up to the camp.
In any case such a task was beyond the few men still fit for duty.

The brigade was hardly functional at all. On the morning of
4 February the 11th Hussars could find only one man fit for picket
duty. The horse he was mounted on had stood out all night in
freezing temperatures. Man and horse together made such a poor
sight that Troop Sergeant Major Smith wished those at home in
England could see this picture of the once splendid Light Brigade:

It was piteous to see him sitting on a frozen saddle, muffled up, looking
perfectly helpless and the poor horse without mane or tail, eyes nearly
closed, with lumps of ice hanging on his legs. I was so struck by his
wretched appearance, that I took a sketch of him and his horse, a copy of
which was sent home to the London Illustrated News [*sic*]. They in their
camp scenes represented horses with flowing manes and tails and looking
quite frisky, much to our amusement.

Smith was not allowing for the several weeks it took British
publications to reach the Crimea. Descriptions of the sad state of

the Light Brigade and of the whole army were by now appearing in the British press. In the edition of the *Illustrated London News* published on 3 February, the day before he made his sketch, there was a shocking report on the condition of the cavalry horses:

I noticed one horse in particular: it was the most pitiful sight I ever beheld. Once upon a day he had been a handsome charger; now he was a skeleton covered with an old hide; no mane, no tail; deep-set ghastly, glaring eyes, and lips shrunk away from the long hungry teeth. You could not tell the colour; his hair was covered with a thick coat of mud which fitted him tight, like a slush-coloured leather jerkin.

Such reports made it clear that the suffering of both men and horses was caused not primarily by engagement with the enemy, nor by the winter alone, but by the inefficiency of the army. Supplies of coal and wood were arriving in Balaklava yet were not reaching the men, so that those sleeping in tents on the snow-covered open plain or on the heights had no campfires to warm them, dry their wet clothes or cook food. Wooden huts were piled in sections on the harbour front, yet by the time these could be transported up and erected as barracks and stabling, the winter would be over and many of the men and horses for whom they were intended would be dead.

There was a public outcry. Everyone wanted to know who was to blame. The government in London appointed Colonel Alexander Tulloch and Sir James McNeil to head the Commission of Inquiry into the Supplies of the British Army in the Crimea, and they sailed out to investigate. It would be a full year before they submitted their report.

While the remains of the Light Brigade struggled to survive the Crimean winter, Lord Cardigan was enjoying his new-found status as a national hero. He had arrived in Dover on 13 January 1855 to the cheers of a crowd gathered on the quay and the approval of the press, both of which were novel experiences for this once reviled aristocrat. Pictures of him were cut from newspapers and pasted in shop windows. The woollen jacket he had worn in the Crimea was copied by a clothing manufacturer and sold under the name 'cardigan'; partly because of his fame and partly because it was a particularly cold winter in England too, it became an instant best-seller.

When Queen Victoria invited Cardigan to dinner at Windsor and Prince Albert asked him to give an account of the charge, he helpfully included the name of the man to blame for it all: Lord Lucan. A banquet at London's Mansion House was held in his honour and he arrived on horseback in the uniform he had worn in the charge, to the cheers and applause of spectators gathered outside. His horse Ronald was considered as much a hero of Balaklava as Cardigan himself and souvenir hunters among the crowd pulled hairs from his tail.

Things were not going so well for Lord Lucan. The Duke of Newcastle had ordered his recall from the Crimea, which by implication placed the blame for the charge upon him. Lucan left Balaklava on 14 February and arrived in England on 1 March. There were no cheering crowds to greet him. While politicians and army commanders were not prepared to blame him publicly, the people, emboldened by the press, had no such inhibition.

Lucan wrote letters to *The Times* in his own defence. He spoke at length in the House of Lords, though in defending himself he attempted to shift much of the blame onto Lord Raglan, a tactic that found little support among the noble members of that House. The most vitriolic response came in the form of a pamphlet, *Remarks in reply to Lord Lucan's speech in the House of Lords by a Cavalry Officer*. This claimed that Lucan had not only proved himself inept but also demonstrated that he lacked the courage to place himself at the head of the cavalry and lead the Light Brigade himself, preferring to follow behind with the Heavies. The author, Anthony Bacon, had been the senior major of the 17th Lancers almost thirty years earlier and in line to take command of that regiment when Lucan, then George Bingham, purchased the command over his head. Bacon had waited a long time to take his revenge. In his pamphlet he listed previous commanders who had led their cavalry from the front and concluded: 'It was not their practice to place a whole Brigade between the enemy and their own persons.' Lucan responded with a pamphlet of his own, *A Vindication of the Earl of Lucan*, which was largely ignored.

Lord Cardigan successfully argued that as the brigade commander he could not be held responsible for the orders and failings of his superior officer, the divisional commander Lord Lucan, but Lucan's attempts in turn to argue that he could not be held responsible for the orders and failings of *his* superior officer, Lord Raglan, found few sympathizers. The logic of their arguments was identical, but the fact that Cardigan led the charge and Lucan turned back had much to do with the differing public reaction to the two men.

While the survivors of the Light Brigade were still in the Crimea, and Lucan and Cardigan in England, the fifty-eight cavalrymen taken prisoner by the Russians at Balaklava were being held in the town of Voronezh. Ironically, they were better cared for than their comrades in the Crimea. One of the captives, Private Wightman of the 17th Lancers, later told how well they lived: 'Our quarters were very comfortable; we had a large house assigned to us, specially furnished for the occasion; we had the liberty of the whole town, and received many invitations to Russian houses. We lived well on white bread, beef, mutton, and plenty of eggs and milk; and we had one rouble each every five days for spending money.' At least one man enjoyed his captivity even more than Wightman. Private Nathan Henry of the 11th Hussars was placed in the custody of a Russian lady. When Britain and Russia agreed to exchange their prisoners, Henry was reluctant to leave.

It was only when these men of the Light Brigade, together with a few of the Heavy Brigade, were being moved to Odessa to be returned to their regiments that trouble occurred. There were many Russian soldiers in Odessa who had fought and lost friends in the Crimea. The prisoners and their escorts had stopped for the night in a village outside the port. Private Wightman described what happened:

We commissioned three of our number to go and buy provisions in an adjacent village on the other side of the river. On their way back, while waiting for a boat, they were suddenly attacked by six men with heavy clubs, who felled and all but stunned them. Recovering themselves, they went vigorously at their assailants, who had made a bad selection, for there were not three finer men in the British Cavalry than Bird (8th Hussars), Cooper (13th Light Dragoons), and Chapman (4th Dragoon Guards). Setting to business in the good old English style, they severely punished their antagonists, who bolted.

Next morning, as the cavalrymen were marched into Odessa, these three recognized their assailants among the soldiers there. Bird, Cooper and Chapman, supported now by their comrades, were eager to take further revenge:

The officer came up and gave the order to march, but we demanded that he should put the six men under arrest. He refused, and struck Bird in the face. Bird knocked the officer down with a straight one from the shoulder; some of us grasped the muskets of the soldiers, others ran to a hut and armed themselves with stakes pulled out of its roof. Discretion, however, was thought the better part of valour when the officer ordered his men to load with ball-cartridge.

HMS *Agamemnon* arrived in Odessa under a flag of truce to collect the British prisoners. Russian soldiers who had been prisoners of war in England and were being exchanged felt no antagonism towards the men of the Light Brigade and seemed to have enjoyed their captivity: 'They greeted us with great warmth, and evidently had found England a very pleasant country. "Very good stout! Very good beer! Very good beef! Brighton very good! Russia got no Brighton! Russia no good! Sorry to come back!" were their exclamations.'

Of the fifty-eight cavalrymen captured on the day of the charge, twenty-one died of their wounds and thirty-seven were returned to their regiments.

★

Spring in the Crimea changed everything, not least as the weather improved dramatically. Steamers arrived from London loaded with comforts for the troops paid for by public donations; the books and tracts were welcomed by some, the potato-baking machine excited much interest, the Godfrey's Cordial and even the jujubes (sweetened gelatine lozenges) found takers, but it was the flannel shirts and leather boots, the potted game and soups, and above all the whisky that had many clamouring.

A sufficient number of huts were carried up to the cavalry camp to accommodate the men and the few horses to survive the winter, and the construction of a light railway from Balaklava up to the plain solved the problem of transporting supplies. Everything was now available at Kadikoi within an hour of it coming off the ships at Balaklava. Fresh meat and fruit was brought in from Malta and the men began to recover their health and their spirit.

Then came a sign that indicated more than physical recovery: outside the camp the men were playing football and cricket. The cavalry officers organized a sport more to their liking, as Fanny Duberly observed in her diary: 'Started on horseback at one o'clock to attend the "First Spring Meeting", the first race of the season. Wonderful that men who had been starved with cold and hunger, drowned in rain and mud, wounded in action, and torn with sickness, should on the third, warm, balmy day be as eager and fresh for the rare old English sport, as if they were in the ring at Newmarket.' It is unlikely that any of the horses to survive both the charge and the winter were fit enough to race at Balaklava's 'Spring Meeting'; the runners were probably selected from among the first remounts to arrive.

The advent of spring brought one less-welcome result. Men who had died during the winter had been buried in shallow graves hacked out of the frozen ground. In some areas these corpses lay only inches below the surface and once thawed by the warmer weather the production of internal gasses threatened to burst them back into the domain of the living. Two limekilns were constructed near Balaklava and the lime they produced was spread thickly over the burial grounds.

During April two cavalry regiments – the 10th Hussars and 12th Lancers – sailed from India to reinforce the Light Brigade. Fresh horses arrived from Spain. In May, detachments of recruits arrived from England for the 4th Light Dragoons, 8th Hussars and 17th Lancers. The brigade was an effective fighting force again.

On 25 May the ground taken by the Russians on the day of the charge was won back, though the cavalry took no part in this action. On 18 June an infantry assault on Sevastopol – the whole point of the campaign – was beaten back with heavy losses. Lord Raglan died eleven days later; of a broken heart due to his failure to take Sevastopol his more fanciful friends and at least one biographer said, though the fact that he was suffering from cholera at the time might have had something to do with it. Many who had served under him in the Crimea agreed with Florence Nightingale when she wrote that he was 'not a very great general' but 'a very good man', which is the most benevolent way of saying that he failed as a soldier. The post of commander-in-chief was taken by General James Simpson.

The allied artillery bombardment of Sevastopol continued through the summer and intensified in the first week of September, when some estimates put the number of Russian casualties along the city defences at almost 1,000 men a day. This was followed by an infantry assault on 8 September. The cavalry again took no part, other than forming a line along the heights to prevent unauthorized personnel – primarily the many 'travelling gentlemen' who had by this time journeyed out from England to observe the war – from interfering with the assault. This task would qualify all officers and men of the Light Brigade for the Sevastopol clasp on their Crimea Campaign Medal, but it was not a role they thought fitting.

This assault also failed to take Sevastopol, and the British and French infantry sustained heavy losses. However, it forced the Russians to conclude they could not hold out for much longer, and that same night they evacuated the city. The allies occupied Sevastopol and the campaign was effectively over except for the demolition of the Russian naval installations and the scuttling of the Black Sea Fleet. First came the plundering. Troop Sergeant Major Smith rode in to claim his share:

As I neared Sevastopol I met numbers of the French, as well as our people, who had been plundering. It was laughable to see them coming to camp laden with all manner of things; some with tables, others with chairs, and crockery of all kinds. Others dressed as Russian officers and soldiers, some as priests, some wearing ladies' bonnets and carrying parasols. I brought as many things back to camp as I could: among them were several framed pictures, a helmet and a greatcoat belonging to the Russian Imperial Guard.

In mid-September the Crimea Campaign Medals arrived and were distributed to the Light Brigade. According to Lord Paget the officers thought the three clasps (for Alma, Balaklava, and Inkerman – the clasp for Sevastopol would come later) looked like decanter labels, and they named them 'Port', 'Sherry' and 'Claret'. All those who had been present at Balaklava on 25 October, not just those who actually rode in the charge, received a medal with the Balaklava clasp.

Then came the long-awaited order for the cavalry to move into winter quarters. On 13 November the first two Light Brigade regiments to leave the Crimea – the 8th Hussars and the 17th Lancers – embarked at Balaklava for Izmir in Turkey. The campaign had not formally ended. Provisional plans were being drawn up for fresh operations against the Russians in the spring of 1856, and as these regiments had been supplied with fresh recruits from England they had every expectation of being returned to the Crimea.

Back in England, Colonel Alexander Tulloch and Sir James McNeil finally presented their report to Parliament early in 1856. This named those responsible for the non-supply of crucial items during the winter of 1854–5. Tulloch and McNeil found that the commissariat – the organization responsible for requisitioning supplies, transporting them to the Crimea and issuing them to the regiments – was largely to blame. Although they found the system to be at fault they also criticized individuals. The main culprits were James Filder, a retired army officer employed as commissary general in the Crimea, and Sir Charles Trevelyan, the purveyor-in-chief based in London. Filder was obsessed with regulations: he refused to issue wood for campfires because regulations stated that troops on campaign foraged for their own firewood, and the fact that there were no trees on the open plains of the Crimea would not persuade him to act otherwise. When Filder did allow a request, Trevelyan often failed to supply the goods. An additional 2,000 tons of hay was requisitioned on 13 September 1854, and although Filder submitted this to Trevelyan no extra hay arrived at Balaklava. After seven reminders the hay finally arrived in May 1855. Virtually all of the horses for which it was originally intended were by then dead.

Despite such negligence, Tulloch and McNeil did not excuse Lucan and Cardigan of all fault. Finding that 932 cavalry horses had died of sickness or exhaustion during the period from October 1854 to March 1855, the report blamed their lordships for 'want of promptitude or ingenuity in devising some means of temporary shelter' for the horses. *The Times* wrote critically of 'those gentlemen' who were 'strutting about our streets with the halo of heroism about their heads', and public acclaim withered. However, no official action was taken against either.

As the spring of 1856 approached, the Light Brigade prepared to return to the Crimea, although this became unnecessary when Russia and the allies signed a treaty of peace on 30 March. Russia agreed that its warships would not enter the Mediterranean. In return the Allies would return Sevastopol and Balaklava to the Russians. The following month the Light Brigade regiments set sail for home. The Russians hired an American engineer, John Gowen, to rebuild Sevastopol and salvage the warships sunk in the harbour. In the Church of the Nativity in Bethlehem, where disagreements between Orthodox and Catholic monks had been the ostensible cause of the war, the arguments and occasional fist fights continued.

12. After the Crimea 1

From the battlefield to the workhouse

The journey home was a great improvement over the voyage out. It had taken five sailing ships twenty-five days to transport the 17th Lancers to Constantinople. Now the whole regiment and its horses were accommodated on a single steamship, the *Candia*, and reached Queenstown in Ireland on 14 May 1856 after only fifteen days at sea. Officers whose first request on disembarking was for a copy of *The Times* were bemused to discover that some things had not changed: the main story concerned their lordships Lucan and Cardigan.

Both lords had demanded that an inquiry be held to correct what they felt were false accusations made against them in Tulloch and McNeil's report. A board of general officers had been convened in the great hall of London's Chelsea Hospital and was taking evidence on the supply of forage and hutted shelter for the cavalry horses. Public interest was at its height as the Light Brigade regiments arrived home. The press attended the meetings in force and on some days as many as 2,000 spectators turned up.

Lucan gave evidence in his own defence. The *Daily News* reported that when cross-examined he appeared bad-tempered and lacking in self-control. In contrast Cardigan's familiar defence was confident: he had acted on orders given him by superior officers and had no choice but to obey. The board reiterated the finding of Tulloch and McNeil that the system was mainly to blame for the supply problems in the Crimea. Nevertheless its members did suggest that their lordships Lucan and Cardigan might have achieved more if they had worked together: 'There is much reason to fear, from the official correspondence of these noblemen, that there had not been between them that cordiality of feeling which is essential to effective co-operation in the field.' That was putting it politely, but it was the strongest rebuke the establishment would hand out to its own. The press was disappointed that neither Lucan nor Cardigan had been found personally to blame and referred to the board as 'the Whitewashing Board'. A public meeting was held in London to protest at the tameness of its findings, to no avail.

On 26 June the newspapers reported a more auspicious reminder of the Crimea. Her Majesty Queen Victoria personally presented the first Victoria Crosses to veterans gathered in Hyde Park. Five VCs had been won 'for valour in the presence of the enemy' by one officer and four men of the Light Brigade.

Every man of the brigade was proud to wear his Crimea Campaign Medal, and of the four clasps that for Balaklava was the most prized. Cavalrymen who visited public houses and told of the hell ride in the hope of earning the gratitude of their fellow drinkers claimed that a medal was worth a slap on the back, but the Balaklava clasp was worth a quart of best ale. Some men who had received the medal and not the clasp now acquired it by other means, creating a flourishing black market. Major Rodolph de Salis of the 8th Hussars had a collar bearing all four clasps made for Jemmy the rough-haired terrier. Boxer, the pet of the 11th Hussars, had a special uniform made for him so that he could wear a medal pinned to it on parade.

Their lordships Lucan and Cardigan slipped quietly out of the limelight. Lucan, spotting an apparent business opportunity in the rising demand for meat in England, adapted his Irish estates to rear and fatten cattle; at the same time the first imports of cheap frozen meat arrived from South America and he lost quite a lot of money. Cardigan was appointed inspector-general of cavalry and took to the round of reviewing (and reprimanding) regiments with a flourish. He married Adeline de Horsey and the couple divided their time between the estate at Deene Park, to which he added a ballroom, their house in Portman Square in London and the *Dryad*, berthed at Cowes.

*

Between Waterloo and Balaklava the British had known 'forty years of peace' – the Afghan War of 1839 and the Sikh Wars in the 1840s were typically discounted, having been fought against native soldiers – yet it was native soldiers employed by the British Army in India who were to rudely disturb the peace little more than a year after the formal end of the Crimean War.

Two of the Light Brigade regiments – the 8th Hussars and 17th Lancers – were among those sent to India to quell the mutiny that broke out in May 1857. *The Times* war correspondent William Russell and Mrs Fanny Duberly, following her husband to war again, went too. The campaign ended in April 1859 and for most men of the old Light Brigade their fighting days were now over. Within a few years, the majority of those who had fought in the Crimea and in India and survived both had served their time and been discharged from their regiments.

Many found work in England, but for the small number who had not yet seen enough of bloodshed the outbreak of civil war in America offered a further opportunity. Their experience guaranteed them rapid promotion in the Union army which, because it was not based on the class system, allowed a man to gain rank on merit. Among the men to volunteer were Thomas Morley, formerly of the 17th Lancers, who joined the 12th Pennsylvanian Cavalry and fought in the action at Bull Run. Watching, notebook in hand, was William Russell, reporting for *The Times* on this latest conflict.

Many of those who had worked on the land before joining the army returned to that employment to find that the horses were now being superseded by steam-driven machines. Private Richard Palframan of the 8th Hussars survived the carnage at Balaklava only to lose a leg in a threshing-machine accident. Others found a new demand for their skills. Police forces around the world were mounted and welcomed recruits with cavalry experience. Private Thomas Robinson (11th Hussars) joined London's Metropolitan Police, Private Samuel Wilson (8th Hussars) became a sergeant in the Otago Mounted Police, New Zealand, and Private Joseph Lane (13th Light Dragoons) joined the Royal North-West Mounted Police in Canada. Troop Sergeant Major William Barker

(17th Lancers) became a mounted coastguard at Mablethorpe in Lincolnshire, Private Robert Briggs (11th Hussars) was employed as a coachman by Miss Lillistone of Beccles in Suffolk, and Private Edward Holland (17th Lancers) worked as a cab driver at the Commercial Hotel in Ormskirk, Lancashire.

Some tried their hand at the new jobs created by industrialization and the success of the railways, and Corporal James Nunnerley (17th Lancers) was appointed stationmaster at Disley, Cheshire. A few had a job created for them by the 'Balaklava industry': Private Nathan Henry (11th Hussars), who had been reluctant to leave his lady keeper while held prisoner in Russia, became manager of the Balaklava Panorama in London's Leicester Square, where visitors paid to view a model of the battle scene.

Private William Pennington (11th Hussars) became a Shakespearean actor with the New Royalty Theatre, London. William Gladstone said that Pennington's Hamlet was the most original he had seen. Despite such high praise, his fame as a survivor of the charge was greater than his reputation as an actor and many in the audience came to see the survivor rather than the performance.

When a reunion banquet was held for Balaklava survivors at London's Alexandra Palace on 25 October 1875 – twenty-one years after the charge – the 120 veterans who came drank a toast to 'The gallant six hundred', and the *Illustrated London News* of 30 October reported that 'to a man they were dressed respectably' and 'seemed to be occupying comfortable positions'. That might have been true of those able to attend, but other survivors were not so comfortably employed. Trumpeter William Perkins (11th Hussars), proud recipient of the Crimea Campaign Medal, the Long Service and Good Conduct Medal and the Meritorious Service Medal, was working as an attendant at a London public toilet. Private James Watts (17th Lancers) became well known in the early 1880s as 'James the crossing sweeper', an elderly gentleman on crutches who swept the mud and horse dung from the streets in front of pedestrians as they crossed, for which each might give him a penny, a halfpenny or a farthing.

Just as Pennington found that his status as a survivor was for many a greater attraction than his performance, so Watts discovered that he was paid more generously if while sweeping he told of his experience in the charge when aged only twenty: before reaching the Russian guns his horse was hit and he fell to the ground, breaking his leg; he was helped back to the British lines by a comrade and after a bumpy ride down to the hospital at Balaklava in a cart his leg was amputated without anaesthetic in a tent with an icy wind blowing through it. He would always conclude the story: 'It fair gives me the shivers whenever I think about it – the pain was summat awful.' Watts must have earned many a penny by his story, but it may not have been totally true. Although recorded as 'Severely Wounded' in the casualty lists for Balaklava, he later served with the 17th Lancers in India, which he could hardly have done with an amputated leg.

Work in a public toilet or as a crossing sweeper provided a meagre income. For those who could find no employment at all there was only the workhouse. Survivors of the charge who took this last resort include Troop Sergeant Major John Linkon (13th Light Dragoons), Private John Smith (17th Lancers), who was in Edmonton workhouse, and Private John Richardson (11th Hussars), who returned from the American Civil War, could find no employment and ended up in Cheetham workhouse.

Richardson was interviewed in 1890 by H. Yeo, publisher of the *Spy*, a popular penny newspaper. Their meeting took place at the workhouse and this is how Yeo described Richardson, then aged sixty-three (he had been twenty-seven at the time of the charge) and destitute.

He entered and I found myself saluted by one of the heroes of Balaklava! But where was the gorgeous uniform of the noble Eleventh Hussars with its bright crested buttons? It was replaced by the workhouse corduroys, with their bright uncrested buttons. The feet which once wore the jack boots, and jingled the spurs to the delight of female England, were now adorned with the low heeled shoes of the Union make. Instead of wearing the spruce Busby, John Richardson now twirled in his hand the round speckled cap of the poorhouse. And this man methought, is one of the

Light Brigade whose heroism is lauded in every household in the land! There stood the old solider paying deep respect to the workhouse master and to me. Oh, Englishmen! Blush with shame!

Yeo asked whether it was true that Lord Cardigan made a promise to the survivors of the charge concerning the future. Richardson replied: 'Yes, sir; that was made at the roll call after it was all over. He said it was certain that every man who rode in the Charge "would be provided for", and [Yeo notes that at this point Richardson glanced down at his workhouse clothes] they "have" provided for us.'

Lord Cardigan died on 28 March 1868, aged seventy-one, from injuries sustained by a fall from his horse possibly following a stroke, while riding in the grounds at Deene Park. Lord Lucan died in 1888, aged eighty-eight; his son, the fourth Lord Lucan, facilitated the sale of much of his land to the Irish peasants evicted many decades earlier. The purchase of commissions, which allowed inept but wealthy men to buy officer rank in the regiment of their choice, and by which their lordships Lucan and Cardigan had reached positions of command in the cavalry for which they were totally unfit, was abolished in 1871. *Punch* magazine gleefully published a 'Notice to Gallant but Stupid Young Gentlemen', informing them that the last date for the purchase of their commissions was 31 October, and 'after that you will be driven to the cruel necessity of deserving them'.

In 1877 the veterans of the charge formed a Balaklava Commemoration Society and held a reunion dinner each year on 25 October. In 1879, 222 survivors of the charge were still living. Twenty years later at the 1899 reunion dinner held at St James's Restaurant in London, only forty-two men were present. By 1913, of the fourteen survivors of the charge still alive, only six were well enough to attend the dinner at the Holborn Restaurant. After that, no more reunions were held. The last survivor, Private Edwin Hughes of the 13th Light Dragoons, died on 18 May 1927, aged ninety-six. He was buried at Blackpool with full military honours.

13. After the Crimea 2

From the facts to the legend

The best-known cavalry charge in history is commemorated by the best-known poem in the English language: 'The Charge of the Light Brigade' by Alfred, Lord Tennyson. Written on 2 December 1854 and inspired by William Russell's first report in *The Times*, the verses caught the public imagination with their rhythm that echoed the beat of the hooves and the constant thunder of the guns. While Tennyson's poem was soon recited by millions, Rudyard Kipling's later poem about surviving veterans of the charge, 'The Last of the Light Brigade', was largely ignored. Tennyson wrote about cavalrymen – heroes all – caught in the maelstrom of battle. Kipling described them after they had returned home, neglected by their countrymen and living in poverty.

Several books written by officers who had made the hell ride or witnessed it claimed to tell what really happened at Balaklava. A number of private soldiers wrote down their experiences too, had them printed at their own expense, and distributed copies among family and former comrades. Neither the officers nor the men were widely read; for the overwhelming majority of the British people the charge had been defined by Alfred Tennyson and there was nothing to add.

Queen Victoria had appointed Tennyson Poet Laureate in 1850 in succession to William Wordsworth. Expected to commemorate important events in verse, he followed the Crimean campaign closely in *The Times* and read William Russell's account of the Light Brigade written on the day of the charge and published on Tuesday 14 November. According to Tennyson he wrote his most famous poem 'in a few minutes'. He described how the poem first took shape in his mind: 'This poem was written after reading the first report of The Times correspondent, where only 607 sabres are mentioned as having taken part in this charge. My poem is founded on the phrase, "Some one had blundered."' Although the inspiration for the poem undoubtedly came from Russell's report, the phrase 'some hideous blunder' was not Russell's, but occurred in a *Times* editorial. In Tennyson's mind it gained a regular beat and became, 'Some one had blunder'd.' Once that line was down, the rest quickly followed.

The Charge of the Light Brigade

Half a league, half a league,
Half a league onward,
All in the valley of Death
Rode the six hundred.
'Forward the Light Brigade!
Charge for the guns!' he said.
Into the valley of Death
Rode the six hundred.

'Forward, the Light Brigade!'
Was there a man dismay'd?
Not tho' the soldier knew
Some one had blunder'd.
Theirs not to make reply,
Theirs not to reason why,
Theirs but to do and die.
Into the valley of Death
Rode the six hundred.

Cannon to right of them,
Cannon to left of them,
Cannon in front of them
Volley'd and thunder'd;
Storm'd at with shot and shell,
Boldly they rode and well,

Into the jaws of Death,
Into the mouth of Hell
Rode the six hundred.

Flash'd all their sabres bare,
Flash'd as they turn'd in air,
Sabring the gunners there,
Charging an army, while
All the world wonder'd.
Plunged in the battery-smoke
Right thro' the line they broke;
Cossack and Russian
Reel'd from the sabre-stroke
Shatter'd and sunder'd.
Then they rode back, but not,
Not the six hundred.

Cannon to right of them,
Cannon to left of them,
Cannon behind them
Volley'd and thunder'd;
Storm'd at with shot and shell,
While horse and hero fell,
They that had fought so well
Came thro' the jaws of Death,
Back from the mouth of Hell,
All that was left of them,
Left of six hundred.

When can their glory fade?
O the wild charge they made!
All the world wonder'd.
Honour the charge they made!
Honour the Light Brigade,
Noble six hundred!

By 9 December when the poem was published in the *Examiner* more detailed accounts of the charge had appeared in *The Times* and Tennyson was upset to discover that 'the noble seven hundred' would have been more correct, though this wrecked the metre of the poem. His wife Emily reassured him that the metre was more important than getting the numbers right.

Copies of the *Examiner* reached the army in the Crimea and the wounded in Scutari. The poem became popular with the men and Tennyson received many letters of thanks. One letter from a surgeon told of a seriously injured cavalryman who lay in a state of torpor and could not be brought out of it until the poem was read to him, after which he opened his eyes and began recounting his own memories of the charge. A letter from a chaplain at Scutari described how the poem was regularly read to the sick and wounded, and asked if it would be possible, as it was proving of such great comfort to them, for Tennyson to send further copies printed on individual sheets for distribution to the men: 'Half are singing it, and all want to have it in black and white.'

Tennyson had 1,000 copies printed and sent some to the hospital at Scutari and some to the Crimea. With each copy he included a personal letter:

> Brave Soldiers
>
> Whom I am proud to call my countrymen, I have heard that you have a liking for my ballad on the Charge of the Light Brigade at Balaklava. No writing of mine can add to the glory you have acquired in the Crimea; but I send you a thousand copies of my ballad because I am told that you like it and that you may know that those who sit at home love and honour you.
>
> A. Tennyson

The poem was published in *Maud and Other Poems* in 1855. This collection was reprinted annually for many years afterwards.

By 1891, when Kipling wrote 'The Last of the Light Brigade', there were twenty survivors of the charge known to be in workhouses. He seems to have taken a particular dislike to Tennyson's poem of the charge – or more precisely to the public acclamation it enjoyed at a time when the veterans of Balaklava were largely ignored. While the nation's schoolchildren learned to 'honour the charge they made' by rote, a public appeal for funds to assist the veterans raised a mere twenty-four pounds. Kipling imagines these twenty impoverished men visiting Tennyson with a request that he complete his story by telling all England of their present state.

The Last of the Light Brigade

There were thirty million English who talked of England's might,
There were twenty broken troopers who lacked a bed for the night.
They had neither food nor money, they had neither service nor
  trade;
They were only shiftless soldiers, the last of the Light Brigade.

They felt that life was fleeting; they knew not that art was long,
That though they were dying of famine, they lived in deathless
  song.
They asked for a little money to keep the wolf from the door;
And the thirty million English sent twenty pounds and four!

They laid their heads together that were scarred and lined and grey;
Keen were the Russian sabres, but want was keener than they;
And an old troop sergeant muttered, 'Let us go to the man who
  writes
The things on Balaclava the kiddies at school recites.'

They went without bands or colours, a regiment ten-file strong,
To look for the Master-singer who had crowned them all in his
  song;
And, waiting his servant's order, by the garden gate they stayed,
A desolate little cluster, the last of the Light Brigade.

They strove to stand to attention, to straighten the toilbowed back;
They drilled on an empty stomach, the loose-knit files fell slack;
With stooping of weary shoulders, in garments tattered and frayed,
They shambled into his presence, the last of the Light Brigade.

The old troop sergeant was spokesman, and 'Beggin' your pardon,'
    he said,
'You wrote o' the Light Brigade, sir. Here's all that isn't dead.
An' it's all come true what you wrote, sir, regardin' the mouth of
    hell;
For we're all of us nigh to the workhouse, an' we thought we'd call
    an' tell.

'No, thank you, we don't want food, sir; but couldn't you take an'
    write
A sort of "to be continued" and "see next page" o' the fight?
We think that someone has blundered, an' couldn't you tell 'em
    how?
You wrote we were heroes once, sir. Please, write we are starving
    now.'

The poor little army departed, limping and lean and forlorn.
And the heart of the Master-singer grew hot with 'the scorn of
    scorn'.
And he wrote for them wonderful verses that swept the land like
    flame,
Till the fatted souls of the English were scourged with the thing
    called Shame.

O thirty million English that babble of England's might,
Behold there are twenty heroes who lack their food to-night;
Our children's children are lisping to 'honour the charge they
    made—'
And we leave to the streets and the workhouse the charge of the
    Light Brigade!

The poem contrasts the lordliness of Tennyson with the lowliness of the veterans who 'lived in deathless song' but were dying of starvation. Their state was not the Poet Laureate's fault and Kipling blames all England, neatly delivering the accusation with the pun on 'charge' in the final line.

Although Kipling was arguably more popular than Tennyson – his verses were generally more accessible to the not-so-literary masses – his poem about the surviving veterans never gained the status of Tennyson's poem about the charge. The Poet Laureate had tapped into an event of legendary status and a nation much in need of heroes was not about to let Kipling's home truths spoil that.

Every schoolchild was taught Tennyson's poem by rote; most of their parents already knew it. In an age before mass literacy, the evocative beat of the Poet Laureate's ballad spawned a legend that not only survived Kipling's challenge, but proved impervious to accounts of the charge written by survivors.

Few read the 'official' histories of the war, in which fine writing sometimes compromised the brute facts, and in any case the objectivity of the authors was questionable. Lieutenant Somerset Calthorpe's *Letters from Headquarters* featured an attack on Lord Cardigan; William Russell's *The Great War with Russia* appeared eager to blame Lord Raglan; while Alexander Kinglake's *The Invasion of the Crimea* seemed equally keen to clear Raglan of all fault.

Despite the publication of these magisterial tomes, when Thomas Morley, who had been a corporal in the 17th Lancers at Balaklava, wrote his account in 1892, he began with these words:

The charge of the Light Brigade has never yet been properly described. This may be accounted for by the bias entertained by the various writers. Having seen many of these accounts, I have felt compelled to write what I know about the action, and to give a plain account without indulging in fine language, but using only soldiers' phrases.

Morley was not the first survivor to do so – Private Albert Mitchell had written his *Recollections of One of the Light Brigade* as early as 1862, and several other men had paid to have their accounts printed. But the small circulation of such works meant that few had read them. Others, like Private 'Butcher Jack' Vahey, spoke their stories for publication in magazines. Yet nothing could dent the legend of the charge; it was as if the facts no longer mattered.

Even today our popular impression of the charge is derived more from Tennyson than from the facts. Legends by their very nature tend to be non-specific, but several constituents of the charge legend can be identified: that Captain Nolan was the officer to blame, that Lord Cardigan deserted the brigade at the Russian guns and was the first man back to the British lines, that virtually all of those who charged were killed or severely wounded, and that Florence Nightingale was the nursing heroine of the wounded.

That these and other beliefs have come down to us as part of the charge legend does not necessarily mean that they are false. Each must however be investigated in the light of the evidence recorded in the first-hand accounts of survivors. As will be seen, the truth turns out to be more astounding – and more horrific – than the legend.

FOUR

Investigating the Charge

The rumour in camp is that someone has been blundering; the truth
will come out some day.
Sergeant Thomas Gowing

14. Finding Fault

Did Captain Nolan – or one of their lordships Raglan, Lucan and Cardigan – lose the Light Brigade?

Alas! Alas! It was a sad business, and all without result, or rather with the result of the destruction of the Light Brigade. It will be the cause of much ill-blood and accusation, I promise you.

Lord George Paget was writing to his wife on the day after the charge. In fact the accusations had begun immediately the survivors reached the safety of the British lines. The men murmured among themselves, blaming Lord Cardigan who, after all, had led them straight at the muzzles of the Russian guns. Perhaps he noticed or felt their venomous stares because his first words to them were: 'It was a mad-brained trick, men, but no fault of mine.'

Raglan, like the men, first blamed Lord Cardigan, but Cardigan knew exactly where to shift the responsibility. Their conversation was recorded by Alexander Kinglake:

RAGLAN: What do you mean, sir, by attacking a battery in front contrary to all the usages of war and customs of the service?
CARDIGAN: My Lord, I hope you will not blame me, for I received the order to attack from my superior officer in front of the troops.

It was the perfect response, and Lord Raglan next blamed Lucan. His words when he confronted the commander of the Cavalry Division were: 'Lord Lucan, you have lost the Light Brigade.' Lucan went away to calm down and replied later in writing: 'I will not bear one particle of the blame.' Just as Cardigan had passed the blame upwards to Lucan, so Lucan passed it further up, to Raglan: 'After careful reading of this order I hesitated, and urged the uselessness of such an attack, and the dangers attending it; the aide-de-camp, in a most authoritative tone, stated that they were Lord Raglan's orders that the cavalry should attack immediately.'

This put Raglan on the defensive. His concern was that Lucan, if accused by the British press, would repeat the same argument and many might believe him. Raglan therefore inserted a crucial sentence in his official dispatch to London on the events of 25 October. While expressed in a most gentlemanly way, this asserts that the fault was not to be found in the order itself but in Lucan's interpretation of it: 'From some misconception of the instruction to advance, the lieutenant-general considered that he was bound to attack at all hazards.'

When the dust had settled, all who feared some part of the blame might fall on them – their lordships Raglan, Lucan and Cardigan – suddenly saw quite clearly whose fault it was: Captain Nolan, the aide-de-camp who had carried the order from Raglan to Lucan, was the culprit. This development came as no surprise to Private John Richardson of the 11th Hussars: 'The blame was put on that poor brave soldier, Captain Nolan, because he was dead, I suppose.' And that is where the blame rested. As the *Daily News* noted, it got everyone else off the hook: 'A very base attempt is being made to stifle inquiry by laying the blame on the late Captain Nolan. Dead men cannot defend themselves; and this fact seems to have suggested the idea of casting blame on a dead and voiceless man in order that the survivors might have no temptation to recriminate on each other.'

This 'base attempt' worked so well that in the 150 years since the charge historians have generally agreed that the blunder was indeed Nolan's. Most argue that he misunderstood the order, and when asked by Lord Lucan what Raglan intended by it pointed towards the wrong enemy guns and sent the Light Brigade to its destruction. In recent years it has even been suggested that he deliberately misled Lucan about which guns were to be attacked. It is time that the matter was looked at again and the officer responsible for the loss of the Light Brigade named *on the basis of the evidence of survivors and witnesses of the charge.*

The man responsible for the loss of the Light Brigade has to be one of these four: Lord Raglan, who gave the order orally to General Airey, who wrote it down; Captain Nolan, who delivered the order to Lucan; Lord Lucan, in command of the Cavalry Division, who passed on the order orally to Cardigan; Lord Cardigan, in command of the Light Brigade, who led the charge.

The case against Lord Raglan

If Lord Raglan was at fault then his error must be evident in the oral delivery of his order to General Airey, as once Nolan had departed to carry the order to Lord Lucan the affair was out of his hands.

Lord Fitzroy Somerset Raglan was sixty-five. He had served on the staff of the Duke of Wellington and lost his right arm at Waterloo, but for the thirty years preceding his appointment as commander-in-chief of the British Army in the Crimea he held only an administrative post in London and had no experience of command.

The absence of his right hand meant that his orders – always expressed by this perfect gentleman as 'wishes' – were written down by General Airey. The order that led to the charge of the Light Brigade could have been better phrased: 'Lord Raglan wishes the Cavalry to advance rapidly to the front – follow the Enemy and try to prevent the Enemy carrying away the guns – Troop Horse Artillery may accompany – French cavalry is on your left. R. Airey. Immediate.' General Airey might be considered to share in the fault if he wrote down the order in words that were more his than Raglan's, but the spasmodic prose and the unnecessarily repeated 'Enemy' suggest that Airey copied the order down as Raglan spoke. If Airey had taken the time to rephrase it in his own words it would have gained a more unified, literary form. We must assume that the words are Raglan's.

The case against Raglan is threefold: first, he issued an order the meaning of which was inherently unclear; second, he failed to properly explain its meaning to the aide-de-camp chosen to deliver it; third, he further confused its meaning by a final, shouted instruction when this officer was already riding away.

First, the order itself. Raglan ordered an advance that was to 'follow the Enemy', yet the Russians were not at this point withdrawing and therefore could not be followed. The cavalry was to advance with the aim of preventing the Russians 'carrying away the guns', yet he failed to indicate which guns he meant or where they were. There were guns at the far end of the North Valley and on the heights to each side, but from where Lucan was positioned with the cavalry he could see no sign of the Russians removing any of them.

Lord Raglan's defence to this accusation is that he intended his fourth order of the day to the cavalry to be understood as a reiteration of his third, which read: 'Cavalry to advance and take advantage of any opportunity to recover the Heights. They will be supported by infantry which have been ordered. Advance on two fronts.' The only heights to have been lost and which could therefore be recovered were the Causeway Heights, where the Russians had occupied the redoubts and taken the British guns positioned there. If the two orders are taken together, the object of the advance is clearly the guns in the redoubts.

This argument in Raglan's defence is weakened by the fact that the fourth order was not merely a repetition of the previous one. It added two new pieces of information: 'follow the Enemy' suggested to Lucan that some part of the Russian force was now withdrawing, and 'prevent the Enemy carrying away the guns' informed him that this withdrawing force was taking guns with it. Neither of these events could be observed from Lucan's position in the valley and Raglan should have realized that. Worse still, there is a high probability that neither of these events was actually taking place. An officer on Raglan's staff, keeping watch on the redoubts through a telescope at a distance of over two miles, had seen Russian horse teams on the move. It was assumed that these were dragging away the British guns, but Russian sources suggest that the guns were not removed until much later in the day.

Even if the Russians had been dragging away the British guns, this would have had little tactical importance and certainly did not warrant any kind of high-risk response. But Raglan was not thinking tactically. Battlefield tradition had it that guns captured were tokens of victory, and guns lost shameful indications of defeat. Raglan assumed that he was about to lose several at once. He gave the order for the cavalry to advance.

The second accusation against Raglan is that he failed to properly instruct the aide-de-camp. When Captain Nolan reached Lord Lucan with the order he would be expected to answer any questions Lucan might ask arising from it. It was Raglan's duty to ensure that the captain understood its contents. Raglan's ADC Lieutenant Somerset Calthorpe had been next in line for duty as galloper; he was standing by and would have paid particular attention to whatever passed between Raglan and Airey prior to the order being dictated. Nolan had no reason to do so. It was only after the order had been written down, when Airey held it out for Calthorpe to take, that Raglan said, 'No. Send Nolan.' Speed was of the essence and Raglan preferred the superior horseman. Whether Nolan was then given some explanation of the order is uncertain. Calthorpe himself, who remained nearby, possibly disgruntled that Nolan had been selected in his place, said that he was given 'careful instruction', and this is crucial evidence in Raglan's defence, although it should be borne in mind that Calthorpe was Raglan's nephew and held his appointment by virtue of that fact.

The third accusation is that Raglan's final instruction confused the issue. Witnesses agree that he shouted 'Tell Lord Lucan the cavalry is to attack immediately' as Nolan rode away. It was this alone that Nolan repeated when asked by Lucan for some elucidation of the written order, suggesting that any previous instruction had made little impression on the aide-de-camp, or had in his belief been superseded by the final, urgent command. Raglan clearly intended the emphasis to fall on 'immediately', his point being that Lucan should now do what the previous order required but which had not been carried out. It is likely that to Nolan the important word was 'attack', which did not occur in either the previous or present order and added something quite new to what was required.

Lord Raglan cannot be totally cleared of blame for the charge of the Light Brigade. The first misconception – that the Russians were dragging away the guns from the redoubts – was his. His reaction was that of a man more concerned with his own reputation than with tactical good sense. His order was so poorly stated that it depended for its meaning on Lord Lucan realizing what was not put in writing: that it was to be read and understood in conjunction with the previous order. And his shouted instruction merely confused the issue further.

Despite that, the case in his defence is sufficient to acquit him of directly causing the blunder. It was reasonable to assume Lucan would read the fourth order as a reiteration of the previous order – which had not yet been acted on and therefore remained pending – and Lucan would have done so if Captain Nolan, who had received some instruction on the order, had understood and properly elucidated its meaning when questioned about it, and not merely blurted out the final, shouted instruction.

The case against Captain Nolan

If Nolan was to blame then his error must be evident either in the manner of his receipt of the order from Lord Raglan or in his delivery of the order to Lord Lucan. In addition his action at an early stage of the advance in dashing ahead of the brigade may help in identifying precisely where any fault lay.

Captain Louis Nolan was thirty-six and had seen active service in India, particularly in the First and Second Sikh Wars, with the 15th Hussars. He was the author of two books, works that had earned him a reputation as an expert on the training of cavalry horses and on cavalry tactics. In *Cavalry: Its History and Tactics*, published in London in 1853, he advised: 'Write up in golden letters in every riding-school and in every stable: "HORSES ARE TAUGHT NOT BY HARSHNESS BUT BY GENTLENESS". Where the officers are classical, the golden rule may be given in Greek as well as in English.'

While the quote contains the crux of Nolan's system of training horses, it is the second sentence that offers an insight into the man himself. Here Nolan, tongue in cheek, pokes fun at the type of senior officer who abounded in the cavalry at that time and whose knowledge of Greek might exceed his experience in the stable or on the battlefield. As a junior officer Nolan could not be overtly critical of such high-ranking and often aristocratic officers in print, but he could attack the extravagant cavalry uniform of the day, which so perfectly represented them, as being wholly unfit for the battlefield. The cavalry, he wrote with muted ambiguity, carried too much dead weight:

To me it appears we have too much frippery – too much toggery – too much weight in things worse than useless. To a cavalry soldier every ounce is of consequence! I can never believe that our hussar uniform is the proper dress in which to do hussar's duty in war – to scramble through thickets, to clear woods, to open the way through forests, to ford or swim rivers, to bivouac, to be nearly always on outpost work, to 'rough it' in every possible manner. Of what use are plumes, bandoliers, sabretaches, sheep-skins, shabraques, etc?

If Nolan had no regard for officers who made up for their lack of experience by an excess of pomposity and show, they certainly had no love for him. The mere fact that the man wrote books was enough to condemn him. It is important to consider this antipathy between Nolan and the senior officers at Balaklava – which proved as fatal as that between Lucan and Cardigan – when assessing the descriptions of Nolan given by those officers, of which this penned by Lord Paget is typical: 'An officer named Captain Nolan, who writes books, and was a great man in his own estimation, and had been talking very loud against the cavalry, and especially Lucan.' Nolan undoubtedly suffered from an excess of enthusiasm for the cavalry, and voiced what he thought of their lordships Lucan and Cardigan when others who thought much the same held their tongues. The frustrations of an experienced officer forced to watch inept commanders misuse the cavalry must have sounded to his superiors like the boasts of one who was 'a great man in his own estimation'.

Nolan's regiment the 15th Hussars was not in the Crimea; he was there as aide-de-camp to General Airey, appointed because of his knowledge of horses and given primary responsibility for purchasing remounts. Socially he enjoyed the company of fellow Indian officers such as Captain Morris of the 17th Lancers and *The Times* correspondent William Russell – already snubbed by Raglan for his irritating habit of telling readers what was really happening. Nolan also went riding with Fanny Duberly and it was said they were lovers; there is no evidence of this, and if Fanny was sleeping with every officer to whom the whisperers linked her then she must have been a very busy lady indeed.

There are three theories of how and why Nolan got it wrong and sent the Light Brigade down hell's mile:

NOLAN: THE RUSSELL–CALTHORPE THEORY
Nolan believed (wrongly) that Raglan intended the Light Brigade to charge the guns at the far end of the North Valley.

William Russell watched the charge from the Sapoune Heights, went down to interview survivors immediately afterwards, and wrote his report for *The Times* that same afternoon:

A braver soldier than Captain Nolan the army did not possess . . . God forbid I should cast a shade on the brightness of his honour, but I am bound to state what I am told occurred when he reached his Lordship . . . When Lord Lucan received the order from Captain Nolan and had read it, he asked, we are told, 'Where are we to advance to?' Captain Nolan pointed with his finger to the line of the Russians, and said, 'There are the enemy, and there are the guns, sir, before them; it is your duty to take them,' or words to that effect . . .

In this very first attempt to explain the loss of the Light Brigade, Russell singles out Nolan as the man who got it wrong. Lord

Raglan's written order was for an advance on the guns, but it did not specify which guns. Nolan did that.

Russell quotes what he had been told was said between Lucan and Nolan; he was not down in the valley to hear it for himself. Captain Walker, ADC to Lord Lucan, certainly was: 'Lord Lucan . . . asked Captain Nolan what he was to attack, and was answered by his pointing to the Russians drawn up across the valley, with the words: "There, my Lord, is your enemy; there are the guns."'

The officers and men of the Light Brigade had their eyes fixed on these two men, seeking some sign of what had been ordered. Among those who saw Nolan point was Captain Arthur Tremayne of the 13th Light Dragoons: 'Nolan gave his message a few yards in front of where I was standing. There can be no doubt that Nolan gave the order to go where we did.'

By the end of 1856, when Somerset Calthorpe's *Letters from Headquarters; or the Realities of War in the Crimea* first appeared in print, this had become the generally accepted version. Calthorpe had been present on the Sapoune Heights on 25 October 1854 and witnessed both Raglan and General Airey instruct Nolan on the order. His became the official explanation of the blunder:

When the order was delivered to Lord Lucan, he demurred for a moment to put it into execution, and asked Nolan what it was he was to attack, who replied, I am told, 'There, my Lord, is our enemy, and there are your guns'; at the same time pointing down the valley to where the enemy had the battery of eight guns, with artillery also on each flank.

Captain Nolan appears to have totally misunderstood the instructions he had just received: 'the guns' in the written order, of course, alluded to those the enemy had captured in the redoubts, and which it was thought they were carrying away; and the direction which he (Nolan) pointed out to Lord Lucan was quite contrary to that intended by Lord Raglan.

Calthorpe claims that Nolan was given instructions and that he 'totally misunderstood' them. If Nolan misunderstood the order, that must have been either because it was inadequately explained – Raglan was certainly in a hurry to get him on his way – or because

Nolan was nodding his assent before the words were half out, himself eager to be away and, to put it bluntly, not listening. Calthorpe puts the blame on Nolan, not Raglan, but his evidence that the latter did give proper instruction is compromised by the fact that he was Raglan's nephew. The Russell–Calthorpe theory thus cannot establish with any certainty whether the fault was Raglan's or Nolan's, but in asserting that the misconception arose between these two men on the Sapoune Heights, it removes the fault from Lord Lucan down in the valley.

The main flaw in the Russell–Calthorpe theory is its interpretation of Nolan's dash forward soon after the advance began. If Nolan truly believed that the guns at the end of the valley were the correct target there was no need to attempt to change the direction of the brigade as it advanced towards them. Why then did he ride out? Proponents of the theory reply that Nolan, having delivered Lord Raglan's order to 'attack immediately' and believing that Lord Cardigan was leading the brigade at too slow a pace, lost his head and rode forward in an attempt to force the pace beyond that set by both Cardigan and cavalry regulations. In support they quote the words Captain Morris is reported to have called after him as he moved ahead: 'That won't do, Nolan; we've a long way to go and must be steady!'

This interpretation of Nolan's dash forward does not sit easily with the evidence. At least two officers of the 17th Lancers later appeared to Cardigan to be attempting to force the pace, and he corrected them verbally and in one case with his sword held across the officer's front. But Nolan is described as drawing level with Cardigan and in some accounts as riding ahead of him, and Cardigan himself believed at the time that the captain was trying to take command of the brigade. This cannot be explained away as impatience with the slow pace of the advance, particularly from one who knew better than most the necessity of preserving the horses and the integrity of the line for the final charge.

The Russell–Calthorpe theory presents a strong case for some misconception of the order arising from either Raglan's rushed instructions or Nolan's inattention, with the result that Nolan believed the guns at the end of the valley were Raglan's intended target. Its fatal weakness is the unconvincing explanation of Nolan's subsequent dash ahead of the brigade.

NOLAN: THE KINGLAKE THEORY

Nolan understood (correctly) that Raglan intended the Light Brigade to prevent the Russians dragging away the guns on the Causeway Heights; when he realized that Lucan and Cardigan had misunderstood the order and the brigade was heading for the guns at the end of the North Valley, he attempted to change its direction towards the guns on the heights.

Alexander Kinglake witnessed the charge from the Sapoune Heights, interviewed many of the survivors and entered into prolonged correspondence with the senior officers involved, particularly Lucan and Cardigan. His history of the campaign, *The Invasion of the Crimea*, ran to eight volumes, the first of which appeared in 1863, seven years after Calthorpe's book. Kinglake's theory rests on a quite different understanding of Nolan's dash to the front:

Nolan audaciously riding across Cardigan's front from left to right, turning round in his saddle, shouting and waving his sword as though he would address the brigade, sought to express by voice and signs something like this – 'You are going quite wrong! Bring up the left shoulder, and incline to the right as you see me doing. This is the way to get at the enemy!'

Kinglake contends that Nolan did properly understand Raglan's order and it was not until Cardigan set off in the wrong direction, leading the brigade straight down the valley instead of turning to the right, that Nolan realized something was wrong. This sudden awareness of a mistake to which he may have contributed – and its likely consequences – explains Nolan's attempt, not to force the pace, but to change the direction of the brigade.

Two objections to Kinglake's theory have been put. First, his explanation of Nolan's dash forward is offered as merely the most likely option, without real evidence. Second, even if this were proven it would beg the question of why, if Nolan knew the guns intended were those on the heights, he pointed down the valley when asked by Lucan which guns were to be attacked. Because of these difficulties most historians have favoured the Russell–Calthorpe theory.

The second objection – the pointing finger – is not as strong as it might appear. It has been argued that from Lucan's (and therefore Nolan's) position there was a twenty-degree difference between an arm pointing directly down the North Valley and an arm pointing to the redoubts on the Causeway Heights, and that this is sufficient for observers not to have been mistaken about which target the captain indicated. But such an angle of difference raises a further possibility: that Nolan flung out his arm, not towards a distant point (the far end of the North Valley), but to indicate a line (the Causeway Heights) by an arm outstretched parallel with it. This latter action would have Nolan signing with his *arm* and believing that he had indicated the guns on the heights, while observers followed the direction of his *hand* and, already conscious of the guns in the valley and unable to see the guns on the heights, assuming that he pointed down the valley.

If this was so, Nolan remains at fault for failing to appreciate that Lucan did not have the benefit of viewing the battlefield from the Sapoune Heights. Lord Raglan made this same mistake and Nolan cannot bear more of the blame than Raglan for an identical error. If Nolan had survived he could have argued – as Raglan did – that it was reasonable to assume Lucan would associate this order with the previous one and already had the Causeway Heights in mind; he merely needed reminding that not only the enemy but also the captured British guns were there. Nolan might additionally have argued in his defence that an order for cavalry to charge guns to the front, along a route with guns on both flanks, was so absurd that he could not have been expected to guess such a misconception had entered Lucan's mind.

It is possible then that Nolan believed he had indicated the guns on the Causeway Heights, and attempted to change the direction of the brigade when it subsequently advanced on those at the end of the valley. This returns us to the first objection to the Kinglake theory: that although this is the most credible explanation of Nolan's dash forward, it cannot stand without evidence. However, Kinglake was unable to present the evidence because it comes from two survivors of the charge who wrote down their memories *after* his history was published.

The first survivor to describe Nolan attempting to change the direction of the brigade was Corporal James Nunnerley of the 17th Lancers writing in 1884:

After giving a kind of yell which sounded very much like 'Threes right', and throwing his sword hand above his head, his horse wheeled to the right and he fell to the rear. As though obeying this death-like order, part of the Squadron wheeled 'Threes right'. I immediately gave the order 'Front forward' and so brought them into line again.

In *Cavalry: Its History and Tactics*, published one year before the charge, Nolan described how to change the direction of a body of cavalry after an advance had begun. It was a tricky manoeuvre but the order required to turn cavalry to the right – which in the case of the Light Brigade would have turned the regiments towards the guns on the Causeway Heights – was 'Threes right'.

One opponent of this explanation, historian Mark Adkin, attempts to discredit Nunnerley by suggesting that what he heard as 'Threes right' was no more than the man's terrible cry on being so grievously hit: 'Nolan supposedly shouting "Threes right" was probably Nunnerley's imaginative mind years later thinking the long-drawn-out shriek sounded similar to "Threees riiight".'

The sounds produced by 'Threes right', even elongated, are not easily confused with a death cry, but given the way Nunnerley's recollection is phrased it is fair argument to suggest that the shriek and the perceived order were one. Another man who witnessed Nolan's final moments – Corporal Thomas Morley also of the 17th Lancers – gave a more detailed description and this makes it clear that the order came before and was quite separate from the death cry:

In the very beginning of the Charge, when the direction we were taking just became evident, occurred Captain Nolan's movement that has been the cause of so much controversy. I was only about seventy yards from Captain Nolan and distinctly saw every movement. As soon as the brigade was fairly in motion, so that its direction down the valley was evident, Nolan rode away at speed, reached a position in front of the centre of the 17th Lancers, gave his order 'three's right' with his horse's head facing the regiment, at the same time waving his sword to the right, which signified 'take ground to the right', then turned his horse and galloped towards the Causeway Heights, still pointing with his sword in that direction. At that moment a shell exploded and a piece of it struck him in the left breast near the heart. Probably the unearthly scream which rang in our ears above the roar of the opening cannonade was a dying effort to make us follow his direction.

Morley confirms Nunnerley's evidence that some men of the 17th Lancers obeyed Nolan's order:

The 17th had instantly followed his direction and gone 'three's right'. The 13th had gone straight on instead of checking, as they should have done to respond to our movement. They were perhaps 25 or 30 yards in front of us when Nolan fell. At that juncture I heard Nunnerley shout in a loud voice, '17th Lancers, Three's Left!' We went three's left.

Adkin rejects Morley's testimony on the basis that this man 'latched on to Nunnerley's idea' – that, to put it more bluntly than he and other opponents of the Kinglake theory dare, this survivor of the charge was making it up. This is hardly an adequate way to deal with uncomfortable evidence, particularly as so much of Morley's detailed account of the charge is confirmed in the writings of other survivors.

Lord Cardigan himself eventually overcame his indignation at what he had thought was Nolan's attempt to take command of the brigade and accepted that the captain was in fact trying to change its direction: 'Nolan did not have the least idea of the mistake which was about to be perpetrated, until he saw the brigade begin to advance without having first changed front. He did not lose a moment in his efforts to rescue the brigade from the error into which he then saw it falling.'

Given the testimony of Cardigan and two survivors of the charge, and the fact that their recollections fit precisely the explanation of Nolan's act suggested by the very first historian of the charge who witnessed it and interviewed survivors, we are bound to accept that the Kinglake theory is more credible than the Russell–Calthorpe hypothesis. Russell and Calthorpe locate the origin of the misunderstanding on the Sapoune Heights, making either Raglan or Nolan responsible – and then plump for Nolan. Kinglake places the mistake down in the valley, where either Lucan or Nolan must bear the blame, and suggests that Nolan's final act was an attempt to correct it.

NOLAN: THE ADKIN THEORY

Nolan understood (correctly) that Raglan intended the Light Brigade to prevent the Russians dragging away the guns on the Causeway Heights, but deliberately misled Lucan by pointing towards the guns at the end of the North Valley.

This is the most grave accusation of all: that far from the charge being caused by a tragic misunderstanding, Nolan deliberately misrepresented the order and sent the Light Brigade charging to its destruction at the muzzles of the Russian guns. It is argued that he was so passionate about the ability of the cavalry, and so exasperated by Raglan and Lucan, who persistently refused to unleash the cavalry on the enemy, that he replaced the commander-in-chief's order with one of his own. The pointing finger *and* the command it gave were Nolan's.

This is the explanation currently in fashion and made so by historian Mark Adkin in *The Charge*, published in 1996. Adkin presents a new and detailed argument in its favour, although as long ago as 1911 C. R. B. Barrett in his *History of the XIII Hussars* considered the possibility that Nolan's act had been 'wilful perversion of the tenor of an order of the import of which he was fully aware' and found no evidence for it.

Barrett found no evidence because there is none. The theory depends wholly on guessing that Nolan's state of mind at the time might have led him to commit such a gross act. Any evidence – a letter or diary entry in Nolan's hand, or a oral confession to another officer indicating what he intended – is lacking. What Nolan did say to fellow officers and to William Russell indicates that he considered Lucan to have mishandled the cavalry throughout the campaign and to have held the Light Brigade back when it should have been sent forward. He undoubtedly felt strongly about the matter. But we cannot, without definite evidence, leap from passion to deliberate falsification.

An army is nothing without hierarchical obedience and Nolan was devoted to the British army. He was a career soldier without an estate or private income to fall back on. The deliberate misrepresentation of Raglan's order to induce Lucan and Cardigan to attack an objective other than that intended would have meant the total ruin of Nolan's cavalry career and reputation. A 'guilty' finding by the inevitable court martial would have shattered the man as surely as the Russian shell smashed the body. Whatever he felt about Lucan and however much he wanted to see the cavalry act, it is improbable in the extreme that he would have knowingly perverted an order.

Advocates of the Adkin theory make much of Nolan's belief that cavalry *could* successfully charge artillery to the front. True enough. Yet Nolan added the condition, in *Cavalry: Its History and Tactics*, that such charges should not be attempted against enemy positions 'unless they have previously been shaken by fire'. The Russian artillery at the far end of the valley and on the heights had not been shaken by fire.

The evidence for Nolan's realization after the advance had begun that Cardigan was heading straight towards the guns at the end of the valley and his attempt to change the direction of the brigade makes nonsense of the claim that he was the one who ordered the initial direction. Adkin can only defend his theory by denying that Nolan attempted to change the direction, and he finds an ingenious way of doing so:

Nolan could not have thought Cardigan was heading for the wrong objective when he suddenly darted forward. The Light Brigade had advanced barely 200 metres when they came under fire and Nolan was killed. That was far too short a distance for anybody who thought the objective was the Causeway Heights to appreciate that the Brigade was not heading the right way. From where the Brigade started, if the destination was the redoubts or the guns at the end of the valley, the route to either would be the same for much further than 200 metres.

Adkin asserts that if Cardigan had wanted to attack the guns on the Causeway Heights he would have led the brigade straight down the valley following the same route that he actually took for 'at least 1,000 metres, possibly more', wheeled to the right when he reached a point immediately below the first redoubt guns, and then advanced directly uphill to take them. Therefore Nolan could not have known so early in the advance that Cardigan intended to attack the guns to the front.

The Causeway Heights ran between the North Valley and the South Valley. If Cardigan had intended to attack the guns on the heights, he had three possible lines of advance. First, he could move down the North Valley and swing uphill to the right; his brigade would come under fire from the guns to the front and on both flanks, and his losses would be similar to those actually sustained in the charge. Second, he could advance along and to either side of the Woronzov Road, which ran up and along the Causeway Heights and passed right by the redoubts and the guns; this would be hard going on uneven ground, and he would come under fire from the guns on the Fedioukine Heights opposite and the guns on the Causeway Heights themselves, but not the guns at the end of the valley, so his losses would be drastically reduced. Third, he could wheel his brigade to the right and into the South Valley, continue until he reached a point directly below the first redoubt, and advance uphill from there; he would come under fire only from the guns on the Causeway Heights, which the Russians had placed facing into the South Valley in expectation of a British advance from that direction, and casualties would be even further reduced.

All three routes would attract some artillery fire and, as the brigade approached the guns in the redoubts, involve engaging Russian infantry and cavalry. But only one route required a ride under artillery fire from the front and both sides – and that is the approach Adkin would have Cardigan take. Cardigan was inept; he was not stupid. Nor was Captain Nolan; he would have been aware almost immediately the advance was ordered and the brigade moved straight down the North Valley that Cardigan was not heading for the Causeway Heights. He dashed out, waving his sabre and shouting, 'Threes right.' Seconds later the first Russian shell exploded nearby.

The Adkin theory has to be dismissed because of the total absence of evidence in its favour. An educated guess based on Nolan's state of mind is not good enough. The suggestion that Nolan deliberately misrepresented an order and sent the Light Brigade to its destruction is no more credible than the possibility that Lord Lucan, nurturing a lifetime's hatred of Lord Cardigan and seeing an opportunity to be rid of him, deliberately misinterpreted the order and sent Cardigan to what both men anticipated would be a certain death. The psychology of Nolan allows the theory, but that is to step from the historical to the preposterous, where evidence no longer counts.

The case against Lord Lucan

If the mistake was Lucan's then this should be evident in the altercation with Captain Nolan, who brought the order from Lord Raglan. The case against Lucan was most cogently put by Raglan himself in a letter to the Duke of Newcastle. Although Raglan's main intent was to deflect blame from himself, he could do so only by explaining where he believed it properly lay. It is indicative of his ramshackle mind that he refers to the third and fourth orders as 'the first' and 'the second', forgetting that two others came before these:

> Not only did the Lieutenant-General misconceive the written instruction, but there was nothing in that instruction which called upon him to attack at all hazards. The result of his inattention to the first order was that it never occurred to him that the second was connected with, and a repetition of, the first. He viewed it as a positive order to attack. I undoubtedly had no intention he should make such an attack.

Raglan argues that he did not order Lucan to 'attack at all hazards'. The written order certainly required an advance and not an attack, implying an altogether more considered movement allowing an assessment of the hazards involved. Yet several of those present on the Sapoune Heights heard him call after Nolan, 'Tell Lord Lucan the cavalry is to attack immediately,' and Nolan quite rightly conveyed this injunction, which, as it came after the written order, was reasonably presumed to elucidate the true intent of that order. Lucan took 'attack immediately' to imply some urgency and therefore to disallow a full consideration of the consequences, in other words 'attack at all hazards'. Raglan suggests to his masters in London that the injunction to attack immediately was part of Lord Lucan's misconception of the written order, when in fact it came directly from Raglan's own lips.

In effect Lucan had to deal with two instructions: the first, Lord Raglan's written order, and the second, Captain Nolan's oral order quoting Raglan and accompanied by an arm flung out to indicate the guns intended. The official case made against Lucan in London rested on his choosing to obey the latter rather than the former and was expressed most clearly by Colonel Munder, Under-Secretary of State:

The Lieutenant-General ought to have acted on the written orders of the Commander-in-Chief and not upon the oral ones of the aide-de-camp. It is evident that he derived his resolution to attack at all hazards, and contrary to his own and Lord Cardigan's expressed opinion, not from Lord Raglan's note, which could by no possibility be construed in that sense, but from the hurried remark of the Staff Officer.

Munder acknowledges that Lucan's decision to 'attack at all hazards' was not his own but was 'derived . . . from the hurried remark of the Staff Officer'. The term 'hurried remark' suggests something unreliable, yet by all accounts Nolan repeated the exact words shouted after him by Lord Raglan. This link back from Nolan's 'remark' to Raglan himself formed the basis of Lucan's defence. By long-established military tradition the oral orders brought by an ADC were to be obeyed as if they had been spoken directly by the original speaker himself.

However, this principle had to be exercised alongside another of equal import and just as firmly established by tradition: that of the discretion accorded one of Lucan's rank not to implement without question an order that he believed to be dangerously misconceived. Both Raglan and the politicians in London argued that in the circumstances the second principle should have overruled the first. The implication is that Lucan lost his head, did not think clearly, failed to question Nolan adequately and made the wrong decision.

Lord George Paget, while asserting that all of the officers concerned in giving, delivering and executing the order should bear some of the blame, had no doubt who was most responsible. He approached the issue from a different angle. Instead of examining the mistakes each had made, he asked which of them had been in a position to identify and correct what was going wrong and had failed to do so. He even suggested how Lucan could have been expected to act differently:

It were perhaps asking of human nature more than one is warranted in doing, to censure Lord Lucan for not keeping his temper at such a momentous crisis, but nevertheless, I venture to think he might better have risen to the occasion.

Thus, Lord Lucan: 'You are in an excited state, Captain Nolan. Calm yourself, and explain to me an order of a very grave nature, which as yet I do not understand. Which, do you believe, are the guns that I am ordered to attack? You come from the heights, and therefore must have had a more commanding view of the scene of operations than I have; besides, you have probably heard the views of those who sent the order, and are, therefore, in a position to give me further information.'

Is it to be believed that even Captain Nolan would have failed in his duty after so temperate a remark? And such a conversation would have saved the disaster.

When Lucan asked where the enemy and guns were that he was to attack, Nolan's response was undoubtedly cocky and insolent, and the arm he flung out was no substitute for a proper response. Yet it is Lucan who must be condemned, not by his first question but by the absence of a second. Given the gravity of the order that Nolan seemed to have brought, Lucan should have queried him further and satisfied himself beyond all doubt about what Raglan intended. If after these questions Lucan was still not convinced of the sense of the order, the discretion allowed his rank permitted him to seek further elucidation by returning a message to Raglan. Lucan's only possible response to this, that sometimes in battle the commander-in-chief is forced to throw a particular unit into an apparently senseless attack in order to prevent a greater ill occurring elsewhere, and that the urgency and authority with which Nolan delivered the order made this appear to be just such an occasion, is a credible but weak defence.

The case against Lord Cardigan

If Cardigan was at fault then his error must be evident in the brief meeting with Lucan when he received the order from his superior officer. Cardigan claimed that Lucan rode across to him and said, 'Lord Cardigan, you will attack the Russians in the valley.' Cardigan pointed out that there were enemy guns to the front and on both flanks. Lucan replied, 'I cannot help that; it is Lord Raglan's positive order that the Light Brigade is to attack the enemy.'

Cardigan's account of what was said between them is confirmed by Lord Lucan: Cardigan did object on the grounds that his brigade would be exposed to flanking batteries and was told that nevertheless the order must be obeyed.

Despite his faults and his obvious ineptness as a cavalry commander, Lord Cardigan cannot be blamed for the charge of the Light Brigade. He received the order from his superior officer and quite properly protested. When Lucan reiterated that the order must be carried out, Cardigan could do no more. He led the brigade and showed great courage under the heaviest fire, particularly in preventing young officers at his back from forcing the pace. There is some question about his behaviour after reaching the Russian guns, but he was not to blame for the charge.

The blame for the loss of the Light Brigade must be shared between their lordships Raglan and Lucan, and Captain Nolan. Lord Raglan dictated an imprecise and badly worded order, gave the aide-de-camp chosen to deliver it only hurried instructions, and confused the issue by adding a further, shouted command as this officer rode away. Captain Nolan did not pay due attention to Raglan's instructions, delivered the order in an unsatisfactory manner, and his flippant swing of the arm to indicate the enemy caused Lord Lucan to misconceive the direction the attack should take. Lord Lucan lost his head in the exchange with Nolan, failed to question the junior officer on the precise enemy and guns to be attacked, and failed to exercise the discretion allowed his rank not to implement a senseless command.

Who lost the Light Brigade? All three officers contributed to a series of fundamental errors that led to the charge. But if we ask (with Paget) which of them could by virtue of his rank and his position in the chain of events have been expected to perceive and prevent the terrible direction those errors were taking, that officer can only be Lord Lucan.

The Duke of Newcastle wrote to Raglan on 27 January 1855: 'Inform Lord Lucan that he should resign command of the Cavalry Division and return to England.' The official reason given for this resignation was that the relationship between Raglan and Lucan had broken down and that Lucan could not therefore properly carry out his duties. There was more to it than that, as *The Times* of 9 March expressed in *its* verdict on Lord Lucan: 'It is not fitting that officers so little gifted with the powers of understanding or executing orders should be entrusted with the lives of men or the honour of nations.'

We can conclude that Lord Cardigan has no case to answer, and that the fault for the loss of the Light Brigade must be shared between their lordships Raglan and Lucan, and Captain Nolan – but the greatest part of it lies with Lord Lucan.

15. The Balaklava Bugle Controversy

*Did Henry Joy or Billy Brittain – or no one at all – sound
the charge of the Light Brigade?*

Visitors to the National Army Museum in Chelsea, London can
see a bugle blown at Balaklava and engraved, 'Presented by the
Colonel of the 17th Lancers to Trumpet-Major H. Joy, on which
the Balaklava Charge was sounded on October 25th 1854'. The
17th Lancers rode in the front line of the charge immediately
behind Cardigan. If that regiment believed Joy to have sounded
the charge, then it can hardly be denied. The marble cross of Joy's
grave in Chiswick, erected by officers of the 17th, is inscribed,
'Sounded the memorable Charge of the Light Brigade at Balaklava'.

But visitors to The Queen's Royal Lancers Museum located
inside Belvoir Castle, the Leicestershire home of the Duke of
Rutland, can see a second Balaklava bugle. The Queen's Royal
Lancers is the descendant regiment of the 17th Lancers and this
instrument is described as 'blown by Trumpeter William Brittain
to sound the charge of the Light Brigade'. Brittain was unhorsed
and mortally wounded during the charge and his bugle is suitably
holed and bent. The sound effects playing over the display – the
jingle of harness, the boom of the Russian guns and above all the
sounding of the charge – are mightily convincing.

The controversy over whether Trumpet Major Henry Joy or
Trumpeter William (Billy) Brittain sounded the charge, and therefore which instrument is *the* Balaklava bugle, has raged for 150
years. It even surfaces every so often in the national press. Under
the headline 'BATTLE OVER THAT BUGLE' the *Daily Mirror*
of 17 April 1964 asked, 'Just who DID blow the bugle that sounded
the Charge of the Light Brigade on the battlefield at Balaklava in
1854?'

Despite having two bugles to choose from, the answer given by most historians of the Crimean War is: no one at all. It is said that under intense fire the cavalrymen dug in their spurs and raced at the guns, coming to the charge long before the order could be given by Cardigan or sounded by any trumpeter. This is considered so certain a fact that evidence is unnecessary. Yet the only men who knew for sure were those who rode in the charge, many of whom recorded what they saw and heard.

In 1854 all cavalry orders were sounded by trumpeters. Cavalry trumpeters carried two instruments, the bugle and the trumpet. The bugle swung free at the man's side and the trumpet was carried slung across his back rolled up in its lines. Trumpeters used the trumpet, a longer instrument, able to produce a wide range of notes, when dismounted for camp calls such as 'Water and feed' which involved a complex musical notation. Because the trumpet was unwieldy on horseback, particularly while on the move, field calls such as 'Trot', 'Gallop' and 'Charge' were sounded on the shorter, handier bugle.

Their lordships Lucan and Cardigan did not have permanent personal trumpeters to sound the orders they gave; the Light Brigade regiments took turns to provide orderly trumpeters for each of them on a weekly basis. Because it was the turn of the 17th Lancers in the week of the charge, both Lucan and Cardigan had a trumpeter from that regiment. The two men provided were Trumpet Major Joy and Trumpeter Brittain.

Henry Joy was thirty-six at the time of the charge. Born in Ripon, Yorkshire, Joy had enlisted on 13 May 1833, aged only fourteen and with a recorded height of four feet, nine inches. By May 1847 he had been promoted to trumpet major and in 1852 commanded the regimental band at the funeral of the Duke of Wellington. In the Crimea, Joy was the regiment's highest-ranking trumpeter and during the week of the charge was assigned to the divisional commander, Lord Lucan.

At just after 11.00 a.m. on 25 October the cavalry was dismounted and waiting at the entrance to the North Valley. There can be no doubt that it was Joy who sounded the order to mount immediately prior to the charge. Sir John Blunt, Lord Lucan's interpreter, was present when Captain Nolan arrived with Lord Raglan's order. Blunt watched Lucan – positioned between the Light and Heavy Brigades – read it, and noted that before speaking to Nolan Lucan turned to Joy and ordered him to 'Mount the division'. That Joy sounded this order was confirmed by Cardigan, waiting in front of the Light Brigade, who, when he heard it, sent an aide to find out what was happening. The order to mount was the first in the series of orders that was to take the Light Brigade to the Russian guns.

Once the advance was under way, each order increasing the pace was signalled first of all by a bugle call from the trumpeter riding beside and a little to the rear of Lord Cardigan, and then repeated by the regimental trumpeters further back. The officers of the 17th Lancers rode several lengths behind their brigade commander and his trumpeter, except for Cornet George Wombwell, who was aide-de-camp to Cardigan and remained close to him. Therefore when Wombwell later asserted that Trumpet Major Joy rode in the charge of the Light Brigade and sounded the several orders increasing the pace to the 'Charge', the surviving officers of the 17th took that as irrefutable proof.

When Joy left the 17th Lancers on 21 April 1860, these officers suggested presenting him with a silver replica of his bugle but he preferred to keep the original and was allowed to do so. It was then that it was engraved. Joy joined the Balaklava Commemoration Society formed in 1877 and continued to attend after its membership was restricted to those who could prove that they rode in the charge of the Light Brigade. When he stopped attending its annual reunion dinners in 1888 it was assumed that he was by then too frail or unwell to travel. He died in August 1893 and was buried in Chiswick cemetery where the marble cross paid for by officers of the regiment marks his grave.

Five years after Joy's death his widow sent his bugle and medals to be sold at Debenham, Storr & Sons auction rooms in London. These items excited much interest, particularly from Mr T. G. Middlebrook, proprietor of the Edinburgh Castle public house, which stood above the rail tracks leaving Euston Station. Middlebrook had established a museum in the pub to display his collection of curiosities, which included Cromwell's helmet, Dr Johnson's spectacles and the spear thrown to kill General Gordon at Khartoum. He was most eager to add the bugle that sounded the charge at Balaklava to his collection.

At the auction on 30 March 1898, Henry Joy's bugle and medals were knocked down to Middlebrook for the sum of 750 guineas. He immediately stood up to make an announcement: 'Mr Auctioneer, there are many gentlemen present connected with the army and the press. Will you allow me, therefore, to announce that at my death this bugle will be the property of the 17th Lancers.' Everyone present shouted and applauded.

The 17th Lancers was then stationed in Ballincollig, Ireland, and sent over Trumpet Major Harrison to sound the 'Charge' on the day that the bugle was first placed on display in the Edinburgh Castle. It was exhibited in a glass case on the bar. Veterans of Balaklava visited to see the bugle and no doubt downed a few pints in honour of the relic. Middlebrook staged bar concerts with female singers and comedians, and at the end of each concert an old soldier blew the 'Charge' on the bugle 'as it had been blown at Balaklava'.

Or had it? Only days after Middlebrook purchased the bugle the sensationalist *Morning Leader* uncovered a story that it ran as a major scandal. William Bird, previously of the 8th Hussars and who rode in the charge with that regiment, claimed that ten years earlier, in 1888, he had confronted Joy, saying that he knew Joy had not ridden in the charge with the Light Brigade. According to Bird, Joy admitted that to be so. Bird had agreed not to speak out about it providing Joy left the Balaklava Commemoration Society and did not attend its reunion dinners. Bird said that he had decided to reveal the truth because Joy was now dead and because of the extravagant claims made for Joy's bugle by Middlebrook.

The publican rejected it all. He replied that when he purchased the bugle Joy's widow had given him a letter written by Sir George Wombwell in which Sir George stated that he heard Joy 'sound the order for the Balaklava Charge'. This was crucial evidence, for as aide-de-camp to Lord Cardigan, the then Cornet Wombwell rode close to both Cardigan and his trumpeter.

The *Morning Leader* stood by its story and sent a reporter to interview Sir George. When the newspaperman pointed out to him that Lord Lucan had confirmed that Joy was *his* trumpeter, Wombwell admitted: 'I heard the charge, but of course that would be by Lord Cardigan's trumpeter.' This was reported in the *Morning Leader* of 4 April 1898. It was a startling development. Wombwell had heard Lord Cardigan's trumpeter sound the charge and only assumed that this man was Joy, his regiment's senior trumpeter. Joy had in fact been Lord Lucan's trumpeter, and Lucan, with his trumpeter at his side, remained behind with the Heavy Brigade when the Light Brigade advanced down the valley.

Triumphant, the *Morning Leader* next sent a reporter to get Middlebrook's reaction. Middlebrook had gained a great deal of publicity by exhibiting Joy's bugle and he was by now despondent: 'I am not at all sure this is the real bugle. Naturally I feel very sorry, but I'm not the man who would show any relic and give it a title which I knew to be false.' When the newspaper moved on in search of its next scandal and the affair was forgotten, Middlebrook changed his mind again. There was still the inscription on Joy's bugle and another on his memorial stone. If those officers of the 17th Lancers who survived the charge had believed Joy to be the man who sounded it, Middlebrook was happy to believe that too.

The Edinburgh Castle continued to be a place of pilgrimage for veterans of the Light Brigade until Middlebrook's death in 1907. On 30 January the following year the contents of his museum were sold at auction. Middlebrook's public declaration that on his death the bugle would go to the 17th Lancers was ignored, and Joy's bugle and medals were knocked down to W. Astor, who presented them to the Royal United Services Institution in Whitehall. They were later transferred to the National Army Museum in Chelsea.

Billy Brittain was twenty-five when he rode in the charge of the Light Brigade. It was his first taste of action – and his last.

Born in Dundalk, Ireland, Brittain enlisted in the 17th Lancers on 11 March 1843 at the age of thirteen years and eleven months. His height was recorded as four feet, ten inches. His regimental service record suggests that he was a bit of a lad: he was promoted to trumpeter in March 1849, reduced to private in November of the following year, and received a sentence of thirty days' imprisonment in March 1851. The nature of his misbehaviour was not recorded, although the punishments might indicate that he enjoyed a drink or two. However, by 1853 he was receiving good conduct pay of one penny a day, and his reputation was such that during the week of the charge in October 1854 he was assigned to the brigade commander Lord Cardigan, as orderly trumpeter.

As Cardigan's trumpeter, Brittain would undoubtedly have been the man who sounded all orders given during the advance down the valley. At or very near the Russian guns when the battery had changed from roundshot and shell to canister in a final bid to stop the brigade, he was badly wounded and unhorsed. No official record was kept of each man's wounds but Private James Mustard, 17th Lancers, wrote that: 'Poor Bill Brittain was wounded in the right groin supposedly by a piece of a shell and after a few weeks when his wound began to heal, an abscess formed in his back and when the Doctor cut it a canister shot fell out.'

Brittain's bugle, displayed at Belvoir Castle, is badly bent and holed in the bell. His nephew Frederick Brittain spoke to several survivors of the charge after their return to England from the Crimea, and one of them had seen what happened after the trumpeter fell: 'The hole in the bell of the bugle was caused by the point of the lance of a Cossack who endeavoured to gain possession of the bugle as he rode past William Brittain who was lying wounded on the battlefield.' The Cossack had expected to collect the bugle on the tip of his lance, but its cord was still wrapped around the wounded man.

Corporal Nunnerley helped bring Brittain in from the battlefield: 'I got the bugle from under Trumpeter William Brittain after placing him on the stretcher, the cord was under his back and to remove it would have given him great pain, so one of the men that was present drew his sword and cut the lines that were under his back from the bugle.'

Severely wounded, Brittain was put on board the steamer *Australia*, which sailed from Balaklava on 26 October with the worst of the casualties, bound for the barrack hospital in Scutari. Mrs Farrell, one of the nurses who tended him, wrote a letter from 'The Hospital, Scutari' dated 14 November 1854 to a Mrs Powell. Although Mrs Farrell finds little use for punctuation, her words provide a revealing glimpse inside the Scutari hospital:

> We had our hands full Miss Nightingale and the french nun with myself Mrs Hutchinson and those other women has had our hands full since that balaklava battle we had some awful sights to witness and attend to night and day without much rest and oh what sights those wounds of some were shot thro bowels legs and chests the trumpeter that sounded the charge for Cardigan was a most pitiful case he begged that his bugle not be taken out of his sight Cardigan spent half hour with him soothing him he belongs to 17 Lancers his name is Brittin, the Sergeant of the 17 calls him billy and keeps telling him to pluck up and get out soon to sound another charge but there never was any chance for him. A very funny Irishman of the 8 hussars named Darby Doyle asked Miss Nightingale for some Cognac as he was nearly faintin, and he golloped it up and winked his eye at me and Mrs Hutchinson.

The assertion by one of Cardigan's biographers that his lordship sat for hours at Brittain's bedside should not be taken literally, but clearly he did visit his trumpeter at Scutari, although his first call was to the bed of Captain Morris, commanding officer of the 17th Lancers, also severely wounded. Significantly, Mrs Farrell had reason to know Brittain as 'the trumpeter that sounded the charge for Cardigan'. Although she was not at Balaklava, Cardigan and 'the Sergeant of the 17' most certainly were, and it was from them that she learned of his part in the charge.

Billy Brittain died at Scutari on 14 February 1855. Cardigan had told him that he could keep the bugle, which was strictly speaking regimental property, and it was sent, possibly in the baggage of a man of the 17th who had recovered sufficiently to be returned to England, to the cavalry depot at Brighton Barracks, and from there delivered to Brittain's father, Corporal William Brittain, who had himself previously served in the 17th Lancers and was by then a Chelsea Pensioner.

On Corporal Brittain's death in 1873 the bugle was left to his third son Henry. Henry died in 1881 and his wife Ellen, on her death, left it to their daughter of the same name. By this time several members of the Brittain family had moved from Ireland to England and were living in Newcastle, although Ellen had remained in Dublin. In 1901 Ellen travelled to Newcastle in order to sell the bugle to a Mr Baker, the proprietor of the Percy Arms public house.

Baker was aware of the debate about whether Joy or Brittain had sounded the charge, but he was convinced by the evidence that only Brittain, as Lord Cardigan's trumpeter, could have done so. His only concern was that two survivors claimed to have heard Brittain sound the first three orders increasing the pace of the advance by degrees, but not the charge itself, suggesting that he was hit before that final order was given. William Butler, previously of the 17th Lancers, wrote: 'Walk, trot, gallop was sounded by William Brittain.' And a letter to the *Evening Standard* of 2 April 1898 quoted another veteran of the 17th: 'Britten was a dead man in a few strides after he had sounded the Gallop.' However, the fact that he had been hit by canister shot – which the Russians fired only at close range – suggested that he remained in the saddle long enough to sound the 'Charge'.

Baker purchased the bugle but by 1904 had begun to think that he had made a mistake. There were still those who claimed that Joy – and thus Joy's bugle – had sounded the charge of the Light Brigade. Worse still, letters from survivors appeared in the news-papers claiming that the charge was not sounded at all. He decided to cut his losses and offer it for sale at auction.

While there is no record of Baker corresponding with Ellen Brittain at this point, he may have done so, for towards the end of that year and prior to the auction she wrote to those survivors who had known Billy, asking them what they had seen or heard of his part in the charge. She specifically wanted to know whether Billy or Joy had sounded the 'Charge', or whether this final order was in fact not sounded at all.

Peter Marsh, formerly of the 17th Lancers, replied on 20 December that the matter could not be doubted:

Each regiment had to find a Trumpeter in turn each week to attend on Lord Cardigan so it happened that the 17th was the regiment to find the said Trumpeter on that week of the Charge and William Brittain was told off for that duty so that he is the Trumpeter that sounded the Charge on that day first and then all the other Trumpeters sounded after him the poor fellow was badly wounded and was taken with the other wounded to Scutari hospital where he died he was in the same troop as I was well respected by all in the regiment I have been asked the question more than once and I have given the same answer for there is no other can be given as to who sounded the Charge first it was decidedly Trumpeter Brittain 17th Lancers.

A few days later Ellen received a reply dated 30 December from William Pearson, also previously of the 17th:

I knew William Brittain perfectly well as we were both in the Band together, he was the best Trumpeter in the Brigade and he was sent out to be Lord Cardigan's Trumpeter and it was him that sounded the Charge. The last I saw of William was in Scutari Hospital we was both wounded together he used to creep on his hands and knees from his bed to mine to see how I was.

The replies continued to arrive and so overwhelming was the evidence that Ellen Brittain asked four of the men to make signed statements, witnessed by solicitors, telling what they knew of the different parts played in the charge by Billy and by Joy. These original statements are preserved in the archives of The Queen's Royal Lancers:

Owing to my position in the Brigade I did not hear the Charge sounded but I can say that the Charge would be sounded by Trumpeter William Brittain and none other as he acted as Orderly Trumpeter to Lord Cardigan. As regards Trumpeter Joy of the 17th Lancers he was not in the Charge of the Light Brigade and neither was Lord Lucan, whose Trumpeter Joy was.

Thomas Morley's signed testimony, 20 March 1905

I rode in the Charge of the Light Brigade. It was the late Trumpeter William Brittain who acted as Orderly Trumpeter to Lord Cardigan and he sounded the Charge for the Light Brigade. As regards Trumpet Major Joy, he did not sound the Charge for the Light Brigade. He was not in the Charge of the Light Brigade neither was Lord Lucan whose Trumpeter Joy was.

William Pearson's signed testimony, 18 July 1905

Trumpeter William Brittain acted as Orderly Trumpeter to Lord Cardigan and it was Trumpeter William Brittain who sounded the Charge of the Light Brigade. He was severely wounded and was taken with others including myself to Scutari Hospital where he died.

James Mustard's signed testimony, 9 September 1905

I took part as a Sergeant in the Charge of the Light Brigade. Trumpeter Brittain was standing by and I saw and heard him sound the Charge of the Light Brigade. He was afterwards mortally wounded and I carried him off the field. Trumpet Major Joy was not attached to the Light Brigade but was in the Heavy Brigade.

James Nunnerley's signed testimony, 19 September 1905

The witnessed testimony of survivors made under the Statutory Declarations Act of 1835 is compelling evidence. These were not the kind of men to swear untruths.

In November 1905 Baker put the evidence collected by Ellen Brittain and his investment in the bugle to the test. He offered it for sale at Glendining & Co. of Argyll Street, London. When the price offered rose to a staggering 1,000 guineas – Joy's bugle had fetched 750 guineas – he withdrew it from sale. Those in the auction room clearly believed that it was Billy Brittain who had sounded the charge.

There was one man who was not convinced. William Pennington had ridden in the charge with the 11th Hussars and was the most vocal of those who claimed that the charge had not been sounded at all. He now contacted several newspapers to say that he had not heard the charge sounded and nor had any other survivor he had spoken to. For good measure he added that the previous calls increasing the pace of the brigade to the trot and then to the gallop had not been sounded either.

Another survivor was incensed at that and wrote to the *Yorkshire Weekly Post* under the pseudonym, 'One of the Six Hundred'. His letter was published on 20 January 1906:

Having read out to me out of 'The Newcastle Daily Journal' an article concerning the Charge of the Light Brigade at Balaklava – that according to every survivor of the charge without exception, the charge was never sounded at all – I beg to state that I was one who rode in that famous charge. I rode in the ranks of the 17th Lancers and I beg to inform you that the charge was sounded. Trumpeter William Brittain, being Lord Cardigan's trumpeter, sounded the charge. He was severely wounded shortly after. I had also read to me an article in the 'Daily Graphic' some weeks back, where Mr Pennington says he rode in the ranks of the 11th Hussars and that there were no bugle calls in the Charge of the Light Brigade. I think it is a mistake of Mr Pennington's when he states there were no bugle calls. The 11th Hussars rode behind the 17th Lancers and it would be impossible for all to hear the calls that were sounded, because with the roar of artillery in front, and right and left of the Brigade, it was impossible for the second line to hear the charge when Trumpeter Brittain sounded it.

This is a crucial point. Undoubtedly many survivors heard no order sounded – hardly surprising, given what Captain Godfrey Morgan of the 17th called 'the whistling and crackling of the shells . . . beyond all description' – but it is quite ridiculous to deduce from this that no order was sounded. Logic dictates that a hundred men may fail to hear a call and yet that call might truly have been sounded, while if just one man truly hears a call then it cannot be denied. A number of survivors *did* report hearing the call. It is likely that the order failed to carry to the regiments and men farthest from Brittain due to the noise of the guns and because some of the regimental trumpeters who would have taken up the call had by then become casualties.

Such reasoning meant nothing at all to Pennington and eight years later, in the year that the Great War began, he was still claiming that no charge had been sounded at Balaklava. Although John Whitehead, who rode with the 4th Light Dragoons, had previously believed that Joy sounded the charge he was in no doubt that it *was* sounded. In a letter dated 7 February 1914 he responded to Pennington's claim: 'I always said it was sounded to whoever put the question to me as I am convinced that I am right I can with truth say that I heard it and it came firstly from Lord Cardigan's Orderly Trumpeter and he was one of the 17th Lancers of course I might be a little wrong saying it was Joy but it was sounded.'

Pennington continued to assert that no charge was sounded and on 20 February, Whitehead wrote a second letter, clearly very angry:

> I feel that I should just like to have five minutes conversation with Pennington to convince him of what I think about his remarks by saying the Charge was not sounded no doubt he was only a Recruit and I believe that might make a lot of difference in how steady he was keeping his head but hearing and seeing what I did there is no one in the world will alter my opinion that the charge was sounded by a Trumpeter of the 17th Lancers who I now know was Brittain of course I always was under the impression it was Joy but it don't alter the situation that I for one heard the Bugle sound the Charge.

'No doubt he was only a Recruit' – Whitehead had guessed correctly. Private William Pennington was twenty-one at the time of the charge and had enlisted in the 11th Hussars only six months earlier. Before that time, according to his father, the full extent of his horsemanship had been 'a pony ride on Blackheath'. Pennington described his part in the charge in a letter to his father and admitted: 'As for myself, I never reached the guns in front.' It is understandable that he failed to hear the charge sounded, either because of the noise of battle or because he was unhorsed and left behind before it was ordered, but quite illogical of him to contend that the call could not therefore have been blown.

In 1964, Billy Brittain's bugle was put up for sale by James Baker, son of the publican who had purchased it from the Brittain family in 1901. Even before it reached the auction room the controversy resurfaced. On 17 April the *Daily Mirror* posed the question of who had truly blown the charge and reported:

Sotheby's, the London auctioneers, are sure that it was trumpeter Billy Brittain – whose bugle they are putting up for sale. But Mrs Bertha Kearns of Isleworth said yesterday: 'It is a lot of nonsense that Brittain sounded the charge. It was my grandfather Trumpet Major Henry Joy who started it all.' Mrs Kearns is backed by Mr W. R. Turner of Westgate-on-Sea: 'My great-great-grandfather, Trumpet Major Henry Joy, sounded the charge.'

The bugle was auctioned at Bond Street on 20 April 1964 and knocked down in less than a minute for £1,600. The successful bidders were actor Laurence Harvey and US television presenter Ed Sullivan. Harvey had recently purchased the film rights for *The Reason Why* by Cecil Woodham-Smith, at that time the most widely read history of the charge. He intended to finance the film himself and star in it, and cynics took the purchase to be a publicity stunt. However, according to Sullivan's agent Peter Pritchard, the two men had heard that the bugle was to be sold and thought it would be a great pity if it did not go where it belonged – to the regimental museum of its original owners, the 17th Lancers.

30. Lord Raglan's order to the cavalry. Dictated by Raglan, hastily written down by General Airey and carried to Lord Lucan by Captain Nolan, this is the order that led to the charge of the Light Brigade

31. The bugle (*left*) blown by Trumpeter Billy Brittain to sound the charge of the Light Brigade, and the bugle (*right*) blown by Trumpet Major Henry Joy to sound the advance of the Heavy Brigade. The damage to Brittain's bugle was caused when it was pierced by a Cossack lance

32. The charger of Captain Nolan bearing back his dead master to the British lines. This depicts the moment when the Russian guns opened fire and Nolan became the first casualty. Although the artist shows a spent cannonball in the foreground, Nolan was hit by a fragment of a shell that exploded overhead

33. *The Charge.* The view that Cossack gunners would have had of the 17th Lancers as the lances came down from the 'Carry' to the 'Engage' in the final seconds of the charge

34. & 35.
The mêlée behind the guns. These two sketches, showing the moment that the
11th Hussars reached the Russian guns, were among the first impressions of the
charge seen by those at home in England

36. *The Roll Call.* Lord Cardigan and survivors immediately after
their return to the British lines, as the first roll call of mounted men
was taken

five

Into the ~~valley~~ of Death
  Rode the six hundred;
For up came an order, which
  Some one had blunder'd;
'Forward the light Brigade!
Take the guns' Nolan said;
Into the ~~valley~~ *five* of Death
Rode the six hundred.

'~~Forward~~ *Honour the* the light Brigade'!
Hearts that were not
~~No men was there~~ dismay'd,
Not tho' the soldier knew
  Some one had blunder'd:

Theirs not to make reply,
Theirs not to reason why,
Theirs but to do ~~and~~ die,
~~Into the valley of Death~~ *So they rode onward*
~~Rode the six hundred.~~

Cannon to right of them
Cannon to left of them
Cannon in front of them
  Volley'd and thunder'd

Half a league half a league
Again Half a league onward
~~Struck in~~ the valley of death
Rode the six hundred.

37. 'The Charge of the Light Brigade'. Alfred, Lord Tennyson's first draft of his
poem in the hand of his wife, Emily, written as he dictated, with alterations in
Tennyson's own hand

38. Alfred, Lord Tennyson. The Poet Laureate said that he wrote his most famous poem 'after reading the first report of *The Times* correspondent'

39. William Russell, war correspondent of *The Times*. Russell spent much time in the cavalry camp at Kadikoi. The British people first learned of the charge from his report published on 14 November 1854.

40. The Valley of Death. This most popular of Roger Fenton's photographs could be purchased in London in 1855 for five shillings. It shows a ravine on the Balaklava plain filled with spent cannonballs, not the site of the charge

41. Four survivors of the charge photographed in August 1855 after their return to the cavalry depot at Brighton. From the left they are Corporal Thomas Smith, Corporal William Dimmock, Private William Pearson, and Corporal Thomas Foster, of the 17th Lancers. All four men are in full dress uniform and hold ash lances as used in the charge

42. Private Benjamin Soley, who rode in the charge with the 17th Lancers. After returning home to Castle Bar Cottage, Ealing, he became known as 'Old Iron' because he insisted on singing 'Any Old Iron' at the reunion dinners held annually by survivors

On the 24 of October 1854 we stood on the Plain all night to our Horses On the 25th inst the Order came for the Light Calvary to retire to one end of the Valley leaving the Heavy Dragoons on the Plain untill Captain Noland brought the Order to Lord Cardigan. The Russians was firing at us two hours before Captain Noland came with the Order also a troup of Artillery firing over us and when he gave it to Lord Cardigan and he tore it up. then told us to Mount our Horses and follow him and he told Captain Noland to turn back. but he would not

had hard biscuits and grapes for breakfast to commence the day nearly all the Officers were Killed or wounded

Benjamin Soley. 17th Lncs
19. Castle Bar Cottage
Castle Bar Park.
Ealing.

do so and he was the first that was shot. When we charged the Russians cut holes in us so that we could turn a horse and Cart round. and we got down to there Guns as quick as we could and Killed a lot of the Artillery men my horse was shot dead and I had three wounds hand leg. and the forehead when we were able to look round we were surrounded by a regiment of Polish Lancers and we had to fight our way through them the best way we could I was taken into the Hospital and had my wounds dressed and was in there for three days we

43. & 44. Letter describing the charge written by Private Soley. Despite three injuries – in the hand, leg and forehead – he was not counted among the seriously wounded and after three days in the regimental hospital in the church at Kadikoi he returned to duty

45. Survivors of the charge with Butcher, one of the few horses to live through both the charge and the winter that followed and to return home. The six men are from the 13th Light Dragoons, photographed after 1861 (when that regiment became the 13th Hussars). On the extreme left is Edwin Hughes, who outlived every other survivor and died in 1927

46. Survivors of the charge photographed with Buffalo Bill (Colonel William Cody) at Earls Court, London, in 1903. Colonel Cody is fifth from the left in the back row and turned to face him is James Nunnerley of the 17th Lancers. The survivors, from all five Light Brigade regiments, wear their Crimean War campaign medals

After the bugle was knocked down, Trumpeter Phillip Costen, in 17th Lancer uniform of the Crimean War period, stood and blew the 'Charge'. The reporters present were eager to know whether this meant the regiment was convinced that Brittain, not Joy, sounded the charge at Balaklava. Major George Graham, representing the 17th Lancers, would say only, none too helpfully, that 'Brittain was the man who sounded something.'

The bugle was later handed to representatives of the regiment live on the *Ed Sullivan Show* in New York, exciting great interest in the charge of the Light Brigade throughout America and, quite incidentally, gaining huge publicity for the proposed film. The regiment got its bugle back and it remains on display in the regimental museum inside Belvoir Castle. Laurence Harvey never did get to star in the film, which was finally released in 1968, starring John Gielgud and Vanessa Redgrave.

Major Graham's equivocal statement on behalf of the regiment – 'Brittain was the man who sounded something' – expresses the heart of the matter. Despite the wealth of evidence that the charge was sounded by Billy Brittain, two crucial pieces of contrary evidence will not go away: the inscriptions on Joy's bugle and memorial cross. The cross was, after all, erected by officers of the 17th Lancers and it categorically states that Joy 'Sounded the memorable Charge of the Light Brigade'. Joy's claim was set in stone by his own regiment.

There are two possible explanations: terminological laxity and human error, both of which seem to have been particularly common at Balaklava.

The first, terminological laxity, arises from the fact that the whole movement of the brigade down the valley, a distance of one and a quarter miles, became known by the cavalrymen and later by the press and the public as the charge of the Light Brigade, while properly speaking it was an advance and only during the final forty yards or so did the pace accelerate to the 'Charge'.

There is no doubt that Henry Joy blew the order for the division

to mount, because that was given by Lord Lucan. It is also possible
that Lucan, after riding along the front line to tell the 11th Hussars
to fall back, indicated that the advance could now begin by having
Joy sound it. As this call ordered an advance that eventually became
known in its entirety as the charge, it might be said that Joy in this
sense sounded the charge of the Light Brigade.

There is evidence from a survivor that this is indeed what
happened. Corporal Thomas Morley of the 17th Lancers wrote:

I first saw Lord Lucan riding about the attacking line and was aware that
we were about to charge. I saw very distinctly what does not appear in
any history, Lord Cardigan gallop on perhaps three hundred yards in
front and to the right to a piece of slightly rising ground, evidently to
reconnoitre the position of the Russian Army and the best way-ground
for his brigade.

I never heard the word of command to go forward from any officer.
If given at all, it must have been by Lord Lucan, for Cardigan was, as I
said, in advance of us planning the line of movement and evidently did
not see what went on in his attacking line at the moment of advance.
The whole movement was executed in the greatest haste and we were
quickly off at a trot.

If Lucan ordered the advance it would have been blown by his
trumpeter, Henry Joy. A degree of terminological laxity might then
have allowed the inscriptions on Joy's bugle and memorial cross to
claim that he had 'Sounded the memorable Charge'. This first
explanation is feasible but unconvincing. Unlike the men (and
almost everyone today), the officers of the 17th Lancers would have
been unlikely to use precise military terms in such a loose way.

The second explanation is all too familiar in the context of this
story: that the two inscriptions owe more to human error than the
careless use of military terms. Cornet George Wombwell knew
that Henry Joy was the senior trumpeter of the 17th Lancers and
believed he was Cardigan's orderly trumpeter on the day of the
charge. He heard Cardigan's trumpeter sound the charge. Simple
logic then required that it was blown by Joy. If Wombwell, who

as ADC to Cardigan was in the best position to see what happened, believed that, then we can assume the other officers of the 17th did so too, taking their lead from him. When eventually Lucan confirmed that Joy was *his* trumpeter, Wombwell admitted it must have been Brittain who blew the charge.

The men too saw only a trumpeter of the 17th Lancers from fifteen yards behind; some simply assumed it was Joy, a more prominent figure in the 17th than Brittain. Finding himself thus acclaimed by officers and men alike, and Brittain dying at Scutari, Joy was not about to disabuse them. No doubt he enjoyed his unwarranted fame until William Bird challenged him in 1888. Joy quietly withdrew from the Balaklava Commemoration Society and attended no more of its reunion dinners in preference to being exposed and shamed.

It is certain that Lord Lucan's trumpeter Henry Joy blew the order to mount the Cavalry Division, and it is possible, though only one source supports it, that he sounded the advance for the Light Brigade. He then remained behind with Lucan and later blew the advance and the trot for the Heavy Brigade as this set off in support.

Only Lord Cardigan's trumpeter Billy Brittain could have sounded the subsequent orders increasing the pace of the Light Brigade by degrees to the charge. There is sufficient evidence from survivors to conclude that the charge was sounded and that it was Billy Brittain who sounded it.

16. Lord Cardigan's Retreat

Did Cardigan desert the Light Brigade at the Russian guns?

Where is Lord Cardigan?
Colonel Mayow (to Colonel Shewell behind the Russian guns)

Where is Lord Cardigan?
Lord Paget (to Colonel Douglas behind the Russian guns)

Holloa, Lord Cardigan! Were you not there?
Lord Paget (to Lord Cardigan after returning from the charge)

Some time after the charge two false rumours about Lord Cardigan circulated in England. The first and most absurd was that he had not participated in the charge of the Light Brigade at all. It may have begun as a misunderstanding of Lord Paget's question to Cardigan back at the British lines – 'Were you not there?' – in the minds of those who knew that the brigade commander slept on his yacht and habitually put in a late appearance with his regiments. Paget was fully aware that Cardigan had led the first line as far as the Russian guns; by 'there' he clearly meant behind the guns.

The second rumour was that after the charge Cardigan retired to his yacht, leaving the desolate survivors of the Light Brigade to sleep on the open plain. Even the redoubtable Cecil Woodham-Smith in her classic history of the war fell for this one – 'Lord Cardigan rode back to his yacht, had a bath and a bottle of champagne with his dinner, and went to bed' – and a host of lesser historians have followed her. Although such behaviour might be thought in keeping with Cardigan's character there is nothing to substantiate this allegation, and Lieutenant Henry Maxse, one of his aides, saw him sleeping on the ground at the cavalry camp that evening, wrapped in his cloak.

While such rumours may have amused the gentleman gossipers in London's clubs, among the officers and men of the cavalry in the Crimea a far more serious accusation was levelled at Cardigan: that after reaching the Russian guns he had immediately turned back, deserting the Light Brigade at its time of greatest need. This was no baseless rumour, for those whispering it had taken part in both the charge and the pursuit. It is implicit in Lord Paget's question which, fully and explicitly put, might have been: Were you not there behind the Russian guns? Did you retire after reaching them while your brigade pursued the enemy cavalry?

This accusation was first made public in December 1856 with the appearance of *Letters from Headquarters, or the Realities of War in the Crimea*. Although the book was published anonymously, 'By an Officer on the Staff', everyone in cavalry circles knew exactly who the author was: Somerset Calthorpe, a lieutenant in the 8th Hussars at Balaklava and Lord Raglan's aide-de-camp. He claimed that Lord Cardigan lost control of his horse as he reached the Russian guns and was immediately carried back towards the British lines, leaving his brigade to attack the Russian cavalry without him. The crucial passage reads:

This was the moment when a General was most required but unfortunately Lord Cardigan was not then present. On coming up to the Battery a gun was fired close to him, and for a moment he thought his leg was gone. Such was not the case, as he remained unhurt; however, his horse took fright, swerved round, and galloped off with him to the rear, passing on the way by the 4th Light Dragoons and 8th Hussars before these Regiments got up to the Battery.

This was far more than an indictment of Cardigan's horsemanship. It was more than a mile from 'the Battery' to 'the rear' and there was an implied accusation that, while Cardigan might have been expected to control his horse and return to his brigade, he

instead allowed it to carry him all the way to safety. Others read
the passage that way too.

Cardigan claimed that Calthorpe's account was so inaccurate and
damaging that it amounted to 'scandalous and disgraceful conduct',
and demanded he face a court martial. The army rejected that, and
when Calthorpe agreed to make changes in the third edition of the
book Cardigan believed that he had won without it. These changes
turned out to be little more than a footnote in which, while
appearing to admit to an error in his description of Cardigan's
conduct in the charge, Calthorpe actually hardened the accusation:

The Earl of Cardigan has stated, since the publication of the first edition
of this book, that he considers the account given of the part taken by him
in the Light Brigade charge 'unworthy of any reply, as it is well known'
that he led the Light Brigade up to the Russian cavalry in rear of the
battery. The author could only rely on statements furnished him by
officers engaged in the charge; but as the excellence of Lord Cardigan's
horsemanship is unquestionable, the idea that his horse ran away with
him is no doubt erroneous! Several officers of the 4th Light Dragoons
and 8th Hussars bear witness to the fact that His Lordship retired between
these regiments as they were advancing.

In admitting to an error – Cardigan's horse had not bolted –
and at the same time reaffirming the testimony of his witnesses
concerning Cardigan's early retirement Calthorpe left the reader
only one explanation for that retirement: Cardigan must have
deliberately deserted his brigade at the guns and dashed back to
safety. With a court martial already denied him, Cardigan applied
to the civil courts.

The case of Cardigan v Calthorpe was heard in London's Westminster Hall in June 1863 by Lord Chief Justice Cockburn and
three other judges. After hearing the testimony of witnesses the
court ruled that although Calthorpe's account did contain errors
damaging to Cardigan, the book had been in print for seven years
and it was too late to seek any form of redress. Moreover, as a
number of witnesses called by Calthorpe – all of them survivors of

the charge – described seeing the brigade commander retiring before the second line had even reached the Russian guns, Cardigan had succeeded only in further publicizing the suspicion that he deserted his brigade.

Because the case had been brought against Calthorpe, accused of libel, these witnesses appeared for the defence. Their testimony is more revealing if it is viewed as evidence for the prosecution in the case that really matters but which was never brought: that against Cardigan, accused of deserting the Light Brigade. In what follows the evidence quoted is that of the original witnesses given in court in the case of Cardigan v Calthorpe, but it is applied to the hypothetical case of the Light Brigade v Cardigan.

The case against Lord Cardigan includes the testimony of officers and men of the first line of the Light Brigade that when they pursued the enemy behind the guns he was not present with them; the testimony of officers and men of the second line that he was seen retreating up the valley while they were still charging towards the guns; and evidence from those waiting on the British lines that he returned before any other survivors of the brigade.

Among those involved in the action beyond the guns was the Victoria Cross winner Private Samuel Parkes of the 4th Light Dragoons: 'Lord George Paget called out to some officers near him "Where is Lord Cardigan?" and I then heard someone (who I always believed and now believe was Captain Low) say "Lord Cardigan has gone back some time."'

Colonel George Mayow, second-in-command of the Light Brigade, lost sight of Cardigan in the smoke from the final volley as they reached the guns. In the absence of the brigade commander it was Mayow who ordered the survivors of the front-line regiments to charge the enemy cavalry massed behind the guns, and Mayow who eventually gave the order to turn back and retreat up the valley:

I was induced to give these orders in consequence of not being able to see anything of Lord Cardigan on emerging from the smoke that hung over the Russian Guns and being the Senior Officer in his absence. Whilst going up the valley I looked in every direction for Lord Cardigan (who would have been conspicuous from wearing the Hussar dress of the 11th) and not being able to see him anywhere I said to myself 'He must be either killed or taken prisoner.'

While Mayow organized the first line and advanced on the Russian cavalry, the regiments coming up behind had not yet reached the now silent guns. None among this second line expected to see the brigade commander already retiring, but Lieutenant Edward Phillips of the 8th Hussars had no doubt about it: 'The 8th Hussars and the 4th Light Dragoons formed the second line. While the Regiment was still advancing down the valley, I saw the Earl of Cardigan coming back. He passed the left flank of the Regiment.'

Private Matthew Keating of the same regiment explained precisely why he was so sure the officer he saw retreating was Lord Cardigan:

I distinctly remember seeing a General Officer with scarlet trousers on a chestnut horse with white heels retiring to the rear of the 4th Light Dragoons as we were advancing to the charge – I knew the horse before we went into action as Lord Cardigan's horse and I knew Lord Cardigan's appearance also and I am perfectly certain it was Lord Cardigan I saw retiring. At the time we were about 200 or 300 yards off the battery.

Several other men said much the same, noting the distinctive appearance of Cardigan's uniform and his horse. Private Daniel Deering of the 4th Light Dragoons testified that while the 4th and the 8th Hussars were still charging they 'met Lord Cardigan alone retiring on a chestnut horse'. The Russians had seen him turn back too and after the charge they questioned their Light Brigade prisoners about him. Private Thomas Lucas of the 4th had been captured by the Cossacks and heard what was said: 'General Liprandi, amongst other questions, asked "Who was the General that went back on the Chestnut horse with white heels?" and he was told it was Lord Cardigan.'

Lord Lucan was with the Heavy Brigade at the British end of the valley. He claimed that Lord Cardigan was the first to return: 'Remaining in advance to watch the movements of the Enemy and to be prepared to support the Light Brigade should they be pursued on their retreat, I saw Lord Cardigan gallop up from the direction of the Enemy. He was at a distance of about 200 yards from me. At this time, no part of the Light Brigade was within my sight.'

Cardigan rode to one side to speak with officers of the Royal Horse Artillery. Captain Brandling was standing nearby and later told Colonel Whinyates that he heard Cardigan say, 'Has anyone seen my regiment?' A group of survivors then came into sight, led by Colonel Shewell and Colonel Mayow, and as they came closer the men of the Heavy Brigade cheered them. What happened next, according to Brandling, seems much like a sketch from pantomime:

When the first cheer was given by some heavies, Lord Cardigan turned about as if to see what it was for, saw it was in compliment to the men returning, trotted towards them, turned about in front of Colonel Shewell, and took up the 'walk'. And now occurred something rather painful to witness. Colonel Shewell was in front, and Colonel Mayow behind on the left of the other officers. The moment Cardigan got his back turned round to them, Colonel Mayow pointed towards him, shook his head, and made signs to the officers on the left of the Heavies, as much as to say, 'See him; he has taken care of himself.' Men here and there in the ranks also pointed, and made signs. Of course Cardigan did not know what was going on behind him while he was smiling and raising his sword to the cheers. He was thus, in a way, held up to ridicule.

It could be argued that Mayow as Cardigan's second-in-command ought not to have stooped to such behaviour, yet the barefaced cheek of Cardigan leading the survivors in proved too much for him – he after all had taken command of the Light Brigade in Cardigan's absence. We can only guess at the precise nature of the 'signs' the men were making at Cardigan behind his back, though these may have involved the use of two fingers.

To conclude the case for the prosecution, no one denied that

Cardigan led the brigade right up to and in among the guns; the accusation is that he then abruptly turned about and retired, deserting both officers and men, and that he was so quick to do so that as he rode back men in the second line were still at the charge and saw him pass by in the opposite direction.

The case for the defence rests on Lord Cardigan's testimony that he was involved in man-to-man combat with Cossacks behind the guns, supported by the testimony of officers and men who saw him in action or heard him shout orders behind the guns, and the testimony of officers and men who saw Cardigan retiring alongside them.

First, Cardigan's own account:

I continued at the head of the first line of the Brigade, and led them up to and into the Battery − as I was leading them into it, one of the guns was fired close to my horse's head, but I rode straight forward through and past the guns, till I came nearly up to a strong force of Russian Cavalry stationed some distance in rear of the guns. I was then attacked by some Cossacks, slightly wounded, and nearly dismounted: I had difficulty in recovering my seat, and in defending myself against several Cossacks who attacked me − I was at this time nearly alone, for the first line of Cavalry, which had followed me into the Battery, had been entirely broken up. Upon disengaging myself from the Cossacks, and returning past the guns, I saw the broken remnants of the first line in small detached parties retreating up the hill towards our original position.

Cardigan appears to overstate his case, implying that he faced the massed Russian cavalry effectively alone − one sabre against so many Cossack lances − while the brigade behind him was 'broken up'. His story is however substantially confirmed by an officer and a sergeant of the 13th Light Dragoons coming up behind him. Captain (then Lieutenant) Percy Smith said: 'I saw one of the Cossacks who were drawn up in the rear of the Guns cut at his Lordship with his sword and I recollect the circumstances particularly as I observed that Lord Cardigan kept his sword at the slope and did not seem to take any trouble to defend himself.'

Sergeant Thomas Johnson had become detached from the 13th, which rode in the first line, and found himself among the second-line regiments:

I passed with some of the second line through the Guns and on approaching the Enemy's Cavalry which I believe was drawn up some little distance in rear of the battery, I and a man named John Heeley found ourselves within a few yards of Lord Cardigan who was also in the rear of the battery and surrounded by and engaged in defending himself against four or five Cossack Lancers. I then saw Lord Cardigan disengage himself from the Cossacks and ride away apparently unhurt but one of the Cossacks then made a right rear point at him with his Lance which I believed and feared had passed through His Lordship's body.

Sergeant Johnson's testimony makes a particularly strong point in Cardigan's defence because if this man passed through the guns 'with some of the second line' and then saw Cardigan still engaged in combat with Cossacks, it cannot be the case that Cardigan retreated before the second line reached the guns.

If Cardigan was ahead of the front line, virtually alone within reach of the enemy cavalry and was attacked by a number of Cossacks, it is crucial to his account that there is a feasible explanation of why he was not killed or taken prisoner. It is claimed that his life was saved by the most unlikely coincidence: the Russian officer waiting forward of the enemy line opposite the point at which Cardigan broke through the smoke was Prince Radzivill, who had met him socially when visiting London and immediately recognized him. The prince supposedly ordered Cossack lancers to take Cardigan prisoner and gave them strict instructions not to harm him.

These men approached Cardigan with their lances held forward and were therefore beyond the reach of his sabre. He was at their mercy – a single thrust would have finished him – but they merely prodded at him with their points. Cardigan wrote that he was 'slightly wounded' and 'with difficulty got away from them'. Sergeant Johnson saw this wound inflicted and supposed it to be

more serious, which it undoubtedly would have been if the Cossacks had not been constrained by Prince Radzivill's order. It is
possible that Cardigan's injury was more bruise than broken skin,
for he later said in Captain Brandling's hearing that 'those instruments of theirs are deuced blunt; they tickle one's ribs'.

Other men saw or heard Cardigan behind the Russian battery.
Corporal Morley of the 17th Lancers saw him about fifty yards
beyond the guns, and Private Wightman of the 17th believed that
Cardigan attempted to rally survivors: 'After passing the guns, I
distinctly heard His Lordship give the order to rally inside the
Guns in the space between those Guns and the Russian Cavalry in
the rear.'

Wightman may have heard Colonel Mayow, who certainly was
trying to rally the men there, although Private Richardson of the
11th Hussars claimed that Cardigan's voice was unmistakable: 'Lord
Cardigan – he was a rough spoke man, was Lord Cardigan, but
good hearted – he shouts, "Give em the points lads; it's no use
slashing at em." And he was right too, because they all wore those
thick ulsters.'

If Cardigan was involved in the mêlée behind the guns then he
must have retired with, rather than ahead of, the men. Captain
Soames Jenyns of the 13th Light Dragoons said that on his way back
he 'observed Lord Cardigan walking his horse'. Private Mitchell of
the 13th saw Cardigan on horseback apparently searching for the
remnants of his brigade. Mitchell had set off on foot towards the
British lines:

Lord Cardigan came galloping up from the direction of the guns, passing
me at a short distance, when he turned about again, and meeting
me, pulled up and said: 'Where is your horse?' I answered: 'Killed, my
lord.' He then said, in his usually stern hoarse voice: 'You had better
make the best of your way back as fast as you can, or you will be taken
prisoner.' I needed no telling, for I was doing so as fast as I was able. He
then rode a little farther down, and in a few minutes returned past me at
a gallop.

Mitchell's evidence suggests that the brigade commander might at this point have turned back towards the guns, though his retreat a few minutes later 'at a gallop' is not so helpful to his case.

It was when Lord George Paget reached the British lines and found Lord Cardigan already there, not having seen him behind the guns, that he shouted his question. Cardigan was alert to the accusation and quick to reply: 'Oh, wasn't I, though! Here, Jenyns, did you not see me at the guns?'

That response sums up the case for the defence: witnesses saw Lord Cardigan in action behind the guns at a time when the second line had already reached this position, while others testify that he attempted to rally the men and later returned to the British lines among them.

Considerable evidence exists that Lord Cardigan did not desert the Light Brigade at the guns because he was still in action behind the guns after the whole of the brigade had reached the battery. That evidence is damaged if two questions that arise from this evidence are not resolved. First, if he remained behind the guns, how could officers and men in the second line have seen him retreating while they were still advancing? Second, why did he not then rally the men and lead the survivors in pursuit of the Russian cavalry – as Colonel Mayow did?

The only possible reply to the first question is that those who believed they saw Cardigan and identified him by his uniform and horse were mistaken. They may have been so. It is likely that they saw Lieutenant George Houghton of the 11th Hussars and took him to be Cardigan. As he neared the Russian guns Houghton was severely wounded on the forehead by a fragment of shell. He immediately turned his horse and headed back towards the British lines; a number of men were wounded and turned back at that same point. Houghton was wearing a similar uniform to Lord Cardigan and most significantly he was riding a chestnut horse with the same leg markings.

Those among the second line who reported seeing Cardigan retreating were young officers and men none of whom had a face-to-face acquaintance with the brigade commander; they knew him by the combination of his uniform and his distinctive horse. Lieutenant Houghton combined these characteristics too and he was retreating while the second line was still some distance from the guns.

Cardigan answered the second question – of why he retreated alone instead of rallying the survivors and continuing the pursuit – in three separate statements: 'The feeble remains of the lines of the brigade could have done nothing more under a general officer than they did under their own officers.' Perhaps not, but it was the first responsibility of the general officer to do what could be done and only in his absence did that duty fall to 'their own officers'. Cardigan argued that he could in fact do nothing because there was no one within his sight to rally: 'On being nearly surrounded by Cossacks, I gradually retreated until I reached the battery. I could see none of the first line or of the supports. The first line did not follow me.' Yet Cardigan rhetorically asked Alexander Kinglake: 'What was the duty of the Brigadier under such circumstances? In such a desperate mêlée to remain to be taken prisoner, or was it his duty to retire?'

Cardigan's second and third points do not sit easily together: if he could see 'none of the first line or of the supports', who exactly was involved in the 'desperate mêlée'? Possibly the mêlée is a reference to his own encounter with the Cossacks, for elsewhere he claimed that on escaping them and returning to the guns he could see only a few individual survivors returning and thought that the brigade had been wiped out or had already turned back. Allowing for the smoke and the confusion, this scenario is not implausible. Part of the first line and much of the second missed the guns altogether and continued down the valley, while the survivors among the guns were quickly rallied by Mayow and led in pursuit of the Russian cavalry. It is just possible that Cardigan returned to the guns as Mayow's force moved beyond them – Cardigan and Mayow thus passing in opposite directions – without each seeing the other. Only a weak form of the case against Cardigan then remains: that he was not as active in seeking out formed groups of survivors as he ought to have been.

In view of the considerable evidence that Cardigan was involved in combat with Cossack lancers behind the guns and the strong possibility that those who reported his early retreat had in fact seen Lieutenant Houghton, the accusation that Cardigan deserted the Light Brigade must be dismissed.

However, he did not pursue the Russian cavalry, unlike a large section of his brigade; he did not seek out formed groups of survivors; and he retired before the majority of his officers and men. There is no suggestion that his actions were due to cowardice or loss of nerve, but they did demonstrate his inadequacy as a senior officer. His orders were to attack the Russian battery and he did exactly that, but no more. Cardigan's declaration that no more should have been expected of him is not an acceptable excuse from the lips of the brigade commander.

17. Not the Six Hundred

Counting them out and counting them in

Into the valley of Death
Rode the six hundred.

Well, no, not exactly.

There are two differing figures for the number of officers and men who charged with the Light Brigade at Balaklava, both provided by officers who were present. Lord George Paget gives a total of 673, based on the regimental returns of those on parade on the morning of the charge, and this is the figure that is usually seen in the history books. The problem with this is that a few men subsequently reported sick and not all of those on parade were available to take part in the charge. Colonel Whinyates makes a calculation from the same regimental records used by Paget, but adjusts his figure downwards in the light of evidence from survivors to exclude known non-combatants, and reaches a total of 658.

Whinyates makes a point of referring to 'combatant officers', suggesting that there was at least one non-combatant officer. After speaking with survivors he may have had to exclude Cornet John Yates of the 11th Hussars from his number. Yates seems to have lost his nerve when the advance was ordered and 'returned to camp'. Troop Sergeant Major Smith of the 11th recorded: 'Cornet Yates remained behind when the brigade was ordered to attack.' Private Pennington of the same regiment wrote in a letter that 'Yates was temporarily indisposed' at the time of the charge and did not take part.

Both Paget and Whinyates took as their starting point the returns from the five regiments, so while Whinyates's 658 is a reliable reckoning of the regimental officers and men who charged, it does not include those who did not belong to one of those regiments. To his 658 we must add Lord Cardigan, his second-in-command Colonel Mayow, Lieutenant Maxse (Cardigan's ADC) and Captain Nolan, who attached himself to the brigade at the last moment. This brings the total to 662.

We now have the number of British officers and men believed to have charged, but two Sardinian officers also rode with the brigade. Major Govone and Lieutenant Landriani were attached to the French cavalry as observers – Sardinia later sent troops to fight alongside the allies – and when the Light Brigade was ordered to charge they saw an opportunity to distinguish themselves and lined up alongside the British cavalry. Both were wounded and one of them was taken prisoner. Including these two in the figure gives a total of 664, and this is now generally accepted to be the total number of officers and men who took part in the charge.

Two men however have been overlooked, and for good reason: neither of them was supposed to be in the charge.

The first was Private Jack Vahey of the 17th Lancers. The starting point for all calculations has been the regimental returns for the morning parade; from there, men known not to have charged have been excluded, and non-regimental and foreign officers included, to reach a final figure. But Vahey was not counted in the regimental returns for the morning parade because at that time he was in the prison tent sleeping off the drink of the night before. We know from Vahey's account, confirmed by other survivors, that he arrived just in time to charge with the Light Brigade. Therefore we must add him to the generally accepted figure to make a total of 665. Vahey escaped from the prison tent along with Private Paddy Heffernan of the 1st (Royal) Dragoons and both men set out to take part in the scrap; no further mention is made of Heffernan in Vahey's account and if this man did become involved, it must be assumed that he rode with his own regiment, which was part of the Heavy Brigade.

The second man who should not have charged but did so was Assistant Surgeon Henry Wilkin of the 11th Hussars. Surgeons and assistant surgeons were not included in the reckoning made by

Whinyates and Paget. Their duties kept them in camp – in the sick tents or the church at Kadikoi being used as a field hospital. Their services immediately following an engagement were crucial and these men were not required to risk themselves in action. Wilkin had other ideas and charged with the men; he was the only surgeon to do so. Therefore we must add him to the generally accepted figure to make a final total of 666 officers and men who rode hell's mile.

The reader is cautioned not to take this or any figure as absolute. There are circumstantial reasons for believing that the number of chargers might have been higher still. Private Vahey was able to escape from the prison tent because the guards had gone. He implies that there had been other prisoners beside himself and Heffernan, and these too had disappeared. When Vahey reached the sick horse line he found only two, useless horses, a surprisingly small number considering the generally exhausted state of the brigade's mounts. Given that the brigade had left England 1,500 strong and now formed up to advance on the enemy with less than half that number, it is feasible that the guards and their prisoners – excluding the two still sleeping it off – had been called on to take part, and were mounted on horses from the sick line.

The known facts allow a total of 666 officers and men in the charge. No fewer. There may have been more.

Alexander Kinglake, the first historian of the war, who watched the charge from Lord Raglan's position, recorded that at the first roll call when the men reformed following the charge, 195 mounted men answered their names. Later historians repeated this fact or at least what they took it to imply, subtracting Kinglake's 195 from Paget's starting figure of 673 to produce a total of 478 Light Brigade casualties – about 70 per cent. These figures created the prevailing impression, which persists to this day, that the majority of those who charged at Balaklava were killed.

Kinglake meant nothing of the kind. The roll call took place soon after the first sizeable groups of survivors reached safety and formed up, and these were men who had been neither seriously wounded nor dismounted. The whole point of this early count was to establish, not the number of survivors, but the number of men still mounted and capable of being deployed in any action that might follow. Many dismounted men were still walking back; wounded men were awaiting rescue; others had been taken prisoner. Sergeant Thomas Johnson of the 13th Light Dragoons was among those present for the first roll call and recorded that of the 112 men of his regiment only 10 were present. True, but 26 were wounded and had yet to be brought in, 13 had been taken prisoner, and some 60 or so were struggling back on foot. When the official regimental return was compiled it showed only 14 men of Johnson's regiment had actually been killed.

What then was the true number of casualties? According to the regimental return of casualties compiled on 26 October and used by Colonel Whinyates, 102 officers and men were killed outright in the charge and 7 more died later that day of their wounds. If we add Captain Nolan, excluded from Whinyates's reckoning, then that makes a total of 110 killed.

Whinyates records 127 wounded, and to this we must add the non-regimental officer Lieutenant Maxse and one of the Sardinian officers to make 129. In addition Whinyates gives the number of men taken prisoner by the Russians as 58, but does not know how many of these were also wounded before their surrender; Lord George Paget records this figure as 31 and to these men we must add the second Sardinian officer, making a total of 32 men wounded and held by the enemy.

The most reliable casualty figures for the charge of the Light Brigade based on returns made on the day after the charge are therefore:

Killed outright or died of their wounds:	110
Wounded and returned to the lines:	129
Wounded and taken prisoner:	32
Total killed and wounded:	**271**

This means that of the 666 who began the advance, 271 became casualties and an incredible 395 (or 60 per cent) rode one and a quarter miles under fire from the Russian guns, attacked and pursued the Russian cavalry behind the guns, and returned up the valley with the enemy at their backs unscathed except for minor wounds not reported to the surgeons. Less than 17 per cent had been killed.

The number of horses killed was considerably higher. Lord Paget recorded 332 horses killed in the charge and a further 43 'shot for wounds' on their return to the lines, a total of 375 (over 56 per cent) killed.

Some of the wounded were later to die at Scutari – though not necessarily of their wounds; disease was rife on the wards – and a number of those taken prisoner died of their wounds in Russia, in most cases following the amputation of a shattered limb. Yet in total contradiction of popular notions of the casualty figures more than 75 per cent of the officers and men who rode hell's mile were either unhurt or recovered from their wounds.

Of course it would have been of little comfort to those who had lost a son, husband or father in the charge to be told that, all things considered, the casualties were remarkably low. Public anger at the blunder was fuelled not so much by the number who died as by the suspicion that not a single man need have done.

18. Death or Glory?

Did the charge succeed or fail?

The motto of the 17th Lancers was 'Death or Glory'. In the aftermath of the charge many of the men must have added a pertinent question mark, wondering which term best summed up their ride down hell's mile.

Some – mostly the survivors, and private soldiers throughout the army – saw the charge as a military blunder in which the ineptness of aristocratic officers had needlessly sent many cavalrymen to their deaths. Others – mostly observers watching from the Sapoune Heights or from England – saw it as a magnificent example of how the dash and esprit de corps of light cavalry could overcome apparently impossible odds.

Historians have neatly combined these two views to declare the charge a 'magnificent blunder'. Because the magnificence is defined as mere spectacle and the blunder is measured by the number of dead and wounded, only one conclusion follows: the charge failed miserably. Thus in the many historical accounts of the charge, no analysis of its success or failure has been thought possible or necessary because the casualties permit only one conclusion. But that is not the case.

The charge cannot be said to have failed on the basis of the number of casualties alone. The immediate and lasting impression gained by the British public was that the losses sustained in the charge made it the most tragic action of the campaign. As we have seen, the numbers turned out to be 110 dead and 161 wounded. But at the Alma, 362 men were killed and 1,640 wounded; at Inkerman the figures were 632 and 1,878. Yet both of these battles were declared successful. Nor can the charge be said to have failed on the basis of the number of casualties expressed as a percentage of those involved. The impression given by the term used on the day by Lord Raglan and taken up by others – that the Light Brigade was 'lost' – is that a majority if not all of the men had been killed or seriously wounded. Sixteen per cent killed and 24 per cent wounded is far from annihilation, and because these casualties were sustained by cavalry in action against artillery, they must be considered remarkably low. It is possible that it was the much higher casualty rate among the horses that, for Raglan, defined the brigade as 'lost', for cavalry regiments were nothing without their mounts. The losses suffered by the men of the Light Brigade were therefore not extraordinary and do not in themselves qualify as evidence that the charge failed.

Later commentators, aware of the figures, shift the emphasis from the number killed to the pointlessness of a charge that achieved nothing, arguing that the futility of the act rather than the casualties defines it as a failure. This again is assumed to be so obviously the case that our question – Did the charge succeed or fail? – remains disallowed.

It needs to be asked. In addition, because popular fascination with this 'magnificent blunder' stems not from the splendour or the failure alone but from the combination of the two, we need to enquire into the nature of a magnificence that can be perceived in an act of such tragic folly.

There are three military criteria by which the charge can be judged: the role of the Light Brigade in the defence of Balaklava, the intended objective of Lord Raglan's order (the guns on the Causeway Heights) and the assumed objective of that order (the guns to the front).

The Light Brigade was part of the defensive screen established by Lord Raglan to protect Balaklava. Whatever the true objective of the Russian attack on 25 October 1854 – to take Balaklava or to cut the lines of supply between Balaklava and the British army besieging Sevastopol – the enemy was successfully turned back. From this it might be argued that the charge of the Light Brigade was a success because it ended any possibility that the enemy might renew the attack on that day.

In fact that issue had already been determined by the action known as the thin red line and by the charge of the Heavy Brigade. The subsequent charge of the Light Brigade was made against Russian defensive, not offensive, positions. Therefore the charge was insignificant in the defence of Balaklava and cannot be considered successful merely because Balaklava was saved.

Raglan's fourth order to the cavalry, which led to the charge, was made on the assumption that the Russians were dragging away British guns from the Turkish redoubts on the Causeway Heights. Whatever action was taken by Lucan could only be considered to have succeeded if, in the precise terms of the order, it prevented the Russians carrying away the guns.

Seven British guns were removed from the redoubts, possibly around the time of the charge or later that day. They were taken into Sevastopol and displayed as proof that Russian forces had won the battle. Church bells were rung as if for a great victory. This was mostly for effect – it raised the morale of those inside the city – although the Russians had gained ground: they had taken and held the Causeway Heights.

Whether the advance of the Light Brigade would have been successful if Raglan's order had been properly understood and Cardigan had led his regiments towards the guns on the heights can only be a matter for conjecture. The Russians might, as Raglan hoped, have withdrawn. It is more likely they would have stood their ground, and in that case it is doubtful that the Light Brigade could have retaken the guns without infantry support, which was coming up but had still not arrived. If Cardigan had pressed home the attack as Raglan required, Light Brigade casualties on the heights, where regiments of Russian cavalry and infantry were massed, might have been as great as those actually sustained in the valley. The intended action was Raglan's blunder from the moment he ordered his cavalry to advance on the heights without infantry support. Only the misunderstanding of that order saved him from later recriminations and made it Lucan's blunder.

If we judge the charge in terms of the intended objective of the order – the guns on the Causeway Heights – it can only be said to have failed. The Light Brigade did not prevent the Russians carrying away the guns.

If we remove the charge from its tactical context, which was at best muddle-headed, it is possible to assess the hell ride on its own terms – that is, not by whether it achieved the objective intended by Lord Raglan, but by how successful it was in achieving the objective Lord Lucan believed had been set.

Lucan believed that Raglan required the cavalry to attack and take the guns visible at the far end of the valley. Neither he nor Cardigan thought that such an objective could be achieved; it seemed far more likely that the brigade would be wholly destroyed. Cardigan did not expect to survive, and when Lucan turned back with the Heavy Brigade it was on the assumption that Cardigan's regiments would be annihilated at the guns and there would be nothing left to support. The Russian gunners thought the cavalrymen mad even to make the attempt.

Remarkably and against all the odds, after charging through the fire of guns from the front and on both flanks, the Light Brigade did take the battery. The Russian cavalry massed behind the guns turned and fled. Officers and men of the Light Brigade laid claim to several of the guns with the intention of returning with them to the British lines until Colonel Mayow ordered them to pursue the enemy cavalry.

For seven minutes the Russian guns had fired on a defenceless mass of men and horses but failed to stop the advance. Given the total number of guns, the time the Light Brigade was within range of each battery and the fact that it took each gun team thirty seconds to reload, about 200 rounds must have been fired. The Light Brigade lost 271 men killed and wounded. Many of these casualties fell to the Russian cavalry; Troop Sergeant Major Smith made a rough survey of the wounded and found that almost half had been cut by sabres or pierced by lances and had not been hit by artillery fire. While it is impossible to be precise, this suggests that far fewer than 200 casualties were caused by the guns. The losses inflicted on such a closely packed enemy riding directly at the muzzles of their guns to the front and offering an easy target for their guns on each flank – less than one man killed or wounded per round – were for the Russian artillery an astonishing failure.

The gunners had their excuses. Those on the flanks found it difficult to align their pieces with the regiments – riding only two men deep – moving across their arc of fire. This continuous movement forward also caused problems for the gunners to the front, who found it difficult to set the correct length of fuse for the shells, so that some exploded in front of or behind rather than directly over the brigade. The Russian artillery preferred a standing or marching prey – infantry. Nevertheless, such a number of guns would have been expected to stop a cavalry advance, and should have done much better.

Despite severe losses the Light Brigade reached the guns and dispersed the gunners. Russian observers were quick to acknowledge the extraordinary success of the brigade in charging and silencing a battery of guns to the front. Lieutenant Koribut Kubitovich wrote: 'The Englishmen charged the guns and not even the canister fire could stop them; they kept on racing forward. The Don Cossack gunners saw that there was no time to save their guns, and withdrew in order to save themselves. But the enemy rode on at their backs and cut them down without mercy.'

Lieutenant Stefan Kozhukhov, a Russian artillery officer, admitted that in reaching the guns the British achieved what he had thought impossible. He described how they went on to do what he could not even have imagined:

Once through our guns the enemy moved quickly and bravely at a gallop towards our cavalry. This was so unexpected that before anyone realized it our cavalry had broken . . . It was chaos. Our cavalry outnumbered the enemy five times over, and yet it fell back in total disorder to the Chernaya, with the English coming hotly forward at the hooves of our horses.

Many survivors believed that had Lord Lucan led the Heavy Brigade up in support at the time the Russian cavalry was in full retreat, a spectacular defeat could have been inflicted on the enemy and a large number of guns taken and held. That Lucan instead turned back is in itself evidence of the wholly unexpected success of the Light Brigade.

If we judge the charge in terms of the assumed objective of the order, it was a remarkable success. In the event no ground was retaken and no guns captured, but this feat of cavalry – which deeply shocked the Russians – had a significant psychological result, which for want of a better term we must call the Tennyson effect.

> O the wild charge they made!
> All the world wonder'd.

Russian officers wondered about the 'wild charge' and at first could come to only one conclusion. They told their men that the spirit shown by the British in the valley had much to do with the spirits consumed by them in camp – the whole brigade had been made drunk before being sent out against the guns. Even General Liprandi suspected as much. When he visited men of the Light Brigade taken prisoner he asked them in English how their commanders had made them charge the Russian guns. Private Wightman remembered how he phrased the question: 'Come now, men, what did they give you to drink? Did they prime you up with spirits to make you charge us in such a mad way?'

Some of the men took that as an insult to their courage and Wightman heard Private William Kirk of the 17th Lancers, who was wounded but still full of fight, answer back with scant regard for the officer's high rank: 'You think we were drunk? By God, I tell you that if we had as much as smelt the barrel, we would have taken half Russia by this time!'

If they had tried, the Russian cavalry might not have stood in their way. Alexander Kinglake had no doubt about the effect of the charge on the enemy: 'For a long time afterwards it would have been impracticable to make the Russian cavalry act with anything like confidence in the presence of a few English squadrons.'

The Tennyson effect was evident in England too, where there was an immediate fascination with the charge of the Light Brigade. When General Bosquet, watching from the Sapoune Heights, famously said, '*C'est magnifique, mais ce n'est pas la guerre!*' he was quite properly thinking like a general. But Tennyson, seeing it from England courtesy of *The Times*, realized with a poet's insight that for the public at home it was the magnificence that mattered most. The Frenchman was not bemoaning the loss of life but its military pointlessness; he would not have minded the loss if it had achieved something tactically significant. For the British public the outcome was irrelevant, given that the enemy had already been turned back from Balaklava; indeed public fascination with the charge might well have been considerably less if it had achieved something. That nothing came before (properly understood orders) or after (a tactically significant achievement) to justify it, left only the pure act of the charge itself, and it is this that sets the charge of the Light Brigade apart.

Captain Morris of the 17th had previously served with the 16th Lancers at Aliwal. That charge against artillery was extolled as an example of the best light cavalry could do when training, dash and esprit de corps conjoined with timely orders to achieve a strategically important objective. Despite that, there was little public interest in Aliwal. Yet there was an immediate national fascination with the charge at Balaklava. The reason, Tennyson saw, was in the wildness of the charge. This was not the wildness of drunks or lunatics, but of men who, while held in check by both Lord Cardigan and their own discipline, had at the same time passed beyond orders that made sense, and perhaps beyond sense itself. The charge of the Light Brigade laid bare the pure will to charge that was otherwise hidden as at Aliwal behind properly understood orders and tactical good sense. The magnificence was in the display of this will to charge that set men free from fear of the enemy, the guns and even death itself.

Because the Tennyson effect was a matter of the way the charge was perceived from the outside, it was not apparent among the officers and men of the Light Brigade in the days and weeks that followed the action. Depressed by the loss of comrades and a feeling that they had been let down by their divisional and brigade commanders, they had no chance to recover before the harsh winter further reduced both their morale and their fighting efficiency. It was much later, when they returned to England and saw the charge as if from afar, that the Tennyson effect struck. Even infantrymen who had jeered the cavalry at the Alma and taunted the men as 'look-ons', came home to give graphic accounts of the gallant charge they claimed to have witnessed, though few could have done so. Many a cavalryman who had not been in the North Valley on the morning of 25 October 1854 and some who had not even been in the Crimea claimed to have taken part in the charge, so that heroes abounded throughout England. When the Balaklava Commemoration Society was formed it was said that so many impostors attended the first reunion dinner in London that the number of men present was more than twice the total known to have survived the charge.

Whether we call the charge of the Light Brigade a success or a defeat is determined by the criteria we use. This writer believes that the charge can only fairly be judged on its own terms; that is, in terms of the assumed objective of the order, as a charge of cavalry against artillery with the primary aim of taking the guns to the front. As such it was an astounding success and a vindication of Captain Nolan's faith in the abilities of light cavalry.

19. The Truth about Scutari

*Was Florence Nightingale – or Mary Seacole – the true
nursing heroine of the Light Brigade?*

Florence Nightingale arrived at Scutari on 4 November 1854, just
five days after the wounded of the Light Brigade – too late to help
some but in time to save many more and to become celebrated
throughout Britain as a nursing heroine. The Victorian image of
her that we have inherited is of the 'Lady with the Lamp'; the truth
may be quite another matter.

And what of Mary Seacole, an overweight Jamaican in a yellow
dress and a blue straw bonnet whom Florence Nightingale refused
to employ as a nurse? Few people today know of her. Yet the men
of the Light Brigade most certainly did.

Florence Nightingale was named after the Italian city in which she
was born in 1820 while her parents were on a two-year tour of
Europe. Taught by governesses and her Cambridge-educated
father, she received the classical education normally available only to
the male members of the British nineteenth-century establishment.
After providing such a privileged upbringing, her father was horrified when Florence, aged twenty-four, announced her desire to
become a nurse at Salisbury Infirmary. He strictly forbade it. Nurses
were women with no other means of support. Nurses were women
of ill repute. Worst of all, nurses were working class. Six years later,
under the guise of the European Grand Tour – an acceptable
pastime for a young lady of her standing – Florence visited hospitals
in Paris and Germany. Her mind was still set on nursing. She
believed that God had spoken to her and that his mind was set on
this role for her too.

It was not until 1853, aged thirty-three, that Florence took up her first nursing post, as superintendent of the Institute for the Care of Sick Gentlewomen in London's Harley Street. The work was purely administrative and she was appointed on the advice of Sir Sidney Herbert, a family friend and influential Member of Parliament. It is likely that her father had a hand in it, hoping that the work would satisfy her desire to nurse while distancing her from bedside practice.

The following year saw the outbreak of the Crimean War, and by the end of September the first major engagement at the Alma river had filled the barrack hospital at Scutari with wounded men. It was *The Times* correspondent in Constantinople, Thomas Chenery, who first alerted readers to the dreadful conditions at Scutari. On 12 October 1854 the newspaper published Chenery's first report from the hospital: 'No sufficient medical preparations have been made for the proper care of the wounded. Not only are there not sufficient surgeons, not only are there no dressers and nurses, but there is not even linen to make bandages.' Chenery's second report, published the following day, stressed that 'there are no nurses to carry out the surgeon's directions and to attend on the sick between his visits'.

On 14 October 1854, Florence wrote to Mrs Herbert, whose husband Sir Sidney was by then Secretary at War: 'I do not mean to say I believe *The Times* accounts but I do believe I may be of use to the wounded.' Sidney Herbert had meanwhile written to Florence suggesting that she lead a party of nurses out to the Crimea; their letters crossed in the post.

Florence set up her headquarters in the Herberts' house in London's Belgrave Square with the intention of recruiting forty nurses. She found most of the applicants unsuitable and accepted only thirty-eight, including twenty-four nuns. On 21 October she set sail with her company of nurses. While she was at sea, the Light Brigade rode hell's mile and the wounded joined the casualties from the Alma at Scutari.

Florence arrived on 4 November. The army surgeons who ran the hospitals shared the accepted notion of nurses as mostly drunken and promiscuous. There was some truth in the view: English hospitals considered prostitutes the only females suitable for nursing because they would not be further corrupted by contact with naked men. Florence had thought to counter this idea by recruiting so many nuns, but the move backfired – only male orderlies had previously attended British troops and the military surgeons thought it indecent to allow women, particularly these women, to do so. Thus while the wounded of the Light Brigade lay moaning in the wards, Florence and her ladies were prevented from nursing them.

So matters might have remained had not their arrival at Scutari been followed a few days later by a flood of horrendously wounded men from the battle of Inkerman. The surgeons could not cope and were forced to allow Florence Nightingale's nurses onto the wards. Their task was formidable. There were no beds: the men lay on the floorboards, still in their blood-encrusted uniforms and covered by filthy blankets. When a man died and was carried away, the patient who took his place inherited his blanket, which was often brittle with the congealed blood of its several previous tenants. There was no soap, no hospital clothing and no laundry.

Florence ordered that everything be scrubbed clean, from the walls to the patients. Drawing on a fund of money donated by readers of *The Times*, she purchased soap and scrubbing brushes for her nurses and hospital gowns for the men, and rented a house in which she had a boiler installed to use as a laundry.

The nurses washed and fed the men, bandaged their wounds, and cleaned up their vomit and diarrhoea. But these women were no angels. Several of them drank so heavily that Florence was forced to keep all alcohol locked away. Others proved so sexually promiscuous that she banned all of them from the wards after 8.00 p.m. The popular image of the Lady with the Lamp patrolling the wards after nightfall to see that all was well with her patients owes as much to her keenness to check that none of her nurses were curled up alongside the men. Several nurses continued to misbehave and had to be returned to England.

Florence had arrived at Scutari to find the wounded from the five regiments of the Light Brigade already there and it has been assumed that these men were the first to benefit from her efforts. For more than a century after her death, biographers made much of the fall in the death rate at the barrack hospital from 42 to only 2 per cent. Although such a phenomenal change clearly could not have been achieved in a single week or even a month, it is reasonable to assume that the rate began to fall soon after her arrival and that some lives must thereby have been saved among the men of the Light Brigade.

That is far from the truth. During her first four months at Scutari the death rate did not fall at all; it rose from 8 per cent in November to peak at 42 per cent the following February. Her own mortality figures, meticulously kept and charted, prove as much. The reason for this, Florence asserted, was that the army sent her those men whose wounds were so severe that most stood no chance of recovery, particularly given their half-starved state. The death rate rose in December and again in January and February because, she said, the worsening weather meant that the men had suffered more from starvation and exposure in the Crimea before incurring the injuries that brought them to her, and were therefore more likely to succumb to their wounds.

This sounds like a reasonable explanation, except that the figures tell a different tale. Of the 4,077 soldiers who died at Scutari during Florence Nightingale's first winter there, only 10 per cent died of battle wounds. The rest, many of whom had arrived free of all disease and might otherwise have recovered, died of typhus, typhoid, cholera or dysentery. Despite the improved conditions she created for the men, most deaths were caused by diseases contracted at Scutari. Seven doctors and three nurses died too.

Although every part of the hospital was permeated by the foul stink of the sewers that lay beneath it, Florence did not believe there could be a connection between the sewers and the diseases rampant among the patients housed above them. She did not believe in germs. What she did believe in was cleanliness. She wrote: 'Cleanliness and fresh air are the only defence against infection.' The men continued to die. They died clean, but they died nevertheless.

Her reputation became untouchable. In February 1855, as

the death rate peaked, a letter writer to *The Times* reported: 'Wherever there is disease in its most dangerous form, there is that incomparable woman sure to be seen. She is a ministering angel without any exaggeration in these hospitals, and, as her slender form glides quietly along each corridor, every fellow's face softens with gratitude at the sight of her.'

The soldiers loved her, not because she was saving them, but because she was there. Allowing them 'the sight of her' was mostly as close as she got. There was little if any hands-on nursing care; nor was it expected. A wounded soldier said: 'She would speak to one and nod and smile to as many more, but she could not do it to all you know. We lay there by the hundreds, but we could kiss her shadow as it fell.'

With the death rate above 40 per cent and rising, the War Office in London sent out a sanitary commission to inspect conditions at the hospital. The commissioners arrived in March and immediately ordered that the sewers beneath the hospital be flushed out. The death rate began to drop and by June had fallen to just 2 per cent. Florence refused to accept that this had been brought about by the cleaning of the sewers, preferring to believe that the passing of winter and improved conditions in the Crimea explained it.

When the Crimean War came to an end, Florence returned to England in August 1856 under an assumed name. She refused all requests for photographs and interviews. The public wanted to idolize her; she wanted to remember the dead: 'Oh my poor men who endured so patiently. I feel I have been such a bad mother to you to come home and leave you lying in your Crimean grave. Seventy-three per cent in eight regiments during six months from disease alone – who thinks of that now?'

She was asked to present evidence to the Royal Commission on the Health of the Army, and as part of her preparation for this she compared mortality rates in various military hospitals. She was profoundly shocked to find that the death rate at Scutari had been far higher than elsewhere, and came to a most painful conclusion – one which she had previously refused to accept – that most of the soldiers who died at Scutari while under her care did so because of diseases rising from the sewers upon which the building stood. Her work had allowed them to die in greater cleanliness and comfort, but it had not saved them.

Biographer Hugh Small believes that this discovery triggered a mental breakdown: 'She suffered a spectacular humiliation when she had to admit that she had been wrong about the cause of death at Scutari. A large number of influential people knew that her image as the saviour of Scutari was a sham.' Florence was however a heroine, and while the authorities knew the terrible truth, they saw no need to disillusion the British public. But when the Indian Mutiny broke out in 1857 and Florence offered to leave for India immediately, the War Office politely declined her assistance.

She settled instead for the life of an invalid, offering advice only from her bed. She used her influence to campaign for improved standards in nursing and wrote numerous books, among them *Notes on Nursing* (1860), the very first textbook for nurses. Public donations continued to pour in and that same year she used the proceeds to establish the Nightingale Training School for nurses at St Thomas' Hospital, London, with a curriculum written by herself.

Florence Nightingale died in 1910, aged ninety. She had previously declined a state funeral and a place in Westminster Abbey in favour of burial beside her parents in a country churchyard. Florence's own sister, Parthenope, revealed that she was 'a shocking nurse' with 'little or none of what is called charity'. That was not the point. Henry Longfellow wrote a poem about her that included the words:

> A lady with a lamp shall stand
> In the great history of the land,
> A noble type of good,
> Heroic womanhood.

To the British, kept ignorant of the facts by the War Office, she remained an icon of heroic womanhood. A statue of her was erected in Waterloo Place, London, in 1915.

Biographies of Florence by Professor F. B. Smith in 1982 and by Hugh Small in 1998 presented a quite different view. Smith claimed that she was a habitual liar, driven more by ambition than compassion,, while Small revealed how the British government deliberately covered up the truth about her 'death camp' at Scutari.

Unison, the union representing 25,000 nurses in Britain's hospitals, voted at its 1999 annual conference to move International Nurses' Day on 12 May, Florence Nightingale's birthday, to 'a more appropriate date'. Speaking in support of the move, health visitor Wendy Wheeler said: 'The nursing profession must, as we enter the new millennium, start to exorcise the myth of Florence Nightingale.' Unison gave some thought to who might replace her. The name that attracted most support was that of Mary Seacole.

Mary Seacole was born Mary Jane Grant in Kingston, Jamaica in 1805. Her Scottish father was an army officer serving there; her Jamaican mother ran a boarding house for British soldiers and sailors, and cared for them when they were sick. In 1836 Mary married Edwin Horatio Seacole, a godson of Admiral Horatio Nelson. She had no children and her husband died after only eight years of marriage. After her mother's death Mary ran the boarding house herself and gained a reputation as a practitioner of herbal medicines.

While visiting her brother Edward in Panama, where he too ran a boarding house, she cared for the sick during a cholera epidemic. The resident Americans praised her nursing skills, though one suggested that her skin be bleached to make her 'as acceptable in any company as she deserves to be'. Mary wrote back: 'I don't altogether appreciate your kind wishes with respect to my complexion. As to the society which the process of bleaching might gain me admission into, judging from the specimens I have met, I don't think that I shall lose much by being excluded from it.'

On returning home she found her boarding house full of soldiers sick with yellow fever. So effective was her care that she was asked to take charge of all nursing at Up-Park Camp, the Kingston headquarters of the British Army in Jamaica. Working in the camp, Mary heard about the outbreak of war in the Crimea. Although

now forty-nine years old and somewhat overweight, she decided
to volunteer her services as a nurse and travelled to England at her
own expense. She felt that her experience with tropical diseases –
which in foreign campaigns regularly killed more British soldiers
than the enemy – might prove vital.

Mary arrived in London in October 1854, donned her best dress
and bonnet, and applied to the War Office, the Army Medical
Department and the Secretary for War. She supplied written references from British officers in Kingston describing her nursing skills
and supreme fitness for this work. All refused her offer.

Then she read about the campaign to recruit forty nurses to
work with Florence Nightingale at the barrack hospital in Scutari.
Mary visited the house in Belgrave Square used as a recruiting
office for the nurses. Her application was rejected by one of Miss
Nightingale's assistants, who hardly glanced at her references and
in whose face she had seen 'the fact, that had there been a vacancy,
I should not have been chosen to fill it'. Mary did not know it, but
Florence had recruited only thirty-eight of the proposed forty
nurses – there were two vacancies. She described how she felt as
she walked back through Belgrave Square: 'Did these ladies shrink
from accepting my aid because my blood flowed beneath a somewhat duskier skin than theirs? Tears streamed down my foolish
cheeks.'

Mary Seacole would not take no for an answer. She used her
own money to purchase a large stock of food and medicines, and
took the first available passage out, virtually in the wake of the ship
carrying Miss Nightingale and her nurses, intending to open a hotel
for the sick in the Crimea.

Mary's ship called en route at Scutari and she took the opportunity to visit the barrack hospital where Florence was by then
installed as superintendent of nurses. Perhaps Mary still hoped to
be recruited to work as a nurse there. The meeting between the
two women was brief:

I am admitted to Miss Nightingale's presence. A slight figure, in the
nurses dress, with a pale, gentle and firm face. She asks in her gentle but

eminently practical and business-like way, 'What do you want, Mrs Seacole – anything that we can do for you?' So I threw myself upon the hospitality of Scutari, offering to nurse the sick for the night. Now unfortunately, for many reasons, room even for one in Scutari Hospital was no easy matter to find; but at last a bed was discovered to be unoccupied at the hospital washerwomen's quarters.

Mary, it seems, had been put in her place.

At Balaklava, Mary paid for the construction of the British Hotel at Spring Hill near Kadikoi, close to the cavalry camp, to provide accommodation, food and nursing care for any soldier in need. The men appreciated its grand name, though the hotel was actually a number of huts built partly from the wood of wrecked ships. One hut served as a store selling everything the troops might require – from a needle and thread to herbal remedies for cholera and dysentery – while another was a canteen selling food and hot tea; a third hut was a sick ward. The store and canteen provided an income to finance her medical work and enabled Mary to dispense medicines free of charge to those who could not afford them.

Mary's ward was open to the wounded, those suffering from the diseases rampant in Balaklava and those who were simply exhausted. Whenever a new patient arrived she would rush to the door calling, 'Who is my new son?' The soldiers soon knew her as 'Mother Seacole'.

Mary Seacole arrived at Balaklava after the charge of the Light Brigade had taken place, but for the men of the five light cavalry regiments, as for the rest of the army, the action at Balaklava occurred near the beginning of a campaign that was to keep them in the Crimea for another twelve months. As we have seen, the winter following the charge was severe and food supplies inadequate. The Russians hardly bothered the allies – the Crimea itself seemed likely to defeat them.

It was a long and difficult journey from the army's position on the Balaklava plain and the heights overlooking Sevastopol down to the hospital at Balaklava; Mary's British Hotel near Kadikoi was much closer, particularly so for the cavalry. A mug of hot tea must have eased many a complaint, and the sick found help too. One officer, Frederick Vieth of the 63rd Foot, wrote: 'She was a wonderful woman. All the men swore by her, and in case of any malady would seek her advice and use her herbal medicines, in preference to reporting themselves to their own doctors.'

Another man was even more impressed: 'She had the secret of a recipe for cholera and dysentery, and liberally dispensed the specific, alike to those who could pay and those who could not. It was bestowed with an amount of personal kindness which, though not an item of the original prescription, she deemed essential to the cure.'

Army surgeons dismissed her as a quack and mocked her herbal remedies, although war correspondent William Russell, who was no fool, described her as a 'kind physician': 'The troops who flock to her hotel had faith in her proficiency in the healing art, which she justified by removing obstinate cases of diarrhoea, dysentery and other camp maladies.' Although not all conditions could be cured, she did everything she could to ease the cramps and vomiting of men with fatal cholera: 'Many a man was later to confess that his most abiding memory of the war was that of Mother Seacole, seated by the death-bed of a young soldier who was comforted by the illusion that the black breast pillowing his head was really that of his mother.'

Her bravest feat was venturing within range of the guns firing from Sevastopol to give first aid to the wounded. She was so overweight that when the Russian guns fired and she took cover by dropping to the ground, she then found it no easy matter to get up again: 'Those around would cry out, "Lie down, mother, lie down!" and with very unladylike haste I had to embrace the earth, and remain there until the same voices would laughingly assure me that the danger was over, or one more thoughtful than the rest, would come to give a helping hand.'

In her eagerness to provide everything the men might need, Mary used the profits from the hotel to buy in extra provisions, and overstocked. When the war came to an end in 1856 and the troops sailed for home, she was left with a store crammed with goods she could no longer sell. She had spent everything she had on the British Hotel, could not pay for the latest consignment of goods, and returned to England to face bankruptcy proceedings.

A letter in *The Times* asked: 'Have a few months erased the memories of the many acts of kindness which made the name of the old mother venerated throughout the camp? While the benevolent deeds of Florence Nightingale are being handed down to posterity, are the humbler actions of Mrs Seacole to be entirely forgotten?' Her supporters established a fund to help her. A four-day music festival arranged for her benefit in London, at which nine military bands played, was attended by 80,000 people. Her autobiography, *The Wonderful Adventures of Mrs Seacole in Many Lands*, was published in 1857 and became a best-seller, solving her financial difficulties.

Mary Seacole died in 1881, aged seventy-six, and was buried in the Roman Catholic section of Kensal Green Cemetery in London. William Russell had done much to ensure the Light Brigade would not be forgotten; he wrote of Mary: 'I trust that England will not forget one who nursed her sick, who sought out her wounded to aid and succour them, and who performed the last offices for some of her illustrious dead.'

Sadly, England did forget her. In 1973 the crumbling headstone of her grave was restored by the Jamaican Nurses' Association. They could not do as much for her reputation. Everyone remembered Florence Nightingale; few had heard of Mary Seacole. Yet in 1984 when Mary Seacole's autobiography was republished, the *Nursing Mirror* commented: 'In many ways she stands head and shoulders above Florence Nightingale, for whereas Florence performed only an administrative role away from the front line, Mrs Seacole was in the thick of things and did not hesitate to go to the battlefield itself in her desire to alleviate suffering and to comfort the dying.' Despite that, a move to have a statue of her erected at the Crimean War monument in London, where a statue of Florence already stands, came to nothing.

★

For Victorian Britain, Florence Nightingale, the slender, well-bred English lady, her uniform starched and spotless, lamp in hand, fitted the image of heroic womanhood; Mary Seacole, an overweight Jamaican in a blue straw bonnet, loud and jolly, did not.

Both Florence and Mary served in the Crimean War. Both did what they could to relieve the suffering of sick and injured soldiers. But that is where the similarity ends. Florence was white, from an influential family, and went out to Scutari with the backing of the British government, a party of nurses at her command, *The Times* fund at her disposal and an agenda that exceeded the immediate nursing needs of the men. Mary Seacole was a black woman whose offer of service was rejected by every authority, who travelled to Balaklava and opened a boarding house for sick soldiers at her own expense, and whose only ambition was to care for the sick.

Of course such a comparison is unfair. At the outbreak of the Crimean War nurses were thought to be drunkards and prostitutes, and in truth a good many of them were. Florence Nightingale understood that if the British public was to accept nursing as an acceptable role for decent women, then this image had to be changed. Even as she travelled out to Scutari, she knew that establishing the right of her nurses to do work previously restricted to male orderlies was more important than any individual patient care she might herself provide.

We can disregard the myth of Florence as the 'Saviour of Scutari' and look beyond it to a woman who single-handedly – for neither her influential friends nor *The Times* fund could have achieved it – established nursing as a proper profession for women in Britain. This great work of her life was achieved only partly at Scutari and mostly from her bed, which she rarely left during the last forty years of her life and from which she wielded her pen and her influence with great effect.

Mary's greatest accomplishment took place in the sick ward and on the battlefield at Balaklava. In concluding that she was the true nursing heroine of the Light Brigade, we do not need to belittle Florence Nightingale's achievement. A statue of Mary should be erected on the Crimean War monument, not to replace that of Florence, but to stand alongside it. The survivors of the Light Brigade would have raised a toast to that.

20. Light Brigade Scandals

Murder, suicide and the Victoria Cross

Of the six heroes of the Light Brigade who were awarded the Victoria Cross for valour at Balaklava, two later died in unusual circumstances. In both cases the inquest reached a verdict that blatantly ignored crucial evidence.

Lieutenant Alexander Dunn of the 11th Hussars was only twenty-one when he won the VC. During the retreat up the valley he turned back to rescue a sergeant surrounded by Russian lancers. Less than three months after the charge he left the regiment, taking with him the wife of his commanding officer. Colonel Douglas refused to divorce his wife and was infuriated by the mere mention of Dunn's name. When Dunn was killed in a shooting accident, the inquest handed down a verdict of accidental death. Many within his old regiment believed he had been murdered.

Sergeant Charles Wooden of the 17th Lancers received the VC for helping to carry the badly wounded Captain Morris to safety during the retreat. The award gained him promotion to lieutenant and his army career progressed. When he was found dying of a head wound with a pistol on the floor beside him it was at first thought that he must have accidentally discharged the gun. Despite evidence from the doctor who attended Wooden which ruled out any such accident, a court of inquiry refused to reach a verdict of suicide.

These men were heroes and their reputations could not be tainted – by a finding of murder in Dunn's case, suicide in Wooden's. The evidence tells a far murkier tale.

Alexander Dunn was born in Toronto, Canada in 1833. He was educated at Upper Canada College, Ottawa and Harrow in

England. At the age of nineteen he enlisted in the 11th Hussars and was promoted to lieutenant the following year.

On 25 October 1854 he charged with his regiment at Balaklava under the command of Colonel John Douglas. During the mad dash back through a line of enemy cavalry, Sergeant William Bentley was wounded and fell behind, and three Russian lancers closed on him. Lieutenant Dunn immediately turned his horse and galloped at the Russians, cutting them down with his sabre.

Colonel Douglas reportedly told the survivors of the charge that he would recommend one officer or man of the 11th Hussars for the VC, and by a unanimous vote they selected Dunn. He became the hero of the regiment and – being in Troop Sergeant Major Smith's words 'a fine young fellow' – was most popular with the ladies. Yet no one suspected the true nature of his friendship with Rosa Maria Douglas, a lady some years his senior.

On 11 November, little more than two weeks after the charge, Dunn announced his decision to sell his commission and retire from the regiment. He told his fellow officers that he wished to return to Canada to manage his family estate there. Another reason became apparent when he left early in 1855, taking Rosa Maria with him. It was not, the gentlemen of the regiment agreed, the 'done thing', though some sniggered behind their commanding officer's back. Colonel Douglas refused to divorce her and his hatred of Dunn was such that, should the man's name be inadvertently mentioned at the mess table, he would fly into a rage.

In 1858 Dunn helped raise the 100th Royal Canadian Regiment and took the rank of major. In 1861 he was appointed its commanding officer. He later took command of the 33rd (Duke of Wellington's) Regiment.

Dunn was a wealthy man and in order to ensure that in the event of his death Rosa Maria would be provided for – as they could not be married – he made a will leaving everything to her. But in 1867, after they had been together for twelve years, he made a second will by which the majority of his wealth went to his sister. Although there is no other evidence, this change suggests a serious breakdown in the relationship between Dunn and Mrs Douglas.

In November of that same year Dunn and the 33rd Regiment joined General Napier's expedition to Abyssinia. On 25 January 1868 Colonel Dunn and the regimental surgeon James Sinclair went on a hunting expedition near the small town of Senafe. At some point they separated, each taking an Indian orderly with him. Soon after that, Sinclair heard a shot and Dunn's orderly came rushing towards him shouting, 'Colonel sahib is dead.' Sinclair ran with the orderly and found Dunn lying on the ground with his rifle, pipe and brandy flask beside him.

The following day a regimental inquest was held to investigate the circumstances of Dunn's death. It found that: 'The death of Colonel Dunn was purely accidental, caused by his own rifle exploding while he was in the act of using his brandy flask, when sitting on a stone, out shooting.'

Not everyone believed the verdict and there were rumours that Dunn had been murdered. Some within his old Light Brigade regiment the 11th Hussars considered Colonel Douglas to have had the most pressing motive for wanting Dunn dead, though no one suggested Douglas himself could have been guilty of murder. Suspicion fell more readily on Rosa Maria. Dunn's second will, which he kept with his campaign kit, was missing. As this will could not be produced, the first will was implemented. Rosa Maria was awarded everything and Dunn's sister received nothing. The latter immediately instituted legal proceedings and Rosa Maria was seen by many as the instigator of a murder plot. There was however no evidence. The court, debating only the legal niceties arising from the disappearance of the second will, awarded both Rosa Maria and Dunn's sister a share of the estate.

The inquest into Dunn's death might have recorded a different verdict if the full facts concerning the lost will had been known. The witnesses to Dunn's second will were Captain Lacey and Private Hastie. Hastie was Dunn's servant and had been left £300 in the first will. As a witness to the second will he could not benefit by it and so Dunn gave him a cheque for £300. After Dunn's death, when the second will was found to be missing and the first had to be implemented, Hastie received that same amount again. Three hundred pounds was a very large sum for a private, and £600 doubly so.

Neither Colonel Douglas nor Rosa Maria was with Dunn or even in the same country when he sustained the fatal wound whereas Private Hastie had accompanied him on the expedition and could have followed the hunting party out from Senafe. There is no conclusive evidence that Hastie murdered Dunn, though his dishonesty is a matter of record: after Dunn's death he worked for the Post Office in Scotland and in 1870 was tried for embezzlement, found guilty and sent to prison.

Rosa Maria overcame her grief and after the death of Colonel Douglas in 1871 she remarried.

Nothing is known of Charles Wooden's life between his birth in Germany in 1827 and his enlistment in the 17th Lancers eighteen years later. By the time he sailed with his regiment for the Crimea he had gained the rank of sergeant. He spoke with a pronounced German accent and had the most distinctive nickname in the regiment, 'Tish Me the Devil', acquired one night when he returned to camp and was challenged by a sentry. Blind drunk, these were the only words Wooden managed to blurt out. Luckily for him the sentry recognized him by his accent and held fire.

On 25 October the survivors of the 17th Lancers had reformed on the British lines when they heard that their commanding officer Captain Morris was lying seriously wounded part-way down the valley. Sergeant Wooden volunteered to accompany Surgeon James Mouat in an attempt to bring Morris back. The two men discovered him lying with blood pouring from a severe cut to the head. As Mouat bandaged the wound they were approached by Cossacks. Both men drew their swords, indicating that they would stand their ground, and the Cossacks moved away without engaging them. Wooden and Mouat then carried Morris to safety.

It was a brave deed and Surgeon Mouat was named among the first to be awarded the VC. Wooden was not. Possibly his German parentage and strong accent made him an unsuitable candidate for the role of British hero. Wooden was livid and wrote to Mouat saying that as both of them had risked their lives to the same extent it was unfair that one should receive the VC and the other not. Mouat agreed and supported Wooden's claim for the award. More surprisingly, after a lengthy investigation the army approved the award and Wooden became the only man to ask for a VC and actually get one.

His military career appeared to prosper. He was appointed regimental sergeant major in the 17th Lancers and served with the regiment in India during the Mutiny. In 1860 he transferred to the 6th Dragoons as quartermaster, which carried the honorary rank of lieutenant – normally such a rank had to be purchased – and in 1865 moved to the 5th Lancers. In 1872 he moved again, this time to the 104th Bengal Fusiliers. At each move he was forced to accept the same position as quartermaster, lacking the funds to purchase a higher rank.

In fact his rise from sergeant to lieutenant had left him impoverished and miserable. Life in the officers' mess was an expensive business and most officers, coming from wealthy families, had private incomes to subsidize their army wages. Wooden had to manage on his lieutenant's wages and support a wife and three children. His accent and his poverty, and perhaps the uncouth manner of a man from the ranks, meant that he was never fully accepted in the mess. There may have been another reason too. To ask for a Victoria Cross, even in circumstances where such an award was clearly justified, was not acceptable behaviour among the snooty officer elite and merely confirmed that he was not one of them.

In 1876 the 104th was stationed at Shaft Barracks in Dover. Wooden had run up large debts and had consulted the regimental surgeon Dr Lucas Hooper about severe headaches. On the afternoon of Sunday 24 April his wife Eliza and daughter Elizabeth found him lying in his quarters with a serious head wound. Despite immediate attention from Dr Hooper, Wooden died at 4.00 a.m. the following day.

An inquest into his death was held at the barracks on Tuesday 26 April, and heard evidence from Dr Hooper, Lieutenant Gordon

Short and Private Richard Kirby, Wooden's servant. Dr Hooper said:

On Sunday afternoon I was called to his room. I found his wife and daughter with him. The first thing that attracted my attention was a great quantity of blood on the floor. The deceased was lying crossways on the bed with a large quantity of blood on the bed as well. He was bleeding profusely from the nose and mouth. He was pointing to the roof of his mouth with his fingers, trying to pull out something. When I asked him what was the matter, he said he had a tooth which wanted pulling out. I induced him to open his mouth, and on examining, I found that the whole roof was smashed.

Dr Hooper told the inquest that he then took Wooden's wife and daughter into an adjoining room and asked them what had happened. Eliza told him that she did not know, but that she had found a pistol on the floor beside her husband. Hooper produced this and continued:

It is a small American pistol, having in it an exploded cartridge. The deceased purchased it very recently. He died at four o'clock on Monday morning. He was under the influence of drink when I first saw him. I attribute the cause of death of injuries sustained by the discharge of the pistol. I believe a bullet was lodged in the brain. Another bullet was found on the floor and an empty cartridge case, showing that there were two discharges. When the deceased was pulling at his mouth I think he was trying to pull a bullet out. The injuries were such that there is no doubt that he inflicted them himself. My impression is that he had recently drunk freely.

Lieutenant Gordon Short testified that 'lately Lieutenant Wooden had been a little ailing and depressed'. Wooden's servant Kirby said that 'for the last four or five days before his death he complained of having a fearful pain in his head'. Wooden's wife and daughter, who had been in his quarters at the time of the incident, were not called as witnesses.

The inquest jury faced a dilemma. The circumstances of the incident suggested a clear case of suicide, but such a verdict would result in this hero of Balaklava being denied burial in consecrated ground. Private Kirby's revelation of Wooden's 'fearful pain in his head' suggested a way out, and they duly found that Wooden had died 'by injury inflicted by himself by the discharge of a pistol while under temporary insanity'. The insane were considered incapable of suicide and this finding allowed him to receive a Christian burial. Wooden was buried with full military honours in St James' Cemetery, Dover. The coffin was transported on a gun carriage; three regimental bands led the funeral procession; and three volleys were fired over his grave. His two sons attended, one of them a private in his old regiment the 17th Lancers. Several officers of the 17th were there too.

One former comrade who stayed away was Thomas Morley, who wrote an obituary of his own for Wooden in a single sentence: 'He got into debt, and shot himself.' Morley's attitude suggests that some in the 17th still harboured a grudge against their old sergeant, thinking that he had asked for and received a Victoria Cross while many others had done much more at Balaklava and received nothing. Morley undoubtedly numbered himself among these and wrote of Wooden: 'He never crossed swords with a Russian. It is a well-known fact that he never went to the battle of Inkerman, but drew out grog and got dead drunk with it.'

Those present at the funeral paid their last respects to a hero and all believed that the controversy over the circumstances of Wooden's death had been laid to rest with him – until the *Dover Standard* reported it on Friday 29 April under the headline, 'DIS-TRESSING SUICIDE'.

What really happened in Lieutenant Wooden's room on the afternoon of 24 April? Dr Hooper confirmed that two bullets had been fired from the pistol: one was found on the floor; the other had shattered the roof of Wooden's mouth and lodged in his brain. Hooper stated: 'He was under the influence of drink when I first saw him,' and: 'My impression is that he had recently drunk freely.' These statements were not followed up and his wife Eliza was not questioned. Victorian society needed its heroes. The death of a VC recipient in questionable circumstances was bad enough; drunkenness would be too much to bear.

Yet the man whose drunken muttering 'Tish me the Devil' had earned him his nickname with the 17th Lancers was known to be a heavy drinker. Given the evidence of severe headaches, it is not improbable that in a drunken stupor Wooden felt that a bullet fired upwards into the mouth was a certain cure but needed two goes to shoot himself. The inquest chose instead to take the headaches as proof of 'temporary insanity'. This term might also in Victorian times have been considered a decent euphemism for 'blind drunk'. It did however mean that Wooden had not in strict legal terms committed suicide.

If after getting drunk to find some escape from his head pains Wooden had shot himself with a pistol he had possessed for many years, no one could argue with the verdict. But the pistol he used was purchased just days earlier. This evidence of premeditation changes everything. Lieutenant Wooden did not shoot himself because he was drunk; he got drunk in order to shoot himself. He committed suicide.

Conclusion

One survivor of the charge, Corporal Thomas Morley, described it as 'the most magnificent assault known in military annals and the greatest blunder known to military tactics'. That is true enough: the Light Brigade swept down the valley, racked by shot and shell, to take the guns and cut down the gunners, and the Russian cavalry, shocked and in awe of men who could ride hell's mile and come on still, fell back in panic; yet the charge was made in error and achieved nothing.

Despite that – perhaps because of it – the charge of the Light Brigade has become the most celebrated cavalry action of all time. Stripped of any reasonable cause or tactical achievement by which it might be justified or understood, it exists as a pure example of the esprit de corps of the cavalry. It leaves us in awe that men can behave in such a way when under fire and expecting every second to be their last. It impresses with the endurance of the human spirit in the face of the most hideous adversity and a meaningless end.

The splendour glitters but has a dark side: the horrific injuries, the suffering and the death. Those at home who lost fathers, brothers or sons must be counted among the sufferers too. We should bemoan the pointlessness of the charge and the losses incurred, yet we insult those gallant men if we do not at the same time recognize the supreme magnificence of their ride down hell's mile. There were lords aplenty at Balaklava, but it was the un-couth cavalrymen who displayed true nobility on the field of battle that day.

This duality – the magnificence and the horror – is polarized most clearly in William Russell of *The Times* as he watched from the Sapoune Heights and Private John 'Butcher Jack' Vahey dashing on horseback down the valley. Russell saw the brigade 'glittering in the morning sun in all the pride and splendour of war', immortal heroes with 'a halo of flashing steel above their heads'. Vahey felt 'the hot air from the cannon's mouth' that kept 'vomiting death upon us' before the men began 'cutting and slashing like fiends'. They described the same action, but from such differing perspectives that they might have been writing about separate events.

At the time of the Crimean War Britain possessed no literary genius capable of a deeper insight. Russia did. Ensign Leo Tolstoy was twenty-five years old and an artillery officer in Sevastopol, in command of a battery of guns defending the city.

Tolstoy wrote several sketches describing the 'heroic spirit' of his men and the terrible conditions of life and death in a city under daily bombardment. He wrote with a deeper perception than his contemporaries on the British side, and as he told of the splendour and the suffering he managed to convey the sense that these two apparently contradictory factors occurred together and were one. Although he was writing of Russian soldiers in Sevastopol waiting for the final allied assault, his words apply as well to the Light Brigade formed up before the advance at Balaklava:

Buried in each man's soul lies the noble spark that will make a hero of him – when the fateful moment arrives, it will leap up like a flame and illuminate great deeds. Yet each one of these men will die under conditions which appal and are characterized by a total absence of the human and of any prospect of salvation – the only relief is that of oblivion, the annihilation of consciousness.

The insight was not welcome. Russian generals who were happy enough to read of the splendour expected a blind eye to be turned to the suffering. In England Tennyson and Kipling produced popular poems by emphasizing the 'noble spark' or the 'conditions which appal' but failed to combine the two.

We cannot understand war or the human response to it until we perceive both the magnificence and the futility, which coexist. The truth about the charge of the Light Brigade lies in the experience of the cavalrymen *and* the observation of those who watched. Both the magnificence seen from the heights and the slaughter in the valley were real, and both are valid descriptions of what occurred. William Russell and John Vahey have to be read together; only then do they reproduce Leo Tolstoy's insight. Noble and appalling: it is in this duality that we find the truth about the charge of the Light Brigade – and perhaps the truth about the human condition.

Appendix 1. Researching the Light Brigade

Did your ancestor ride in the charge?

The primary source of information about officers and men who charged with the Light Brigade is the Public Record Office (PRO), now part of the UK National Archives, which preserves the medal rolls and soldiers' records from the Crimean War period. Light Brigade records are arranged by regiment and the key to researching a particular individual is to discover the regiment in which he served. If he rode in the charge then my own list of officers and men of the Light Brigade known to have been present at Balaklava on 25 October 1854, arranged alphabetically by name, will indicate his regiment (see Appendix 2).

The Public Record Office houses millions of documents and to find an individual record you will need to know its letter code (in this case WO – for War Office) and number code. The medal rolls for the Light Brigade regiments are in WO100/24 and it is on these that my own list is based, although I have corrected mistakes that are known to have occurred in the original rolls. These rolls give each man's name, rank and regimental number, and a list of the clasps he was entitled to wear on his Crimea Campaign Medal.

Casualty returns are in WO25. These give each man's name, rank, place of birth and trade; the date, place and nature of the casualty; and the next of kin. Muster rolls for the five regiments give each man's date of enlistment, where he served and his date of discharge, and these can be found in WO12, WO14 and WO15.

While it is possible to visit the PRO and make a personal search, it is advisable to hire a professional researcher to do the work, as he or she will be aware of the many different documents and locations in which information on a particular man may be found. A list of accredited researchers is available from the Public Record Office, Kew, Richmond TW9 4DU.

The next best source of information on officers and men of the Light Brigade is their regimental museums. Note that the museums do not hold individual service records; these can only be found at the PRO. There may however be additional records held in regimental archives and it is worth writing to find out. Staff time costs money and you should expect to pay for a search of the archives and for photocopies of anything found. In exceptional cases a search may uncover a letter in a man's own handwriting, or you may be told that the museum owns and displays his medals.

Each of the five Light Brigade regiments has long since been amalgamated with others and you will need to know which present-day regimental museum incorporates the original regiment in which your ancestor served.

Light Brigade Regimental Museums

- 4th Light Dragoons: now The Queen's Royal Hussars
  Redoubt Fortress Museum, Royal Parade, Eastbourne BN22 7AQ
  www.qrh.org.uk

- 8th Hussars: now The Queen's Royal Hussars
  Redoubt Fortress Museum, Royal Parade, Eastbourne BN22 7AQ
  www.qrh.org.uk

- 11th Hussars: now The King's Royal Hussars
  The King's Royal Hussars Museum, Peninsula Barracks, Winchester SO23 8TS
  www.krh.org.uk

- 13th Light Dragoons: now the Light Dragoons
  Canon Hall Museum, Cawthorne, Barnsley S75 4AT
  www.lightdragoons.org.uk

- 17th Lancers: now The Queen's Royal Lancers
  The Queen's Royal Lancers Museum, Belvoir Castle, Grantham NG32 1PE
  www.qrl.uk.com

  Additional information and links to the museums can be found at
  www.balaklava.co.uk

Light Brigade medals

Every officer and man in the Light Brigade who was present at Balaklava on the day of the charge received the Crimea Campaign Medal with a clasp for Balaklava. This has become known as the Queen's Crimea Medal because it shows the head of Queen Victoria. All of these men were also awarded the Turkish Crimea Medal issued by the Sultan of Turkey. Some received the Distinguished Conduct Medal. One officer and five men were awarded the Victoria Cross.

The Crimea Campaign Medal was instituted in December 1854. Suspended on a pale blue ribbon with yellow edges, the silver medal shows the profile of the young Queen Victoria by William Wyon previously used on coins of the period. For officers and men of the Light Brigade, an additional three clasps are possible, representing their presence at the Alma, Inkerman and Sevastopol.

There is a particular problem about the authenticity of individual examples of this award. The medals were originally issued unnamed but could be returned for naming (always on the rim) and the majority were. Many were engraved officially by the Mint, but some were named by the regiments and others by private engravers. Thus there are several different styles of naming and it can be difficult to know whether a particular medal is genuine or not, for unscrupulous persons have been known to purchase an unnamed medal, which is of relatively low value, and add the name of a man known to have charged with the Light Brigade, making it very valuable indeed. Potential purchasers should seek expert advice.

The Turkish Crimea Medal was awarded by the Sultan of Turkey to all British, French and Sardinian troops who fought in the Crimea. The silver medal, suspended on a crimson ribbon with green edges, shows a cannon and the flags of the four allies. It was issued unnamed but many recipients had their names privately engraved.

The Distinguished Conduct Medal is silver and its crimson ribbon has a dark blue stripe down the centre. Each medal has the name of the recipient on the rim.

The Victoria Cross was instituted in January 1856 at the suggestion of Prince Albert as the premier award for conspicuous acts of
bravery; the design was chosen by Queen Victoria. Suspended on
a crimson ribbon, the bronze medal is a cross pattée showing a lion
above a royal crown, with the words 'FOR VALOUR'. The name of
the recipient and the date of the act of gallantry for which the medal
was awarded are engraved on the reverse. The bronze used to
manufacture this medal was taken from Russian guns captured in
the Crimea, although the latest research suggests that bronze from
guns captured in other conflicts may also have been used.

Seven Victoria Crosses were awarded for actions during and after
the charge of the Light Brigade – one to an officer and five to men
of the Light Brigade regiments, and one to a surgeon of a Heavy
Brigade regiment:

4th Light Dragoons	Private Samuel Parkes
6th Dragoons	Surgeon James Mouat
11th Hussars	Lieutenant Alexander Dunn
13th Light Dragoons	Corporal Joseph Malone
17th Lancers	Sergeant John Berryman
	Sergeant John Farrell
	Sergeant Charles Wooden

Private James Lamb of the 13th Light Dragoons later claimed
that the commanding officer of each regiment had been allowed to
put forward one name only for the award. It is a matter of record
that Lamb assisted Corporal Malone in the rescue of Captain Webb,
and both men appear to have played equal parts in that action, but
Malone received the VC and Lamb did not. Lamb claimed that he
and Malone had drawn straws for the award, and that he was the
loser. His story is supported by men of the 11th Hussars, who
reported that they were asked to recommend one officer or man
for the VC and selected Lieutenant Dunn.

Contradicting this claim is the fact that three men of the 17th
Lancers received the VC. However, Sergeant Wooden actually
requested the award and was proposed at a much later date (by the

War Office not his regiment), which leaves two names put forward at the time. It is possible that as Sergeants Berryman and Farrell cooperated in the same act, and as the commanding officer of the 8th Hussars had not used his option to propose one name, two from the 17th were allowed.

The evidence is inconclusive, but at the time of the first recommendations the five regiments of the Light Brigade put forward precisely five names for the Victoria Cross.

Appendix 2. Roll of the Light Brigade

An alphabetical list of officers and men

This roll is compiled from the five regimental rolls listing the officers and men of the Light Brigade who were present at Balaklava on 25 October 1854 and who therefore qualified for the Balaklava clasp on their Crimea Campaign Medal. It is important to note that the Balaklava clasp was awarded for being present at Balaklava and not specifically for riding in the charge. Of approximately 1,000 men entitled to the clasp, only 666 rode in the charge. No regimental records were kept naming those who rode and those who did not because they were sick or assigned to other duties. It is only possible to be certain a man charged if:

a) he was killed or wounded – official casualty lists were compiled at the time;

b) he was taken prisoner – a list of these men was provided by the Russians;

c) he was a long-term member of the Balaklava Commemoration Society – in 1878 membership was restricted to those known to have charged;

d) he is mentioned as charging in a letter or account written by a man known to have charged.

It is also important to be aware that errors occurred in the original rolls compiled in 1854. Crimean War scholars hotly debate the inclusion of a number of names. 'C' in the roll which follows indicates those known to have charged. Some of those recorded as 'Wounded' on the day died later at the barrack hospital in Scutari.

Adams, Albert	Private, 1464	13th Light Dragoons	
Adams, Joshua	Private, 899	8th Hussars	C Killed
Aldous, Charles	Private, 1064	17th Lancers	C Wounded
Alexander, Joseph	Private, 989	17th Lancers	
Allen, John	Corporal, 1199	13th Light Dragoons	C
Allen, Thomas	Private, 807	17th Lancers	
Alliston, Thomas	Private, 1128	11th Hussars	
Allured, Charles	Private, 1340	11th Hussars	C Killed
Allwood, Job	Private, 1534	13th Light Dragoons	C
Anderson, George	Surgeon	8th Hussars	
Anderson, Robert	Private, 1250	4th Light Dragoons	
Anderson, Thomas	Quartermaster	13th Light Dragoons	
Andrews, David	Private, 1444	11th Hussars	C Wounded
Andrews, Henry	Private, 998	17th Lancers	
Andrews, James	Corporal, 1447	11th Hussars	
Andrews, John	Corporal, 1262	4th Light Dragoons	C
Andrews, John	Private, 516	17th Lancers	C Wounded
Andrews, Lewis	Private, 746	13th Light Dragoons	C
Andrews, William	Private, 1028	11th Hussars	
Archer, George	Hosp Sgt Major, 707	11th Hussars	
Armes, Thomas	Private, 1535	4th Light Dragoons	C Wounded
Armiston, William	Private, 878	17th Lancers	
Armstrong, Joshua	Corporal, 1292	4th Light Dragoons	C Prisoner
Armstrong, Lancelot	Assistant Surgeon	13th Light Dragoons	
Ashton, Robert	Private, 828	11th Hussars	C
Audin, James	Private, 1375	13th Light Dragoons	
Avison, Charles	Farrier Major, 644	11th Hussars	
Badger, George	Private, 1545	13th Light Dragoons	C
Bagshaw, James	Private, 1581	4th Light Dragoons	C Prisoner
Bainton, William	Private, 830	13th Light Dragoons	C Wounded/ Prisoner
Baker, J. G.	Sergeant, 888	4th Light Dragoons	C
Baker, John	Private, 828	17th Lancers	C
Baker, William	Private, 846	11th Hussars	
Baker, William	Private, 749	17th Lancers	C Killed
Ballies, Alexander	Private, 1407	13th Light Dragoons	
Balme, George	Private, 1049	4th Light Dragoons	C
Bambrick, John	Private, 1465	11th Hussars	C
Barber, J.	Farrier, 1298	11th Hussars	
Barker, William	Troop Sgt Major, 655	17th Lancers	C
Barker, William	Private, 983	17th Lancers	C Killed
Barnes, Edward	Trumpeter, 1236	4th Light Dragoons	C Killed
Barrass, James	Private, 801	11th Hussars	
Barry, John	Private, 1144	8th Hussars	C Killed
Barter, James	Private, 1085	8th Hussars	

Bassett, W.	Corporal, 1027	11th Hussars	
Baxter, J.	Private, 1518	11th Hussars	
Baynes, Henry	Private, 1029	11th Hussars	
Beard, George	Private, 1116	4th Light Dragoons	
Beck, Thomas	Corporal, 1378	11th Hussars	
Becket, John	Private, 585	8th Hussars	
Beeson, Benjamin	Private, 1570	11th Hussars	C
Beetham, William	Private, 898	17th Lancers	C
Bell, Huntley	Private, 1486	4th Light Dragoons	
Bennington, Stephen	Private, 839	11th Hussars	
Bentley, William	Sergeant, 863	11th Hussars	C
Berckleman, Arthur	Private, 871	17th Lancers	
Berry, John	Private, 1306	11th Hussars	C Wounded/ Prisoner
Berryman, John	Sergeant, 735	17th Lancers	C
Best, Walter	Private, 1201	4th Light Dragoons	C
Bevil, John	Private, 723	8th Hussars	
Bevin, John	Private, 1060	8th Hussars	C Wounded/ Prisoner
Bingham, John	Private, 1412	11th Hussars	C Wounded
Birch, James	Private, 1568	4th Light Dragoons	
Bird, William	Private, 1209	8th Hussars	C Wounded/ Prisoner
Blackett, Thomas	Private, 1426	13th Light Dragoons	C Killed
Blackwell, Battye	Private, 1237	13th Light Dragoons	
Blissett, E.	Private, 1430	11th Hussars	
Bloomfield, James	Private, 484	17th Lancers	C
Blower, George	Private, 1550	13th Light Dragoons	
Bolton, James	Private, 868	4th Light Dragoons	C Prisoner
Bond, Seth	Sergeant, 1091	11th Hussars	C
Bonis, George	Private, 1352	13th Light Dragoons	
Bow, John	Private, 1039	17th Lancers	C Wounded
Bowen, George	Private, 965	8th Hussars	
Bowen, John	Private, 957	17th Lancers	
Bowen, William	Private, 933	8th Hussars	
Bowler, Frederick	Private, 1103	17th Lancers	
Bowler, Michael	Private, 1322	4th Light Dragoons	C
Boxall, John	Private, 1550	4th Light Dragoons	C Wounded/ Prisoner
Bradley, Edward	Private, 1542	4th Light Dragoons	C Wounded
Braithwaite, Ernest	Sergeant, 1355	13th Light Dragoons	C
Bray, Francis	Private, 511	8th Hussars	C Wounded
Brennan, James	Private, 636	17th Lancers	
Brennan, Michael	Private, 852	8th Hussars	C Killed
Brewington, John	Private, 1510	4th Light Dragoons	C

Briers, Daniel	Private, 1539	11th Hussars	C
Briggs, Robert	Private, 1473	11th Hussars	C
Brittain, William	Trumpeter, 726	17th Lancers	C Wounded
Brooks, John	Private, 1516	13th Light Dragoons	C Wounded
Brooks, Walter	Private, 747	17th Lancers	C Killed
Broom, George	Private, 486	17th Lancers	C Killed
Broughton, William	Private, 1565	11th Hussars	
Brown, Henry	Private, 1168	13th Light Dragoons	C
Brown, John	Captain	4th Light Dragoons	C Wounded
Brown, John	Private, 887	8th Hussars	C Wounded
Brown, John	Trumpeter, 476	17th Lancers	C
Brown, John	Trumpeter, 926	17th Lancers	C Wounded
Brown, John	Private, 455	17th Lancers	C Wounded
Brown, Joseph	Private, 1492	13th Light Dragoons	
Brown, Peter	Private, 862	17th Lancers	C Wounded
Brown, Richard	Private, 1153	11th Hussars	C
Brown, Robert	Private, 894	17th Lancers	
Brown, Samuel	Private, 1231	11th Hussars	C
Brown, Thomas	Private, 714	17th Lancers	C Prisoner
Bruce, John	Private, 1022	13th Light Dragoons	
Bruges, William	Orderly Room Clerk, 1578	4th Light Dragoons	
Brunton, Joseph	Private, 1176	11th Hussars	C Killed
Bryan, James	Private, 1293	13th Light Dragoons	
Bubb, Robert	Private, 1588	11th Hussars	C Killed
Buck, James	Private, 1160	17th Lancers	C Wounded
Buckton, John	Corporal, 1413	11th Hussars	C
Bull, George	Sergeant Major, 1057	11th Hussars	C
Bullock, John	Private, 864	17th Lancers	
Bunce, Frederick	Private, 1419	11th Hussars	
Bunn, Richard	Private, 1036	4th Light Dragoons	
Burgess, Henry	Private, 1232	11th Hussars	
Burling, John	Private, 1256	11th Hussars	
Burnett, James	Private, 1577	4th Light Dragoons	C
Burns, William	Private, 796	17th Lancers	C
Burton, John	Private, 624	11th Hussars	
Bury, P.	Private, 1452	11th Hussars	
Bushell, William	Private, 1051	13th Light Dragoons	
Butler, William	Private, 1452	4th Light Dragoons	C
Butler, William	Private, 840	17th Lancers	C Wounded
Byrne, Charles	Private, 1481	13th Light Dragoons	
Byrne, John	Veterinary Surgeon	4th Light Dragoons	
Cain, Francis	Private, 1391	13th Light Dragoons	
Callaghan, Timothy	Private, 931	17th Lancers	
Calthorpe, Somerset	Lieutenant	8th Hussars	

Cameron, James	Private, 412	13th Light Dragoons	C Wounded
Cammell, David	Hospital Sergeant, 904	8th Hussars	
Campbell, Edward	Sergeant, 1329	4th Light Dragoons	C Killed
Campbell, Hutchison	Private, 1366	13th Light Dragoons	C
Campbell, Michael	Private, 907	8th Hussars	
Canning, Walter	Private, 1604	11th Hussars	
Cardigan, Lord	Major General	Brigade Commander	C
Carr, William	Private, 1430	4th Light Dragoons	
Carroll, Peter	Private, 1515	4th Light Dragoons	C Wounded
Cart, Charles	Private, 1046	11th Hussars	
Carter, Eli	Private, 1158	4th Light Dragoons	
Carter, Henry	Private, 1145	17th Lancers	C Wounded
Carter, Joseph	Private, 1494	4th Light Dragoons	C Wounded
Catlyn, Thomas	Private, 847	13th Light Dragoons	
Cattermole, William	Troop Sgt Major, 483	17th Lancers	C Wounded
Chadwick, John	Cornet/Adjutant	17th Lancers	C Wounded/ Prisoner
Chadwick, Richard	Corporal, 1448	13th Light Dragoons	
Chamberlayne, Denzil	Cornet	13th Light Dragoons	C
Chambers, R.	Private, 1252	11th Hussars	C
Chapman, Edward	Private, 1070	17th Lancers	
Chapman, Robert	Private, 1182	8th Hussars	
Cheshire, Henry	Private, 1201	8th Hussars	C Wounded
Chetwode, George	Captain	8th Hussars	
Clark, Edward	Private, 1471	11th Hussars	
Clarke, Michael	Troop Sgt Major, 453	8th Hussars	C Wounded
Clarke, Thomas	Private, 1113	17th Lancers	C
Clement, James	Private, 1189	8th Hussars	C Wounded
Cleveland, Archibald	Cornet	17th Lancers	C
Clifford, Frederick	Private, 1088	17th Lancers	C Wounded
Clifford, James	Corporal, 1142	13th Light Dragoons	
Clowes, George	Cornet	8th Hussars	C Wounded/ Prisoner
Clutterbuck, Daniel	Lieutenant	8th Hussars	C Wounded
Coldwell, John	Private, 1364	4th Light Dragoons	
Collin, John	Private, 1163	17th Lancers	
Colson, William	Private, 1433	13th Light Dragoons	C
Comley, Samuel	Private, 705	17th Lancers	
Connolly, Alexander	Private, 835	8th Hussars	
Connor, Dennis	Private, 1125	4th Light Dragoons	C
Constant, Stephen	Veterinary Surgeon	17th Lancers	
Cook, Edwin	Captain	11th Hussars	C Wounded
Cooke, Thomas	Private, 1048	13th Light Dragoons	C Wounded/ Prisoner
Cooper, Charles	Private, 1603	11th Hussars	C Killed

Cooper, George	Private, 1526	13th Light Dragoons	C Wounded/ Prisoner
Copas, Edmund	Private, 1244	8th Hussars	
Cope, James	Private, 1034	17th Lancers	C
Cope, William	Private, 837	17th Lancers	
Corcoran, Thomas	Private, 643	17th Lancers	C Killed
Cork, Charles	Corporal, 1437	11th Hussars	C Wounded
Cornelius, Charles	Private, 1482	4th Light Dragoons	
Cornelius, John	Private, 1523	4th Light Dragoons	
Corson, William	Private, 1512	11th Hussars	
Cosgrove, Peter	Private, 930	8th Hussars	
Coultate, George	Private, 752	11th Hussars	
Coulter, Joseph	Private, 1390	13th Light Dragoons	
Court, Charles	Private, 1421	13th Light Dragoons	C Killed
Cousins, Charles	Private, 1482	4th Light Dragoons	
Cox, Samuel	Private, 1573	11th Hussars	
Crane, Charles	Private, 747	4th Light Dragoons	
Crawford, Hugh	Trumpeter, 1296	4th Light Dragoons	C Prisoner
Creed, George	Private, 1164	17th Lancers	
Creed, Michael	Private, 971	8th Hussars	
Crene, George	Private, 1474	11th Hussars	
Cresswell, Josiah	Private, 1240	13th Light Dragoons	
Crichton, Robert	Assistant Surgeon	4th Light Dragoons	
Crisp, Frederick	Private, 788	8th Hussars	
Crocker, Rowland	Private, 1551	11th Hussars	
Crosse, John	Surgeon	11th Hussars	
Croydon, George	Private, 1440	4th Light Dragoons	C Wounded
Cullen, William	Private, 1520	11th Hussars	C
Cunningham, James	Private, 1298	13th Light Dragoons	C Wounded
Curteine, Thomas	Private, 987	8th Hussars	
Daley, John	Private, 1005	8th Hussars	
Dalton, Charles	Private, 1136	8th Hussars	C
Daniel, Thomas	Private, 1262	11th Hussars	
Davies, Robert	Sergeant, 1495	11th Hussars	C Wounded
Davies, Samuel	Private, 1632	11th Hussars	
Davies, William	Private, 1406	11th Hussars	C Killed
Davis, Richard	Corporal, 1530	11th Hussars	C
Davis, Richard	Trumpeter, 1108	13th Light Dragoons	
Davis, Thomas	Private, 772	17th Lancers	C
Dawn, William	Private, 1180	8th Hussars	C
Deaball, William	Private, 852	17th Lancers	
Dearlove, George	Private, 1055	13th Light Dragoons	
Deason, Alfred	Private, 1494	13th Light Dragoons	
Deering, Daniel	Private, 1302	4th Light Dragoons	C
Delworth, James	Private, 940	13th Light Dragoons	

de Salis, Rodolph	Major	8th Hussars	C
Devlin, James	Corporal, 1447	4th Light Dragoons	C Wounded
Dickenson, Francis	Sergeant, 847	17th Lancers	C
Dickenson, Thomas	Private, 1488	13th Light Dragoons	
Dickie, Alexander	Private, 876	17th Lancers	
Dies, James	Private, 1033	8th Hussars	C Killed
Dimmock, William	Private, 653	17th Lancers	C
Dobson, Benjamin	Private, 874	17th Lancers	
Doherty, Charles	Lieutenant Colonel	13th Light Dragoons	
Dollard, Richard	Private, 916	17th Lancers	C Killed
Donald, William	Corporal, 579	8th Hussars	C Killed
Donaldson, James	Private, 961	4th Light Dragoons	C Killed
Donoghue, Bernard	Private, 1088	8th Hussars	
Donoghue, James	Trumpeter, 1064	8th Hussars	C
Donovon, John	Private, 1067	8th Hussars	
Doogan, William	Private, 605	13th Light Dragoons	
Doolan, Patrick	Private, 936	8th Hussars	C Wounded
Dorell, William	Private, 1503	13th Light Dragoons	C Killed
Doughton, Joseph	Private, 1422	13th Light Dragoons	C Wounded
Douglas, John	Lieutenant Colonel	11th Hussars	C
Douglas, John	Private, 1410	13th Light Dragoons	
Dowling, Patrick	Private, 1027	17th Lancers	C Killed
Downing, Frederick	Private, 1524	4th Light Dragoons	C Wounded
Doyle, John	Private, 1131	8th Hussars	C
Doyle, William	Private, 1278	13th Light Dragoons	
Doyle, William	Private, 576	17th Lancers	C Wounded
Dray, J. E.	Private, 1528	4th Light Dragoons	
Dryden, John	Private, 1617	11th Hussars	C Wounded/ Prisoner
Duberly, Henry	Paymaster	8th Hussars	
Dudley, Thomas	Private, 1134	17th Lancers	C Wounded
Duff, John	Private, 804	17th Lancers	
Duggan, John	Private, 579	17th Lancers	C Wounded
Duggan, William	Private, 580	17th Lancers	
Duke, Robert	Private, 1340	13th Light Dragoons	C Wounded/ Prisoner
Dumayne, William	Private, 1429	13th Light Dragoons	C
Duncan, James	Sergeant, 688	17th Lancers	C
Dunn, Alexander	Lieutenant	11th Hussars	C
Dunn, Charles	Private, 1088	4th Light Dragoons	
Dunn, John	Trumpeter, 1090	8th Hussars	C Wounded
Dunn, Martin	Private, 1112	8th Hussars	
Dunn, Patrick	Private, 931	8th Hussars	
Dwan, James	Private, 1079	8th Hussars	C
Dyer, John	Farrier Sergeant, 431	8th Hussars	

Dyer, Thomas	Private, 562	17th Lancers	C
Dyke, John	Private, 1265	11th Hussars	C
Eastick, John	Private, 1129	13th Light Dragoons	
Eastoe, George	Private, 1432	4th Light Dragoons	
Eastoe, Nehemiah	Private, 1578	11th Hussars	C
Eastwood, George	Private, 1531	13th Light Dragoons	
Eaton, Edmond	Private, 1056	17th Lancers	
Eaton, William	Private, 900	17th Lancers	
Eccles, William	Private, 1468	13th Light Dragoons	C
Eccleshall, John	Hospital Sergeant, 769	17th Lancers	
Edden, John	Private, 1481	4th Light Dragoons	C
Edge, Robert	Private, 969	17th Lancers	C Wounded/ Prisoner
Edge, William	Private, 975	8th Hussars	
Edmunds, James	Private, 977	17th Lancers	
Edwards, George	Private, 1036	13th Light Dragoons	
Elder, James	Private, 1140	11th Hussars	C Killed
Ellis, Henry	Private, 1022	17th Lancers	C Prisoner
Ellis, William	Private, 1456	11th Hussars	C
Ellison, Henry	Private, 768	11th Hussars	
Elvey, George	Private, 1066	11th Hussars	
Emery, James	Private, 1437	4th Light Dragoons	
Ettridge, John	Private, 1483	13th Light Dragoons	C Wounded
Evans, John	Private, 1217	13th Light Dragoons	
Evans, Robert	Private, 1510	13th Light Dragoons	C Wounded
Fairbanks, Henry	Private, 1478	4th Light Dragoons	
Farmer, John	Private, 521	17th Lancers	
Farquharson, Robert	Private, 1277	4th Light Dragoons	C Prisoner
Farrell, John	Private, 1420	4th Light Dragoons	C
Farrell, John	Sergeant, 705	17th Lancers	C
Farrington, Stephen	Private, 1316	13th Light Dragoons	
Fegan, Patrick	Private, 333	17th Lancers	
Fellowes, Edward	Captain	11th Hussars	
Ferguson, Robert	Private, 1192	4th Light Dragoons	C
Ffennell, Charles	Regt Sgt Major, 699	17th Lancers	C
Field, George	Private, 1183	17th Lancers	
Finch, Charles	Private, 1297	13th Light Dragoons	
Finlay, William	Private, 1312	13th Light Dragoons	
Finnegan, Francis	Private, 385	8th Hussars	C Killed
Firkins, Edward	Private, 1477	13th Light Dragoons	
Firth, Wilson	Private, 1612	11th Hussars	C Wounded
Fisher, George	Private, 1488	4th Light Dragoons	
Fisher, Richard	Private, 1395	4th Light Dragoons	
Fitzgerald, John	Private, 1227	13th Light Dragoons	
Fitzgerald, Richard	Private, 972	8th Hussars	

Fitzgibbon, John	Lieutenant	8th Hussars	C Wounded
Fitzgibbon, John	Private, 1091	8th Hussars	C Killed
Fleming, John	Private, 1156	11th Hussars	C Wounded
Fletcher, Thomas	Private, 1271	4th Light Dragoons	C Wounded/ Prisoner
Flowers, George	Private, 524	17th Lancers	C Killed
Forbes, John	Corporal, 1330	4th Light Dragoons	C
Ford, John	Private, 1547	4th Light Dragoons	C
Foreman, Samuel	Private, 1149	13th Light Dragoons	
Foster, Charles	Orderly Room Clerk, 935	13th Light Dragoons	
Foster, Thomas	Private, 1108	17th Lancers	C Wounded
Fowkes, William	Private, 1535	13th Light Dragoons	
Fowler, William	Troop Sgt Major, 831	4th Light Dragoons	C Wounded/ Prisoner
Fox, Charles	Private, 1314	4th Light Dragoons	
France, Thomas	Corporal, 1334	11th Hussars	C Killed
Frazer, Robert	Private, 1435	13th Light Dragoons	C Killed
Frazier, Richard	Private, 825	13th Light Dragoons	
Frederick, Charles	Private, 1450	4th Light Dragoons	C Prisoner
Frevillier, William	Private, 661	8th Hussars	
Friend, James	Private, 982	17th Lancers	
Frith, Edmund	Paymaster	13th Light Dragoons	
Fry, George	Private, 1137	11th Hussars	
Fry, William	Private, 1562	11th Hussars	
Fulton, William	Private, 1153	8th Hussars	C Wounded
Gammage, Joseph	Trumpeter, 1029	13th Light Dragoons	C
Gammon, J.	Private, 1350	11th Hussars	
Gardiner, William	Private, 1405	13th Light Dragoons	C
Gardner, George	Regt Sgt Major	13th Light Dragoons	C
Garland, William	Sergeant, 954	17th Lancers	C
Garnham, George	Private, 1480	13th Light Dragoons	C
Garvey, John	Private, 921	4th Light Dragoons	
Gaskin, James	Private, 1318	13th Light Dragoons	
George, Thorne	Paymaster	4th Light Dragoons	
Gibson, George	Private, 1471	13th Light Dragoons	C Wounded
Gifford, Thomas	Private, 1558	4th Light Dragoons	
Gilchrist, John	Private, 1312	4th Light Dragoons	C
Gillam, David	Corporal, 1130	4th Light Dragoons	C
Glanister, James	Private, 1564	11th Hussars	C Wounded
Glendwr, Robert	Private, 1192	8th Hussars	C Wounded
Gloag, John	Veterinary Surgeon	11th Hussars	
Glyn, Riversdale	Cornet	8th Hussars	
Glynn, William	Corporal, 1345	13th Light Dragoons	
Goad, Maxwell	Cornet	13th Light Dragoons	

Goad, Thomas	Captain	13th Light Dragoons	C Killed
Goodall, George	Private, 1161	8th Hussars	
Gordon, Sir William	Lieutenant	17th Lancers	C Wounded
Gorman, James	Private, 1538	13th Light Dragoons	
Goshall, Joseph	Private, 1085	4th Light Dragoons	C Wounded
Gough, Joseph	Private, 740	8th Hussars	
Gould, Henry	Private, 1206	4th Light Dragoons	
Gowings, George	Private, 1445	4th Light Dragoons	C
Graham, William	Orderly Room Clerk, 961	17th Lancers	C
Grant, Robert	Private, 817	4th Light Dragoons	C
Grantham, David	Private, 1486	11th Hussars	C Wounded
Gravenor, John	Private, 1157	17th Lancers	C Wounded
Gray, Charles	Private, 1413	4th Light Dragoons	
Gray, John	Private, 1485	4th Light Dragoons	C Wounded
Gray, William	Trumpet Major, 392	8th Hussars	C Wounded
Green, Henry	Private, 1475	11th Hussars	
Green, John	Private, 1259	13th Light Dragoons	
Greening, William	Private, 743	4th Light Dragoons	
Gregory, Henry	Private, 1169	13th Light Dragoons	
Gregory, James	Private, 1417	4th Light Dragoons	C Wounded
Grennan, Edward	Private, 1425	4th Light Dragoons	
Grey, Edward	Veterinary Surgeon	8th Hussars	
Grey, Henry	Private, 1058	17th Lancers	C Killed
Griffiths, Thomas	Private, 1301	13th Light Dragoons	
Grigg, Joseph	Private, 1180	4th Light Dragoons	C
Groombridge, William	Private, 1027	4th Light Dragoons	
Groome, H.	Private, 1569	11th Hussars	C Wounded
Groves, Herbert	Private, 1466	4th Light Dragoons	C
Guill, Martin	Private, 525	8th Hussars	
Gully, Augustus	Hospital Sergeant, 1353	13th Light Dragoons	
Gusterson, James	Private, 1618	11th Hussars	C
Guthrie, Thomas	Private, 1319	4th Light Dragoons	C
Guttridge, G.	Troop Sgt Major, 1329	11th Hussars	
Gwinnell, Reuben	Private, 1616	11th Hussars	C Killed
Hackett, Martin	Private, 1031	8th Hussars	C
Halkett, John	Major	4th Light Dragoons	C Killed
Hall, James	Corporal, 1051	17th Lancers	C Prisoner
Hallaway, John	Private, 1580	4th Light Dragoons	C Wounded
Hallowell, William	Private, 865	8th Hussars	
Halpin, James	Private, 937	8th Hussars	
Hammond, John	Private, 1079	4th Light Dragoons	
Hampson, George	Private, 1310	11th Hussars	
Hancox, John	Private, 1245	4th Light Dragoons	
Handley, John	Private, 756	17th Lancers	

Hanlon, Christopher	Private, 1334	13th Light Dragoons	C Wounded/ Prisoner
Hanrahan, Dennis	Private, 939	8th Hussars	C Killed
Hanrahan, Thomas	Private, 979	8th Hussars	
Harding, John	Private, 1382	13th Light Dragoons	C
Harding, Robert	Sergeant Major, 545	8th Hussars	
Hardy, Thomas	Saddler Staff Sgt, 382	8th Hussars	
Harling, Richard	Private, 1393	4th Light Dragoons	
Harris, Amos	Private, 1346	13th Light Dragoons	C Wounded/ Prisoner
Harris, Richard	Private, 884	13th Light Dragoons	
Harris, Robert	Private, 652	17th Lancers	
Harris, William	Private, 1159	8th Hussars	
Harris, William	Private, 1221	8th Hussars	
Harrison, Charles	Private, 1119	8th Hussars	
Harrison, Henry	Troop Sgt Major, 370	8th Hussars	C
Harrison, Isaiah	Private, 1097	13th Light Dragoons	
Harrison, Joseph	Private, 692	8th Hussars	
Harrison, Stephen	Private, 1403	13th Light Dragoons	
Harrison, Thomas	Private, 1389	11th Hussars	C
Harrison, William	Private, 1131	17th Lancers	C Prisoner
Hart, Walter	Private, 1143	17th Lancers	C Wounded
Harvey, James	Private, 1433	11th Hussars	
Haughton, John	Private, 646	11th Hussars	
Hawkes, James	Private, 714	8th Hussars	
Haxhall, Daniel	Private, 1536	4th Light Dragoons	C Killed
Hefferon, James	Trumpeter, 1151	8th Hussars	C
Hefferon, Thomas	Private, 1152	8th Hussars	C Killed
Hellet, Amos	Private, 1365	11th Hussars	
Hely, Joseph	Paymaster	11th Hussars	
Hemmingway, Jacob	Private, 657	13th Light Dragoons	
Heneage, Clement	Lieutenant	8th Hussars	C
Henry, Nathan	Private, 1584	11th Hussars	C Prisoner
Herbert, Edmund	Private, 793	8th Hussars	C Killed
Herbert, Frank	Troop Sgt Major, 1134	4th Light Dragoons	C Killed
Herbert, James	Private, 1460	4th Light Dragoons	C
Herbert, Thomas	Private, 1205	4th Light Dragoons	C Wounded
Hermitage, Joseph	Private, 1068	8th Hussars	
Heron, Bartholomew	Private, 1432	13th Light Dragoons	
Heron, Denis	Private, 1327	4th Light Dragoons	C Wounded
Herriott, George	Private, 803	17th Lancers	C Wounded
Hickey, John	Private, 1379	4th Light Dragoons	C
Hill, John	Quartermaster	4th Light Dragoons	
Hindley, Edward	Private, 1540	13th Light Dragoons	C
Hinton, Edwin	Corporal, 920	17th Lancers	

Hitchcock, James	Private, 1516	4th Light Dragoons	
Hoarne, George	Private, 1590	11th Hussars	C Killed
Hodges, James	Private, 1550	11th Hussars	C
Hodges, John	Private, 1396	4th Light Dragoons	
Hogan, John	Private, 1006	8th Hussars	C
Holland, Edward	Private, 1147	17th Lancers	C
Holland, Matthew	Private, 1543	11th Hussars	C
Holland, Richard	Private, 1531	4th Light Dragoons	
Holland, William	Private, 1504	4th Light Dragoons	
Holliday, Algernon	Private, 1365	13th Light Dragoons	C Killed
Holmes, Henry	Private, 1224	8th Hussars	C
Holston, Samuel	Corporal, 1450	11th Hussars	
Holt, J.	Private, 1576	11th Hussars	
Holton, George	Private, 1133	8th Hussars	
Home, Anthony	Assistant Surgeon	8th Hussars	
Hook, Alfred	Private, 1264	13th Light Dragoons	
Hooper, Robert	Troop Sgt Major, 1101	13th Light Dragoons	
Hope, Henry	Private, 1614	11th Hussars	
Hopgood, Charles	Private, 1175	17th Lancers	
Horan, Michael	Private, 581	8th Hussars	
Horan, Patrick	Private, 808	8th Hussars	C Prisoner
Horn, Henry	Private, 1573	4th Light Dragoons	
Horn, Philip	Paymaster Sergeant, 977	11th Hussars	
Houghton, George	Lieutenant	11th Hussars	C Wounded
Howard, Henry	Private, 1225	8th Hussars	
Howarth, William	Trumpeter, 669	13th Light Dragoons	C Prisoner
Howes, John	Sergeant, 1274	4th Light Dragoons	C Wounded
Hudson, Edward	Corporal, 1142	11th Hussars	C Wounded
Huggard, Richard	Private, 914	8th Hussars	
Hughes, Edwin	Private, 1506	13th Light Dragoons	C
Hughes, James	Private, 905	17th Lancers	
Hughes, John	Private, 1584	4th Light Dragoons	C Wounded
Hulton, Thomas	Private, 1458	4th Light Dragoons	C Killed
Hunniball, Joseph	Private, 1071	4th Light Dragoons	
Hunscott, Samuel	Private, 944	17th Lancers	
Hunt, Edward	Sergeant, 1195	13th Light Dragoons	C
Hunt, George	Cornet	4th Light Dragoons	C
Hunt, Henry	Private, 1009	4th Light Dragoons	
Hunt, Henry	Private, 1495	13th Light Dragoons	
Hunter, Thomas	Surgeon	4th Light Dragoons	
Hurley, James	Private, 1273	13th Light Dragoons	
Hurst, Thomas	Private, 1121	8th Hussars	
Hutton, Thomas	Captain	4th Light Dragoons	C Wounded
Hyde, Walter	Private, 1601	11th Hussars	C Wounded/ Prisoner

Hynes, Bartholemew	Private, 1256	13th Light Dragoons	
Ireland, Joseph	Private, 935	17th Lancers	
Isaac, John	Private, 1219	4th Light Dragoons	
Jackman, John	Private, 1476	11th Hussars	C Killed
Jackson, Alfred	Private, 1058	8th Hussars	
Jackson, Robert	Private, 915	17th Lancers	C Killed
Jackson, Simon	Private, 1236	11th Hussars	
Jackson, Thomas	Private, 1014	17th Lancers	
Jackson, William	Private, 1599	11th Hussars	
Jackson, William	Private, 1388	13th Light Dragoons	
Jamieson, Samuel	Private, 1593	11th Hussars	C
Jay, John	Private, 1253	13th Light Dragoons	
Jeakins, Robert	Private, 509	17th Lancers	
Jenner, Alfred	Private, 1118	17th Lancers	C Prisoner
Jennings, Henry	Regt Sgt Major, 1102	4th Light Dragoons	C
Jenyns, Soames	Captain	13th Light Dragoons	C
Jervis, Edward	Lieutenant	13th Light Dragoons	C
Jewell, Henry	Private, 1403	11th Hussars	C Wounded
Johnson, Robert	Private, 1126	8th Hussars	C
Johnson, Robert	Private, 1327	11th Hussars	
Johnson, Thomas	Sergeant, 1300	13th Light Dragoons	C
Johnston, John	Private, 725	8th Hussars	
Joliffe, Hedworth	Lieutenant	4th Light Dragoons	C
Jones, G.	Private, 1365	4th Light Dragoons	
Jones, John	Sergeant, 1423	11th Hussars	C Killed
Jones, William	Private, 1349	4th Light Dragoons	C Wounded
Jordan, John	Private, 1321	4th Light Dragoons	
Jordan, Thomas	Sergeant, 1209	11th Hussars	C Killed
Joseph, John	Sergeant, 1127	11th Hussars	C
Jowett, Gregory	Private, 1357	11th Hussars	C
Joy, Henry	Trumpet Major, 416	17th Lancers	
Kauntz, Henry	Quartermaster	11th Hussars	
Kearney, Robert	Private, 1108	8th Hussars	
Kearney, William	Private, 1049	8th Hussars	
Keates, Joseph	Trumpeter, 914	11th Hussars	C
Keating, Matthew	Private, 1031	8th Hussars	C Wounded
Keating, Michael	Private, 802	8th Hussars	
Keegan, Henry	Private, 1446	4th Light Dragoons	C Wounded
Keeley, John	Private, 1363	13th Light Dragoons	
Keen, John	Private, 1529	13th Light Dragoons	C Wounded
Keenan, William	Private, 1426	4th Light Dragoons	C Wounded
Kelleher, Cornelius	Private, 969	8th Hussars	
Kelly, Edward	Private, 571	17th Lancers	
Kelly, James	Troop Sgt Major, 1229	4th Light Dragoons	
Kelly, James	Private, 1613	11th Hussars	C

Kelly, Thomas	Private, 1120	8th Hussars	
Kendall, Henry	Surgeon	4th Light Dragoons	
Kennedy, Richard	Private, 1007	8th Hussars	C Wounded
Kennedy, Stephen	Private, 566	17th Lancers	C
Kent, Henry	Private, 1005	11th Hussars	
Kilmurray, Patrick	Corporal, 1277	13th Light Dragoons	
Kilvert, John	Corporal, 1513	11th Hussars	C Wounded
Kincart, James	Private, 1473	13th Light Dragoons	
King, George	Cornet	4th Light Dragoons	C
King, Thomas	Private, 1509	4th Light Dragoons	C Prisoner
Kirk, William	Private, 842	17th Lancers	C Wounded/ Prisoner
Kitterick, Patrick	Private, 1130	8th Hussars	C Wounded
Kneller, Frederick	Private, 1485	13th Light Dragoons	
Lamb, James	Private, 1406	13th Light Dragoons	C Wounded
Lane, Henry	Quartermaster	8th Hussars	
Lane, Joseph	Private, 1502	13th Light Dragoons	
Lanfried, Martin	Trumpeter, 986	17th Lancers	C Wounded
Lang, Henry	Private, 1270	4th Light Dragoons	
Lark, Thomas	Private, 1110	17th Lancers	C
Larkin, James	Private, 1270	11th Hussars	C Killed
Larter, Daniel	Private, 1102	13th Light Dragoons	
Lauder, David	Private, 1421	4th Light Dragoons	
Law, Richard	Private, 679	8th Hussars	
Lawson, John	Sergeant, 1415	11th Hussars	C Wounded
Lawson, William	Private, 1041	13th Light Dragoons	C Killed
Lay, James	Sergeant, 1237	4th Light Dragoons	
Layzell, Robert	Private, 1335	11th Hussars	C Killed
Leaney, Edwin	Sergeant, 648	13th Light Dragoons	C
Learey, James	Private, 493	8th Hussars	
Lees, Harry	Private, 1474	4th Light Dragoons	
Lees, John	Private, 841	17th Lancers	C Killed
Lennon, Martin	Private, 942	8th Hussars	C Killed
Levett, Robert	Private, 1260	11th Hussars	C Killed
Light, William	Private, 1254	4th Light Dragoons	
Liles, George	Private, 1197	17th Lancers	C Wounded/ Prisoner
Ling, Robert	Private, 1136	17th Lancers	C Killed
Linkon, John	Troop Sgt Major, 762	13th Light Dragoons	C Prisoner
Linser, George	Private, 1589	4th Light Dragoons	C Wounded/ Prisoner
Lockwood, Augustus	Surgeon	8th Hussars	
Lockwood, George	Captain	8th Hussars	C Killed
Lodge, Martin	Private, 712	13th Light Dragoons	
Loftus, Edward	Private, 389	17th Lancers	C Killed

Long, Matthew	Corporal, 1123	13th Light Dragoons	
Lovelock, Thomas	Trumpeter, 1247	4th Light Dragoons	C Killed
Low, Alexander	Captain	4th Light Dragoons	C
Lowthorpe, Robert	Private, 1140	13th Light Dragoons	
Lucas, Thomas	Private, 1540	4th Light Dragoons	C Wounded/ Prisoner
Lymbrey, John	Private, 1462	4th Light Dragoons	
Lynch, Richard	Sergeant, 968	4th Light Dragoons	C Killed
McAllister, James	Private, 997	17th Lancers	C Prisoner
Macaulay, Charles	Private, 1057	8th Hussars	C
McBrine, John	Private, 1418	13th Light Dragoons	
McCabe, Michael	Private, 639	17th Lancers	
McCann, John	Private, 1341	13th Light Dragoons	C Prisoner
McCausland, John	Private, 1114	8th Hussars	C
McCluer, Harry	Troop Sgt Major, 859	8th Hussars	C Killed
McDonald, Edward	Private, 1272	8th Hussars	C Killed
McDonald, James	Private, 1059	11th Hussars	
McDonough, John	Private, 916	8th Hussars	
McGeorge, John	Private, 1385	11th Hussars	C Killed
McGorrine, Thomas	Private, 1332	13th Light Dragoons	C
McGrath, Martin	Private, 925	17th Lancers	
McGregor, George	Private, 1382	4th Light Dragoons	C
McHeath, Wallace	Private, 1598	11th Hussars	
McInnes, David	Private, 1425	13th Light Dragoons	
McKenna, William	Private, 541	17th Lancers	
McKimm, Graham	Corporal, 1397	13th Light Dragoons	
McKimm, Robert	Private, 1356	13th Light Dragoons	
McLean, Peter	Private, 573	8th Hussars	
Macnaghten, Francis	Lieutenant	8th Hussars	
McNally, Thomas	Private, 1272	13th Light Dragoons	
McNeil, James	Private, 1339	4th Light Dragoons	
McNeill, David	Private, 684	17th Lancers	C Wounded
McNeill, Robert	Private, 901	17th Lancers	C Killed
McNulty, John	Private, 1269	11th Hussars	
McVeagh, John	Hospital Sergeant, 906	4th Light Dragoons	C Wounded
Magee, Thomas	Private, 934	17th Lancers	C Wounded
Malanfy, James	Private, 1276	13th Light Dragoons	
Malone, Joseph	Corporal, 1440	13th Light Dragoons	C
Mann, James	Private, 943	17th Lancers	
Mansell, George	Private, 1106	17th Lancers	
Markland, William	Private, 1649	11th Hussars	
Marsh, Peter	Private, 1025	17th Lancers	C
Marshall, Charles	Private, 1128	4th Light Dragoons	C Killed
Marshall, Thomas	Private, 1010	17th Lancers	C Prisoner
Marshman, Thomas	Private, 882	4th Light Dragoons	

Martin, Alfred	Private, 1562	4th Light Dragoons	
Martin, Edward	Sergeant, 1208	13th Light Dragoons	C Wounded
Martin, Fiennes	Cornet	4th Light Dragoons	C
Martin, John	Private, 992	8th Hussars	C
Martin, Robert	Private, 1337	11th Hussars	C Wounded
Martin, William	Private, 1068	13th Light Dragoons	C Wounded/ Prisoner
Martin, William	Private, 1536	13th Light Dragoons	
Martindale, Henry	Private, 1254	8th Hussars	
Mason, Thomas	Private, 1015	17th Lancers	
Massey, Hampden	Surgeon	17th Lancers	
Matthews, George	Private, 1605	11th Hussars	
Maule, George	Private, 1602	11th Hussars	C
Maxse, Henry	Lieutenant	ADC to Cardigan	C Wounded
May, G.	Private, 1555	11th Hussars	
Mayhew, James	Private, 1153	13th Light Dragoons	C
Mayow, George	Lieutenant Colonel	Brigade Major	C
Meade, James	Private, 1000	8th Hussars	
Meally, Thomas	Private, 1237	4th Light Dragoons	
Medders, Frederick	Private, 1436	4th Light Dragoons	
Melrose, Frederick	Private, 975	17th Lancers	C Killed
Mepham, John	Private, 1571	4th Light Dragoons	
Middleton, Isaac	Private, 1422	11th Hussars	
Milburne, S.	Private, 741	11th Hussars	C Wounded
Miller, James	Private, 1087	8th Hussars	
Minshull, William	Private, 1229	8th Hussars	
Mitchell, Albert	Private, 1401	13th Light Dragoons	C
Mitton, John	Private, 881	17th Lancers	C Killed
Mock, William	Private, 1266	8th Hussars	
Moloney, William	Private, 1389	13th Light Dragoons	
Moneypenny, Robert	Private, 934	8th Hussars	C
Montgomery, Hugh	Cornet	13th Light Dragoons	C Killed
Moody, Henry	Private, 1094	4th Light Dragoons	C Killed
Moody, Thomas	Private, 1517	13th Light Dragoons	
Mooney, Nicholas	Private, 1125	8th Hussars	
Moore, John	Private, 855	4th Light Dragoons	
Moore, Joseph	Private, 1224	13th Light Dragoons	C Wounded
Moran, Thomas	Private, 1165	17th Lancers	
Morgan, Charles	Private, 988	17th Lancers	C
Morgan, Godfrey	Captain, The Hon.	17th Lancers	C
Morley, Thomas	Corporal, 1004	17th Lancers	C
Morris, George	Private, 1136	8th Hussars	
Morris, William	Private, 1255	8th Hussars	
Morris, William	Captain	17th Lancers	C Wounded
Morrissey, Patrick	Sergeant, 1248	13th Light Dragoons	

Mortimer, John	Private, 938	8th Hussars	C
Mugg, Henry	Private, 1085	17th Lancers	C
Mulcahy, John	Sergeant, 1230	13th Light Dragoons	C
Mullins, Thomas	Private, 1095	17th Lancers	C Wounded
Murphy, Phillip	Private, 690	17th Lancers	
Murray, John	Corporal, 1317	13th Light Dragoons	
Murray, Robert	Corporal, 1083	8th Hussars	
Mussenden, William	Cornet	8th Hussars	C
Mustard, James	Private, 1149	17th Lancers	C Wounded
Myers, John	Private, 1409	11th Hussars	
Nagle, Benjamin	Sergeant, 1315	13th Light Dragoons	C
Nally, Thomas	Private, 943	8th Hussars	
Naylor, Henry	Private, 1460	13th Light Dragoons	C Wounded
Naylor, James	Private, 697	13th Light Dragoons	C Wounded
Neal, James	Corporal, 1185	8th Hussars	
Neille, Edward	Private, 985	8th Hussars	
Newbrey, George	Private, 1104	4th Light Dragoons	
Newitt, William	Private, 1261	8th Hussars	
Newman, Frederick	Private, 817	17th Lancers	
Newman, Owen	Private, 1204	13th Light Dragoons	
Nichol, Robert	Private, 1027	8th Hussars	C
Nicholson, John	Private, 1026	17th Lancers	
Nicholson, William	Private, 1378	13th Light Dragoons	C Wounded
Normoyle, James	Private, 918	4th Light Dragoons	C Wounded/ Prisoner
Notley, William	Private, 1438	13th Light Dragoons	
Nowlan, Michael	Private, 615	17th Lancers	
Nunnerley, James	Corporal, 870	17th Lancers	C
Nye, James	Private, 624	8th Hussars	
Oakley, Luke	Private, 709	11th Hussars	
O'Brien, Edward	Private, 1021	4th Light Dragoons	
O'Brien, Michael	Private, 1461	4th Light Dragoons	C Prisoner
Ockford, Samuel	Troop Sgt Major, 1198	4th Light Dragoons	
Odlam, Henry	Private, 908	8th Hussars	
O'Gorman, James	Private, 882	17th Lancers	C Wounded
O'Hara, Denis	Troop Sgt Major, 600	17th Lancers	C
O'Hara, James	Private, 716	17th Lancers	
O'Keefe, John	Private, 1036	8th Hussars	
Oldham, John	Captain	13th Light Dragoons	C Killed
Olley, James	Private, 1543	4th Light Dragoons	C Wounded
Oram, Caleb	Private, 1551	4th Light Dragoons	
Page, Francis	Private, 1114	13th Light Dragoons	
Paget, Lord George	Lieutenant Colonel	4th Light Dragoons	C
Paine, John	Private, 692	17th Lancers	C Wounded
Palframan, Richard	Private, 1218	8th Hussars	C Prisoner

Palin, John	Private, 1381	4th Light Dragoons	C
Palmer, Roger	Lieutenant	11th Hussars	C
Pamplin, James	Private, 1254	13th Light Dragoons	C
Pantry, James	Private, 1303	11th Hussars	
Parker, Henry	Private, 1484	11th Hussars	C Prisoner
Parker, W.	Corporal, 954	13th Light Dragoons	
Parker, William	Private, 1591	4th Light Dragoons	
Parkes, Samuel	Private, 635	4th Light Dragoons	C Prisoner
Parkinson, John	Private, 1521	11th Hussars	C Wounded
Paynter, Joshua	Surgeon	13th Light Dragoons	
Peake, Frederick	Sergeant, 1309	13th Light Dragoons	C Wounded
Pearce, Henry	Private, 790	17th Lancers	C Killed
Pearson, John	Private, 861	8th Hussars	
Pearson, William	Private, 1353	4th Light Dragoons	C
Pearson, William	Private, 939	17th Lancers	C Wounded
Pedrick, John	Private, 1071	13th Light Dragoons	
Pegler, Henry	Private, 1436	13th Light Dragoons	C Wounded
Penn, John	Corporal, 1168	17th Lancers	C
Pennington, William	Private, 1631	11th Hussars	C Wounded
Percival, Enoch	Private, 1469	13th Light Dragoons	
Percy, John	Private, 1291	13th Light Dragoons	
Perkins, James	Private, 850	17th Lancers	C
Perkins, William	Trumpeter, 1304	11th Hussars	C
Perry, Thomas	Private, 597	8th Hussars	C Wounded/ Prisoner
Phelan, Michael	Private, 1513	4th Light Dragoons	C Killed
Phelan, William	Private, 964	17th Lancers	C Wounded
Phillips, Edward	Lieutenant	8th Hussars	C
Phillips, James	Private, 651	17th Lancers	
Phillips, Joseph	Private, 1404	4th Light Dragoons	C Wounded
Phillips, William	Private, 1370	11th Hussars	C
Philpot, Humphrey	Private, 770	13th Light Dragoons	
Picking, William	Private, 1231	8th Hussars	C Prisoner
Pickles, Joseph	Sergeant, 908	11th Hussars	
Pickworth, John	Sergeant, 684	8th Hussars	C
Pitt, William	Farrier, 1193	4th Light Dragoons	C
Plummer, William	Private, 1241	8th Hussars	
Pollard, Benjamin	Private, 1627	11th Hussars	
Pollard, Thomas	Private, 478	13th Light Dragoons	C
Poole, Richard	Private, 594	4th Light Dragoons	
Porley, Thomas	Private, 1145	13th Light Dragoons	
Portal, Robert	Captain	4th Light Dragoons	C
Potter, Samuel	Private, 1480	4th Light Dragoons	
Powell, Charles	Private, 1587	11th Hussars	C
Powell, Harry	Trumpeter, 1228	13th Light Dragoons	C Wounded

Power, James	Private, 1234	13th Light Dragoons	
Price, G.	Private, 1174	4th Light Dragoons	C
Prince, Benjamin	Private, 656	4th Light Dragoons	
Prior, William	Private, 499	17th Lancers	
Proctor, John	Private, 1467	11th Hussars	
Pumfrett, George	Corporal, 1082	17th Lancers	
Purcell, David	Private, 1591	11th Hussars	C Killed
Purvis, J.	Private, 1441	11th Hussars	C Wounded
Purvis, William	Private, 868	17th Lancers	C Wounded
Pyne, John	Corporal, 928	17th Lancers	C Wounded
Quill, Martin	Private, 525	8th Hussars	
Rafferty, Patrick	Private, 980	17th Lancers	C Wounded
Randall, Charles	Private, 1062	17th Lancers	
Ranson, Abraham	Troop Sgt Major, 493	17th Lancers	C
Ratcliffe, John	Private, 681	17th Lancers	
Rawlins, James	Private, 1265	8th Hussars	
Reardon, John	Private, 1244	13th Light Dragoons	
Reilly, Edward	Sergeant, 619	8th Hussars	
Reilly, John	Regt Sgt Major, 1398	4th Light Dragoons	C
Reilly, John	Private, 868	8th Hussars	
Reilly, Joseph	Private, 815	17th Lancers	C
Reilly, Michael	Sergeant, 917	8th Hussars	C Killed
Reynolds, John	Private, 912	8th Hussars	
Rhodes, Joseph	Private, 694	13th Light Dragoons	C Wounded
Rhys, W.	Private, 1498	11th Hussars	
Richardson, John	Private, 1567	11th Hussars	C
Rickman, James	Private, 1065	4th Light Dragoons	
Ridge, George	Private, 1125	17th Lancers	
Rivers, George	Private, 1146	8th Hussars	
Roberts, Thomas	Private, 1198	11th Hussars	C Wounded
Roberts, Thomas	Private, 1286	13th Light Dragoons	
Roberts, William	Private, 1484	4th Light Dragoons	
Roberts, William	Private, 1172	17th Lancers	
Robinson, Charles	Armourer Sergeant, 1492	11th Hussars	
Robinson, George	Private, 1305	4th Light Dragoons	C Killed
Robinson, George	Private, 1025	11th Hussars	
Robinson, John	Corporal, 1449	13th Light Dragoons	
Robinson, Thomas	Private, 1600	11th Hussars	
Robinson, William	Private, 828	4th Light Dragoons	
Robinson, William	Private, 1596	4th Light Dragoons	
Roche, William	Private, 1131	13th Light Dragoons	
Rogers, Thomas	Private, 986	4th Light Dragoons	
Ross, Joseph	Private, 1222	8th Hussars	C Wounded
Rowe, James	Farrier Major, 1124	4th Light Dragoons	

Rowley, Richard	Private, 984	13th Light Dragoons	C Wounded
Russell, Archibald	Private, 1120	11th Hussars	C Killed
Russell, Patrick	Private, 1449	4th Light Dragoons	
Ryan, James	Private, 1155	17th Lancers	C
Ryan, John	Private, 631	17th Lancers	
Ryan, Patrick	Private, 955	8th Hussars	
Ryan, Thomas	Private, 1555	4th Light Dragoons	C
Ryan, Thomas	Private, 983	8th Hussars	
Ryan, William	Private, 1004	8th Hussars	C Wounded
Saker, William	Private, 703	17th Lancers	
Salter, Jabez	Private, 1479	13th Light Dragoons	
Saltern, Joseph	Private, 1212	4th Light Dragoons	
Samer, S.	Private, 1364	11th Hussars	C Wounded
Sampson, George	Private, 1402	11th Hussars	
Saunders, William	Private, 978	4th Light Dragoons	
Sawbridge, T.	Private, 1507	11th Hussars	
Scarfe, James	Sergeant, 481	17th Lancers	C Wounded
Seabrook, Michael	Private, 618	17th Lancers	
Seager, Edward	Lieutenant	8th Hussars	C Wounded
Sealy, Henry	Private, 1222	11th Hussars	
Sedgwick, James	Private, 826	4th Light Dragoons	
Senior, George	Sergeant, 1386	13th Light Dragoons	
Sewell, Edward	Sergeant, 1104	8th Hussars	C Wounded
Sewell, John	Corporal, 1197	8th Hussars	C Wounded
Sewell, Johnson	Private, 1111	17th Lancers	C Killed
Sewell, William	Private, 1452	13th Light Dragoons	C Wounded
Shackle, John	Private, 985	4th Light Dragoons	
Sharpe, Thomas	Private, 940	17th Lancers	C Prisoner
Sheargold, Henry	Private, 1704	11th Hussars	C Wounded
Shearingham, John	Sergeant, 539	17th Lancers	
Sheppard, William	Private, 1580	11th Hussars	C Wounded/ Prisoner
Sharman, Andrew	Private, 1123	17th Lancers	
Shergold, Thomas	Sergeant, 1482	11th Hussars	
Sheridan, Anthony	Private, 468	8th Hussars	C
Sherriff, George	Private, 906	17th Lancers	
Shewell, Frederick	Lieutenant Colonel	8th Hussars	C
Shoppee, Leonard	Private, 1528	11th Hussars	C Killed
Short, Charles	Private, 1517	11th Hussars	C
Short, Frederick	Sergeant, 1250	4th Light Dragoons	C
Shrive, Thomas	Private, 1523	11th Hussars	C Killed
Simpson, George	Private, 1383	11th Hussars	
Sims, William	Private, 1285	13th Light Dragoons	
Slack, Joseph	Private, 832	17th Lancers	
Slattery, James	Private, 1247	13th Light Dragoons	C Killed

Smith, Aubrey	Corporal, 1491	13th Light Dragoons	C Killed
Smith, George	Troop Sgt Major, 766	11th Hussars	C
Smith, George	Troop Sgt Major, 1106	13th Light Dragoons	C Wounded/ Prisoner
Smith, George	Private, 1003	17th Lancers	
Smith, Henry	Private, 1264	8th Hussars	C
Smith, John	Private, 1446	13th Light Dragoons	
Smith, John	Private, 924	17th Lancers	C
Smith, Percy	Lieutenant	13th Light Dragoons	C
Smith, William	Trumpeter, 1586	11th Hussars	C
Smith, William	Private, 849	13th Light Dragoons	
Smith, William	Private, 867	17th Lancers	
Sneezum, John	Private, 1432	11th Hussars	
Soames, Thomas	Corporal, 1099	13th Light Dragoons	
Soley, Benjamin	Private, 1120	17th Lancers	C Wounded
Somers, Henry	Assistant Surgeon	8th Hussars	
Spain, Christopher	Private, 568	8th Hussars	C Wounded
Sparke, Henry	Lieutenant	4th Light Dragoons	C Killed
Spence, Henry	Corporal, 1344	4th Light Dragoons	C Killed
Spring, William	Private, 1608	11th Hussars	C Wounded/ Prisoner
Staden, William	Private, 870	11th Hussars	
Stanger, Robert	Private, 1424	13th Light Dragoons	
Stanley, David	Private, 1009	17th Lancers	C Wounded
Stanley, Ferdinand	Private, 1039	4th Light Dragoons	C
Stanley, William	Private, 1306	13th Light Dragoons	
Stannage, James	Private, 1016	17th Lancers	C Killed
Stannicliffe, Henry	Corporal, 1261	11th Hussars	
Steele, Hugh	Private, 952	8th Hussars	
Stephenson, James	Private, 1538	11th Hussars	C Killed
Stephenson, John	Paymaster	17th Lancers	
Stewart, Thomas	Private, 974	17th Lancers	C Wounded
Stine, Andrew	Private, 1060	17th Lancers	
Stoddard, William	Private, 706	17th Lancers	
Storey, John	Private, 852	4th Light Dragoons	
Strutt, J.	Private, 1421	11th Hussars	C Wounded
Styles, Benjamin	Private, 1157	8th Hussars	
Sutcliffe, W.	Private, 1234	4th Light Dragoons	C Wounded
Swan, George	Private, 1585	4th Light Dragoons	C Killed
Swiney, John	Private, 1036	17th Lancers	C
Talbot, Edward	Sergeant, 556	17th Lancers	C Killed
Taylor, George	Corporal, 405	17th Lancers	C Wounded
Taylor, Henry	Private, 1141	13th Light Dragoons	C
Taylor, John	Private, 1523	13th Light Dragoons	
Taylor, Thomas	Private, 1091	17th Lancers	

Taylor, William	Corporal, 872	8th Hussars	C Wounded/ Prisoner
Taylor, William	Private, 836	8th Hussars	
Taylor, William	Private, 1541	11th Hussars	C Wounded
Teehan, Cornelius	Private, 1339	11th Hussars	
Teevan, Patrick	Troop Sgt Major, 1159	11th Hussars	C Wounded
Terry, George	Sergeant, 721	17th Lancers	C
Thomas, David	Private, 1181	4th Light Dragoons	C
Thomas, John	Private, 936	11th Hussars	
Thomas, William	Sergeant, 969	4th Light Dragoons	C Wounded/ Prisoner
Thompson, Hugh	Private, 1248	8th Hussars	
Thomson, John	Lieutenant	17th Lancers	C Killed
Thorburn, Thomas	Private, 1362	11th Hussars	
Thorne, William	Private, 1203	4th Light Dragoons	C Wounded
Thornton, John	Private, 974	8th Hussars	
Thorpe, John	Private, 1273	4th Light Dragoons	
Tiggle, Samuel	Private, 1178	17th Lancers	C
Tobin, James	Private, 991	8th Hussars	
Tohey, John	Private, 968	8th Hussars	
Tomkinson, Edward	Captain	8th Hussars	C Wounded
Tomsett, Thomas	Private, 1586	4th Light Dragoons	C Killed
Topham, William	Private, 820	8th Hussars	
Towers, John	Veterinary Surgeon	13th Light Dragoons	
Townrow, William	Private, 797	11th Hussars	
Towson, Thomas	Private, 838	17th Lancers	
Travers, William	Private, 1075	8th Hussars	
Travis, William	Private, 678	17th Lancers	C
Tremayne, Arthur	Captain	13th Light Dragoons	C
Trevelyan, Harington	Lieutenant	11th Hussars	C Wounded
Trowman, Edward	Private, 923	17th Lancers	
Tully, Patrick	Private, 918	8th Hussars	
Turby, George	Private, 775	17th Lancers	
Turner, Edward	Private, 1238	8th Hussars	C Killed
Turner, George	Private, 1358	11th Hussars	C Wounded
Turner, Henry	Private, 1263	4th Light Dragoons	
Turner, William	Private, 1115	4th Light Dragoons	
Twamley, Thomas	Private, 1078	8th Hussars	C Wounded
Tyler, James	Private, 1194	4th Light Dragoons	C Wounded
Tyrrell, Lawrence	Corporal, 1333	13th Light Dragoons	
Vahey, John	Private, 598	17th Lancers	C
Veitch, John	Private, 1431	13th Light Dragoons	C Wounded
Venables, Edward	Private, 1561	11th Hussars	
Vick, Joseph	Corporal, 725	4th Light Dragoons	C
Viner, Frederick	Private, 1454	13th Light Dragoons	C

Waight, Charles	Private, 1527	4th Light Dragoons	C Killed
Wainhouse, Thomas	Private, 1009	13th Light Dragoons	
Wakelin, Henry	Private, 1526	11th Hussars	C Killed
Walker, William	Private, 1621	11th Hussars	C Wounded
Waller, Frederick	Private, 1035	17th Lancers	C
Wallis, John	Private, 725	4th Light Dragoons	
Walls, William	Private, 1186	8th Hussars	
Walpole, Edwin	Private, 1031	11th Hussars	
Walters, William	Private, 694	8th Hussars	
Ward, David	Private, 1080	11th Hussars	C Killed
Ward, George	Sergeant, 1166	13th Light Dragoons	
Ward, James	Private, 1357	13th Light Dragoons	
Ward, William	Sergeant, 517	8th Hussars	
Wareham, William	Private, 938	11th Hussars	C Killed
Warnes, S.	Private, 1208	11th Hussars	
Warr, Thomas	Private, 1481	11th Hussars	C
Warren, Christopher	Private, 1515	13th Light Dragoons	C Prisoner
Waterer, Charles	Private, 1228	8th Hussars	C Killed
Waters, William	Private, 812	13th Light Dragoons	
Waterson, William	Troop Sgt Major, 1215	4th Light Dragoons	C
Watkins, Joseph	Private, 1459	11th Hussars	
Watlen, William	Private, 1442	13th Light Dragoons	
Watling, Robert	Private, 1568	4th Light Dragoons	
Watson, Charles	Private, 872	17th Lancers	C
Watson, James	Private, 1413	13th Light Dragoons	C Killed
Watson, John	Armourer Sergeant, 433	8th Hussars	
Watters, Richard	Corporal, 1123	8th Hussars	
Watts, James	Private, 1153	17th Lancers	C Wounded
Watts, John	Private, 1506	4th Light Dragoons	
Weatherley, George	Corporal, 673	17th Lancers	C
Webb, Augustus	Captain	17th Lancers	C Wounded
Webster, James	Private, 902	17th Lancers	C
Wells, John	Private, 1559	11th Hussars	
Weston, John	Troop Sgt Major, 715	13th Light Dragoons	C Killed
Wheeler, George	Private, 1449	11th Hussars	
Wheelhouse, Samuel	Private, 643	13th Light Dragoons	
Whelan, John	Private, 741	8th Hussars	
Whitby, James	Private, 1508	4th Light Dragoons	C
Whitby, Joseph	Private, 1493	4th Light Dragoons	C Wounded
White, George	Private, 1420	11th Hussars	
White, John	Private, 1011	8th Hussars	C Killed
White, Morris	Private, 1231	13th Light Dragoons	
White, Robert	Captain	17th Lancers	C Wounded
White, Thomas	Private, 975	13th Light Dragoons	C Wounded

Whitechurch, James	Private, 855	8th Hussars	
Whitehead, John	Private, 1289	4th Light Dragoons	C
Whitehouse, John	Private, 830	8th Hussars	
Whitworth, Samuel	Private, 1363	4th Light Dragoons	
Whyte, Charles	Private, 981	8th Hussars	C
Wickham, Henry	Private, 1499	13th Light Dragoons	C
Wightman, James	Private, 1177	17th Lancers	C Wounded/ Prisoner
Wilcox, Edward	Private, 1202	11th Hussars	C Wounded
Wilde, George	Private, 1119	13th Light Dragoons	C Wounded
Wilder, Anthony	Private, 1445	11th Hussars	C
Wilkin, Henry	Assistant Surgeon	11th Hussars	C
Williams, Edward	Private, 919	8th Hussars	
Williams, George	Private, 1348	13th Light Dragoons	C Wounded
Williams, James	Corporal, 663	11th Hussars	C Wounded/ Prisoner
Williams, Richard	Sergeant, 750	17th Lancers	C
Williams, Samuel	Troop Sgt Major, 420	8th Hussars	C
Williams, Thomas	Private, 1479	11th Hussars	C
Williams, Thomas	Private, 879	13th Light Dragoons	C Killed
Williams, William	Sergeant, 804	8th Hussars	C Killed
Williamson, James	Private, 1609	11th Hussars	
Williamson, William	Sergeant, 1122	11th Hussars	
Wilsden, Henry	Private, 1361	4th Light Dragoons	C
Wilson, John	Private, 1017	17th Lancers	
Wilson, Peter	Private, 1379	11th Hussars	
Wilson, Samuel	Private, 911	8th Hussars	C
Wilson, William	Private, 1204	8th Hussars	C
Wimset, Richard	Private, 961	13th Light Dragoons	
Winan, Thomas	Private, 1427	4th Light Dragoons	
Winter, John	Captain	17th Lancers	C Killed
Wombwell, George	Cornet	17th Lancers	C
Wood, John	Private, 1522	4th Light Dragoons	
Wooden, Charles	Sergeant, 799	17th Lancers	C
Woodham, Edward	Private, 1355	11th Hussars	C
Wootten, George	Private, 1533	11th Hussars	C Killed
Worley, John	Private, 1528	13th Light Dragoons	
Wright, Edmund	Private, 1458	13th Light Dragoons	C Wounded
Wright, Robert	Private, 1625	11th Hussars	
Wright, Thomas	Private, 1097	17th Lancers	C
Wrigley, Constantine	Private, 469	17th Lancers	C Killed
Wroots, Thomas	Private, 1235	11th Hussars	C
Wynne, Peter	Private, 1387	13th Light Dragoons	
Yates, John	Cornet	11th Hussars	

Yates, John	Private, 1102	17th Lancers	C Wounded
Young, Henry	Private, 1078	17th Lancers	C Wounded/ Prisoner
Young, Richard	Private, 1463	11th Hussars	C Wounded

SOURCES

Documents in the Public Record Office, UK National Archives:
   Medal Rolls for the Queen's Crimea Medal – WO100/24
   Muster Rolls 1854/1855: WO12, WO14, WO15
   Casualty Returns – WO25

ADDITIONAL INFORMATION

Cook, Frank and Cook, Andrea, *The Casualty Roll for the Crimea*, Savannah Publications, London, 1976

Lummis, William and Wynn, Kenneth, *Honour the Light Brigade*, Hayward and Son, 1973

Sewell, Andrew, *Lummis and Wynn: Some Revisions*, Crimean War Research Society, 1994

Bibliography

Accounts of Survivors

The main accounts used – books, magazine articles and letters by survivors – are listed below. Many of these include the comments or observations of other men who charged, but who did not publish accounts of their own. The ranks shown in parentheses are those held at the time of the charge, not at the time of publication.

Cardigan, Lord (Major General, Light Brigade commander), *Eight Months on Active Service*, Clowes and Sons, London, 1855

4th Light Dragoons

Farquharson, Robert (Private), *Reminiscences Of Crimean Campaigning And Russian Imprisonment*, privately printed, Glasgow, 1882

Grigg, Joseph (Private), his account in the collection, *Told From The Ranks*, edited by Milton Small, Melrose, London, 1897

Joliffe, Hedworth (Lieutenant), letters, National Army Museum, London

Paget, Lord George (Lieutenant Colonel, commanding officer), *Crimean Journal – The Light Cavalry Brigade In The Crimea*, Murray, London, 1881

Portal, Robert (Captain), *Letters From The Crimea*, privately printed, 1856

8th Hussars

Anonymous (Private), 'The Charge of the Light Brigade by one who was in it', *United Services Journal*, April 1856. Although anonymous, this man was known to and vouched for by the editor of the highly respected *United Services Journal*.

Doyle, John (Private), *A Descriptive Account Of The Famous Charge Of The Light Brigade at Balaclava*, privately printed, Manchester, 1877

Seager, Edward (Lieutenant), letter, National Army Museum, London

11th Hussars

Pennington, William (Private), *Left of Six Hundred*, privately printed, London, 1887; *Sea, Camp and Stage*, privately printed, Bristol, 1906

Smith, George Loy (Troop Sergeant Major), *A Victorian RSM*, D. J. Costello, Tunbridge Wells, 1987, from his original diaries

13th Light Dragoons

Mitchell, Albert (Private), *Recollections Of One Of The Light Brigade*, privately printed, Tunbridge Wells, 1884

Tremayne, Arthur (Captain), letters, National Army Museum, London

17th Lancers

Butler, William (Private), *A Descriptive Account Of The Famous Charge Of The Light Brigade*, privately printed, Preston, *c.*1890

Morley, Thomas (Corporal), *The Man Of The Hour*, privately printed, 1892; *The Cause Of The Charge Of Balaclava*, privately printed, Nottingham, 1899

Nunnerley, James Ikin (Corporal), *Short Sketch Of The 17th Lancers And Life Of Sergeant-Major J. I. Nunnerley*, privately printed, Liverpool, 1884

Wightman, James (Private), 'One Of The Six Hundred', *Nineteenth Century Magazine*, May 1892

Wombwell, George (Cornet), letters, The Queen's Royal Lancers Museum

Accounts of Observers

All of these men (and the indomitable Fanny Duberly) watched the charge either from Lord Raglan's position on the Sapoune Heights or from the valley itself. Several, but particularly Alexander Kinglake, interviewed survivors after the charge. Both Lucan and Cardigan wrote lengthy accounts specifically for use by Kinglake.

Blunt, Sir John (Lord Lucan's interpreter), personal papers, National Army Museum, London

Calthorpe, Somerset (Lieutenant, ADC to Lord Raglan), *Letters from Headquarters*, Murray, London, 1856

Cattell, William (Assistant Surgeon, attached 5th Dragoon Guards), unpublished autobiography, National Army Museum, London

Clifford, Henry (Captain, 1st Rifle Brigade), *Letters and Sketches from the Crimea*, Michael Joseph, London, 1956

Duberly, Fanny (wife of Captain Duberly, 8th Hussars), *Journal Kept During The Russian War*, Longman, 1856

Ewart, J. A. (Captain, ADC to Lord Raglan), *The Story of a Soldier's Life*, Sampson Low, London, 1881

Fisher-Rowe, Edward (Cornet, 4th Dragoon Guards), *Letters written during the Crimean War*, R. D. Stedman, Godalming, 1907

Forrest, William (Major, 4th Dragoon Guards), letters, National Army Museum, London

Godman, Richard Temple (Lieutenant, 5th Dragoon Guards), *The Fields of War*, letters edited by Philip Warner, Murray, London, 1977

Kinglake, Alexander (travelling gentleman and historian), *The Invasion of the Crimea*, William Blackwood and Sons, London, eight volumes, 1863–87

Raglan, Lord (commander-in-chief of the army), papers, National Army Museum, London

Russell, William (war correspondent of *The Times*), *The British Expedition to the Crimea*, Routledge and Sons, London, 1858; *The Great War with Russia*, Routledge and Sons, London, 1867

Strangways, Fox (Lieutenant, Royal Horse Artillery), chapter on Balaklava in *From Coruña to Sevastopol* by Colonel F. Whinyates, W. H. Allen and Co., London, 1884

Walker, Beauchamp (Captain, ADC to Lord Lucan), *Days of a Soldier's Life*, Chapman and Hall, London, 1894

Secondary Sources

Among the many secondary accounts of the Crimean War, these have made a substantial contribution to the study of the charge of the Light Brigade.

Adkin, Mark, *The Charge*, Leo Cooper, London, 1996

Anglesey, Marquess of, *History of the British Cavalry, Volume 2*, Leo Cooper, London, 1975

Barker, A. J. *The Vainglorious War*, Weidenfeld and Nicolson, London, 1970

Harris, Stephen, *British Military Intelligence In The Crimean War*, Frank Cass, London, 1999

Hibbert, Christopher, *The Destruction of Lord Raglan*, Longman, London, 1961

Lummis, Canon W. M., and Wynn, K. G., *Honour the Light Brigade*, Hayward & Son, London, 1973

Mollo, John and Mollo, Boris, *Into The Valley Of Death*, Windrow & Greene, London, 1991

Moyse-Bartlett, Lieutenant Colonel H., *Louis Nolan and his Influence on British Cavalry*, Leo Cooper, London, 1971

Royle, Trevor, *Crimea*, Little, Brown and Company, London, 1999

Seaton, Albert, *The Crimean War*, B. T. Batsford, London, 1977

War Correspondent, quarterly journal of the Crimean War Research Society

Warner, Philip, *The Crimean War*, Arthur Barker, London, 1972

Whinyates, Colonel F., *From Coruña to Sevastopol*, W. H. Allen and Co., London, 1884

Woodham-Smith, Cecil, *The Reason Why*, Constable, London, 1953

Index

93rd Highlanders, 71, 84, 86, 88–9, 91–2

Abdelal, Major, 123

Aberdeen, Lord, 7, 8

Adkin, Mark, 251–2, 253–6

Airey, General Richard, 51, 99, 101, 103, 241

Alma, battle of the, 53–9

Annersley, Cornet, 49

Astafev, Cornet, 162

Bacon, Major Anthony, 20–21, 216

Balaklava, 59, 63–5, 71, 75, 85–6, 88, 91, 207, 212, 213, 215, 219

Balaklava Commemoration Society, 228, 264, 265, 277, 302

Barker, Troop Sergeant Major William, 225–6

Belbec, river, 57–8

Bentley, Sergeant William, 166–7, 317

Berryman, Sergeant John, 61, 136, 138, 180–81

Bingham, George, see Lucan, 3rd Earl of

Bird, Private William, 218, 265

Blishen, Private Henry, 54

Blunt, Sir John, 106, 112, 122, 183, 264

Bond, Sergeant Seth, 55

Bosquet, General, 190, 202, 301

Brandling, Captain, 95–6, 184, 283, 286

Breese, Sergeant John, 208

Briggs, Private Robert, 226

Brittain, Private William, 113, 205, 262–3, 266–7

Brooks, Private John, 13

Brooks, Private Walter, 125

Brown, General Sir George, 44

Brudenell, James, see Cardigan, 7th Earl of

Bulganek, river, 49–53

Burgoyne, Sir John, 59, 64–5

Butler, Private William, 125, 143, 176, 269

Calthorpe, Lieutenant Somerset, 29, 38, 61–2, 69, 88, 103, 104, 119, 235, 243, 246–8, 279–81

Cambridge, Duke of, 98, 99

Cameron, Private Donald, 92

Campbell, Sir Colin, 71, 77, 83–4, 88, 91–2

Canrobert, General, 206

Cardigan, James Brudenell, 7th Earl of: life and career, 24–9; relationship with Lucan, 18–19, 21, 23–4; in Turkey, 35, 36, 38, 39–40, 41, 42–3; in the Crimea, 48, 49–52, 58, 61, 67, 70; and the charge, 83, 87, 93, 97–8, 100, 107–18, 132, 137, 138, 145–7, 185, 188, 199, 202, 206, 208, 211, 215–16, 222, 223–4, 228, 236, 239–41, 252, 259–60, 268, 278–89

Cathcart, General Sir George, 64, 98–9, 182

Cattell, Assistant Surgeon William, 96, 183

Cattley, Charles, 67–8, 75–7

Causeway Heights, 71, 73, 81–3, 91, 98–100, 102, 106, 107, 119, 128–9, 141, 160, 169, 175–6, 187, 250, 255

Chadwick, Cornet John, 132, 144

Chamberlayne, Cornet Denzil, 172

Charteris, Captain Walter, 122, 123

Chasseurs d'Afrique, 101, 123

Chernaya, river, 61, 63, 66, 74–5, 82, 100, 115, 151, 152, 153, 155

Chenery, Thomas, 304

Clarendon, Lord, 9

Clifford, Private Frederick, 153

Clifford, Captain Henry, 93, 203, 211

Clowes, Cornet George, 34, 172

Constantinople, 7, 10, 35–7, 205

Cook, Captain Edwin, 135, 160, 176

Cooper, Private George, 218

Cowley, Lord, 9

Crawford, Trumpeter Hugh, 157

Daily Graphic, 272

Daily News, 32, 223, 240

Daily Mirror, 262, 274

Davis, Elizabeth, 214

Deering, Private Daniel, 282

de Salis, Major Rodolph, 224

Devna, 38–9

Dies, Private James, 14

Doherty, Colonel Charles, 211

Douglas, Colonel John, 83, 153, 154, 155, 160, 161–2, 165, 317–19

Doyle, Private John, 101

Duberly, Fanny, 31, 34, 37, 38, 40, 43, 44, 67, 83, 87–8, 91, 99, 141, 170, 219, 225, 246

Duberly, Captain Henry, 31, 83

Dudley, Private Thomas, 130

Dunn, Lieutenant Alexander, 166–7, 316–19

Elliott, Lieutenant, 92, 96

Evelyn, George, 70

Evening Standard, 269

Ewart, Captain, 98–9, 182–3

Examiner, 232

Farquharson, Private Robert, 35, 73, 82, 111, 156, 158, 173

Farrell, Sergeant John, 181, 182

Fedioukine Heights, 115–16, 119, 123, 127, 129, 139, 148, 160, 255

Filder, James, 222

Firkins, Private John, 177, 178

Fisher-Rowe, Cornet, 45, 68, 73

Fletcher, Private Thomas, 179

Forrest, Major William, 28, 41, 74

Franks, Troop Sergeant Major Henry, 94

George, Private Henry, 14

Glanister, Private James, 139

Goad, Captain Thomas, 172

Godman, Lieutenant Richard, 65–6, 93–5, 170

Gordon, Lieutenant William, 137

Gough, Corporal, 95

Govone, Major, 291

Gowing, Sergeant Thomas, 237

Graham, Sir James, 9

Grieve, Sergeant Major, 94

Grigg, Private Joseph, 156, 158

Hall, Corporal James, 153

Harrison, Troop Sergeant Major Henry, 141

Heavy Brigade, 10, 39, 45, 65, 84, 91, 93–6, 98, 112, 121–3, 160, 170; 1st Dragoons, 65, 84; 2nd Dragoons,

65, 93–4; 4th Dragoon Guards, 65, 68, 96; 5th Dragoon Guards, 65, 93–4; 6th Dragoons, 65, 93
Heneage, Lieutenant Clement, 40, 41, 213
Henry, Private Nathan, 217, 226
Herbert, Sir Sidney, 304
Hodge, Colonel Edward, 29, 123
Holland, Private Edward, 226
Houghton, Lieutenant George, 121, 287–9
Housden, Private Alfred, 4
Hughes, Private Edwin, 228
Humphries, Private, 139
Hunt, Cornet George, 157
Hutton, Captain Thomas, 110, 134, 177, 185

Illustrated London News, 195, 215, 226
Inkerman, 207–208

Jenyns, Captain Soames, 42, 133, 286
Jervis, Lieutenant Edward, 147, 153
Johnson, Sergeant Thomas, 285, 293
Jowett, Private Gregory, 74
Joy, Trumpet Major Henry, 93, 105, 122, 124, 262–6, 269–77

Kadikoi, 63–5, 71, 75–6, 83, 90, 98, 205, 211, 212, 219, 292, 311
Kalamita Bay, 46–9
Katcha, river, 57
Keating, Private Matthew, 282
Khutor Mackenzie, 59–61
Kinglake, Alexander, 64, 106, 108, 124, 149, 150, 235, 239, 249–53, 288, 292, 300–301
Kipling, Rudyard, 229, 232–5
Kirk, Private William, 300
Kozhukhov, Lieutenant Stefan, 152, 163, 167–8, 299

Kubitovich, Lieutenant Koribut, 152, 163, 179, 299

Lamb, Private James, 120
Landriani, Lieutenant, 291
Lane, Private Joseph, 225
Lawrenson, Lieutenant Colonel, 4, 55–6, 74
Light Brigade, 3–5, 10–17, 31–45, 47–9, 50–52, 54–9, 61, 62, 65–7, 97, 100–101, 112–14, 119, 143, 170, 199, 205–209, 212–14, 220; 4th Light Dragoons, 3, 11, 33, 35, 39, 49, 50, 109, 118, 128, 140, 155–8, 161, 165–6, 199–201, 220; 8th Hussars, 3, 11, 24, 31, 32, 35–6, 42, 49, 109, 118, 126, 128, 140, 155, 158–60, 162–4, 199–201, 220, 221, 225; 11th Hussars, 3, 11, 25–8, 28, 32, 47, 49, 50, 55, 97, 109, 113, 116, 118–19, 121, 127, 139, 153, 160, 165, 199–201, 214; 13th Light Dragoons, 11, 3, 32, 42, 48, 49, 50, 98, 109, 113, 132, 142–5, 148, 150, 160–3, 199–201, 211; 17th Lancers, 3, 4, 11, 19–21, 24, 31, 32, 35, 36, 49, 55, 109, 111, 113, 126–7, 132, 142–5, 148, 150, 160, 162–3, 199–201, 220, 221, 223, 225
Linkon, Troop Sergeant Major John, 145, 227
Liprandi, General, 75, 282, 300
Lovelock, Trumpeter Thomas, 206
Low, Captain Alexander, 82, 134, 156, 165, 281
Lucan, George Bingham, 3rd Earl of: life and career, 18–24; relationship with Cardigan, 18–19, 21, 23–4; in Turkey, 35, 36, 38, 41–2; in the Crimea, 44–5, 50–52, 55, 56–8,

Lucan, George Bingham – *cont.*
61, 69, 74, 76; and the charge,
82–5, 89, 93, 98, 100, 101,
105–109, 112, 118, 122, 123–4,
150, 188, 199, 206, 210, 213,
216–17, 222, 223–4, 228, 239–41,
256–61
Lucas, Private Thomas, 282

McMahon, Major Thomas, 82–3
McNeil, Sir James, 215, 221–2, 223
Malone, Corporal Joseph, 181, 182
Mansell, Private George, 183
Marsh, Private Peter, 130–31, 270
Martin, Cornet Fiennes, 126
Maude, Captain George, 53, 69, 72
Maxse, Lieutenant Henry, 146, 279
Mayow, Colonel George, 145, 148,
150, 151, 153, 155, 160, 162, 163,
278, 281–3
Melrose, Private Frederick, 138
Menshikov, Prince, 60, 65, 75–6, 188
Mitchell, Private Albert, 32, 33–4,
39, 40, 44, 51, 57, 86, 98, 101, 105,
120, 126, 129, 136, 140, 171, 173,
174, 175, 186–7, 210, 236, 286
Mouat, Surgeon James, 183, 319–20
Monks, Trumpet Major, 93
Morgan, Captain Godfrey, 115, 116,
117, 135, 137, 138, 145, 273
Morley, Corporal Thomas, 118, 125,
127, 130, 136, 139, 143, 146, 147,
153, 168, 169, 178–9, 225, 235–6,
251–2, 271, 276, 286, 322, 327
Morning Advertiser, 4
Morning Chronicle, 27
Morning Leader, 265–6
Morris, Captain William, 12, 97, 105,
107, 115, 117, 127, 136, 143,
148–51, 156, 180, 182–4, 246, 248,
301

Munder, Colonel, 257–8
Mustard, Private James, 267, 271

Naylor, Private Henry, 117, 120, 132
Newcastle, Duke of, 44, 216, 256, 260
Nicholas I, Tsar, 4, 6–7, 9, 10
Nightingale, Florence, 205, 220, 236,
303–309, 310–11, 313–15
Nolan, Captain Louis, 36, 43, 51, 56,
69, 77, 79, 88, 103–107, 116–19,
182–4, 199, 236, 240, 243–56,
259–61
Nunnerley, Corporal James, 39, 131,
138–9, 173–4, 188, 226, 251–2,
267, 271

Obolensky, Colonel, 125, 136, 143
Oldham, Captain John, 67, 133

Paget, Lord George: 29, 33, 35, 42,
47, 49–50, 56, 71, 73; and the
charge, 82–4, 87, 102, 109, 118,
121, 126, 128, 134, 140, 155–8,
161–2, 166, 176, 177, 185, 207,
211, 239, 245, 258–9, 278–9, 287,
290, 293
Palframan, Private Richard, 225
Palmer, Lieutenant Roger, 52, 74, 165
Pardoe, Sergeant Joseph, 196–7
Parkes, Private Samuel, 157, 281
Pasha, Omar, 38
Paulet, Lord William, 82, 124
Pearson, Private William, 270, 271
Penn, Private John, 136, 144, 168
Pennington, Private William, 51, 81,
111–13, 128, 129, 141, 163, 164,
165, 177, 185, 226, 272–4, 290
Perkins, Trumpeter William, 226
Phillips, Lieutenant Edward, 209,
210, 282
Pickworth, Sergeant, 101

Pollard, Private Thomas, 171, 173
Portal, Captain Robert, 35, 41, 49, 56, 131, 209, 212
Priestly, Sergeant Joseph, 52
Punch, 3–4, 11, 12, 228

Radzivill, Prince, 285–6
Raglan, Fitzroy Somerset, 1st Baron: 29, 39, 42, 44, 48, 50–51, 53, 56–9, 61, 63, 71, 74, 76; and the charge, 84–5, 87–91, 98–104, 112, 119, 141, 188, 189, 206, 207, 211, 213, 220, 239, 241–4, 256–7, 260–61
Reilly, Sergeant Michael, 159
Reynolds, Captain John, 26
Reynolds, Captain Richard, 26–7
Richardson, Private John, 110, 111, 116–17, 153, 171–2, 227–8, 240, 286
Robinson, Private Thomas, 225
Royal Horse Artillery, 43, 53, 69, 71, 95–6
Russell, Troop Sergeant Major, 123
Russell, William, 29–30, 56, 61, 77, 86–7, 91, 96, 112, 113, 132, 141, 188, 189, 190, 197–201, 202, 211, 225, 229, 230, 235, 246–8, 312, 313, 327
Russia, 7
Russian army: cavalry, 5, 46, 73, 80, 82, 85–6, 92–4, 148–53, 162, 171–2, 175–80, 299; Cossack artillery, 5, 15–16, 99, 119, 125, 135, 137–8, 142–3, 151, 201, 299; 16th Artillery Brigade, 115; 6th Hussar Brigade, 125; 12th Artillery Brigade, 129
Ryzhov, General, 125, 151, 163, 167

St Arnaud, General, 46, 59, 206
Sapoune Heights, 87, 96, 101, 104, 112, 131, 141, 170, 175, 189

Scarlett, General James, 91–4, 122, 123–4
Scott, Private John, 91
Scutari, 205, 232, 268, 303, 305–308, 310–11
Seacole, Mary, 303, 309–13, 314–15
Seager, Lieutenant Edward, 34, 102, 128, 164
Sevastopol, 44, 46, 64, 72, 75, 99, 208, 220–21, 222
Seymour, Sir George, 9
Shakespear, Captain, 43, 92
Sheridan, Private Anthony, 159, 196
Shewell, Colonel Frederick, 101, 126, 158–9, 162–4, 283
Silistria, 7, 10, 36, 37–8, 39, 42–3
Simpson, General James, 220
Simpson, William, 201–2
Small, Hugh, 308, 309
Smith, Troop Sergeant Major George, (11th Hussars), 3, 39, 47, 50, 57–8, 63, 85, 90, 110, 115, 121, 127, 139–40, 154–5, 161, 165, 167, 180, 186–7, 208, 213–14, 221, 298
Smith, Troop Sergeant Major George, (13th Light Dragoons), 145
Smith, Private George (17th Lancers), 183
Smith, Private John, 147, 227
Smith, Lieutenant Percy, 120, 172, 284
Smith, Trumpeter William, 13
Strangways, Lieutenant Fox, 96, 184

Talbot, Sergeant Edward, 131
Tennyson, Alfred Lord, 8, 111, 129, 190, 200, 229–32, 233, 235, 300–302

The Times: 1, 7, 8, 11, 25, 27, 28, 29, 38, 45, 56, 77; and the charge, 86, 112, 189, 190, 197, 216, 222, 223, 225, 229, 230, 232, 246, 301, 304, 305, 307, 313, 314, 327

Todleben, Colonel Franz, 72

Tolstoy, Ensign Leo, 328, 329

Tomsett, Private Thomas, 13

Tremayne, Captain Arthur, 106, 133, 247

Trevelyan, Sir Charles, 222

Tuckett, Captain Harvey, 27

Tulloch, Colonel Alexander, 215, 221–2, 223

Turkey, 7

Turkish army, 82, 84, 88–91

Turner, Private George, 121

Vahey, Private John, 189, 190–97, 236, 291, 292, 327

Varna, 10, 36–8, 39, 44–5

Victoria Cross, 157, 167, 181–4, 224, 316–17, 319–20, 322

Victoria, Queen, 4, 7, 8, 10, 216, 224, 229

Voronezh, 217

Walker, Captain, 106, 122–3, 247

Ward, Private David, 121

Wathen, Captain Augustus, 25

Watts, Private James, 226–7

Webb, Captain Augustus, 180–81

Wellington, Duke of, 28

Westminster Review, 9

Wetherall, Captain, 60

White, Private George, 208

White, Captain Robert, 111–12, 114, 127, 138

Whitehead, Private John, 134, 273–4

Whinyates, Colonel, 212, 283, 290, 293

Wightman, Private James, 55–6, 74, 97, 105, 111, 116–17, 127, 130–31, 133, 136, 138, 142, 146, 151, 168–9, 178, 179, 217–18, 286, 300

Wilkin, Assistant Surgeon Henry, 291–2

Willett, Major Augustus, 74, 97

Williams, Sergeant William, 101, 159

Williamson, Private James, 52

Wilson, Private Samuel, 225

Wilson, Private William, 14

Windham, Colonel Charles, 72

Winter, Captain John, 136

Wombwell, Cornet George, 41, 48, 55, 73, 126, 138, 140, 144–5, 180, 181, 188, 210, 213, 264, 265–7

Wooden, Sergeant Charles, 183–4, 316, 319–23

Woodham-Smith, Cecil, 274, 278

Wootton, Private George, 13

Yates, Cornet John, 290

Yeni Bazaar, 39–41, 44

Yorke, Colonel John, 84, 122, 196

Yorkshire Weekly Post, 272

Young, Private Richard, 121